FIGHTING
AUTHORITARIANISM

FIGHTING AUTHORITARIANISM

AMERICAN YOUTH ACTIVISM IN THE 1930s

BRITT HAAS

Empire State Editions
An imprint of Fordham University Press
New York 2018

Fordham University Press has no responsibility for the persistence or accuracy of URLs for external or third-party Internet websites referred to in this publication and does not guarantee that any content on such websites is, or will remain, accurate or appropriate.

Fordham University Press also publishes its books in a variety of electronic formats. Some content that appears in print may not be available in electronic books.

Visit us online:
www.empirestateeditions.com
www.fordhampress.com

Library of Congress Cataloging-in-Publication Data
available online at https://catalog.loc.gov.

Printed in the United States of America

20 19 18   5 4 3 2 1
First edition

This book was written for the young people it discusses in the hopes of resurrecting their significance and reclaiming their vision.
It is dedicated to my sons, Jared and Aden, who help me see the wonders and promises of youth, and to my husband, Matthew, whose love and support know no limits.

Contents

PART III   Disillusion and Dissolution

Abbreviations

ACLU   American Civil Liberties Union

AFL   American Federation of Labor

ASU   American Student Union, umbrella group formed
            in 1935 through the amalgamation of the NSL
            and SLID; the ASU is the more narrow of the
            two most important youth organizations of the
            decade in that it included only student groups; led
            primarily by New York native Joseph Lash; James
            Wechsler and Molly Yard were also important
            leaders; headquartered in New York City; published
            The Student Advocate newsletter, maintained active
            membership of 20,000 though its Annual Strike
            Against War mobilized at least 500,000 students
            or one-half the college population at the time;
            dissolved in 1941

AYC   American Youth Congress, umbrella group formed
            in 1934; the most important youth organization
            of the decade; membership of affiliated groups
            extended to 5 million young people; included broad
            cross section of youth groups; leaders included
            Joseph Cadden, William Hinckley, and Jack
            McMichael; dissolved by 1942

CCC	Civilian Conservation Corps, New Deal program that became a *de facto* youth program
CCNY	City College of New York, many youth leaders, including Joseph Lash, hailed from CCNY
CIO	Congress of Industrial Organizations, labor organization established in 1935, led by John L. Lewis
CPSU	Communist Party of the Soviet Union
CPUSA	Communist Party of the United States of America
FERA	Federal Emergency Relief Administration, the first major relief program of the New Deal, later replaced by the WPA
JCC	Junior Chamber of Commerce, a conservative youth organization
LID	League for Industrial Democracy, an adult socialist organization
NAACP	National Association for the Advancement of Colored People
NEC	National Executive Committee (of the ASU), democratically elected leaders of the ASU charged with carrying out the ASU program designed by delegates at its annual conferences
NSFA	National Student Federation of America, a liberal umbrella group founded in 1925, comprising representatives of student governments; 150 schools were members by 1933; the NSFA was a member of the AYC; NSFA leaders were also leaders in the ASU and AYC (Joseph Cadden, for example, served simultaneously as NSFA Secretary and AYC Executive Secretary); important leaders include John A. Lang and Mary Jeanne McKay; disbanded during WWII and succeeded by National Student Association in 1947
NSL	National Student League, an autonomous radical student organization whose membership overlapped with the YCL; founded at CCNY in 1931; perhaps 3,000 members at its height before dissolving in order to merge with SLID in 1935 to form the ASU

NYA	National Youth Administration, the primary New Deal youth program, created in 1935
NYU	New York University
ROTC	Reserve Officers' Training Corps
SDD	Students in Defense of Democracy, a pro-Roosevelt group formed in 1941 by Joseph Lash after he withdrew from the ASU and AYC
SLID	Student League for Industrial Democracy, autonomous socialist youth group that developed originally as the student arm of the LID; members were referred to as SLIDers; dissolved when SLID merged with NSL in 1935 to form the ASU; reactivated in 1946; changed name to Students for a Democratic Society (SDS) in 1960
USOE	United States Office of Education
WPA	Works Progress Administration
YCAW	Youth Committee Against War, an ad hoc committee to coordinate anti-war activities
YCL	Young Communist League, youth branch of the CPUSA whose members were referred to as YCLers; membership overlapped with NSL; combined YCL/NSL membership was around 5,000 people
YMCA	Young Men's Christian Association
YWCA	Young Women's Christian Association
YPSL	Young People's Socialist League, youth group affiliated with the Socialist Party founded in 1907; members were referred to as Yipsels; in 1930 it had 1500 members in 65 branches (called circles) in 25 cities in 9 states

Introduction

Young people between the ages of 18 and 25 experienced the Great Depression rather differently than adults. Their shared experience involved not only concern about finding a job and getting married, but also a deep-seated concern about the future of America for that future was *their* future. Millions of these young people, who were not even legally considered adults until the age of 21, came together in the 1930s to form organizations dedicated to actively shaping that future. Their vision for America rested securely on their collective idea of what America was supposed to be: a democratic nation based on the equality of man and freedom for all. As the foundation of their ideological outlook, this notion guided their actions.

Youth perspectives on the events of the 1930s were often radically different from those of adults and stand in stark contrast to current images of the Great Depression. Understanding those perspectives sheds new light on how the decade of the Great Depression affected America. It was not simply youthful naïveté that drove young people to seek fundamental change to American political, economic, and social structures; it was hope in what they saw as *the* moment for such change to occur. Bleak images of stark hopelessness had no home in young activists' vision. Instead, they saw opportunity amidst the economic devastation to develop a free and equal political and social system. And those who came of age during the 1930s took the lessons they learned from their experiences with them into adulthood, helping to forge the movements that would later take up their calls for freedom and equality.

In this study, *youth* refers to young people who were generally 18–25 years of age and belonged to at least one youth organization. They were activist young people, not young activists. That is, their goal was to implement the egalitarian and democratic vision they shared in order to cultivate freedom and a secure future. They were not activists for specific causes, nor were they simply the younger coterie of adult organizational efforts. They developed autonomous organizations that furthered youth's agenda. Together, those organizations catalyzed the youth movement, which then took up causes, such as freeing the Scottsboro Boys and supporting the Spanish Republicans, as a means to further the wider objective of reforming America to live up to its promises.

To implement such a broad-based and profoundly held vision, young people needed to organize. They did this first at the local level. Being involved in local civic-minded, character-building organizations was widely encouraged and began at an early age, as evidenced by the widespread popularity of organizations such as the Boy Scouts and Girls Scouts of America. Later, young people became involved in organizations of their own choosing, such as the Young Men's Christian Association (YMCA) or the local branch of the Young Republicans or even the Future Farmers of America (FFA). They joined organizations where their personal interests and inter-personal relationships could be fostered. These local organizations tended to reflect their members in terms of race, class, ethnicity, and gender and up through the 1920s such organizing largely occurred outside the college campus.

Activist youth in the 1930s embodied a new zeitgeist. Even as more people were attending college than ever before, students in the 1920s tended to focus on cultural change based on personal freedom rather than political engagement. As historian Paula Fass has argued, in that decade "the young did not get below the surface of American political life to engage in a debate with America's leaders or to challenge her basic institutions. They did not agitate for change."[1] Instead of serious study, intellectual meditation, and social activism, it was football, petting, drinking, dancing, and fraternities that consumed the college co-eds' attention. "They had little interest in changing political or social structures," Fass explains, "because they were also the heirs apparent of American industrial capitalism and the political party system."[2] In a decade of prosperity, the young middle class white college students Fass focuses on had little to object to aside from adult attempts to restrain their behavior to align with strict Victorian moral codes the young saw as terribly out-of-date, impractical, and personally limiting. Yet, their willingness to stand up against efforts to repress their personal freedoms laid the seeds for the torrent of outspoken resistance on social, economic, and political issues in the 1930s. Relegated to the fringes of campus society in the 1920s, the activist groups became the voice of young people in the 1930s. And when youth leaders protested against campus authoritarianism, racism, economic exploitation, and impending war during the Depression, they targeted not only adult policymakers, but the frivolity and misguided nature of both their peers and the previous youth cohort.

What amounted to fits and starts in the 1920s led to full-scale youth mobilization in the 1930s.[3] The tables turned on the fulcrum of the stock market crash. Capitalism no longer meant security, even for middle class white youth. The personal became political in the 1930s and individualism gave way to collectivism. Focus on specific instances of injustice led to demands for systemic change: to help a person, the entire system must serve the general welfare. Suddenly, the serious-minded intellectual concerned about social, economic, and political issues garnered much more attention and respect as his explanations for current events and calls for fundamental reform reverberated not so much in the classroom, but in the campus clubs and social spaces.

One such place was Alcove #1, a corner of the cafeteria at City College of New York where Irving Howe, Daniel Bell, and Irving Kristol regularly debated political ideology and the course America should take. Attending CCNY in the late 1930s, this group followed in the footsteps of earlier New York radicals, like Joseph Lash, who said that "the real learning experience at college, the cauldron in which readings and lectures were precipitated into usable knowledge ... the crucible in which tastes were shaped and values confirmed was the talk that went on endlessly in the corridor and alcove, at lunch tables and on long walks along St. Nicholas Heights with one's classmates."[4] There were certainly still other groups prominent on campus, such as the athletes, but it was this group of politically minded intellectuals whom Lash referred to as the literati that increasingly steered the direction of the student body and this is because in the 1930s young intellectuals moved beyond study and inquiry to action.

Sometimes they were influenced by professors. For example, Lash credited philosophy professor Morris R. Cohen, himself a CCNY graduate, with his intellectual development. Another CCNY graduate who earned his advanced degree at Columbia and then taught philosophy at New York University, Sidney Hook, certainly influenced student thought, as well. Hook's philosophical disposition tended to align with

John Dewey, who, though he retired from Columbia in 1930, remained
an active writer living in New York, thus sustaining his widespread influence. The impact of Reinhold Niebuhr also reached from his teaching
post at Union Theological Seminary into the ranks of young people.
However, adult influence was indirect. Even Lash, who came the closest
to becoming an actual devotee of his mentor, said that the influence was
not about imparting information or creating protégés, but rather about
honing one's ability to question, debate, and think critically. Of more
practical import for Lash was his own experiences in the college newspaper office where he engaged fellow journalists, interviewed college
authorities, and took a broader view of campus life than that dictated by
his own individual path to graduation. Many young radicals remember
attending class only enough to earn a passing grade and some, like James
Wechsler, mention no professorial influence at all.[5]

Youth activists agreed with the ideas of H. L. Mencken, but here, too,
it was not about personal influence. Young radicals tended to attribute
their political ideology more to what they read, especially in left-leaning
newspapers and magazines, such as *The New Republic* and *The Nation*.
Adult influence, then, should not be entirely discounted, but the impetus
behind youth activism rested more with young people themselves. They
sought autonomy and bristled at adult attempts to control them. This is
perhaps why a radical editor could easily spark a college-wide student
protest against an administration's authoritarianism simply by publishing an article critical of the college president's actions. It was in youth-
centered places like the Alcove that students were likely to hear about
the Social Problems Club and there, too, that they would be invited by a
member to a meeting. Planning protests began in just such places. Turning
students into activists did, too. Youth-devoted groups off campus served
the same function.

Crucial to effective protest and to the mobilization of youth generally
were those groups both on and off campus that advocated serious change
through immediate action. In the 1920s, such radicalism tended to be tied
to religious pacifism. Thus, Christian groups' support for internationalism
then laid the groundwork for much more encompassing efforts later. In
addition to denominational groups, the YMCA and YWCA were also
instrumental in provoking a new political awareness, especially on issues
relating to war and peace.[6] That awareness became an awakening in the
1930s as young people organized on their own behalf. Starting as localized groups in the early 1930s, these organizations came together under
umbrella groups forging the Popular Front by mid-decade, marking a
distinct and significant development.

The two most important umbrella groups were the American Youth Congress (AYC), founded in 1934, and the American Student Union (ASU), established in 1935. The AYC was the more inclusive of the two. It included fraternal, political, religious, civil rights, educational, farming, professional, settlement house, business, trade union, student, and other organizations. Combining the member lists from its affiliated organizations, the AYC claimed to represent as many as five million young people. The ASU, in contrast, was focused on its college student membership, though it did have high school branches, as well. Like the AYC, the ASU was an amalgam. Campus organizations affiliated with the ASU, which then served as an umbrella organization representing students. Most of its member organizations were politically slanted. In particular, the National Student League (NSL) and Student League for Industrial Democracy (SLID), representing the communists and socialists respectively, were instrumental in the creation of the ASU. Other organizations, such as the National Student Federation of America (NSFA), a liberal organization made up of student government representatives; the Young People's Socialist League (YPSL), the youth branch of the Socialist Party; and the Young Communist League (YCL), the youth branch of the Communist Party of the United States of America would also come to play a significant role in the ASU. While its 20,000 members paled in comparison to the five million represented by the AYC, the ASU was still a remarkably large organization representing an important segment of the youth population.

The leaders of the member organizations (particularly, those mentioned here—the NSFA, YPSL, and YCL) helped shape executive policy in the ASU, but it was the ASU National Secretary, Joseph Lash, and the Director of Publications, James Wechsler, who became his *de facto* second in command, along with the leaders of the AYC that most effectively expressed the voice and vision of American organized youth. Lash, a New York city native, began his involvement in the youth movement while attending City College of New York first through the SLID and then through the ASU. He served as the leader of the ASU from its inception through December 1939. Like so many others who belonged to more than one organization, he also served on the executive committee of the AYC through May 1941. James Wechsler, a YCL member from Columbia College, was Publications Director of the ASU, and thus served as editor of its newsletter, *The Student Advocate*. Like other youth leaders, Lash was paid a stipend by the ASU for his work on behalf of young people. Unlike other youth leaders who aged out of the movement, though, he made youth activism a career he pursued until he was 31 years old and thus was a principal spokesman for the movement throughout the decade. Together with the money he earned from publishing, the stipend assured his financial independence. The ASU and AYC were able to provide such stipends and to fund their leaders' attendance at international conferences through the dues collected from their members. When funds fell short, youth leaders adeptly solicited donations from patrons like Eleanor Roosevelt, who was instrumental in securing money from a wide variety of sources for them and their organizations.

Such leaders, many of whom hailed from New York, projected the voice, expounded the perspective, and executed the will of young people from across the nation. New York City–based college students were often elected leaders of the national organizations as well as the umbrella groups because they effectively articulated young people's worldview and worked tirelessly to institutionalize that worldview. These leaders tended to be radicals, but they were not extremists. They wanted to bring about fundamental positive change in America's political, economic, and social systems, but they did not seek to overthrow those systems. While some expressed revolutionary rhetoric, none fomented a revolution. They worked within the system to change the system. Their own personal ideology, then, was often further to the left than the organizations they led. However, they were democratically elected and thus could legitimately claim to represent young people. Lash and Wechsler, for example, certainly tried to move the ASU further left; however, they were bound by the agenda of the organization they represented, which was determined not by executive fiat, but by parliamentary procedure during the ASU's annual conferences. Furthermore, the executives, themselves, were chosen by ballot at those conferences. They had to convince people to vote for them. The same was true for the AYC leadership. Someone like Lash or Wechsler, then, could not speak *as* a poor farmer's son from the Midwest, yet they were elected to speak *for* that young man and the millions like him.

Women were actively involved in the youth movement, too. Indeed, Viola Ilma was the original architect of the AYC. And people like Molly Yard and Celeste Strack played significant roles in the ASU. Molly Yard, the daughter of Methodist missionaries, who was born in China, served on the executive board of the ASU from its inception until 1940. Although she would later become a leader of the National Organization for Women, campaign for the Equal Rights Amendment, and claim that she was "born a feminist,"[7] she did not promote a women's rights agenda nor was she the leader of a women's bloc in the 1930s. This is because, as far as the youth movement was concerned, there was no women's bloc.

Young women did join gender-specific organizations such as the Young Women's Christian Association (YWCA), but in the youth movement, it seems there was no need for a women's rights agenda because such rights were subsumed within the broader goals of fuller democracy, freedom, and equality.

Truth be told, I fully intended to focus on gender when I began the project that would become this book. That project initially grew out of research focused on Eleanor Roosevelt whose support for the youth movement piqued my interest. Given her advocacy for women's rights and her efforts to secure positions for women within the New Deal Administration, I fully expected to see a reflection of that female centeredness in discussions of and about young women within the youth movement. The sources, however, do not support such a focus. The papers left behind are woefully silent on matters relating to gender. Given the prominent positions young women held, it is not because they had no seat at the decision-making table. They were very much involved in both shaping and instituting young people's vision of and for America. And they, too, spoke for young Americans. It is *because* they were so involved that they did not think they needed to advocate specifically for women. They were working for a future where all Americans would have equal opportunity. Gender equality was assumed—so much so that when Joseph Lash went to Belgium in 1934 to attend an international socialist student congress, he was shocked that European socialists there believed women were not as good as men, should adhere to strict gender roles, and should never smoke.[8] In this regard, American youth organizations of the 1930s were much more inclusive, perhaps even more than current advocacy groups.

Not only were the umbrella groups inclusive in terms of gender, they were racially integrated and religiously tolerant, as well. Member organizations often had to adhere to their local segregationist laws and so there were all-white and all-black groups, but the ASU and AYC, themselves, abided by no such separation. The two organizations were rather progressive when it came to race and religion. African-Americans William Bell and George Streater both rose to prominent positions in the ASU. Like female leaders, though, they did not represent a bloc within the larger organization; they were elected to represent all American youth.

All Protestant denominations, Catholics, and Jews were welcomed in the youth movement. They sometimes became involved through their own religious groups, like Young Judea, but just as often through secular social or political groups. Their religious faith was not a deterrent for someone to become a youth leader. In fact, during a time of rampant anti-Semitism, Joseph Lash and James Wechsler, both Jews, were just as highly regarded as Methodists Molly Yard and Jack McMichael. Moreover, although the majority of students at CCNY were Jewish and at the beginning of the Depression there formed what Richard Pells calls a family of young Jewish intellectuals, religiosity tended to give way to a general commitment to social justice among young activists.[9] Lash remembers growing up in a mixed ethnic neighborhood where his Orthodox grandmother seriously disciplined him for cavorting with the Irish and Italian Catholics as well as the Protestants, whose friendship had a much more immediate impact on him than his family's Judaism.[10] Rather than concentrate on what separated them, youth activists were intent on bridging the gaps, bringing people together, and fighting for their common cause to make America live up to its ideals.

The umbrella groups' desire to unite young people throughout the nation made them inclusive and diverse. Unity strengthened their voice and augmented their influence, but that unity should not be confused with uniformity. Unlike Depression-era youth movements in Germany and Italy that emphasized group conformity and submission to adult authority, the youth movement in America thrived because it brought together disparate groups that found common cause resulting from their shared experiences. When local organizations started working within and through the autonomous national umbrella organizations, they did so based on a common worldview that allowed them to work together even when—or perhaps, especially when—they did not see eye-to-eye on specific issues. This is what makes the AYC and ASU so exceptional. They became the voice for young Americans and the means by which to seek implementation of their vision for America.

Both the AYC and ASU were established in New York City largely through the efforts of native New Yorkers and both organizations' headquarter remained in New York City. Before the 1930s, there were national organizations made up of local chapters spread throughout the country. The national headquarters for those organizations were likewise at great distances from one another. The NSFA was headquartered in New York City, for example, while the Young Republicans was headquartered in Washington, D.C. The YWCA was likewise headquartered in the nation's capital, but the YMCA headquarters was in Chicago. Some organizations, like the Future Farmers of America, had no national headquarters (land was bought in Alexandria, Virginia in 1939 to establish a national headquarters for the FFA) and small local groups unaffiliated with a national organization remained completely isolated. The umbrella groups, and the

AYC in particular, brought all these organizations together. Young people from every corner of the country and from every sized organization attended the annual conferences of the AYC and ASU to have a say in the direction the movement as a whole took.

But the locus was New York City. In 1937, at least eight of the twenty-three members of the AYC National Council lived in New York City and it was not unusual for a meeting of the National Council to be almost exclusively attended by New Yorkers.[11] To balance the New York–centeredness of the leadership, the AYC also included eight Regional Representatives and thirteen Representatives-At-Large on its Executive Council though nothing prohibited those at-large representatives from being New Yorkers.[12] From its inception, New Yorkers also dominated the ASU leadership, accounting for at least thirteen of thirty seats on the National Executive Committee.[13] In between national conferences, leaders met regularly in New York City, worked to disseminate information to member organizations as well as to the wider public, and pursued the agreed upon agenda. This organizational structure that relied on the national headquarters' staff maintained the momentum necessary for the movement. And that staff relied heavily on the networking and other resources available to them in New York City.

One particularly important resource was the press. From their experiences as editors of their college newspapers, Lash and Wechsler established a national organ for the ASU, *The Student Advocate*, which was published in New York City. They continued to write features for their campus papers even after they graduated and were often interviewed by them. From its headquarters in New York City, the AYC regularly published pamphlets and bulletins, issued press releases, and printed flyers to be distributed among member organizations and the general public. The AYC and ASU leaders routinely sent articles about youth efforts and achievements to be published in the New York City–based newspapers and magazines. They granted interviews as well as broadcast speeches over the radio. Both organizations thus garnered publicity from the national press.

New York City–based leaders brought with them their activist fervor and network of contacts when they took the helm of the AYC and ASU. These leaders tended to be the most active in local groups in the early 1930s, which prepared them to assume prominent roles in their national organizations. When they moved beyond the local chapter to participate in the national organizations, they broadened their scope. That experience, in turn, provided both the practical and ideological basis with which to lead the umbrella groups by mid-decade. Astute debaters and parliamentarians, they knew how to work within a committee system of governance. Even more significant, their ability to couple a focus on immediate issues and concerns with long-term objectives resulted in them being elected leaders of the ASU and AYC. In short, they became the movement's visionaries.

The vision young activists sought to implement had much to do with the influence of a nebulous idea called the American Dream they had been brought up to revere: They wanted a truly free, truly democratic, and truly equal society. The only way to make such an America was to fundamentally alter the economic, political, and social structures then in place. That meant, for many, embracing radical ideologies, especially socialism and communism, which were widely discussed, debated, and promoted on New York City college campuses. It is absolutely imperative to understand: Youth believed that in embracing these ideologies, they *were not* turning their backs on American values. Instead, they believed that such ideologies were the *only* way to make America live up to its promises. For them, there was no inherent contradiction between radicalism and faith in America.

Youth activists, then, were idealists. Yet they were also practical and very much grounded in reality, a reality defined by the Great Depression. To them the crash of 1929 was nothing less than the death-knell of capitalism. To some extent they were right. The American economic system could not go, and has not gone, back to the nineteenth and early-twentieth-century laissez-faire system that helped produce such a catastrophe. This, of course, was assured by the institutionalization of the New Deal, many of the programs of which grew out of plans first implemented in New York. Youth activists readily assessed the New Deal as a good start, but not nearly enough. These young people, therefore, continually pushed Franklin D. Roosevelt, Eleanor Roosevelt, and other members of the administration to do more to address not only economic distress and the need for more inclusive politics, but also the problems associated with social inequality. Their access to New Dealers in Washington, D.C. was amplified because youth leaders hailed from New York City. Members of the Brains Trust, such as Rexford Guy Tugwell, Raymond Moley, and Adolphe A. Berle (all Columbia University professors) along with New Dealers, such as Harry Hopkins and Frances Perkins, could be accessed through their New York connections. Moreover, youth leaders were regularly invited for conferences and meetings at both Eleanor Roosevelt's New York City townhouse as well as the president's home in Hyde Park, New York. Youth leaders used this access to great advantage in lobbying for more far-reaching programs. Proximity to New York City—based New Dealers made access at least possible, but it was their successful networking that allowed youth activists to turn that access into sustained relationships necessary to influence adult policymakers.

Employing political lobbying as well as investigative and expository journalism techniques, they became skilled at convincing policymakers to at least begin to implement youth's vision for America. In meetings with politicians, they were quick to point out the parallel between themselves and their adult counterparts: As elected representatives, they, too, were duty bound to advocate policies to address their constituents' concerns. Youth leaders used their New Deal connections to pressure both the federal and the state government to do more for young people and they objected when their vision of America was undercut by policies, like the Nunan Loyalty Oath Bill passed by the New York State Senate in 1935. Youth leaders became astute politicians maneuvering the layers and branches of the American governmental structure to pursue the youth movement's agenda.

Youth activists, in using politics as a means to accomplish their goals, remained steeped in civics. In meeting with government-appointed officials, youth leaders reminded them of their responsibility to execute policies fully and to promote the general welfare. Their high-mindedness certainly irked some, but it also won them avid supporters, most notably among them, Eleanor Roosevelt. Sincerely believing that their vision for America was just and right, they steadfastly pushed for its implementation, congratulating adults when their proposals fell in line with youth's vision and chastising them when they did not.

Regarding foreign policy, youth were especially and outspokenly critical of FDR's Administration. It was not until the second half of the 1930s that the Roosevelt Administration's attention turned, markedly, from domestic to foreign policy; youth, however, were consistently concerned with international relations and foreign affairs throughout the decade. To them, a truly free, democratic, equal American society was contingent on a peaceful world that would foster freedom, democracy, and equality both at home and abroad. Their allegiance to peace, however, was tested against their devotion to freedom and democracy, especially evident in their desire that America do something for China in the early 1930s and for Spain in the late 1930s.

Fascism and militarism abroad, then, had a profound effect on American youth, inducing young people to reevaluate their priorities, resulting in a public debate in New York City college newspapers. That reevaluation crystallized around the Nazi-Soviet Pact of 1939, over which the decade-long developing solidarity of youth activists crumbled. Although some activist youth leaders remained committed to transforming America, many others "matured" from their youthful idealism to adult diffidence as a result of the kaleidoscopic transformation of policies generated by the advent of World War II. *Fighting Authoritarianism: American Youth Activism in the 1930s*, then, corrects misconceptions about the 1930s at the same time it sheds light on what young people thought and did. It shows the limits of the New Deal in its short-sighted misunderstanding and neglect of young people's problems. It questions the interventionist versus isolationist paradigm in that young people sought to focus on *both* domestic and international affairs. And it explores the era not as a precursor to WWII but as a moment of hope.

Until now, the scholarship concerning youth activism in the 1930s, though sparse, defined the youth movement in three ways: as a student movement, as a political movement, or as a peace movement. Despite historians' proclivity to compartmentalize youth activism and to focus mainly on only academic freedom and peace, these three interpretations are not mutually exclusive and ought not to narrow our understanding of young people's agenda. Youth activists writing in the 1930s embraced a holistic view that identified economics, academic freedom, and peace as central, overlapping issues confronting young people. They never solely focused on just one issue, one method, or one goal. It is important, therefore, to go back to what the young people had to say in the 1930s to learn about their perspective on what the Depression decade meant for America.

Because most scholars have relied on George P. Rawick's 1957 unpublished dissertation, "The New Deal and Youth: The Civilian Conservation Corps, the National Youth Administration, and the American Youth Congress," many of the arguments about activist youth's perspective have been skewed. Steeped in Cold War rhetoric, Rawick's argument is that the American Youth Congress was a communist front organization and that the youth movement was communist controlled. For his analysis, Rawick relied almost entirely on newspaper articles, the findings of the House Un-American Activities Committee, and the testimony of former student activists who quit the youth movement—all of which were rather dismissive of youth's policies and positions; most were decidedly hostile to youth's efforts. Writing before the student activism of the 1960s, Rawick believed the youth movement in the 1930s was an aberration in American history and therefore explains it as foreign-inspired. The influence of his analysis has been immense. The research presented here seeks to correct the interpretation of youth's perspective and youth's activism as a product not of Soviet manipulation, but a product of the events of the 1930s that formed youth's vision of and for America.

The published literature on activist youth in the 1930s is scant. There are only four serious studies. Philip G. Altbach's 1974 book, *Student Politics in America,* discusses various groups' political activism in order to lay the groundwork for the later student movement of the 1960s. His study of the 1930s movement, then, is not to understand the context of the time, but rather to support his argument that student activism in the 1960s was not an aberration. The emphasis is decidedly on that later time period. In *The First Student Movement: Student Activism in the United States During the 1930s,* Ralph Brax examines the psychological and sociological make up of student activists and claims that the student movement served as a training ground for political and intellectual leaders who would emerge after the war. Again, the focus is on explaining the roots of the post-WWII era. Further, Brax relied on articles, periodicals, and student publications for his conclusions that student activists were the avant garde liberals on the cusp of cultural change rather than looking at manuscript collections because his purpose was to trace the growth of liberal thought in America. Eileen Eagan, in *Class, Culture, and the Classroom: The Student Peace Movement of the 1930s,* published in 1981, offers a different orientation for the youth movement of the 1930s, but similarly argues that it was a student movement and that it paved the way for the social movements of the 1960s. Eagan contends that political action was merely a means for maintaining peace. Eagan sees World War I as the most significant molder of youth consciousness and the effects of the Great War as the catalyst for the peace movement rather than focusing on the events of the 1930s.

Fighting Authoritarianism, in contrast, relies on what youth activists said and did. Many of the youth leaders were New York City natives who attended New York City colleges. They and the organizations they headed left behind a wealth of manuscript collections filled with copious notes, meeting minutes, biographical information, letters, conference programs, pamphlets, and other valuable information, which form the basis for this analysis. In addition, I consulted New Dealers' manuscript collections because they so carefully catalogue how often and how much youth leaders were able to influence policymakers. New York City college newspapers, especially Columbia's *Daily Spectator* and City College of New York's *The*

Campus, explain what youth leaders thought and why they advocated the positions they did through their editorial pages. Sources written by youth inform and shape my argument.

Until now, Robert Cohen's *When the Old Left Was Young: Student Radicals and America's First Student Movement, 1929–1941*, published in 1993, was the most recent book-length study, which Cohen himself justified as a way to address historians' "pattern of neglect" when it came to America's first student movement.[14] His study, however, perpetuates two misconceptions: first, that it was a student movement rather than a widespread youth movement, and second, that it was a communist-controlled and therefore doomed experiment. *Fighting Authoritarianism* corrects that Cold War perspective so that the events of the decade can be understood through the voices and vision of those who participated in them. I seek to situate youth activists in the context of their time by removing the Cold War lens. This requires a rethinking of the 1930s. It was not the static black-and-white image of desperation perpetuated by popular perception. It was a dynamic moment when anything seemed possible and youthful idealism led activists to implement their vision. This study also refocuses the 1930s so that questions of progress and possibility are not grounded in the desperate farmer, but the urban-based movements for change. This builds on the Progressive Era's efforts to institutionalize progress and is in line with much of New Deal historiography that has set about emphasizing the continuities of reform.

Despite the tendency among historians to assume otherwise, American youth activists were protective of their autonomy and vigorously resisted adult efforts to control their organizations' platform positions on policy no matter from which political camp such efforts emanated. Simply stated, the Young Communist League was not controlled by the Communist Party of the United States of America, which, in turn, recent scholarship has shown, was not entirely under the command of the Comintern. The Comintern's policies and positions, likewise, were not always dictated by the government of the Soviet Union. Localized groups, events, and ideas had a much more trenchant influence on the communist world than has largely been heretofore acknowledged. Communists were, like other youth activists, young *Americans*. They adopted Marx's radical ideology, but they did so to bring about the very American goals of equality, freedom, and democracy. They may have hoped for a revolution to hasten the establishment of a classless society, but they did not actively seek to precipitate such a revolution.

The closest thing to revolutionary action that young people undertook in the 1930s was the Student Strike Against War. Despite some people's hope that this strike foreshadowed the spark for an internal revolt in the event that war broke out, it was really more about gaining publicity for young people's anti-war stance. When the publicity showed government officials just how widespread their pacifism was, those officials would be less likely, it was hoped, to pursue hawkish policies. Rather than furthering or even reflecting revolutionary fervor among young people, then, the strike served as another way to pressure adults to adopt measures in line with youth's vision for America. Youth activists did not try to incite an actual uprising. Even the most radical among them caucused, lobbied, proposed policies, and used the press. All of these activities enmeshed them in the American system of government they hoped to reform. Youth leaders, as the link between young people and the government, worked *with* the FDR Administration even when they protested against the shortsightedness of its programs. Indeed, later many went to work *for* the government.

Instead of creating an actual revolutionary vanguard, in all sincerity, youth activists forged the popular front, an otherwise typically American effort of coalition-building and compromise committed to carrying out the vision American youth had for America. The communists did not sabotage the youth organizations in a slavish self-sacrificial attempt to promote the Soviet Union's positions, as so many have supposed. The youth organizations fell apart because other groups (first the socialists, and then the liberals) opted out of the Popular Front in the face of imminent war. Indeed, it was the New York City branch of the Young People's Socialist League that precipitated the dissolution of the movement.

The youth movement was a social movement heavily influenced by historical events, whose goal was to make America live up to its promises. Those events engender a discussion of economics, politics, foreign affairs, and ideology as ways to determine how youth evaluated 1930s America and planned for its future. The way young people responded to those events, then, is a lens through which to gain a better understanding of youth's vision of and for America as they molded that vision. The events discussed in this book were chosen for their importance to youth; they do not necessarily align with what was most important to adults, to the FDR Administration, or to a specific political party. There is no discussion, then, of the Glass–Steagall Act, Social Security, or the American First Committee. The events explored here—from the Harlan County coal miners' strike to the expulsion of Columbia University student Reed Harris to the Student Strike Against War—were instrumental in defining and expressing youth's vision of and for America.

The organizational structure of this book mirrors the three distinct stages of the youth movement. In Part I, "Seeing the Problem and Envisioning a Plan," three events and the issues they laid bare are discussed because they galvanized young people into organizing on their own behalf. Chapter 1 depicts the bus trip departing from Columbia College to Harlan County, Kentucky, as the starting point for explaining how the National Student League (NSL) turned New York City college students' activism on behalf of the striking coalminers in Kentucky into an inclination to put forth demands to address their own hardships caused by the Great Depression. To do so, young people needed first to organize. The formation of the NSL in 1931 and its sponsorship of the Harlan County trip therefore represents the birth of the movement. Young people not only faced widespread unemployment, but decreased academic opportunities as well at the beginning of the decade. Chapter 2 therefore focuses on academic issues. Here, though, it was not merely a decline in educational opportunities that concerned students, they were also concerned with what kind of education they could get. Chapter 2 explores the ramifications of the expulsion of Reed Harris from Columbia, situating that event in young people's wider call for increased freedom. Out of this incident, another organization, the Student League for Industrial Democracy (SLID) established itself as a leading proponent of the youth movement. A different form of freedom is discussed in Chapter 3, where young people in New York City move beyond their own personal agenda to fight for the freedom of the wrongfully accused and convicted Scottsboro Boys of Alabama. In doing so, they begin to focus on the need to agitate for equality more broadly.

These three events—the Harlan County trip, the expulsion of Reed Harris, and the trials of the Scottsboro Boys—led to the consensus that young people should fight for economic opportunity, democratic freedom, and equality. The purpose of discussing these events is not to explain what youth did for those people, but to explain how getting involved in the issues endemic to these incidents served as catalysts for young people coming together to find their own voice and to develop their own vision for how to make America live up to its promises. Part I explores these three specific incidents with a birds-eye view to reveal the coalescing circumstances that created the need for a youth movement. It serves as the foundation for understanding how and why later events unfolded as they did and it introduces youth activists who were in the process of organizing.

Part II, "Implementing a Vision," explains the detailed origins of the AYC and the ASU, the two most important organizations of the decade, and the platform those organizations developed to make America live up to its ideals. Chapter 4 details youth's forging of the Popular Front while Chapter 5 dissects the ways in which youth leaders and the organizations they represented sought to implement policies to carry out their program for more economic opportunity, democratic freedom, and equality. Chapter 6 explores how the youth movement in general and youth leaders in particular began to reconsider one of their major tenets: their anti-war stance. Young people agreed that war was a threat to freedom, democracy, and equality, but so was fascism. The growing belief that only armed conflict could halt the fascists caused fissures that presaged the rift within the umbrella groups as many lent their support to the Republicans in the Spanish Civil War. These three chapters present a worms-eye view to explain what youth leaders thought and what the youth movement actually did. Whereas Part I explains how young people extrapolated meaning from events they participated in to develop a common vision regarding issues they held dear, Part II details the actions they took to implement that vision.

In Part III, "Disillusion and Dissolution," the unraveling of the youth movement is explored in detail. Chapter 7 covers a complicated series of events that has been misunderstood and misrepresented. The communists are often blamed for the youth movement's collapse. However, the sources show that it was first the liberals and then the socialists who abandoned the movement. This becomes clear in examining the ASU and AYC leaders' responses to the Nazi-Soviet Pact and the advent of WWII. Just as the birth of the movement was more of a prolonged process than a sudden event, so, too, was its demise.

This book, then, follows not only the chronology of the Depression decade, but the birth, coming of age, and death of the youth movement. Its conception involved a series of distinct episodes where the focus is not on what young people did for coalminers, Reed Harris, or the Scottsboro Boys, but rather on what Harlan County, Columbia University, and Scottsboro, Alabama meant for young people. In discussing their creation of the Popular Front and the program they developed, young people were taking charge of their destiny by expounding their vision of and for America. Youth activists were not reactive protestors, they were proactive policymakers who protested injustice while simultaneously engaging the adult establishment in order to effect change. Their energy is not reflected in the monochromatic grey of black-and-white Depression-era photographs. Informed, independent, and emboldened by a sense of nothing to lose, youth activists strove to enact their hopes for a better America. Essential to Depression-era youth activism was a sense that positive change was, indeed, possible, and that it would result from both a broad base of support and all-inclusive goals that benefit everyone. Despite its descent into oblivion, the legacy of the youth movement lived on in both its worldview and in its leaders.

The story of how they sought to do this revolves around the young activists. I have used this ambiguous term because this is how young people at the time labeled themselves. In the early 1930s, they were not yet organized, but they were active. While the organizations, particularly the AYC, were inclusive, the leaders were left-leaning and many of whom were drawn to and emanated from New York City college campuses. New York City was, simply put, the epicenter of the movement. The leaders helped formulate youth's vision and then espoused that vision by operating as youth's voice. *Fighting Authoritarianism* projects that voice so that we may understand more about the Depression decade from young radicals' vision of and for America.

PART I

Seeing the Problem
and Envisioning a Plan

1

The Effects of the Crash
The Youth Problem from New York City to Harlan County, Kentucky, and Back Again

> I make an appeal to your heart, your
> understanding, your prescience, that you tell
> me, a boy of eighteen years, what hope there
> is for me in this world, for the future.
>
> —*John D. Bell to Franklin D. Roosevelt*[1]

The Great Depression's effects reached all strata of society, leaving virtually no one unscathed. There were social, cultural, and political effects to be sure, but the economic effects were, by far, the most pressing, even for America's youth. Young people were generally unconcerned with the stock market, having no vested interest, and thus the crash of 1929 barely registered a mention in the documents they left behind. For them, the Great Depression was not about money lost, but about the present and future viability of making a living. The stock market crash provides a context for understanding what young people hoped America's economy would become rather than a siren's call for what it once had been. They did not yearn for a gilded age gone by; they sought to implement their burgeoning radical vision by using the economic catastrophe to usher in more equal and just economic and political systems for America.

The catalyst for the maturation of both their vision and their method was their attempt to aid striking coalminers in Harlan County, Kentucky. Activist youth were appalled by the conditions of the miners. James Wechsler, a New York City native and Columbia College freshman at the time of the strike, who would soon become a radical youth leader, later explained that the coal miners

21

faced hunger and starvation. Their children continue to die of flux because they lack sufficient and proper food. Attempts of the miners to preserve and broaden their National Miners Union, the only instrument for improving the conditions under which they live and work, are still met with the bullets and black-jacks of the coal operators and their faithful servants, the state and county administrations.[2]

It was the National Student League (NSL), whose members were more inclined to practice "trade union communism" than the members of other radical groups that organized a bus trip of 80 students to Harlan County as a show of solidarity with striking coal miners.[3] Yet the NSL's radicalism sprung not from foreign inspiration, but something very near to home for City College of New York students. The college newspaper's editor was suspended in 1930 for criticizing the college president and the NSL was created by outraged students to spearhead protest efforts for the months-long fight for student rights.[4]

The trip to Harlan County took weeks of planning by NSL leaders, who invited students from all over the Northeast and beyond to participate, irrespective of their social or economic beliefs. James Wechsler, writing in 1935, noted that instead of political ideology, "the one common denominator was their curiosity and their courage"[5] to undertake this journey, which its coordinators hailed as "a student laboratory in political science."[6] Only those attended who could cover the costs of travel themselves, or raise funds to defray those costs. One participant, noting the varied nature of the group, reported that they "had in common only the fact that they were students, a rather indefinite interest in labor problems and a somewhat vague liberal sympathy with the working class."[7] Once they made the commitment to go to Harlan, the volunteers raised relief funds from other students and faculty members to be given to the striking miners.[8]

The students, from colleges mostly located in New York City, though some were from Boston, Cincinnati, and Tennessee, as well, left from Columbia University on March 23, 1932 with moral support officially provided by 175 professors. They hoped, once they reached Harlan County, to be able to support and assist miners who had been on strike since the spring of 1931.[9] Foreshadowing the freedom rides of the 1960s, one of their goals was to investigate allegations of repression, brutality, and violence against the strikers and to then publicize the miners' plight in order to gain public sympathy for the oppressed.[10] They were armed "with questionnaires and plans to interview miners, coal operators, representatives of the Red Cross, local officials and the townspeople."[11] However, they were never able to conduct their investigation, validating their worst suspicions because, they argued, "we should not have been kept out if there were nothing to hide."[12] Their belief that a "reign of terror" was being carried out against American citizens was thus substantiated.[13]

Students were warned by previous investigative missions—one taken just a few weeks before by a committee that included Theodore Dreiser, who had published a piece called "Harlan Miners Speak"—about the brutal treatment one could expect in coal country.[14] This trip, then, was no mere publicity stunt. After being confronted by the Harlan Country sheriff, district attorney, and an angry crowd of local citizens, the participants were harassed and threatened and finally forced to leave the state under police escort.[15] James Wechsler believed the students "were admittedly fortunate to escape" because some of the armed throng that swarmed the bus were yelling the "ominous lynch-cry—string 'em up."[16] Students, Wechsler recalled, "never [even] got to see the miners whose conditions [they] had prepared to study; they were concealed from [them] by an army of deputy-thugs."[17]

The episode, though it did not immediately aid the strikers, accomplished the larger goal of drawing national attention to the strike and the miners' working and living conditions. Despite the fact that news coverage superficially focused on the novelty of the students' trip and the sensationalism of their conflict with political authorities, rather than on the actual conditions of the miners and their conflict with the mining company's owners, it nevertheless helped attract the attention of other workers and students to those conditions.[18] Organizers remained hopeful that, at a minimum, more relief funds would be collected and sent to the miners.

Whatever the effect on miners, their experience in Kentucky had profound effects on the students involved. They had anticipated economic distress, but what they found in Kentucky, according to NSL member and Columbia College student Robert F. Hall, was a "reign of terror" where "the solidarity of the ruling class, employers, investors, and governments, was revealed with all its implications."[19] When youth protested their treatment, they found that the Kentucky press, local law enforcement officers, and state political officials were unsympathetic and often downright hostile. Dismissed by the governors of Kentucky and Tennessee and believing that "miners have no recourse now except a federal investigation," youth leaders took their story to Washington. But "only in the case of one lone senator,"[20] Hall bitterly reported, "was there any show of interest in a situation which we recognized as intolerable, unconstitutional, and, in terms of our earlier values, inhuman."[21] Hoping that public servants would indeed serve the public, they even took their story to the Attorney General and the Office of the President, where, Hall noted, "the secretary of the secretary of the secretary of Mr. Hoover accepted the statement with the remark that it would be placed in the hands of the Department of Labor."[22] While political officials ignored what was happening, Hall confirmed that for those who went on the Harlan trip, "their future thinking and perspective could not fail to be conditioned by what they had seen."[23] Disillusioned youth, like Hall, concluded: "Constitutional rights are a fiction. Democracy is a myth. The figures who sit in the seats of authority are not concerned with the denial of what we were once pleased to call civil liberties."[24] Thus what had initially been conceived as a deplorable economic situation for coalminers quickly transformed into a political tribulation for students, about which something must be done.

The NSL concluded that a genuine student movement must shoulder the responsibility for rectifying this situation—to make American democracy function as it ought—by struggling "against reaction and conservatism," lest "the fascist regime in the coal fields, with its . . . palpable denial of constitutional rights," spread.[25] While the NSL hoped this would lead to students and workers "fighting shoulder to shoulder" against the "ruling class," most young activists, radicalized by the Harlan County experience, understood this rhetoric as an expression of their desire to work more adeptly from within the system.[26] They envisioned young people, instead, as an interest group that should stake its claim as a rightful member of the American polity.

For many, like Joseph Lash, then a Columbia College graduate student who had earned his Bachelor's degree from City College of New York in 1931, and who later became one of the most prominent youth movement leaders, the trip to Harlan County was a turning point:

> I was induced into going on the Harlan expedition. What I saw would not let me rest. When I returned I quickly became active in the Socialist movement. I put out a magazine for the LID, fought on picket lines, went to conventions, began to formulate policy, went abroad to a socialist student congress. My history from this time on becomes the history of the student movement. I took part in the bonus march, helped in the 1932 Socialist campaign, and reluctantly came to the conclusion that I would not become a professor

[of English Literature] and began to equip myself toward becoming a professional revolutionist.[27]

The Harlan trip inspired other young people to take action, too. A similar incident undertaken by 150 students and teachers from Midwestern universities, intending to investigate conditions in the Illinois coal belt, met a similar fate—except that, in this case, some refused to leave the state and were unceremoniously jailed.[28]

Youth radicalism increased as a result of the Harlan experience as reflected in a 1934 study of over 850 students from nine eastern colleges and universities, which concluded that a majority of those students were either quite liberal or radical in many of their social and political views.[29] Michael B. Smith, elected to the Washington State legislature in 1934, did not go to Harlan, Kentucky in 1932, but was similarly transformed. Smith recalled that his "first experience in the radical movement was in an unemployed organization" that was created "in response to a desperate need for organized opposition to the retrenchment in relief standards."[30] For his participation in the longshoremen's strike he "was arrested as a dangerous radical" because "open season had been declared on the reds."[31] As his organization became more popular, it "assumed a position of major significance as a political force in the state" and therefore launched his political career as a "left wing Democrat."[32] Smith, like the young activists with whom he sympathized, became intent on remaking America.

This is not to say that young people were overly optimistic children banking on quixotic dreams. Like so many, they, too, suffered during the Great Depression and their vision was conditioned by that reality. According to Norman Ball, who later became a member of the American Student Union, young people "have known from bitter and cruel experience just what poverty is. Many times we have been without any food in the house, and without money or a job."[33] Youth, approximately one-sixth of the population (and thus totaling 21.2 million people in 1938), faced diminished prospects for marriage, few constructive recreational outlets, limited educational opportunities, and a troubling international situation. All of these issues sprang from economic instability. As young people recognized, and Leslie Gould, later a member and defender of the American Youth Congress, attested: "The simple, elemental, unassailable crux of the youth problem is *the chance to hold down a job*."[34] The question of whether they would find gainful employment weighed on the minds of young people, and the statistics were not encouraging.[35]

For youth, unemployment was particularly formidable. Unemployment estimates among young people *start*, conservatively, at 25 per cent and range from a low of about three million to a high of seven million or more.[36] According to the American Youth Congress, "out of a total of 12,000,000 unemployed persons in the United States in 1935, Young America appropriated for itself a full 5,000,000. It ate up almost half of the whole unemployment pie all by itself."[37] Young people, notably un-skilled and not recognized as family providers, were often the first fired and last hired once the Depression began. As the trough of the Depres-sion continued to deepen, young people were caught in a vicious unem-ployment cycle in which employers would not hire them because they had no experience (or rather, because there were so many experienced workers who could be hired at low wages) and they could get no ex-perience because no one would hire them. Solicitous New Dealers and supporters like Eleanor Roosevelt identified this as a serious problem because, she said, "young people today have got to have a good deal of practical experience before anyone will think they are worth taking on a job."[38] A study undertaken by pro-New Deal journalists Betty and Er-nest K. Lindley, who were also concerned about the long-term effects of joblessness, posited that by 1938 at least one-third of all unemployed workers in America were young people aged 16–24, thus making the unemployment rate for this age group higher than any other.[39] In some states, the official unemployment rate among youth reached 39 percent.[40] Moreover, of the youth who were employed, 1.8 million had only been able to secure part-time or seasonal work.[41]

Perpetual unemployment struck at a time in their lives when young people should have been building their economic viability in preparation for future family and career development. It was a time in the nation's life when families became more dependent on the income older children could provide to help keep the family financially afloat. Yet employing young people was not a priority, and young people knew it. This, one young journalist claimed, was society's self-inflicted crime.[42] Needing to work in a society that said their work was not needed created a grow-ing skepticism about the possibility of pursuing happiness in that society. For many young people coming of age in the 1930s, disaffection with the status quo began because of the impasse created by the inability of society to meet their needs.[43] They believed they were living on the brink of catastrophe and that the worst was yet to come.[44] Hoping to amelio-rate this situation, the leaders of youth organizations eventually began to pressure their policymaking elders to adopt long-term programs that, if fully implemented, would begin to restructure the American economy

into a socialist system. Theodore Draper, a Brooklyn native who attended
City College and was a member of the NSL, believed like so many young
radicals that this was the key to cure the country's ills, but was especially
critical to what he referred to as the "locked-out generation."[45]

Joseph Lash and James Wechsler were two such radicals. The diminished prospects for economic prosperity helped convince them that fundamental change was necessary. In stark terms they argued that "the onset
of the depression gave rise, too, to a new and popular theory of economics in which the present generation became the 'surplus population.' Unemployment increased and with it a growing apprehension that, whatever
partial restoration might be made, the 'surplus' would continue to exist."[46]
What that might mean for the young generation instilled a fear that can
only be understood in the context of the time. Lash and Wechsler pointedly alluded to the New Deal program to help farmers that entailed the
plowing up of surplus crops and predicted that the surplus generation
would be similarly disposed of by the agents of imperialist war. Such
a situation was simply not acceptable. Frustrated by the status quo and
eschewing the exploitation inherent in a capitalist system, both young
men became adherents of leftist ideologies: Lash turned to socialism and
Wechsler to communism. Two decades later, even after he had become an
avid anti-communist, Wechsler still remembered the attraction to radical
ideologies as *the* logical course of action in the 1930s:

> Generally overlooked or forgotten now is the sense of breakdown
> which for several years swept large areas of American life. Forgot-
> ten too is the absence of clear, affirmative and plausible alternatives
> to Marxism, the hesitancy of scholars and statesmen in the face of
> the Marxist critique. It was not merely what the communists said
> that enthralled us; it was what other men failed to say. The self-
> assurance of the communists proved contagious; the liberal loss of
> nerve repelled us.[47]

At a time when they felt both abandoned and deterred by America's liberal leaders, Wechsler recalled, "the Marxists came breathing certitude
and salvation."[48] The full equality of opportunity provided by a socialist
system attracted youth leaders and, in turn, was championed to varying
degrees by many young people, including those outside the academy. Indeed, a poll conducted by the Institute of Public Opinion in 1936 indicated that, if anything, college students were actually more conservative
in their political views than their out-of-school peers.[49]

While a socialist economy was a far-sighted goal, in the short term, young people needed work experience and/or training; they were largely denied both. The educational system was, in a practical sense, incapable, and in a philosophical sense, unwilling, to fulfill youth's demand for vocational training. A college professor admitted that "education in America came to have the authority of the medieval church," and was nearly as imposing, in the 1930s.[50] Without academic promise, youth had been pushed out of school. Without experience, youth were now pushed out of regular wage work. To level the employment playing field with out-of-work adults (many more of whom, comparatively, had skills), young people began to demand opportunities to develop skills or, alternatively, to stay in school.

Yet staying in school became more of a challenge. During the 1930s, many teachers were fired (as many as 200,000 by 1933),[51] and between 1929 and 1934, 20,000 schools were closed because of a lack of funding. Or, from the perspective of youth, "schools declared a lockout" in order to balance budgets, which resulted in federal, state, and local governments spending $408 million less for education in 1935 than they had in 1929.[52] This meant that more young people, joining those who had already quit school in order to help support their families financially, were forced to abort their education to search for employment. For young people, such as W. D. Coley, a 14-year-old high school sophomore, the financial burden of attending school was too much to bear. In a letter to President Roosevelt, he noted that by October he and his three siblings had to miss more than a month of school because "the tuition [was] $20.00 and books $7.00," which he could not pay because "there is no work anywhere," and he had only gotten "1½ days cotton picking this fall." For a family who could not afford clothes and shoes for the children, education was simply an expendable luxury.[53] Coley's experience was not unique. In 1935 alone, 700,000 high schoolers had to quit school, and by that time, according to official reports, "not more than sixty percent of the youth of normal high school age [were] actually in school."[54] Income from all sources to institutions of higher education dropped 35 percent between 1930 and 1936,[55] and as colleges and universities were forced to make sacrifices, so were families. Even upper and middle class students attending Columbia College felt the pinch; 140 students, cutting convenience and cost, left the dormitories in 1931 and decided to commute from home.[56] The number of college attendees decreased 4 percent in 1932 and a further 4 percent in 1933, which meant, as historian Robert Cohen concluded, that "80,000 youth who would have been in college [were] unable to attend."[57] These young people were the ones most likely to feel cheated by a system that had cast them aside.

Relatively few adult politicians were concerned enough about the plight of American youth to try to do something constructive for them. Eleanor Roosevelt was one of those few. However, the little attention youth garnered during the Depression would be outmatched by the disregard for their experiences after the economic catastrophe subsided. "Many people," Eleanor Roosevelt later lamented, "seem to have forgotten how worried we were about the young people in our country during the early days of the Depression."[58] Her profound concern for youth led to her activism on behalf of young people, their organizations, and their movement's leaders. And it was that concern, coupled with her deeply held liberal beliefs on political inclusion that sustained her public advocacy for youth. While she felt a personal affinity for youth's leaders, whom she befriended, what motivated Roosevelt even more on this matter was her own political convictions. As with many of the causes with which she was involved, such as civil rights and women's issues, the youth movement represented Eleanor Roosevelt's belief that in a democracy individuals have rights and duties toward government and government has certain responsibilities to its citizens. In this, her thinking was very much in tune with what young people were themselves saying.

Eleanor Roosevelt's background in the education field[59] was at the heart of her advocacy of youthful citizenship, and she therefore vested teachers with the responsibility of continuing the political education process begun by parents. Through their years in school, students were to learn about America's democratic process. According to Roosevelt, they should study the nature of political parties and campaigns in order to understand how government worked and then apply that knowledge in their lives. It was important to understand government-citizen interaction in everyday life in such activities as obeying traffic laws and buying postage stamps. But even more important was the understanding of how those laws were implemented and individuals' ability to shape the laws they were obliged to obey. In a democratic republic, individuals have the opportunity to influence politicians who draft legislation, and Eleanor Roosevelt wanted young people to be aware of this power that they, too, possessed. Young people quickly began to act upon this power by engaging authority figures at home, in the streets, at schools, and, eventually, in Washington, as well.

Along the way, they adopted a more radical paradigm through which to judge the American social, political, and economic systems. This radicalism did not frighten Eleanor Roosevelt the way it did many political leaders (especially later in the decade). She was a firm believer that only an educated person could decide on adherence to a political ideology.

This meant that young people should be taught about all political systems, including communism. She thought that a course on communism should be offered in American public schools because she believed "it would be extremely helpful to young people to understand the basis of Communism, the Party line and the Party tactics."[60] If they understood what communism really entailed, she explained, then young people would agree that the most advantageous political system to adhere to was democracy. Whether that democracy was of the social democratic type did not seem to concern her.

It was also in school, Eleanor Roosevelt said, that basic democratic ideals of serving the community and participating in politics were to be passed from one generation to the next. That sense of putting the welfare of the community over one's individual desires was quite in line with young people's socialist ideas of the time. Implicit in her argument, though, was the sense that young people needed to be able to stay in school because although they were expected to become conscientious citizens, she did not think that they were born as such. Nor did she think that these values could be conferred by any means other than education, provided both at home and in the schools.[61] If students could not afford to stay in school, then the repercussion would be felt not just by them and their families, but by the American political system, as well.

In the classroom, students learned how to become active, informed participants in the democratic process. By participating, young people could ensure that their voice would be heard. The most effective way to accomplish this was to join a political organization. In an article for *Future* magazine, Eleanor Roosevelt pointed out that being "active in your political organizations and in various civic groups ... if they [the youth] were organized" could be beneficial because young people could then get their "ideas over to the appropriate departments of government and to the Congress."[62]

The two viable options for youth in the Depression decade were: Stay in school to learn skills needed later in life or find gainful employment. Yet if they were lucky enough to find a job, other problems followed. The nation's youth recognized that their early admission into the work force denied them the time to develop skills necessary to obtain a well-paying job conducive to supporting a family. Concern over marriage weighed heavily on young people as they became increasingly pessimistic about the possibility of raising a family. Marriage would have to be postponed. By 1937, there was, according to the American Youth Congress, "a marriage deficit of 748,000 couples."[63] Without the security of spouse and children of their own, young people would be denied the happiness and stability their parents and grandparents had enjoyed.[64]

Even if young people found work, they could expect no help in securing favorable working conditions, pay, or advancement from their adult worker representatives. They faced hostility from organized labor, whose leaders' loyalty rested with adults.[65] Radical youth leaders, then, quickly decided that youth's economic interest, to the disappointment of Socialist and Communist Party functionaries, would not be served through worker solidarity via labor organizations. Instead, youth turned to reforming the educational system to meet their employment needs. In Eleanor Roosevelt, they had a loyal partner to promote their position because she, too, recognized that the schools were failing the nation's youth. She pointedly asked: "Is education in our public schools today fitting young people,

   a. To earn a living?
   b. To be intelligent and useful citizens?
   c. To lead satisfying lives?
   d. To enjoy their leisure periods?"[66]

Young people knew the answer to all these questions was "no." Eleanor Roosevelt was amenable to hearing that reality in order to construct a better educational foundation since she believed that "school is the beginning of the child's life work."[67] Meanwhile, young people argued that

> Free, widespread vocational training has been an ideal in this country from the days of William Penn down through Abraham Lincoln and Woodrow Wilson to President Roosevelt and Secretary of Labor Frances Perkins.... If this ideal is to be realized, if America is remain the land of equal opportunity, vocational training would have to become a permanent fixture in our public schools.[68]

It took political leaders time to fall in line with this thinking, in part because it required increasing budgets, not slashing them. Many policymakers, unmoved by the pleas and demands of young people, were only convinced to support such programs by the argument that reforming schools would be a constructive vehicle for reducing unemployment.[69] Beginning in 1935, the National Youth Administration (NYA) began to fulfill youth's educational needs. (By then there were already 3.1 million people aged 16–24 on relief rolls, though Works Progress Administration chief Harry Hopkins, who began his career as a New York City settlement house worker, expected there were many more in need and therefore called for a census to collect more accurate data.[70]) The NYA was meant to create an alternative to classical education by providing vocational training at the same time it helped high school and college students remain in school by providing part-time work relief. Since working one's way through college was not a viable option any longer in the face of widespread unemployment, students would go to work for the NYA, instead. At the same time, the NYA furnished aid to schools that faced retrenchment in educational budgets.[71]

While the NYA would bring some relief for many young people, 1935 was five hard-pressed years away from where youth found themselves at the beginning of the Depression. In the meantime, they had found their collective voice by coming together in youth organizations where they practiced the democratic ideals with which Eleanor Roosevelt had hoped they might be imbued. Formulating and implementing agendas within their organizations led to their sense of ownership over youth policy and their presumption that their voice should be heard concerning it. Few were as prescient as Charles Taussig (Chairman of the National Advisory Committee of the National Youth Administration) in understanding the demands of young radicals on their own terms. He tried to explain that "they ask for the opportunities promised them by every Fourth of July orator since the signing of the Declaration of Independence—the opportunity to be educated, the opportunity to work and the opportunity to be heard."[72]

Youth organizations fell into three general (and overlapping) categories: social, religious, and political. Social organizations ranged from the Boy Scouts and Campfire Girls to fraternities and sororities. The YMCA, YWCA, Young Judea, the National Council of Methodist Youth, and various other denominational organizations made up the religious organizations. The political organizations included the Young Democrats, Young Republicans, Young People's Socialist League, and the Young Communist League. Many of the youth organizations of the 1930s had their roots in long-established adult organizations. Various religious youth groups such as the Young Methodists, Young Judea, and the YM-YWCA, for example, had existed since the nineteenth century. Radical political youth organizations, such as the National Student League (NSL), Young Communist League (YCL), Young People's Socialist League (YPSL), and the Student League for Industrial Democracy (SLID) grew out of their parent (communist or socialist) organizations. In the 1930s, however, the NSL and SLID (unlike the other groups) became autonomous youth organizations operating to varying degrees beyond adult control. This independence empowered their members to demand sustained change to benefit young people. The epicenter for these organizations was New York City, where they maintained their respective headquarters and where their executive committees met regularly. There were branches and chapters of each organization through the country, but it was New York City where young radical activists came together to discuss, implement, and disseminate their ideas.

Students made up the majority of these organizations' memberships, though not all youth activists were students. Indeed, youth leaders were employed full-time by the organizations they represented, and students whose time was otherwise occupied were therefore not likely to fill these positions. Leaders had, however, generally been active in the youth movement as students and typically assumed leadership positions after graduation.

Of all the groups that made up the youth movement, socialists and communists were most often the ones to hold prominent leadership positions—largely because their activism was supported by organizations interested in young people. In addition, deeply held ideologies gave them an understanding of the world to adhere to at the same time they provided a solution and a way to achieve their goals, creating more-or-less disciplined functionaries well versed in the art of political maneuver.[73] It is no wonder, then, that young radicals would lead the youth movement. Though generally characterized uniformly as dogmatic radicals, it is important to bear in mind that socialists and communists spent most of the 1930s quarreling with each other and fellow radicals and thus represented no coherent unity of interests. Moreover, there were various socialist and communist organizations, further contributing to a fragmented left. Simply put, socialists and communists led the movement because they were the best equipped to do so and because their ideas were most in line with what young people thought would alleviate the suffering of the Great Depression and prevent its recurrence. The specter of an unruly mass being led in lock-step by those bent on overthrowing the American system was more a figment of a Cassandra mentality than the reality. Young radicals of the 1930s, by and large, wanted to make America live up to its ideals; they did not want to dismantle it.

Not only was there considerable friction between socialists and communists in the 1930s, but communism itself was not a cohesive ideology. Aside from the Young Communist League (YCL) and National Students League (NSL), the communists were further fragmented into competing factions, including the Trotskyists and Musteites; at the same time communism also attracted a broad range of left-leaning liberals. Many young people, disillusioned by their previous faith in the American Dream, found the Soviet experiment alluring. In the Soviet Union, they saw images of factories in full-scale production and farmers working the land. Compared to the images of breadlines, farmers slaughtering pigs while millions went hungry, Hoovervilles, and bastions of unemployed workers that their experience living in a capitalist society afforded them, there is little wonder that a system promising to guarantee equality and sustenance should seem palpably better and at least worth trying. Historian Ralph S. Brax readily admitted that "at a time when many people believed that capitalism was responsible for the horrors of both the first world war and the worst depression in American History, it was only natural that students should be curious about the Soviet experiment."[74] YCL leader James Wechsler was even more to the point in explaining to his brother, a government employee, why he had chosen to become a communist:

> When, as a simple fact, there are 13,000,000 still unemployed and Roosevelt promises jobs for 250,000, I can't help feeling that Washington life has made you too hopeful about how things will turn out. . . . I don't expect a revolution in America to parallel that of Russia's [sic]; there will be many variations of pure communist doctrine. But I hope that you recognize the need for change.[75]

He "agreed with the communists that the world was in dreadful shape and that any possibility of achieving tranquility hinged on men's capacity to change the system."[76] Many young people shared this sentiment.

It has been estimated that there were never more than 5,000 members of the YCL and NSL combined. The NSL, a year before its merger with the Student League for Industrial Democracy (SLID), had, at most, 3,000 members.[77] Other radical groups were even smaller. The Trotskyites' membership, for example, was probably less than 1,000.[78] For those who concur with Martin Dies's characterization of youth leaders, the committed few orthodox communists formed vanguard organizations that set the tone and agenda of the youth movement.[79] "Communists," according to historians concerned with the youth movement, "represented not a normal political party, but rather a conspiratorial group. . . . Communists . . . could not be counted on to be honest about their goals or affiliations . . . they often hid their motives and identifications."[80] They were devious, "faceless people" who worked behind the scenes, like puppet masters, of the youth movement.[81] This characterization denies the attractive qualities of communism and youth's disillusionment with capitalism during the Depression. It also credits the CPUSA (and the Socialist

Party) more power and control over its members than is warranted. While leaders might have desired party unity and uniformity, the oft-repeated admonition found throughout young people's radical literature that such un-socialist behavior as carrying on intra-party disputes in the public eye cannot be tolerated indicates that young radicals were not brainwashed nor hoodwinked, but rather continued to think and speak for themselves.[82]

Communism seemed to be a viable option during the 1930s. Stalin's purges and subsequent show trials would do much to shatter the illusion of Soviet grandeur; however, they did not begin until 1936. Even so, during the 1930s, communism, as an ideology, was not yet as widely recognized as inherently evil, as it would be during the Cold War. Many people, especially youth, in all their stereotyped rebelliousness and radicalism, traveled through the party. Some were undoubtedly convinced that to break the vicious cycle of unemployment created by the Great Depression, drastic measures were necessary; the most radical groups advocated, in true Marxist terminology, "the abolition of the profit system and the establishment of a democratic cooperative commonwealth in which industries shall be run by the people for their own welfare, instead of for the welfare of absentee owners who sit home and collect profits."[83] Yet many CPUSA members, who never religiously adhered to Communist dogma but, rather, as James Wechsler later contended, embraced it as "a democratic humanism,"[84] would nevertheless find solace in the Communists' attempts to offer solutions and provide aid and support when the economic system and governmental response seemed to have failed them. Wechsler, a member of the YCL from 1934 to 1937, argued that youth "had good reason to believe that the American system had lost control over events; and many of those disposed to think much about the chaos were captivated by the view that the Soviet 'experiment' showed us how to resolve the grotesquerie of poverty in a country so richly endowed as ours."[85] Clearly, something had to be done, and communism offered an alternative to the suffering so many were enduring. Moreover, the Communist Party moved perceptibly to the right during the 1930s, thereby increasing its attractiveness to an audience that since the 1920s had defended radicals' right to be heard.[86]

The two most prominent communist organizations for youth were the Young Communist League (YCL), created in 1922 (out of the former Young Workers League that had been established the previous year) by the Communist Party, and the National Student League (NSL), created in 1931,[87] which was not established by the Communist Party, according to Hal Draper.[88] Draper, though, in addition to being Theodore's brother and thus also a Brooklyn native, attended Brooklyn College where he joined the YPSL and, later, became a Trotskyist, so he was likely trying to free the organization he was affiliated with from any connection to the Communist Party and *ipso facto* to Stalin. Some historians nevertheless claim that the NSL was indeed formed by the Communist Party even though the NSL contended its roots were in the League for Industrial Democracy—a Socialist organization. Whatever its parentage, the impetus for its creation was the general feeling that the adult organizations were too conservative. The NSL was kept separate from the YCL, though it was formed by radical students and the two groups had overlapping memberships. The YCL was technically a subsidiary of the CPUSA, which attempted to define its program. It has been assumed, most notably by the first historian of activist youth, George Rawick, that CPUSA policies were determined by the Comintern. Earl Browder, the titular head of the CPUSA from 1930 to 1945, argued that this was not the case. He insisted that the Communist Party, while following the Russian lead, was able to exert a certain degree of autonomy in order to advance the Communist cause in America, whose culture and socio-political systems were markedly different from Russian or European models.[89] The degree to which American Communists were controlled by the Soviet Politburo, which, Browder realized in hindsight was controlled by Joseph Stalin, is therefore questionable. While the YCL did generally follow the Soviet line throughout the Third Period (1928–35), its leaders reached out to socialist leaders in the interest of forming a broader leftist coalition as early as 1934—before the Soviet adoption of the Popular Front. That effort at coalition-building had its roots in the cosponsoring of events, such as the trip to Harlan County, and found expression in the YCL's stated policy of "collective action of the democracies to stop aggression, and the unity of all peace forces to achieve this."[90]

James Wechsler, in unmasking his own communist past before Joseph McCarthy's committee in 1953 and thereby trying to redeem his subsequent turn to liberalism, claimed that the reason he left the YCL in 1937 was not that he and his wife had discovered evil in naked form. "Indeed," he remembered, "we saw much individual goodness and selflessness. It was primarily that the atmosphere was suffocating; we had come to communism in a spirit of rebellion and we found ourselves imprisoned in the most ruthless orthodoxy any political faith ever imposed."[91] Yet Wechsler offers no examples to corroborate this debilitating sense of powerlessness. Instead, there are several key points when he notes that the Communist

Party did *not* exert control over his actions: He decided to write a book (*War Our Heritage*) instead of immediately taking on his leadership role within the YCL, he published that book without pre-approval of its contents (and when there were points the party hierarchy decided were unflattering, he was not forced to omit them), there was very little oversight concerning his work in student organizations (he claims he spent most days talking amicably with—not recruiting—other student leaders, many of whom, like Joseph Lash, were not communists), he was not asked to make speeches about what he had seen on his 1937 visit to the Soviet Union, and he was not pressured to give up bourgeois notions when he decided to leave student work to pursue a career in journalism.[92] Even after leaving the YCL,[93] Wechsler continued to sympathize with the communist perspective on world affairs and maintained that he "thought the Soviet regime had probably improved the living standards of the populace."[94] Whatever aspersions have since been cast upon communism, a much more positive image emerges when focus is placed on what communists—especially young communists—said and did in the 1930s.

While the YCL, generally, could be said to be more oriented toward garnering support for the Soviet Union, the policy positions of the NSL were more certainly a result of native American communism; the NSL agenda was not dictated from above but evolved from below.[95] Members were disenchanted with the direction of American capitalism altogether, for they believed American capitalism was oxymoronic: Capitalism kept America from fulfilling its egalitarian potential. Combating the evils of capitalism, then, was the primary goal of the NSL, but a violent, truly Marxist-Leninist overthrow of the American political and economic systems was not. In this, the NSL had much in common with social democratic groups. It was young people in the NSL who pioneered the Popular Front pattern, according to Theodore Draper, which was for them, manifested not in Soviet foreign policy directives but in American cultural reality.[96] That cultural reality was replete with celebratory homage to American notions of compromise and coalition-building.

In protesting the unfair treatment of the Great Depression's economic casualties—whether on behalf of themselves or others—young people undertook their first significant political steps. Given the impetus for their initiation into the political system, young people were seen as dangerous malcontents. Yet it was in adults' best interest to shore up youth's confidence in America because some young people were losing hope. Leslie Gould testified that "with the crash, the bandwagons that carried all the sleepy dreamers of the American Dream, the reciters of the catechism of the American Way, broke down . . . then began the violation of the spirit of youth."[97] As the Depression became more entrenched, young people were the ones most likely to become permanently jobless, and this "forced, involuntary idleness," it was believed, would ruin "the moral energy of more than a few thwarted young men and women."[98]

The average adult, meanwhile, viewed the "youth problem" quite differently, for they had been influenced, in part, by articles in the national press that focused on the deviance of young people.[99] Witnessing an increase in juvenile delinquency as well as their increased political activity, many adults viewed young people as out of control and on the brink of rebellion. For these adults, youth, particularly organized youth, represented a threat to society. They believed youth were responsible for the communist, Nazi, and fascist regimes coming to power in Europe, and they feared that such revolutions could take place in America.[100] Not recognizing youth as the forerunners of anti-fascist sentiment, these adults also denied youth's right to fashion the future of America, instead calling for more control of unruly *children* at the beginning of the Great Depression.[101] Thus, while young people were lobbying for educational and vocational opportunities, citizens were writing letters to the president warning him of the societal dangers young people posed. One such concerned citizen, Edward Browning, Jr., pointedly asked the president to decrease the minimum entry age for the Army, Navy, and Civilian Conservation Corps (CCC) to 16 in order to keep young people from hanging around street corners, which, he said, was detrimental to everyone's morale.[102] Young people, popular opinion attested, must be controlled.

Youth were seen as social detritus, not as citizens intrinsic to the nation's political fabric. The "youth problem," according to popular belief, was one that faced society; something had to be done to protect society from unruly youngsters. It took most adults some time to realize that unless something was done to improve the situation of youth in America, then their worst fears would be more likely to come to fruition despite the warnings from Charles Taussig, chairman of the NYA National Advisory Committee. He argued that "at the present time, this situation [of increasing radicalization] is not dangerous providing we make a genuine effort to convince the great bulk of the youth of this country that we mean to do well by them."[103] Ignoring youth's problems or trying to suppress young activists' initiatives only bred more radicalism. And then, as more young people turned to radical ideologies, they would unwittingly solidify the older generation's negative perception of them. That, as Wechsler recalled, it was the works of H. L. Mencken and not Karl Marx that most young radicals "recited as scripture, as the last virile voice in a stagnant atmosphere" was irrelevant to adults.[104]

Young activists were committed to changing America for the better regardless of what anyone thought of their efforts to do so. Young people, despite the name-calling that would be leveled at them, wanted to make the system work; they did not revolt. AYC member Leslie Gould, writing in 1940, summed up this notion:

> We knew all this pain and sickness and skinny babies and grain rotting in storehouses wasn't the America we'd been told was waiting for us . . . we knew somehow that it was in our power to fashion the kind of America we'd heard about in song and story . . . We had to get together. . . . Together we could do something for ourselves, for America. Together we could help the older folks see more clearly the way out. We could help with our strength, our courage.[105]

Young people came together for that purpose, forming the youth movement of the 1930s. The development of that movement began in 1931, with the creation of the first national student organization of the era—the National Student League (NSL) at City College of New York. In response to the suspension of the City College newspaper editor, young people came together to form the NSL, which quickly moved beyond local issues to sponsor the trip to Harlan County. That trip, instead of creating a solidarity movement between students and workers, galvanized young people to come together to voice their demands to meet their own needs. Sponsoring the Harlan County trip brought the NSL national attention and made it the most visible youth organization of the time. Consequently, the NSL had 129 local chapters by 1933.[106] Other organizations quickly followed suit. The creation of such national organizations in New York City during the first half of the decade represented the uniting of youth, who generally suffered a common fate during the Depression: unemployment and decreased educational opportunities in a corrupt system where the American Dream was no longer conducive to success. This was the first step in building a youth movement. The NSL, with is small membership, quickly saw the benefits of joining with other groups in order to achieve the vision of America young people espoused and this laid the groundwork for the subsequent creation of an umbrella group, and one of the most important organizations of the 1930s youth movement, the American Student Union.

2
The Reed Harris Affair
Youth Claim Their Rights and Freedoms at Columbia University and Beyond

Trying to voice their concern about the conditions under which coalminers suffered in Harlan County came to no avail for young people in 1932. Yet they had come together through the efforts of the National Student League (NSL), and their unity only grew stronger thereafter. The NSL intended to transform sympathy for workers into a genuine student-worker bond that could one day (soon, members hoped) have real influence over public policy, hastening the transition to a socialist economy. While activist students were inclined to side with workers against employers in any given situation, the link between students and workers remained tenuous due, in large part, to the class barrier: Most college students were members of the middle class or above, and despite what the Great Depression might have done to their families' finances, they retained their middle-class mindset and lifestyle to a great extent. Blue collar workers were lucky if they maintained wages that kept them above the poverty line. As James Wechsler noted in 1935, the idea of America as a land of opportunity where "the working-man's son goes to college with the youthful Duponts, has long ago been exploded."[1] Workers' sons did not go to college, and college students did not go to work in coal mines or on assembly lines. Students' concerns, then, were not the same as workers' concerns. Students "saw" the workers' problems—which were not *their* problems—as philosophical or ideological issues. Their attention was more likely to be held by, and their sustained efforts likely to be expended upon, concerns that had more direct bearing on *their* lives, not someone else's. The Reed Harris affair made this quite clear. They could see themselves walking in the shoes of Columbia student Reed Harris, and so when he was mistreated, students protested because they felt that mistreatment personally, proving that empathy is a good deal more potent than sympathy. Moreover, by this time outrage sparked by campus authoritarianism was normal youth behavior as any affront to personal freedom or attempts to control and repress self-expression met with widespread condemnation on college campuses throughout the previous decade.[2] That they could also claim to be concerned about the exploitation suffered by dining hall workers allowed them to feel secure that they had, indeed, secured the moral high ground from which they could voice their demands regarding how institutions of higher learning ought to be operated. In protesting what they saw as the deplorable treatment meted out to Harris, students (activist and non-activist, alike) were really fighting for their own rights: the right to free speech, the right to be heard, and the right to have a say in policies that affected them.

Within a week of the Harlan County trip, Reed Harris, the editor of Columbia College's student newspaper, the *Spectator*, was expelled for his "insolent" editorials. Harris had a rather common undergraduate experience (playing football, joining a fraternity) until he became editor his senior year.[3] Radicalized by the deepening Depression, Harris began to question everything.[4] He wrote editorials criticizing "king football," a secret society known as Nacoms, and compulsory ROTC training. In advocating the eradication of military training from college campuses, Harris won the support of radical groups, such as the NSL.[5] The NSL was further impressed that "although several persons high in administrative circles of the college heartily disapproved of the student trip to Kentucky, *Spectator* supported the expedition with some enthusiasm and plenty of space. (The Alumni Bulletin, on the other hand, expressed intense opposition.)"[6] While Harris had won the support of radicals, none of these editorial topics stood him in good stead with the administration.

It was his editorial decrying the poor treatment of John Jay Dining Hall workers and the administration of those dining halls for profit that precipitated his expulsion. He charged that prices were inflated and student waiters were exploited in order for the dining halls to earn a profit, proving that they were not being run for the benefit of the students as they were supposed to be—another example of the appalling effects of capitalist greed.[7] Incidentally, the previous editor had claimed that the management of the dining service was incompetent a year before Harris aired his grievances, and he suffered no consequences for those accusations. But much had changed in one year.[8] In 1931, such complaints could simply be ignored. In 1932, however, there was a force (the NSL) to organize efforts for reform. Students would not be pacified until something was done to rectify the situation. Exploitation when times were so difficult had already proven to be an issue among students (resulting in, among other things, the Harlan County trip), but now it was students— both waiters and those who had to pay unduly high prices—who were suffering. Harris believed he was justified in writing this article and likely anticipated consonant outrage from his readers. That he had, by this time, angered and embarrassed members of the administration was a certainty. Thus, this last article was no more the *reason* for his expulsion than the expulsion was the reason for the consequent protests. The article and subsequent expulsion were merely the occasions for retribution for both parties.

Harris's punishment was swift, but the NSL was just as quick to swing into action, galvanizing widespread student support. The group's first order of business was to publicize the proceedings (or lack thereof) that led to Harris's expulsion. On March 31, 1932, the NSL informed students:

> The day after the dining rooms case was reopened, Harris was called before Dean Hawkes and informed that his "registration had been cancelled." Harris was taken before the committee on instruction, sitting at that time, for reasons, which no one has been quite able to understand, inasmuch as everyone, including the Dean, stated that the committee had no powers to veto or modify his expulsion order.... A statement was issued almost simultaneously from the office of the dean which said: "Material published in *Spectator* during the last few days is a climax to a long series of discourtesies, innuendoes and misrepresentations which have appeared in the paper during the current academic year and calls for disciplinary action."[9]

Harris was forced to account for his actions in a written statement to the Dean. In it, he protested both the fact that he had to write such an explanation as well as the dictatorial tone Dean Herbert E. Hawkes adopted in forcing it, likening Hawkes to a drill sergeant more fit for the Marine Corps than an educator responsible for nurturing young minds.[10] Given the general antipathy toward militarism among leftist students, this was a pointed insult. Harris also took this opportunity to list all his complaints, including the poor quality of the food in the dining hall.[11] But what really incensed college officials was that he accused Mabel Reed, the dining hall administrator, of corrupt business practices. Specifically, he claimed that she received rebates from wholesalers, passed the sub-par food to students at inflated prices, and pocketed the profit.[12] Against the dean's claim that the charges were unfounded, Harris defended the statements he had made in *Spectator*, but would not reveal his sources by name because, he said, the student waiters feared losing their jobs.[13] Administrators were quick to jump to Reed's defense, not just in the interest of protecting female honor, but because Reed was the sister of Nicholas Murray Butler, president of Columbia University.[14] Students rejected the administration's perceived vengefulness and were, instead, won over by Harris's plain-spoken explanation of the situation: "I have no personal bones to pick in this matter, no matter what view you may take. I believe firmly that the student body should have the benefit of cheaper food, better food and better service from the John Jay Dining Service, and have it soon."[15] Yet in the course of one day, the controversy had been transformed into something else entirely; the operation of the dining hall was no longer the issue. For administrators, the issue was Harris's impertinent attack on Reed and thus on the college, itself; for students, the issue was Harris's right to free speech. This imbued the Reed Harris Affair with much larger significance, so much so that the *New York Times* gave it front-page coverage, only further galvanizing student feelings of duress.

Nicholas Murray Butler refused to acknowledge that Harris had a case. He viewed it as a simple matter: Students entered a contractual agreement when they entered college, and if one behaved in a manner deemed unacceptable by the college administration, then the college was within its rights to expel such a person. Butler explained in a letter to the university's lawyer that "the dean ... had no alternative but to cancel [Harris's] registration, since he had plainly failed in exhibiting the conduct becoming a gentleman which is one of the essentials for graduation from college. Failure in this respect is certainly as significant as would be failure in a course in mathematics or in history; in my judgment it is much more significant."[16] Furthermore, Butler believed that Harris had endangered the ability of a governing body to effect its will and thus had overstepped the bounds of liberty.[17] To say that Butler disparaged youthful radicalism would be an understatement. He took the college's *in loco parentis* role seriously and set out to make an example of Harris. It was his misfortune that he decided to do this at a time when students increasingly rejected the notion that they should act as obedient children deferring to adult omniscience and omnipotence. Unlike their 1920s predecessors whose insistence upon personal freedoms nestled into their general conformity to American political, social, and economic conservatism, in the 1930s activists rejected not just repressive policies, but the whole system that produced such policies. Such radicalism rankled authorities.[18]

In painting a picture of his alma mater's president, Wechsler, who enrolled at Columbia in 1931 at the age of 16, said of Butler that he would have been considered a "good administrator," which is to say "he is essentially a drill-sergeant, dedicated to the assignment of keeping everyone, student or teacher, in step along the same paths which thousands of others have walked before."[19] This was because Butler, like so many other university presidents, was beholden to the members of the Board of Trustees who ruled higher education indirectly through their subordinates' willingness to submit to the Board's every whim. Above all, Wechsler contended, the Board could never be allowed to think that its power was in jeopardy.[20] Wechsler noted in 1935 that the "trustees are far more than guardians of the treasury; they are the supervisors of the intellectual life of the university—and they do not hesitate to say so in order to resurrect capitalism and its institutions."[21] Trustees were entrenched in the very system that had left so many young people disillusioned. The *Student Outlook*, a socialist newspaper produced by college students whose readers crossed the boundaries of individual college campuses, reflected Wechsler's frustration in claiming that "college trustees are notoriously out of step with social change. . . . They are recruited from the privileged classes. As directors of the college they take it to be their job to preserve the domination of the privileged classes, to preserve the old loyalties, the old customs, the old emotions. They are usually absolute rulers."[22] They, and the broader alumni associative network they represented, were, as Harris referred to them, a "campus Tammany" that ruled, ultimately, to maintain their own positions of power.[23] Harris's editorials were threatening to everything the trustees stood for and promulgated what they stood against: radical visions of reorganizing higher education to serve the needs of students as determined by those very same students—a system that benefited the student body, not the capitalist hierarchy of which academe was a part. Harris's expulsion rid the university of a dangerous rabble-rouser as far as Butler and the administration were concerned.

However, for young people, Harris's expulsion meant something else. It was not about what was good for the university; it was about the rights of students, for his expulsion centered on issues of academic freedom and the protection of civil liberties. Within a week, the Social Problems Club, with help from the NSL, had called a mass meeting attended by approximately 4,000 students, where widespread support was sounded for a student strike to be held two days later. In urging students to strike, the NSL reviewed Harris's editorial stances, stressing his advocacy of students' rights.[24] In explaining the need for student participation, the NSL said that "this was obviously a free speech fight [though] the Social Problems Cub was attempting to get to the deeper political significance of the issue. It was not only the right of free speech, but the right to defend student rights and to campaign for their interests that was at stake. It was because Harris had done this that he was denied the right of free speech."[25] The student committee, consisting of members from the Social Problems Club and the NSL, clarified the issue even further: "The rights of an editor of a newspaper, in acting on information which he considers reliable, to make charges and demand an investigation in a matter of public interest, is a fundamental aspect of the right of free speech and free press."[26]

The protestors were able to secure the reinstatement of Reed Harris on April 20, 1932, with the aid of Raymond Wise, whom the university's lawyer, John G. Saxe, described as "a gentleman, a republican, and a holder of two Columbia degrees." He was also an attorney for the American Civil Liberties Union, which stepped in to represent Harris in his meetings with university administrators.[27] The protestors' other demand, the creation of a student-faculty board to investigate the John Jay Dining Service, had already been granted.[28] As prearranged, Harris then promptly resigned from the university.[29] He had agreed to this because, he said, the activities of the previous three weeks had left him no time to study for the final exams that were fast approaching. Harris was also required to write a letter of apology to Dean Hawkes, but he steadfastly refused to agree with Butler that his dismissal had no connection to the freedom of the press or the right to free speech.[30]

Harris was expelled the same day the election took place to choose his successor as editor of *Spectator*. Ironically, that turned out to be Wechsler, who led the newspaper ever more leftward, paralleling his road through socialism to communism.[31] His scathing editorials would allow it to remain, he insisted, "the most independent, outspoken college paper in the country," and, he predicted, if it were able to survive, "it will be because of the awareness of a student body which long ago learned that, even in the 'most liberal university world,' academic freedom endures only so long as it is militantly defended."[32] Harris was subsequently voted most likely to succeed by his fellow seniors.

By then, even many passive students had become politicized, as more than 75 percent of the student body (1,500 out of 2,000 students plus an additional 2,000 students in other schools of the University) had participated in the student strike on April 6, 1932. The NSL, though it helped organize the strike, never had more than 3,000 members nation-wide, indicating the popular appeal of its position among the Columbia student body.[33] During the strike, students picketed and bound the Alma Mater statue located in the middle of campus with black crepe to denote the gagging of free speech, which sparked violent protest from the Spartans, a pro-Administration group.[34] They thought the "radicals" had gone too far; Butler agreed.

The very same day that the agreement was reached in the Harris case, Butler received, upon his request, a report from the Director of Admissions on twenty-one students that listed their intelligence test scores, family information, and general disposition.[35] In summing up the students' confidential files, the Director also noted how the students had scored in response to the loyalty questions on their admissions applications, suggesting that the connection between their responses and their recent actions exposed serious character flaws. These twenty-one students were not self-proclaimed revolutionaries; they were the students who had visited Butler on April 5, 1932, the day before the strike, to plead for a reversal of Harris's expulsion and thus avert the coming showdown. To Butler, though, guilt by association was thereby substantiated, as at least one of the students had been an avid supporter of the Harlan County trip.[36] This proved, in his mind, that Harris's expulsion was not only warranted, but necessary.

To those sympathetic to the striking students, however, the expulsion was at best a terrible mistake, and at worst a grim symbol of the state of American civil liberties. An article in *The Nation* entitled "Free Speech at Columbia" described the expulsion as "a hideous blunder" resulting from a failure of due process. Reverberating with the fear of what this might mean for college students' rights in the future, it pointed out that "the damage is done whether Mr. Harris himself was guilty or innocent of any misconduct. . . . The fact remains that no effort was made to prove his guilt and . . . the expulsion was affected by the authority of one man without the formality of a hearing before even a faculty committee."[37] Had the reporter been privy to Butler's private correspondence, he would have been even more disturbed to find that there was a committee formed to help advise the president on this matter—a committee that was fed information by Nicholas Murray Butler, including the confidential student reports, and which did not ever condescend to speak to Reed Harris at all. The same writer pointed out that the administration had shown poor judgment in siding with the "conservative rah-rah boys," who are "the least serious, the least intellectual, and the least articulate of the student body" against the "liberal intellectual element."[38] At Columbia University in the spring of 1932, student activists raised their voices, convinced the student body to rise, and achieved results, both concrete and psychological, through their collective power.

As Wechsler, writing in 1935, remembered, the Reed Harris Affair was a galvanizing moment because "the event . . . served to dramatize the need for organized student force to combat similar moves. Perhaps even more important than the mere fact of undergraduate thought—however extraordinary—was a conviction of power which the triumph of the strike engendered."[39] The strike, in particular, had garnered national publicity and thus, he said, "established the place of the student movement and the paths of procedure for it to follow," and so the protest action on behalf of Harris served as a model for later action.[40]

Indeed, the Reed Harris Affair was not unique. Other students suffered a fate similar to Harris. During that school year (1931–32), eight other student editors were expelled or lost their jobs, and another twelve left their positions due to pressure placed on them by their schools' administrations; however, it should be noted that no editors left their posts as a result of student body dissatisfaction, indicating that students either agreed with what the editors were writing or agreed that they had a right to express themselves.[41] Moreover, it was not just Columbia students who were protesting. Students were challenging authority on campuses across the nation.

Not far from Columbia, at City College of New York (CCNY), similar confrontations between students and administrators had begun even earlier and were sustained even longer. It was at CCNY in 1925 that student agitation against ROTC began, setting a precedent replicated on campuses across the nation.[42] In 1930, the CCNY administration invoked a 1927 ruling by the board of trustees to prevent political talks and meetings on campus on questionable grounds.[43] The original ruling prohibited the use of campus premises in the interests of one political party during an election campaign; however, as applied in 1930 it prevented a series of talks by the leaders of three leading parties. With the ban on political meetings in place, involvement in political issues subsequently played out in the context of club meetings and the articles published by the college's newspaper, *The Campus*.

To maintain control over the newspaper, the editor was suspended in 1930 for criticizing CCNY president Frederick B. Robinson.[44] Youth activist and CCNY student at the time, Joseph Lash, who characterized Robinson in the most derogatory term by calling him a "Babbitt," later remarked, in explaining Robinson's actions, that he "cannot brook criticism, and when he has the whip hand he retaliates, sometimes in a very petty fashion."[45] Underlying the outrage over the editor's suspension was the general dissidence among *The Campus* editorial staff concerning alumni censorship of the newspaper through the Campus Association, which oversaw the newspaper's operations in its downtown offices. The staff saw this as an attempt to hamstring student efforts at self-government by denying student editors any autonomy over the newspaper and by physically separating the publication of the newspaper from the uptown campus.[46] The Campus Association was ultimately able to maintain its control over the newspaper in the face of four editors (including Joseph Lash) resigning in protest; however, the administration found it more difficult to rein in student outrage initiated by the editor's suspension.[47]

Even after the alumni board reinstated the editor, the escalating cycle of student demonstrations and reprisals continued. Wechsler, reporting on the situation at CCNY, said Robinson "tried to disrupt and terrorize every left-wing student group, [erecting] an even more oppressive network of espionage and intimidation"[48] than the one Wechsler was familiar with at Columbia. Like Butler, Robinson, who was celebrating his twenty-fifth year at CCNY, believed that radicalism (defined as students acting in any way he interpreted as a challenge to the administration's authority) had to be snuffed out. To that end, the president and eight other members of the Social Problems Club were suspended for handing out the club's newsletter, *Frontiers*, without prior approval and in direct violation of Robinson's earlier edict to disband the club.[49] The showdown continued unabated for a full month, as campus groups came out in support of the Social Problems Club and its members, who numbered only twenty-one out of more than 6,000 day session students.[50] In the face of campus turmoil, the board of trustees restored the Social Problems Club, granted it permission to publish and distribute its newsletter, and brokered a compromise between Robinson and the suspended students that allowed for their reinstatement.[51] And while Lash had resigned as editor, he remained a columnist for *The Campus*, assuring that radical views would continue to be voiced. Despite the compromises, the disputes between student radicals and administrators did not end.

When the furor over the Reed Harris expulsion began at Columbia, students at CCNY protested in sympathy. *The Campus* circulated a petition to more than 200 colleges in support of Reed Harris, sent an official protest letter to President Butler, and called for a thorough investigation to expose the administration's wrongdoing.[52] It also reported with some pride that Tudor R. Harris, father of Reed Harris and a CCNY student during the 1892–93 academic year, stated that "he would consider it a 'stigma' if his son were to receive a degree from Columbia."[53] Illustrating that *Spectator* articles were, in fact, circumspect in their reporting of the conditions at John Jay Dining Hall, *The Campus* reported details taken from a worker's affidavit noting the "instances of lice-nests being found in rolls, of dead worms being scraped from foods, of rats living in the cabinets, and of corn grit being used in hamburger sandwiches."[54] The intended effect was achieved: CCNY students were outraged. Not even the summer hiatus subdued their ire, which simmered and then flared up again the following semester.

In the fall of 1932, a student forum was denied the right to hold a political symposium at CCNY because the symposium planned to have speakers from four political parties: Republican, Democratic, Socialist, and Communist. Socialists and Communists were not entitled to the right to free speech, as far as the administration was concerned. The Student League for Industrial Democracy therefore sponsored an outdoor meeting so the symposium could be held off campus.[55] Subsequently, the faculty advisor to the Social Problems Club was dismissed and nineteen more students suspended for "left-wing" activity. Yet the more the administration tried to repress radicalism, the more students protested.

There were further disturbances at CCNY in the fall of 1932 when Oakley Johnson, an English professor who had been teaching there for twelve years, was fired, which the administration claimed was a budgetary decision but students believed was the result of Johnson's membership in the League for Industrial Democracy, his previous membership in the NSL when he was a student, his sponsorship of the Liberal Club, and (most damning) the fact that he had accompanied students to Harlan County, Kentucky. A march on the administration building by several hundred students led to the arrest of twenty of them, which then sparked a second march to the courthouse, where another demonstration was held.[56] A public hearing orchestrated by the NSL and attended by 1,500 student sympathizers, demanded Robinson's resignation.[57] An additional nineteen students were later suspended (and subsequently reinstated by the Board) for holding a mock trial of Robinson.[58] Their suspension also sparked mass meetings in protest. Student outrage over the abrogation of their rights was not only prolonged but seemed to be infectious.

The Campus routinely expressed the importance of students' right to fight for free speech. By 1932, that fight, as well as the newspaper's defense of it, had been going on for nearly three years. In an editorial calling for a repeal of the "gag rule" the paper proclaimed: "The restriction prohibiting political activity within the college is not only an un-American violation of the freedom of speech and press, it is a distinct impediment to an important phase of our college education."[59] The Liberal Club held yet another public meeting four days later at which Robinson defended his actions to an audience of 1,000 students. During the question and answer period that followed, one student asked if Robinson would allow Oakley Johnson, who was in attendance, the right to present his version of events, to which Robinson responded: "I think that it would be an affront to the college to have a man named Oakley Johnson ever say anything in these halls. . . . This man has no right to address this meeting or any other within the protection of the college."[60] And then, when the chairman of the meeting refused to deny Johnson's right to defend himself, Robinson promptly left the dais, saying that "no self-respecting and honorable person can remain in the same room with the person who expects to speak now."[61] Robinson's disdain was palpable and was the source of his decision to expel forty-three students, suspend thirty-eight others, bring hundreds before disciplinary boards, and ban every radical publication and organization at some point during the three-year period between 1931 and 1934.[62]

The effect of this repression, according to Wechsler, was that "by 1933 the college was riddled with rulings which virtually barred any semblance of undergraduate expression on the issues of their immediate environment or of larger spheres."[63] That same year, students held a counterdemonstration numbering 500 people on Jingo Day to protest the ROTC, and during a confrontation with the protestors, Robinson struck students with his umbrella.[64] Robinson, it appeared to many, did not represent the calm voice of reason, but rather the shrill voice of hysteria.

At the end of 1932, when the focus shifted back to Columbia, where Donald Henderson, an Economics instructor, was let go, purportedly because he had not finished his doctoral degree and had a poor teaching record, CCNY students continued their inter-campus support.[65] Wechsler, who was at the time a student at Columbia, admitted that Henderson was not a great teacher, but insisted that was not the cause for his dismissal because, on this basis, 80 percent of Henderson's colleagues should have been let go as well. Instead, Wechsler explained, Henderson was dismissed because he was a radical: "He refused to accept the breach between thought and action to which his colleagues were inured."[66] Specifically, Henderson had organized unemployed workers in Harlem, helped found the NSL, and participated in the Reed Harris strike (one of only sixteen faculty members who publicly supported Harris).[67] In turn, Harris called on students to protest the firing of Henderson. "Education," Harris claimed "is a little like beer. It needs ferment to keep it from becoming flat. It needs activity and teachers like Henderson provide this activity to dispel the unhealthy serenity of college studies."[68] Activists organized an initial strike of 150 students, a subsequent demonstration of more than 1,000 that turned into a near riot, and dramatically made their point by carrying across campus a black-draped coffin inscribed with the message "here lies academic freedom."[69] In an expression of solidarity, Henderson was invited to speak at CCNY by the Social Problems Club, illustrating activist students' common quest to safeguard their rights.[70]

Students in New York City were at the forefront of such protests, and they helped spark similar ones across the nation because they were so capable of using both the college and national press outlets. Such protests became more than a New York City phenomenon as other students around the nation read about what was going on at Columbia and CCNY. Students also protested administrations' attempts to curb their rights at institutions such as the University of Michigan, University of California at Los Angeles, Ohio State University, Massachusetts Institute of Technology, University of California—Berkeley, University of Pittsburgh, Yale University, and the University of Chicago.[71]

Vital to these protests was the mouthpiece of students—the college newspaper—whose editors, like Wechsler, outspokenly tried to "resist the tide of Trustee-domination."[72] Fifty college newspaper editors gathered together in New York in September 1933 to form an Association of College Editors to serve as an information network for reporting newsworthy events; at the same time, it allowed them to act in concert, especially when one of them was threatened with suspension or expulsion for speaking out. This group also took upon itself the task of countering the Hearst Press that regularly attacked organized youth as the red menace. Young activists had formed a network, had identified their enemies, and now intended to set the record straight in order to carry on their efforts to establish a more just and democratic system.

Activist youth's concern over academic freedom and civil liberties was sincere and, it turns out, merited. They were right to feel targeted. Young people's freedoms were abrogated by college administrators who were working with the Federal Bureau of Investigation, which was intent on stamping out all signs of radicalism. Historian Robert Cohen has argued that in providing confidential data regarding the political affiliations, activities, and ideas of thousands of student activists to the FBI, college administrators tore away the rights of students and thereby rent the entire fabric of higher education: "This trampling of student civil liberty compromised the very ideal of the university as a center of free intellectual discourse and pursuit of truth."[73] Legislators, mistakenly thinking that students had been inculcated with radicalism from their professors, instituted loyalty oaths. In 1935, New York State Senators passed the Nunan Bill, which required students at publicly financed institutions to take a loyalty oath.[74] The Nunan Bill provided young radicals with further proof that there was a concerted effort afoot to silence them and thus this bill was widely protested by college students as an infringement of their rights as American citizens.[75] An editorial in *The Campus*, calling on students to protest the Nunan Bill, saw through the ruse: "The Nunan Bill is avowedly aimed 'to keep communists out of the College of the City of New York....' We hardly think it necessary to repeat that communists have as much right to go to City College as anyone else and it should be obvious that the Nunan Bill, if adopted, would be patent discrimination."[76] Within a week, the paper was publishing articles linking the Nunan Bill to red-baiting by the Hearst Press and identifying it as an indication of the "INCREASING MENACE OF FASCISM IN AMERICA."[77] Such well-organized efforts helped ensure the bill's quick defeat in the New York State Assembly. Despite government officials, college administrators, FBI agents, and the Hearst Press working together to combat American student radicalism, their actions only drove more students further left and made them more likely to protest.

This reached down to the high school level, as well. Robert Spivack, for example, was the editor of his high school newspaper his senior year and used that position to challenge the Dayton, Ohio Board of Education for unjustifiably removing the principal. He remembered that throughout the campaign to rectify the situation, he "led a delegation of students to see the Governor of Ohio, [was] threatened with dismissal from office, [and] threatened with cancellation of academic credits."[78] Although his (and other students') efforts did not lead to the reinstatement of the wronged principal, he was vindicated when "five of seven members of the Board of Education were defeated the following election as a result of our fight."[79] Spivack, for one, had become a player in the American political system even though he, like all other young people under the age of twenty-one, could not vote.

Despite the pressure to lower the voting age to eighteen by such groups as "March of Youth,"[80] most political leaders agreed with Eleanor Roosevelt, who, for all her liberal sentiments, said she "did not particularly favor a change in the voting age" even though she realized "it is a change which is advocated by a number of young people who think that as it is usually considered possible to put young people to work at eighteen, that this should also mean that they should be given the right to vote at that age."[81] She might have noted that young people that age could also enter militarily service as well. Unlike most nay-sayers who wanted to keep radical elements or immature people from the voting booth, Eleanor Roosevelt believed that young people between the ages of eighteen and twenty-one should "think more about preparation for their participation in government and use those three years as years of preparation," because then both "they and our democracy would profit."[82]

Activist youth envisaged no better way to "prepare for participation" than to engage in protests to protect academic freedom and civil liberties. Freedom and liberty, they believed, were essential to a functioning democracy and thus young activists imbued localized events at such places as Columbia University or Harlan County, Kentucky, with much more significant meaning. Adults who thought young people were exaggerating were blinded by their own gullibility; for young people, the molehill was a mountain whose façade did not need to be scaled so much as it needed to be sculpted to democratic perfection.

For youth (activist and non-activist, alike), then, academic freedom and civil liberties spoke to a much larger issue: the functioning of democracy. They were American citizens, and as such they believed they had a right to influence policy. One such concerned young person, Bill Hagen, pointedly asked "how youth, tomorrow's leaders, may preserve American democracy" if they were not allowed to voice their concerns and be heard.[83] Events like the Reed Harris Affair made their voice audible, and it was, if one listened closely enough, a political voice that was coming of age. Youth activists believed that "the student movement in this country now has strength" and therefore demanded "participation in the government of the college; not merely a partial control of extra-curricular activities" and not "illusory self-government," but rather "a voice in the vital affairs of the college," which would include an end to the trustee domination of higher education and/or the inclusion of students and faculty on boards of trustees.[84] The purpose and parameters of higher education were thus being questioned and sometimes rejected.

Like so many other youth activists who encountered the American political system through confrontation and opposition, Robert Spivack, too, became a member (and eventual president) of the socialist League for Industrial Democracy (LID) chapter upon entering college. And, like so many other young people, he simultaneously maintained membership in various other organizations, including the International Relations Club and the YMCA. He explained that he was "a radical . . . in large part because of study and analysis and in smaller part because of a desire to aid the underdog."[85] His radicalism did not motivate him to overthrow the American system. Instead, Spivack wanted to help those less fortunate than he.

The LID was the most organized and widely respected radical group on the college campus.[86] By 1933, the students involved in the LID split off to form the Student League for Industrial Democracy (SLID), an autonomous youth organization and the most successful socialist student organization of the 1930s. According to historian Philip G. Altbach, its success hinged on the way "it marked a change in orientation, away from an educational perspective to activism."[87] In promoting action, the more ideological SLID leaders, like Joseph Lash, who edited the group's newsletter, *The Student Outlook*, were able to attract a less ideological membership, which included many people who became identified with leftist and liberal causes, including labor leader Walter Reuther, sociologist (and CCNY graduate) Daniel Bell, philosopher (and CCNY graduate) Sidney Hook, journalist Max Lerner, humorist Will Rogers, and writer Irving Stone, among others.[88] Peace was the SLID's main concern (it sponsored the annual student strike for peace from 1934–1940 and adopted the Oxford Pledge as its manifesto) although it also supported economic relief and academic freedom for American youth. All of these positions made it attractive to young people in the 1930s. Within a year of its founding in New York City, the SLID had 4,000 members and 120 chapters while its publication, *The Student Outlook*, published in New York City, reached an even wider audience.[89]

In jumping to Harris's defense, then, the NSL had initiated another crusade that increased the momentum of the youth movement established by the Harlan County trip because it had inspired the creation of another powerful student organization: SLID. Though the NSL and SLID, and, more particularly, the leaders of the two organizations, were leftists, they nevertheless claimed the right to speak for all youth. Claiming to speak for all students was reasonable because undergraduates had, as a whole, moved to the left, especially in their ideas about the government's role in society and the economy.[90] While students voted staunchly Republican in straw polls throughout the 1920s, socialist Norman Thomas won the majority of student support in a Columbia University poll in October 1932. The polling was spread over six days, and the results showed Thomas with an early lead.[91] Student participation was high (about 67 percent), and the end result gave 1,033 votes to Thomas, 833 to Herbert Hoover, 547 to Franklin Roosevelt, and 81 to William Z. Foster.[92] This was a much better showing for the Socialist Party than among the American electorate as a whole, from whom Thomas garnered only 2.2 percent support. There were Thomas for President Clubs on over 150 campuses.[93] And while Hoover won the nationwide student ballot, leftists felt strength in the fact that when the Democratic, Socialist, and Communist Parties' support was taken together, more students voted for change than not.[94] Wechsler explained the general confluence between activist leaders and students: "There is no divergence between our interests and those of the vast body of students; our problems are alike and our quest for a solution inspired by the same conditions."[95] The straw poll results, the growing incidences of protest demonstrations, and the increasingly radical rhetoric employed by college editors indicated growing disillusionment with the American political and economic systems as they then functioned. Added to this was the ferment caused by an antiquated educational system unfit to meet youth's needs and a rejection of adults' desire to treat them like children when they believed they were American citizens whose rights should be protected. Growing discontent was matched by commensurate radicalism, creating the conditions for a genuine youth movement.

Yet student activists claimed to speak for all *youth* and felt justified in doing so. This was because, in the end, they had much in common with others in their cohort; the Depression economy had no place for them, and they shared similar expectations about American democracy. Activist leaders tethered themselves to their memberships. If they moved too far to the left, in advocating Marxism, for example, they would have no organization left to lead. If they were sincere ideologues (and it is doubtful that many were true Marxists; it is more appropriate to say that they had a Marxist orientation), they nevertheless had to bend to the will of the majority. This became clearer as mass organizations were erected later in the decade.

Both the Communist Party of the Soviet Union (CPSU) and the CPUSA have been credited with more influence over young communists than they rightfully deserve. The CPSU had to use murderous purges to control communists in the Soviet Union. It could not possibly control young people in America to the point of dictating every move, as so many have supposed. Neither William Z. Foster nor Earl Browder enjoyed widespread support among left-leaning youth. Young people, radical activists included, were uncommitted to Communist Party leaders and adhered even less to communist doctrine concerning how to take over power. Although they had alternative ideas about how America should be run, young people did not physically attack the establishment. In fact, demonstrations were likely to erupt into "riots" only when rightist groups such as the Spartans at Columbia attacked peacefully assembled leftists. Wechsler still recalled more than twenty years later, even after he had become an anti-communist, that "there seemed to be nothing funny about the way the defenders of free speech were being attacked and heckled and pelted with water-bags and pushed around by those who refused to understand the solemnity of the occasion."[96] The rightists believed the leftists were wedded to Marxist-Leninist theory much more than the leftists actually were. They did not try to set up Soviets. They rarely railed against bourgeois American decadence, partly because such decadence was scarcer during the Depression, but also because they were not leading a proletariat against the bourgeois state.

Indeed, young people (activists included) hoped to become part of the revered brotherhood called the American bourgeoisie. They wanted to protect what was left of the middle class and enlarge it through a social democratic vision of equality of opportunity, which helps explain how so many of the radical leftists of the 1930s became mainstream liberals later in life.[97] It is not that they changed so much as America had changed. The radicals of the Great Depression, like Harris, Wechsler, and Lash, were products of their time.[98] Once the Depression was over and the New Deal institutionalized, the political and economic systems in America looked like they might just live up to their potential after all (with the social system to make significant strides shortly thereafter through the civil rights movement and its progeny). Former activists could believe in America once again. The promise was still there, but that was not how the situation looked in 1932.

To prove the point, one should consider the less obviously radical groups, which were, nevertheless, radicalized by the effects of the Great Depression. The YMCA, the oldest national religious group, for example, was quite active on campus and was becoming rather left-leaning. It earned a reputation for being one of the first groups on campus to be concerned about issues affecting the working class, particularly those revolving around the relationship between worker and employer in an exploitative capitalist system.[99]

The largest liberal student organization in the 1930s was the National Student Federation of America (NSFA), created in 1925 (and thus the oldest of the student organizations) and made up of representatives from collegiate student governments. It acted as a clearinghouse to provide information and services to the college population and worked tirelessly in encouraging student participation in all levels of government.[100] It organized conferences, such as the National Institute for Public Affairs in 1934, which was co-sponsored by the United States Office of Education, to get students involved in discussions on topics of national importance.[101] One historian has noted that the NSFA "was recognized by many adults, on and off campus, as the voice of the American student community. Thus its statements received some attention and university administrators and others listened to these 'legitimate' student leaders."[102] It was a firm supporter of academic freedom and revision of college curricula in addition to advocating increased appropriations for New Deal youth programs and economic support for students. Yet even a self-avowed moderate group such as the NSFA moved substantially to the left in the 1930s, supporting a generally pacifist platform more commonly associated with left-leaning groups.[103] It protested the Nunan loyalty-oath Bill, passed resolutions calling for the abolition of compulsory ROTC, and supported the League of Nations as well as American participation in the World Court and the Geneva disarmament talks.[104] Moreover, the NSFA considered itself a trade union, representing students in collective bargaining relations with college administrators and trustees and saw publicizing student concerns as its *raison d'être*.

Thus, in both outlook and activity, the NSFA was operating on a track parallel to the NSL and SLID, and even though its members might insist its destination was different, all three groups envisioned an America where young people had a place at the decision-making table, and together they undertook radical actions to gain that place. Historians tend to view liberal students as having been swept away by more disciplined radical groups, but, in reality, liberals, socialists, and communists were uniting in a common cause. The resulting synergy propelled the incipient youth movement. The liberals were not hoodwinked; they were willing partners. Because 150 colleges and universities, representing approximately 500,000 students, affiliated with the NSFA by 1935, it was much larger than the NSL and SLID, and thus it was this liberal organization that served as a bellwether for the youth organizations that would subsequently unite in a popular front against war and fascism.[105]

When the socialists, communists, and liberals united to form the American Youth Congress in 1934 and the NSL and SLID came together in 1935 to form the American Student Union, their commensurate power, youth activists believed, would be undeniable. In that, they were not mistaken because even the Roosevelt Administration, for a period, accepted the voice of activist youth as the legitimate expression of American youth, thus increasing the prestige and influence of the movement and its leaders.[106]

Ever vigilant in protecting their right to free speech, the editors of *The Campus* published an open letter to President Robinson in 1935, warning him that "The faculty and the undergraduates will not countenance any infringement on free student expression.... You said 'the time might come when it will be clear that a college can not permit its students to publish papers.' We trust that that time has not yet come. We trust that it will never come."[107]

By this time the movement to remove Robinson had picked up steam, enlisting the support of powerful alumni, including President Roosevelt's advisor and future Supreme Court Justice, Felix Frankfurter.[108] *The Campus* quoted a report by the Alumni Association, which found that "the [CCNY] president [Robinson] lacks the human qualities necessary to achieve the widespread confidence of his faculty and his student body and to provide genuinely inspired, resourceful and socially imaginative leadership."[109] Both the Student Council at CCNY and the American Federation of Teachers adopted resolutions asking the Board of Higher Education to remove him as president because he was "one of the most dangerous enemies of academic freedom in America."[110] In December 1938, while he was on sabbatical leave, Robinson's "retirement" was announced.[111] Eight years of radical student agitation had come to fruition.

The Reed Harris Affair was a catalyst for that radicalism. Looking back, the *Columbia Spectator* noted in 1935 that "every time two or more college editors get together for a discussion, if the session lasts long enough, one of them is bound to bring up the name of Reed Harris."[112] He became a legend for *Spectator* editors, but also, according to a *Spectator* editorial published in 1961, "a symbol of the early 1930's—a time of questioning and reappraisal on college campuses."[113] Remembering this period of his life, Wechsler noted that "the year was 1932, the time of Hoovervilles and a Bonus Army marching on Washington and angry farm revolts and everywhere the pall and frustration.... At seventeen I was a sophomore and a socialist. Life had really begun, I was convinced, with the Reed Harris strike."[114]

Reed Harris went on to a storied career. After leaving Columbia in 1932, he wrote *King Football*, which a reviewer called a "biting commentary on colleges."[115] Publishing this book led to employment at *The New York Times* and *The New York Evening Journal*. He then went on to be an editor and productions manager of an advertising agency before going to work as the Assistant Director for the Federal Writers' Project in 1935. In 1945, he began an eight-year stint working for the Voice of America within the State Department, only to be called before Joseph McCarthy in 1953 to account for his radical past. He resigned his position at Voice of America, but in standing up to McCarthy, he won the respect of Edward R. Murrow, who hired him in 1961 to work in the International Information Administration. Like Murrow, Wechsler, editor for the *New York Post* at the time, also publicly decried McCarthy's trampling of civil liberties despite the fact that Wechsler had by then turned his back on his radical past and become a staunch anti-communist.[116] Wechsler, too, was called before McCarthy's committee where he provided five hours of testimony.[117] Whether or not they disavowed their youthful radicalism (Wechsler did; Harris did not), both men were just as wedded to freedom of thought, speech, and press in the 1950s as they had been in the 1930s.

Columbia University, meanwhile, followed its path toward suppressing academic freedom and civil liberties in an effort to quell the growing radicalism engendered by the Reed Harris Affair. Six months later, and as a direct result of the public protests against his expulsion, outdoor meetings were banned at Columbia, in an effort, *Spectator* claimed, "to keep Communists out;" indoor meetings required faculty members' approval and sponsorship.[118] Consequently, the Thomas for President Club had to hold its meeting off campus on October 7, 1932, which necessarily lowered turnout and perhaps affected the result of the 1932 straw vote. The decree brought enough widespread protest that it was rescinded by the Committee on Student Organizations five days later, with the caveat that outdoor meetings could only be held on the South Field and not on the Low Library steps where they had been held in the past, and indoor meetings had to be scheduled in advance (thus there could be no impromptu protest gatherings inside), supposedly in order to find adequate space.[119]

In the midst of this new controversy, the investigative committee established as a result of the negotiations between the ACLU and the university administration regarding the Harris expulsion, submitted its report on the John Jay Dining Service, declaring the two most serious charges against the management unsubstantiated. It claimed that the food was as clean as could be expected in view of the large number of meals prepared and that the managers were not receiving rebates. The complaints about the mistreatment of student employees was "partly confirmed," but was the result of "a lack of coordination" between management and students and thus did not qualify as real mistreatment, the report claimed.[120] Six of ten front-page stories in the *Spectator* the next day criticized the administration; four of those stories supported the claim that it was a bogus report that whitewashed the charges. The two remaining critical articles discussed the general censorship of student opinion, one of which was written by Harris himself. The other article was titled "Boesling Denies Censorship: Columbia Board to Continue Control of Editorial Policy."[121] Clearly, students chafed at the stifling of their voice and still found ways to publish opinions with which the administration disagreed.

Even after Harris left and Wechsler graduated, the *Columbia Spectator* continued its vigilance in pointing out breaches of civil liberties. In 1938, a front-page editorial lambasted President Butler for denying free speech to radicals who came to speak to students, a fact that was particularly galling because he had previously accepted a request from fascist delegates to visit Columbia.[122] The clash on campus quadrangles between those who wanted to carry on the vestiges of an earlier milieu and those who rejected it continued unabated.

Before Harris died in 1982, there was an effort to get Columbia University to grant him an honorary degree, which the university steadfastly refused to do, much to the chagrin of the college's newspaper, which pointed out the hypocrisy of championing human rights advocates abroad, but not those who hailed from within the college's own walls.[123] Administrators had come and gone, but the Columbia administration remained wedded to the idea that students who spoke out deserved punishment, not respect. Harris was never officially recognized for the stand he took for academic freedom and civil liberties.

Nevertheless, the *Spectator* accurately understood in 1932 that Harris's expulsion "fired the shot heard 'round the undergraduate world" in an opening salvo that would lead to increased confrontation between young radicals and adult authority figures throughout the decade.[124] Spearheading young people's efforts were the SLID and NSL, both established and headquartered in New York City. Coming together in a genuine youth movement, as a result of the Harlan County trip and the Reed Harris Affair, would allow activist youth to push for further democratic ideals; their attention turned next to the issue of racial equality. It was not enough for authority figures to listen to youth's demands for economic opportunity and civil liberties; they would also have to entertain the notion of universal freedom and equality if America was going to carry the mantle of democracy. Working in concert on behalf of racial equality and justice would bring about the merger between the NSL and SLID to form the American Student Union.

3

The Scottsboro Boys
Demands for Equality from the Deep South to New York City

I n March 1931—a full year before the Harlan County, Kentucky, trip and the Reed Harris expulsion—nine black boys ranging in age from 13 to 19 years old were arrested on a freight train near Scottsboro, Alabama. Within twelve days of their arrest, they were indicted, tried, and all but one were convicted of raping two young white women aged 17 and 21. Their many retrials would keep the cases of these young men in the national spotlight for the remainder of the decade and beyond.[1] Already in October 1932, a month before the U.S. Supreme Court, in *Powell v. Alabama*, remanded the decision of the Alabama State Supreme Court, holding that the Scottsboro Boys' right to due process had been violated, the National Student League was drumming up support for such a ruling. An article in the *Student Review*, the official newsletter of the NSL, provided a detailed review of the case up to that point. The article stressed the unfair treatment the defendants had suffered while calling to light the travesty of justice American jurisprudence had suffered because the whole trial had been nothing but a show:

> The stage was already set.... A special grand jury had already indicted the boys. Legal formalities had been dispensed with.... The nine terrified, helpless boys, chained, and bearing marks of brutal beatings, were dragged into the court-room. The oldest boy was twenty; the youngest just thirteen—all poor, illiterate, and absolutely at the mercy of the mob.... The court tried to bribe them and threaten them, but they held out courageously. They

did not commit the crime. When the two oldest boys were found guilty wild applause broke out in the courtroom, followed by loud cheers from the mob outside. The brass band struck up a lively tune "There'll be a Hot Time in the Old Town Tonight".... Mass demonstrations have aroused the world against the barbarous injustice committed against nine innocent boys. American embassies have been picketed.... As Sacco and Vanzetti became the symbols of the suppression of revolutionary workers the world over so have these nine Negroes become, the world over, the symbols of the oppression of a national minority.[2]

The author then called on young people (students, in particular) to rally to the Scottsboro Boys' defense by tying together the precarious status of all working class people:

If we students, intellectual workers, fail to put up a strong fight for the liberation of these nine Scottsboro boys, we shall betray not only the cause of the Negro people whose desperate plight these boys symbolize, but the cause of the whole working class in the U.S. and all over the world. "Labor in the white skin cannot be liberated as long as labor in the black skin is enslaved!"[3]

The editorial brought the issue home to students. It was not merely a matter of feeling sorry for the Scottsboro Boys. The Great Depression had forced many students out of school and into a hostile workforce and thus into the ranks of the unemployed. They, too, experienced the wage-reducing impact of competing with black workers for employment in a Jim Crow system.[4] Their fate was wrapped up in the fate of these young African-Americans, they argued, because of the exploitative nature of capitalism. Historian Dan Carter echoed the sentiment of the college editor who spoke the minds of many young radicals when he said that "The Scottsboro Case was destined to be the decade's equivalent of Sacco and Vanzetti, a test of the growing strength of the masses against the capitalist bosses of the South and their cohorts throughout the United States."[5]

The economic plight of African-Americans aroused sympathy from youth activists who felt a sense of solidarity with a group of surplus workers hard-hit by unemployment, but they also realized that this situation was compounded by racism. Many of them found the communists' argument that this case was the inevitable result of an economic system based upon racism and class exploitation convincing.[6] African-American unem-

ployment was estimated to be at least 29 percent higher than general unemployment, while African-Americans also made up the majority of the
farmers suffering most from the Great Depression: sharecroppers.[7] New
York City college students were apprised of the full gamut of economic
oppression suffered by African-Americans through their college newspapers, and they, unlike many sympathetic white northern adults, perceived racism not as a regional (southern) problem, but a national one.[8]
Leslie Gould, youth activist and chronicler of the youth movement, noted
that "the downward spiral of 'economic determinism' spins much more
rapidly for the Negro" and therefore advocated, in concert with many
young activists, an end to racial discrimination.[9]

Young radicals sympathized with the plight of African-Americans,
in general, and with the Scottsboro Boys, in particular, not just because
they had a shared feeling of having been excluded from achieving the
American Dream, but because that nebulous goal had concrete bench-
marks (job, career, home, family) they, too, feared would pass them by.
The Scottsboro Boys were not just young and unemployed; they were also
transients, a condition that befell at least 250,000 young people by 1933.[10]
Kingsley Davis, commissioned by the American Council on Education to
investigate the transient population, estimated that as many as one-half of
the 1.25 million people living on breadlines and on the highways in 1932
were young men between the ages of 15 and 25.[11] Further, he claimed,
one out of every twenty young men in the United States was a transient.[12]
These young transients were not at fault for their situation, Davis argued,
for it was "the machinery by which young people are drawn into the
work of the nation [that] had broken down; and youth, bearing the bur-
den of this breakdown, was seeking blindly for some way out."[13] Because
African-Americans were almost always the last hired and first fired, they
were thus commonly found among the transient population.[14]

Some adults concerned about the future of American youth and
American youth themselves could see that the transients' living conditions—perpetually riding the rails, looking for work, being harassed
by law enforcement agencies, not knowing when the next meal would
come—marked "the lowest point of social and economic degradation to
which American youth [had] sunk."[15] Reduced to living as a transient was
not just a worst-case scenario, but seemingly an increasing likelihood for
the "locked out generation." Davis warned Americans that if something
was not done for American youth, they would follow in the footsteps of
German, Italian, and Russian youth by turning against the government
that had turned its back on them. Davis called for increased funding for

programs that kept students in school or provided them with employment skills, thus championing the New Deal programs then in place that at least allowed young people to apply for aid: the Federal Emergency Relief Administration and Civilian Conservation Corps.

But, the government would have to do more, Davis warned, because although "[young people] have not lost faith in their own ability to work out a better future within the framework of the government . . . they inherited," the proverbial clock was ticking, and it was not the "hardiness of a dollar alarm clock" that "you could drop it, or bang it around, and still it would keep on running," but rather "an expensive, many jeweled wrist watch. Jar it and you ruin its sensitive mechanism."[16] The American government was alienating its youth by not addressing their economic needs.

Although many young people were becoming more disenchanted with the economic system, they recognized the inseparably unjust social system it had created and the unwillingness of American politicians to address those problems, thereby intensifying their desire for radical change. If America were to live up to its promises, then all people would have to have the opportunity to work and to receive just compensation for their labor.[17] Racial equality, then, was not simply an abstract idea for youth activists. It was grounded in the economic conditions they were weathering at the time and a necessary requirement to remake America into the democratic republic they envisioned—one that shed all vestiges of the race-based caste system of the South and the no less insidious *de facto* racism of the North.[18]

The NSL was, once again, at the forefront of a contentious issue around which young activists rallied. Its monthly newsletter of October 1932 issued its call to battle:

> It is time that the student body should play a decisive part in the fight against race oppression. We must uproot it on the campus by fighting against Jim-Crow clubs and schools, fighting against all forms of race discrimination aimed at Negro and other minority students. We must organize student protest meetings against the Scottsboro verdict. . . . Students and student groups should flood the Supreme Court with protest telegrams and participate in the movement for the freedom of the Scottsboro nine! . . . The Scottsboro Boys must not die! They shall not die![19]

The Scottsboro Boys' case symbolized racial oppression; however, fighting for their acquittal was not just an effort to secure their freedom, it was the first step in achieving true freedom for all black people—and all

Americans—whose destiny, the NSL said, was inextricably linked to that of the nine boys on trial. Students who wanted a better America could not afford to ignore the plight of the Scottsboro Boys, for Scottsboro had become synonymous with racism, repression, and injustice.[20] It was the morality play of its time.[21]

The NSL went further than most organizations in pushing for racial equality, but it was nevertheless advancing an agenda supported by many young people. The NSL sought to make that support apparent by publicly challenging racism whenever possible. Ever aware that actions speak louder than words, the NSL chose to hold its annual conference at Howard University in 1933. Encamping at an all-black university in the nation's capital was sure to make its message of racial solidarity clear. The NSL followed this up by organizing a conference on Negro student problems in April 1933. Such a show of good faith won many black students to the youth movement's ranks. By 1936, the majority of students attending black colleges participated in the youth movement's most public act: the annual anti-war strike.[22]

Other groups were soon to follow the NSL's example. The NSL and SLID meetings at CCNY in December 1934 were concerned not just with student expulsions but with collecting funds for the International Labor Defense to aid the Scottsboro Boys.[23] When the American Youth Congress met in Detroit for its second annual conference in 1935, members were indignant about patronizing a segregated establishment. The manager may not have been swayed by their interpretation of American idealism, but faced with the options of canceling their reservations and/ or playing host to a protest demonstration, he capitulated, and, in the end, African-American delegates were allowed to stay at the hotel.[24] This scenario was repeated in Cleveland in 1936.[25] There, students picketed the Euclid Hotel for its discriminatory policies, chanting "Black and white ... fight ... fight ... fight."[26] One report by youth delegate David Blunt claimed that while the lone policeman at the scene did nothing to break up the protest, he physically would not allow any pictures to be taken by the press.[27] Stifling their media outlet did not thwart the young protestors. This was not a publicity stunt; they were looking for concrete change. In the end, the protestors won their immediate goal: Black delegates were allowed to stay at the hotel. It was not enough to say one was against discrimination; members of youth organizations often put their principles into practice. Those principles were clearly expressed in The Creed of the American Youth Congress to which all members pledged themselves: "I dedicate myself to the service of my country and mankind. I will uphold the American ideal, which is the democratic way of life. I will help assure its bounty to all races, creeds, and colors."[28] Ending with the Pledge of Allegiance, the creed clearly enunciated young activists' position that racial justice was an American democratic ideal they were determined to see implemented.[29]

While the NSL and AYC confronted segregation and discrimination in dramatic, public pronouncements and demonstrations, the YMCA-YWCA was just as busy crossing the color line in quieter, though no less effective, ways.[30] In the name of Christian brotherhood, many Y leaders opened their meetings and activities to all races and thus provided a protected space for integrationist impulses while preaching the message of interracial good will.[31] Jack McMichael was profoundly affected by such an experience. McMichael was involved in the student YMCA at Emory University, which was led by black minister Emmet Johnson, who instituted integrationist policies. In an interview with historian Robert Cohen, McMichael recalled the breakdown of his own personal prejudice resulting from his work with Johnson. He said, "these experiences made a big difference. You can read these things in a book, but when you know people who are black and you know that the taboos about them are not true you see you get this kind of deep feeling [against segregation]."[32] Even when they ventured outside their Y buildings, YMCA groups insisted on adherence to their racially progressive policies. When his YMCA group went to North Carolina for a conference, for example, Johnson insisted that the facilities be integrated regardless of local segregationist laws. Racial equality, then, was not merely a theoretical principle, and adherence to integrationist policies was not just a way to show one's belief in racial equality. Exposure to integrated experiences led to a firmer belief in the necessity of racial equality. McMichael, introduced to integration through the YMCA, advocated such policies as Chairman of the American Youth Congress after he moved to New York City where he attended Union Theological Seminary and did doctoral work at Columbia University.[33]

Students were kept aware of racial injustice through the dramatic reporting of their campus newspaper staffs. Within a week of Reed Harris's expulsion (and the same day of the student strike to support him), *The Campus* ran a story for CCNY students titled "Murder in the South." It lambasted the sorry state of freedom and equality in America by exposing the circumstances surrounding the death of Juliette Derricotte, Dean of Women at Fisk University. Injured in a car accident, she was refused treatment at the segregated hospital because she was black. In striking its blow against Jim Crow, the article indignantly intoned: "She died, but the nice, beautiful, modern Hamilton Memorial Hospital remained clean and uncontaminated, except for the red stain of murder at its door."[34] Stories like this found wide coverage in the college press, and authors whose published works uncovered the harrowing effects of racism in the South found sympathetic audiences on New York City campuses and were repeatedly invited to speak at student forums.[35]

Students responded to such outrages, but activists were careful not to channel their fury solely at the Jim Crow South.[36] Overcoming northern activists' ignorance was a top priority. Racism was a problem endemic to the North, too, as the young delegates to the AYC conferences were well aware. A group at CCNY calling itself the Douglass Society came up with a seven-point platform to be introduced as resolutions at the annual American Student Union conference. The planks represented immediate needs to redress racial discrimination as well as far-reaching policies to end racism in America:

1) Demand for equal educational opportunities for the Negro in the South, specifying by equality, abolishment of jim-crow [sic] schools.

2) Campaign to include courses of Negro history and, in particular, the contributions of the Negro to American culture in the curricula of the various colleges and universities.

3) Emphasis on freedom for the Scottsboro boys as epitomizing the underlying principle of de facto disfranchisement of the Negro in the South, together with all the political, social and economic implications consequent to it.

4) Enactment of Federal anti-lynching legislation, specifically, immediate consideration of the Wagner-Costigan Bill.

5) Cessation of discrimination against Negroes within the AFL as well as within all other labor organizations.

6) Appointment of qualified Negroes to instructorial [sic] and professorial positions in institutions of higher learning, as well as the broadening of Negro instructorship in secondary and grammar schools.

7) Emphasis upon non-invitation of outstanding Negro athletes to AAU meet in Miami, physical jeopardy faced by Ozzie Simmons, case of Wilson and Hotel Normandie, etc. to exemplify criminal, if not homicidal, tactics employed in discrimination against Negro athletes.[37]

Wilson (referred to in plank number seven) added a handwritten note to this platform indicating that he thought it could focus the upcoming discussion of conditions in the South for the ASU because it concretely depicted the problems faced by African-Americans throughout the nation. He hoped it would allow the ASU delegates to address the larger parameters of racism existing beyond the Mason-Dixon line.[38]

Like fellow collegiate athlete Jesse Owens from Ohio State University, who laid bare the fallacy of Nazi Germany's Aryan myth by winning four gold medals in the 1936 Summer Olympics in Berlin, Welford Wilson was also a young African-American track star. Wilson attended CCNY, and unlike Owens who acquiesced to American segregationist policies by living off-campus with other African-Americans and eating at blacks-only restaurants when the team traveled, Wilson rejected such racist treatment. In the spring of 1935, he quit the team after the manager at a Philadelphia hotel refused to allow him to stay there with his white teammates, offering, instead the option to stay at the home of one the hotel's black maids.[39] Wilson did not receive support from his team or his coach, but he did find support back on campus. The Liberal Club met to discuss the matter, and a mass protest ensued, prompting the student council to investigate not just the Wilson case, but other allegations of Jim-Crowism on campus, as well.[40] Some may have hoped the ensuing end of the school year would dampen student ardor over race problems, but they were taken up again with the very first issue of *The Campus* in the fall.

The committee set up to investigate the Wilson case pressured the administration to hire more African-American instructors, supporting one of the suggestions made by the Douglass Society.[41] While waiting for that day to come, *The Campus* gave full coverage to the story of Edward Atkinson, who was denied admission to a fraternity smoker despite having received an invitation. The doorkeeper claimed there must have been a mistake in the address because, he said, "this fraternity has certain requirements that it must keep," which included no admittance of black students.[42] Coverage of Atkinson's story convinced many there was a pattern of discrimination at CCNY; activist students hoped such awareness would be a catalyst for widespread student action to alter that pattern. In this, they were not disappointed.

Activist students were not the only ones protesting segregation. In December 1935, the members of the CCNY senior class voted in near unanimity to cancel their prom—the most important social event of their four year college career—because the Park Central Hotel said African-

American attendees would have to enter through a side door. The editor of *The Campus* lauded the stand taken by the senior class, noting that "it is startling for a northerner to run face to face into practices of this kind. While everyone has read of 'Jim-Crowism' down south, it became far more ugly and brutal when seen at first hand."[43] The editor felt confident that the negative publicity this stand for principles engendered would cause the Park Central management to rethink its policies while, at the same time, the hotel's decision to acquiesce to the students' position would reinforce students' beliefs that such efforts were not only morally justified, but effective.[44]

Protesting discrimination in isolated episodes, though, was not enough to effect lasting change. Students therefore continued to push for more long-range solutions: They insisted that African-American instructors be hired and African-American history classes be offered.[45] By October 1935, a petition was circulating for "a course on the Negro race," which, the signatories believed, "would serve as a valuable factor in establishing better race relations between students at the college."[46] Although African-American studies classes would have to wait for a later era, the students scored a significant achievement when Dr. Max Yergan was hired for the 1937–38 academic year as the college's first African-American instructor.[47] In his first article for *The Campus*, Yergan told his student audience that although "the Negro's problem is a special problem . . . the cause of the Negro in America" was "in a general sense the struggle for democracy,"[48] highlighting the connection between racial equality and democracy that student activists espoused.

As had happened in the fight for free speech, integration advocates faced hostile college administrators. Indeed, the two issues of free speech and racial equality were often inseparably intertwined. A professor involved in forming the Liberal Club at Syracuse University in 1931 was fired in 1932, supposedly as a result of his poor teaching record. James Wechsler, however, believed it was because of his support for radical students and their causes: He had just published a well-documented report of prejudice against African-Americans at the University.[49] Following the precedent recently set at Columbia University and City College of New York to curtail the burgeoning radicalism of students, the administration forced the Liberal Club off campus, abolished the Peace Council, and set up a process for selecting editors of the *Daily Orange* to allow for administrative control over the publication.[50] Such actions, however, did not stifle students' increasingly outspoken indictment of American social relations.

College newspapers were vigilant in reporting racial discrimination, especially when it took place on campus. Their criticism was particularly venomous when noting the segregationist policies of the ROTC, a hated institution among the student left. In April 1936, *The Campus* followed up on a story first published in *The Daily Worker* about Winston Simms, an African-American sophomore at CCNY enrolled in the ROTC advanced course who was obliged to attend a segregated summer training camp maintained by the War Department.[51] One of the commissioned officers was reported to have said that "if he were a self-respecting colored man, he would not force himself on people who did not want his company."[52] *The Campus* reporter went on to surmise that this attitude was the reason another black student had resigned from the course seven years before, indicating that the race issue would not be put to rest. Six months later, an issue of *The Campus* was almost entirely devoted to unmasking Dean John R. Turner's racism. In the presence of William McDonald, the president of the Douglass Society, the dean had made some rather revealing remarks. As reported by McDonald:

> The dean, in commenting on a poem by Langston Hughes, had said to his secretary . . . "Now, Miss Brenman, can't you just get the picture down there in (he names some small town in West Virginia)—these niggers—ag, Negroes—sittin' on the railroad sidin', just a-laughin', shootin' craps, and a-bettn' on the numbers on the box-cars a goin-by. . . . It takes a man of letter to see it, but you notice in the colored people a different walk and laugh. They just seem to be so happy-go-lucky a-singin-and-laughin-, just a driftin-along in the hands of fate." . . . When I differed and sought to show that these qualities were not intrinsic to the Negro as the dean charged, he laughed and ended by saying that this seeming indifference on the part of the Negroes seemed "intrinsic to him."[53]

McDonald called for a public apology; Turner refused to make any statement to *The Campus*. The fissure between activist students and the administration already created by the Reed Harris expulsion was developing into a deep chasm because of ongoing race issues. On the one side were the administrators determined to maintain the status quo; on the other side were the activist students determined to create a more democratic society through which they could exercise their freedoms and achieve racial equality.

Similar to the issue of free speech, the issue of racial equality publicized so adeptly by the college press in New York City transformed this from a local phenomenon to a more widespread issue garnering sustained attention. Students meeting to discuss the plight of the Scottsboro Boys were threatened with expulsion from Ohio State University—where Jesse Owens was then a student—in 1935.[54] Although they faced severe punishments for speaking out and were not optimistic that the reactionary leaders of higher education would entertain their integrationist ideas, such students did not capitulate. They continued to speak out even though issues relating to racial equality were carefully policed and segregation was rigidly enforced at places like Ohio State University, where Owens was denied admission to Bucket and Dipper, the campus athletic honor society.[55]

The issue of racial equality was raised in America's heartland, too. At the University of Kansas, four students, three of whom were African-American, attempted to use the college's pool in May 1935, but were refused the privilege by the lifeguard on duty, backed up by Herbert Allphin, the physical education instructor and swim coach. This went against the Athletic Director's decision to allow a trial period during which both races could use the pool together. That decision resulted from the campaign launched two months earlier by the four students to change the segregated pool hours. The signatures of 160 white students had been gathered in support of the policy to allow both races to use the pool, thereby disarming the Athletic Director's original objection that although he supported such a measure, public sentiment on campus would not countenance the pool's interracial usage. During the poolside dispute, the four students were told to take the matter up with the Athletic Director, but he was conveniently attending an out-of-town track meet.[56] Allphin, it seems (and perhaps with the Athletic Director's blessing), did not agree with the new rule. He personally fired all lifeguards who refused to use physical violence to forcibly eject African-Americans from the pool when white students were present. When one such lifeguard, Harlan Jennings, was fired as a result, concerned students took the case to the college chancellor, Ernest H. Lindley. While Lindley promised to investigate the affair and reverse the decision if the students' account was verified, no such action was taken. More disturbing to the students was Lindley's comments about the "negro question" during the meeting. According to the students' statement, sworn before a notary public, Lindley said that

K.U. was a white man's school, built by white money and for white people, and that he intended to keep it so. That if the bars against negroes were let down the school would be over-run by negroes. That we had already granted them more privileges than

other schools. . . . That public opinion justified his stand and would
uphold him in it despite the [state] constitution. . . . That this university was to be run as the board of regents chose to run it even
if that was counter to the letter and certainly the spirit of the constitution.[57]

When the students tried to publish reports of this ongoing affair in the
college's newspaper, *Daily Kansan*, they found their efforts blocked by
faculty member censors who claimed such articles were inappropriate to
publish because they attacked the university's administration. The students
who were spearheading this anti-discrimination campaign thus found
themselves simultaneously pursuing the goal of free speech, as well. By
this point, though, they had a national organization to support their cause:
The American Student Union, headquartered in New York City, published both the censored article and the students' letter of concern about
Chancellor Lindley's attitude toward race in *The Student Advocate*, giving
the Kansas Affair national coverage.

Yet the most serious obstacle to effecting change was neither hostile college administrators whom young radicals had stared down before,
nor northern activists' ignorance, which was easily overcome through
the educative means of the college newspaper. Much more debilitating
was the northern activists' arrogance. George Streator, an ASU member and writer for its newsletter, *The Student Outlook*, who would later
become the first African-American reporter for the *New York Times*,
warned that the patronizing attitude adopted by many of the African-
Americans' would-be friends did more damage than any lynch mob.[58]
Young white activists' insistence that they wanted to do something for
African-Americans, he said, was "a mere verbal exploitation of their
wrongs" because "there are many Negro students who are convinced that
there can be no end to discrimination until we change the system that
makes it profitable."[59] The focus needed to be on the causes, not just the
effects, of racial discrimination. Activists could only end racism by first
throwing off their own subtle race prejudice that led them to believe they
could help their less fortunate brothers, and then by advocating a new
social and economic order that would bring about "the leveling of the
races."[60] Streator was calling for true solidarity between blacks and whites
without any hint of inferiority/superiority. Then black students could
fully trust the good intentions of young activists, but only if they also
advocated economic equality as a necessary corollary to social equality.
    Streator's position was fully adopted by the ASU, though not everyone

had been convinced of its methodological necessity. In January 1936, John J. Bednarz, a student council member of Connecticut State College, resigned from the National Executive Committee of the ASU because, he said, "I am not ready to accept a movement which has for its fundamental principle the aim to overthrow the present social order and to put in its place a new one."[61] While Bednarz went on to explain that he was primarily concerned with what he believed to be the ASU's determination to overthrow capitalism, the jab at the ASU's position on the social order could not be overlooked. Joseph Lash, Executive Secretary of the ASU, responded publicly to Bednarz's letter of resignation by publishing it along with his own response in an article titled "Are Liberals Immune?" Lash adroitly pointed out that although socialist and communist members of the ASU did believe in the need to replace capitalism with socialism, it was not the ASU's position. The ASU, Lash argued, was a forum where all young people—socialists, communists, liberals, and even conservatives—could come together to figure out the best solutions to the shared problems they faced.[62] Those problems, Lash insisted, were not simply economic, and thus the ASU's goals were not limited to changing the economic system. Just as important, the ASU advocated peace, the democratization of education, academic freedom, and racial justice.[63] These were issues that Bednarz had championed with enthusiasm in the committee's development of the ASU's program. Sidestepping the issue of whether or not those issues *could* be addressed without radical economic change, Lash maintained simply that those issues *would* not be addressed without organizations such as the ASU. To turn his back on the ASU was to turn his back on the fight for all those issues. Liberals, Lash warned, should not be blinded by the Hearst Press or by their own insecurities; more than anything else the ASU was advocating that their voice be heard. To withdraw from the ASU was to silence one's own voice. Furthermore, when the ASU condemned the "inner oligarchy of high finance, industry and politics" for the problems facing America, Lash maintained that

> it [was] using the language, not of the socialists and communists, but of the liberal *New York Post*, which is supported by capitalist advertisements, of the LaFollettes and western agrarians, who still rally to President Roosevelt, of Epic and the American Federation of Labor all of whom acknowledge the evils of capitalism and have denounced the arrogant "inner oligarchy" for its responsibility in this crisis.[64]

To allay liberals' fears of unwittingly supporting a radical revolution, Lash went on to explain that "the Young Peoples Socialist League and the Young Communist League [did] not want the ASU to have a revolutionary objective because that is the purpose of their organizations, and they have indicated no wish to liquidate themselves."[65] Socialists and communists, he said, supported the ASU because it was the most progressive organization espousing many goals they held in common, and they hoped to be able to convince liberals of the folly of their allegiance to the corrupt status quo. He ended his response by asking liberals in general, and Bednarz in particular, "whether the responsibility for the fight against reaction and war is only that of the radicals as your letter would seem to indicate. Is it not as much yours?"[66]

Lash was by no means the only member of the ASU National Executive Committee to support racial equality. William Bell, an African-American student at Northwestern University and another leader of the ASU, brought a lawsuit against the college in 1936, demanding $5,000 in damages resulting from the college's refusal to allow him to use the campus beach. This slight was the last insult in a long train of abuses: An editorial in *The Daily Northwestern* concluded its discussion of the Bell case by saying that "Negroes at Northwestern . . . are discriminated against in the boarding house, the dining room, the theater, the athletic field, and the classroom."[67] It called for "all liberal organizations on the campus and the Y.M.C.A., to take up the defense of Negro rights. The status of the Negro at Northwestern makes ridiculous our claim to glory as a liberal institution. To fight for Negro rights is the fight of every person who believes in democracy and freedom."[68] The ASU called for a mass meeting, the result of which was the creation of a committee to investigate allegations of racial discrimination on campus.

The committee's recommendations were conciliatory. It proposed that the Athletic Director propose a meeting of the Big Ten schools to discuss permitting African-Americans to play on their colleges' basketball teams, an integrated dorm at Northwestern if student body sentiment favored it, and the division of the campus beach into a white section and an integrated section.[69] While the committee bowed to the limits of how far popular opinion would allow forced integration and was willing to work with the administration to broker some kind of compromise, the ASU went beyond these proposals. It contacted the YMCA, YWCA, Hillel, International Relations Clubs and other organizations on the campuses of the Big Ten schools asking for cooperation with a more comprehensive anti-discrimination campaign. Again young activists were using a local situation to bring about more universally applied change.

At the same time he was carrying out his correspondence with Bednarz, Lash was also working with the rest of the ASU National Executive Committee to support the Southern Negro Youth Conference that was held February 13–14, 1936. The ASU issued the call for delegates to attend that conference, which promised to "discuss all economic, social, political, religious, and educational problems of Negro youth" and "decide upon concrete measures necessary to solve these problems."[70] The delegates were to carry on the "great tradition" of Frederick Douglass, Harriet Tubman, and Nat Turner. In "recall[ing] the Scottsboro frame-up, the shame of America!" they would address lynching,[71] unemployment, sharecropping and peonage, and educational retrenchment under the slogan "No school, no work, no opportunity for the Negro youth in 1936!"[72] Their call was loud enough that it reached the ears of President Roosevelt, for whom Richard R. Brown, Deputy Executive Director of the National Youth Administration (NYA), compiled a dossier of the conference leaders along with other related documents.[73]

Young people's urgent calls for change hit their mark: The following year, the NYA sponsored its own conference to consider the problems facing the Negro and Negro Youth in America.[74] That conference identified four problems facing young black people and issued the following recommendations to alleviate them: increased opportunity for employment and economic security, adequate educational and recreational opportunity, improved health and housing conditions, and security of life and equal protection under the law.[75] Its specific recommendations were a pale echo of those espoused by activist youth. They did not seek to replace the existing social, political, or economic systems. They simply advocated more appropriations for New Deal programs, like the NYA, with earmarked funds for hiring, training, and educating black youth. They were in line with the demands of the Douglass Society at CCNY but did not confront racism directly. Adult government employees, however well-meaning, had no inclination to support radical measures.

The agenda of the second National Conference on the Problems of the Negro and Negro Youth, held in 1939, conformed more to young activists' perspectives on youth's problems and goals. Its statement of purpose declared that "no such 'united democracy'[76] can possibly exist unless ... common opportunity is available to all Americans regardless of race, color or creed. Only when these objectives are fully achieved will our country be able to stand before the world as the unsullied champion of true democracy."[77] The committee reports indicated that very little progress had been made in alleviating the problems identified at the last conference. Only the NYA was singled out for commendation for its steadfast adherence to democratic principles and practices. Much of the rest of the report catalogued the dismal showing for efforts to secure racial justice: The anti-lynching bill had not passed in Congress, the military was not integrated, the Fair Labor and Standards Act did not apply to farmers and domestic workers and thus neglected 70 percent of the black labor force, and not enough blacks had been appointed to administrative and policy making bodies.[78] In summarizing the committee reports, Mary McLeod Bethune, the highest-ranking African-American official in the New Deal Administration, lauded the NYA for its efforts at integration, but even that, she cautioned, could backfire because

> one of the great tragedies of American life has been and still is the denial of opportunity to a rising army of trained Negro youth. We are equipping them for service and then slamming the door of opportunity shut in their faces. They grow restless and may prove fertile ground for the seeds of resentment and of false political and economic doctrine.[79]

Bethune supported far-reaching reforms including making the NYA a permanent youth service agency because, in helping youth, "we contribute not only to the strengthening of our own racial group, but to the cause of democracy."[80]

While Bethune pushed for more recognition of African-American needs in New Deal policy, the two New Dealers most aggressively progressive on matters of race equality—who also worked for the National Youth Administration—were Charles Taussig (chairman of its National Advisory Council) and Aubrey Williams (its Executive Director). Their concern about the causes and effects of racial discrimination was not limited to the college campus, but extended to the high schools and vocational schools, as well. Taussig, for example, was deeply troubled by the use of textbooks across the country that reinforced racist stereotypes and claimed that "Negroes ... came to this country; lived for two hundred years in a condition of servitude and enjoyed that condition which suited them because they were not fit for anything else."[81]

Williams, though interested in rectifying such issues, was more focused on making sure New Deal policies were devoid of racial injustice. In July 1941, he sent written instructions to all regional directors and state youth administrators reminding them that "the National Youth Administration, in keeping with the provisions of this Executive Order [No. 8802],[82] reaffirms its policy of providing employment for eligible citizens of the United States without discrimination because of race, creed, color, or national origin."[83] He even included a copy of the Executive Order with his letter, thereby ordering compliance.[84]

The story of the NYA Resident Center in Auburn, New York demonstrates the degree to which Williams was able to implement his racial integrationist policies. Congressman John Taber (R-NY) claimed, before the House Appropriations Committee, that this NYA Resident Center located in his hometown fostered interracial relations whereby "Negro boys were permitted and encouraged to court white girls."[85] Williams recognized this for what it was: an attempt by a conservative congressman to dismantle a progressive New Deal program. Though he longed for a more racially equal society, Williams knew that calling for complete racial equality by defending interracial relationships would only add to the already growing opposition to him and the NYA, and, by extension, the New Deal, itself.[86] He therefore set out to clear the name of the NYA on this matter. He gathered statements to refute Taber's charges from local residents and business leaders that, at the same time, recognized the good work being done at the training center.[87]

Similar grass roots mobilization had saved the Auburn Resident Center from dismantling through appropriations reductions the year before. At that time both the Auburn Chamber of Commerce and the Department of the Navy had stepped into the Congressional debate then underway by writing to Senators James M. Mead (D-NY) and Robert F. Wagner (D-NY) about the vital need the center was fulfilling by shipping material to the Brooklyn Navy Yard.[88] Nothing could save the NYA, though, once the charge of interracial dating was leveled. While Williams was trying to salvage both the NYA and the American ideals it sought to implement, conservatives believed the NYA was causing the destruction of American society. The NYA was eventually abolished in 1943, but its progressive policies had, in the meantime, won it the support of a broad spectrum of young people, thus helping to bring them into the New Deal fold.

In marked contrast to the previous decade when little attention was paid to such issues, in the 1930s, concerns about racism extended not only to African-Americans but to Jews as well, and in this more comprehensive view of race relations, youth activists' internationalist perspective was manifest.[89] Some youth leaders, including James Wechsler and Joseph Lash, were Jews and thus felt the anti-Semitism on college campuses and in the larger society personally. Wechsler remained pessimistic that anti-Semitism in America would abate without frank recognition of it. He therefore wrote about the unofficial quota system that was used to limit the concentration of Jews on any one campus and further explained that once Jews were admitted, they were often barred from the fraternity system, the very center of undergraduate social life and the venue for pre-professional networking.[90] Much more serious ramifications of anti-Semitism, as embodied by Nazi policies in Germany, were also of concern. *The Campus* consequently urged student support for the move to boycott the 1936 Berlin Olympics.[91]

But anti-Semitism in America was not the result of a party's program; instead, it was understood as part of the much larger context of racial prejudice—a racial prejudice that terrorized African-Americans.[92] And so it was racial prejudice in general that youth activists sought to overcome. In a society where the anti-lynching crusade was still unsuccessfully pressing its stand on an unsupportive president, Jewish activists like Wechsler recognized that African-Americans were more often the target of violent oppression in the United States: "Vigilantism uses the Negro; in many places it will employ him as a scapegoat far more fiercely and unremittingly than the Jew."[93] In linking racism in America to Nazism, though, Wechsler warned that "minorities are the first—and only the first—victims of fascism."[94]

Young people were continually reminded of the links between racism and anti-Semitism by the news reports coming out of Alabama. Jewish New Yorker Samuel Leibowitz, lead defense attorney for the Scottsboro Boys, needed the protection of two New York police bodyguards sent by Mayor Fiorello LaGuardia against the death threats leveled at him, some of which spawned from comments made during Warren Country solicitor Wade Wright's closing argument that the Scottsboro Boys' defense was underwritten by "Jew money from New York."[95] Newspapers across America depicted Scottsboro as Hitlerism come to America, and a writer for the *New York Evening Post* said that if Americans wanted to know what Nazism was like, they should simply imagine a Klan takeover of America.[96]

Thus, even when the antipathy toward Jews became virulent, it was often intricately interwoven with racism toward African-Americans. In 1937, an anti-Semite mailed an anonymous letter to *The Campus* promising to launch a campaign against the "degraded and degenerate race" that possessed "thoroughly rotten racial characteristics and schemes."[97] In threatening tones, the vigilante said that "It is time to call a spade a spade and a Jew a monkey" and promised to begin his/her campaign by posting the following slogans all over campus:

PERISH JEWRY—CHRISTIANITY OR COMMUNISM, WHICH?—GHETTO
BENCHES FOR JEWS—VIGILANCE THE PRICE OF LIBERY—AMERICA
FOR AMERICANS DOWN WITH THE SIX POINTED STAR OF INTERNA-
TIONAL JEWISH DOMINATION—KKK KKK KKK KKK—THE KNIGHTS
OF THE WHITE CHAMELIA RIDE AGAIN—HEIL HITLER—VIVA
FRANCO—VIVA MUSSOLINI[98]

In linking together racism, anti-Semitism, and fascism, the anonymous
writer reflected what was already going on within youth organizations
themselves: the linking of social, economic, and political problems that
had to be overcome collectively so that America could fulfill its promises.
In attacking the "separate but equal" ideology of education and public
accommodations, then, young activists were creating a bulwark against
fascism—the most serious threat to democracy—in America.

In their demands for full racial equality, young people unearthed the
connections among social, economic, and political factors that privileged
one group and denigrated another. Many came to believe that radical ideologies—like communism—that addressed racism by recognizing those
inherently inseparable factors offered prescriptions for real change. Young
activists' support for the Scottsboro Boys highlights this, as does their
championing of Angelo Herndon, an African-American Communist
Party member arrested in Atlanta in 1932 and convicted of inciting insur-
rection, not because he led a riot or made a speech in which he proposed
such a course of action, but because he possessed communist literature
and had tried to organize industrial workers. Young activists believed their
efforts helped keep Herndon (who was released in 1934, after serving
two years of his 18–20 year sentence) off the chain gang.[99] The Herndon
case came up during a question and answer session between AYC leaders
and Eleanor Roosevelt in 1936. When she was asked if she thought the
murder of 33 men killed in the previous year as a result of "their activities
on behalf of economic justice" represented the decline of democracy in
America, Eleanor Roosevelt said she did not agree with such an assessment, and when the questioner pointed to the Herndon and Scottsboro
cases, she replied that "when things like that happen, we must make it our
business to really try and see that justice is done."[100]

For the Scottsboro Boys, there was, ultimately, no justice. The defendants spent no less than six, and as many as nineteen, years in jail not
just for a crime they did not commit, but for a crime that most people
have come to believe never happened.[101] Youth activists were unable to

secure their release, but in championing this case they identified racism as an endemic American problem to be addressed. Their tireless effort on behalf of racial equality is young activists' crowning achievement. No law was passed during the Great Depression forbidding all forms of racial discrimination. No court decision decreed once and for all that African-Americans were entitled to all the legal rights enjoyed by white Americans. Racist attitudes remained the social norm among whites. The anti-lynching bill was not passed. Nevertheless, smaller victories were scored against racism. Every time young activists successfully pressured a business proprietor to treat black customers just as they did white customers, every time they forced an educational institution to acknowledge (if not address) a racist policy, every time they publicized an act of discrimination in the student press, every time they insisted that a federal program—like the NYA—pay equal wages regardless of race, they were building momentum toward social, political, and economic equality. They were, in so doing, making their vision of equality a reality; they were making America live up to its promises. Much like their fights for free speech, academic freedom, and economic opportunity, this was an ongoing struggle that lasted well beyond the Depression decade. Their accomplishments, then, were in these individual, often localized, situations. Perhaps their greatest achievement, though, was articulating an ideology of racial equality that would become a cornerstone of 20th century liberalism. They lobbied government officials and found support from some sympathetic politicians and this began the process of institutionalizing that ideology.

While Herbert Hoover waited for prosperity, it was the radicals, especially the communists, who were trying to alleviate the suffering of the Great Depression and, it seemed, trying to make America more American by exposing racial injustice.[102] They believed, as James Miller's chronicle of the Scottsboro Boys attests, that if not for the communists stirring up a public outcry and keeping their plight continually before the people, the eight boys originally sentenced to die would have been executed on July 10, 1931 by the state of Alabama—that is, if they had not already been lynched by an angry mob.[103] This placed many young people more firmly in the radical political camp as once again they found themselves working side by side with the Communists.[104] Many young people supported (or were at least understanding of) alternative political belief systems—like communism—because they offered a convincing critique of America at the same time they offered an alternative system that seemed to more fully live up to American ideals.[105]

Even as youth organizations were disbanding during World War II, they remained committed to racial justice. The American Youth Congress launched an aggressive campaign to end the poll tax in the spring of 1941.[106] At the same time, it was galvanizing support to pressure the Chancellor of New York University not to suspend seven students who had protested against the discrimination experienced by track team members at a meet in Washington, D.C.[107] Going even further, the American Youth Congress had, by this point, drafted an anti-discrimination bill to be introduced in Congress by Representative Vito Marcantonio, a member of the American Labor Party from New York City, which was designed to protect both Jews and African-Americans.[108] Young activists had, for all their radicalism, become active policymakers in order to institutionalize their positions on civil liberties and civil rights.

Before this transformation could be fully carried out, though, young activists needed to both consolidate their organizational structures and expand their support base. This would allow them to become political players representing an important constituent group of the American polity. The creation of the two largest youth organizations—the American Student Union and the American Youth Congress—galvanized youth's political agency into vehicles that young activists hoped would drive American democracy forward. At the same time they wished to substantiate American ideals, young activists were acutely aware of the incongruity of an American democracy based on freedom and equality in an increasingly totalitarian and militarized world. Thus the uniting of youth groups into these two umbrella organizations was meant to address American youth's needs while responding to the foreign threat by creating a popular front against war and fascism, which is the focus of Part II: "Implementing a Vision."

PART II
Implementing a Vision

4
The Popular Front: Strength in Unity
New York City Organizations Come Together in Solidarity

Young activists had tried, with some limited success, to make the educational system more amenable to their needs and more responsive to their worldview by demanding free speech and racial equality. Compared to their goals for a free, democratic, and equal society, though, their gains were meager and frustratingly difficult to attain. They realized administrators, board members, and even teachers were determined to maintain the educational system's conservative status quo, and thus they clearly understood the opposition they had to overcome in order for their vision of America to materialize. They came to believe that the only way to implement real economic and social change was to become enmeshed in the political system, but that also engendered a transformation of the political system itself. America, they believed, must be wrested from the elite power brokers and made truly democratic before their other goals could be achieved. In a true democracy, the voice of young people would be listened to, and they would be involved in making decisions that affected them. Young people would have to become policymakers. Before they could be accepted as representatives of a valued constituency, however, activists had to bring young people together, for only in mass unity would their voice be heard and their ideas be given serious consideration in America's new brand of interest group politics.

To that end, two organizations were created by young people to represent them in the political arena: the American Youth Congress, established in 1934 to represent all youth, and the American Student Union, formed in 1935 to represent all students. Dedicated to addressing youth's needs, these organizations came to exert influence in the formulation of New Deal youth policy.

In becoming political players, young activists did not realize that many of their number would abrogate their radicalism. Socialists and communists held fast to their desire to restructure the social, economic, and political systems; however, they took a significant step away from revolutionary action in their willingness to see what the New Deal could provide in the meantime, and upon taking that first step, many of them would never return to the revolutionary fold.[1] They adopted this course not just because the New Deal seemed to move toward the restructuring they favored, but also because radicals' hands became tied to those of the liberals by the menace of fascism. Radicals joined Popular Front organizations as a way to work toward their goals in the face of an increasingly hostile global environment. Meanwhile, liberals, who might have shunned working with radicals before this time, came to see that they had much in common. One liberal who called for a genuine youth movement in America distinct from both the fascist and Russian models expressed this point of view when he said that what bound American youth together was that "we do have a sense of the traditions upon which our country was established—the American Dream, if you will, of a classless society with equality of opportunity—and we know that that tradition has been violated."[2]

Aside from occasional background checks on youth activists, New Deal policymakers largely ignored American youth in the early Depression years: They seemed to be both oblivious to their plight and neglectful of their needs. It was not until 1934 that activist youth, as representatives of young people's organizations, began to pierce New Dealers' consciousness with any kind of frequency. By June, Linton M. Collins, personnel director and division administrator for the National Recovery Administration, was strongly advising the president to reach out to pro–New Deal–youth organizations such as the Junior Chamber of Commerce (JCC), which had 200,000 members in 250 cities across the nation and, according to Collins, was "one of the most potent forces in our national life."[3] In compliance, FDR sent a letter in "sincere appreciation for their contribution to our national program of recovery."[4] Collins seemed to have recognized, as only a few others did at the time, that large youth organizations' support was essential if the younger generation was to bear the New Deal mantle in the future. By this time, young people had already begun to come together to make that specific point as well as a broader one: recognition of youth's role in defining the future of

America, itself. Even a conservative group like the JCC was committed to that goal by working within the popular front ideology. The program it adopted in 1935[5] was dedicated to "selling Americanism—American traditions, American ideals and the American system of government—to our citizens generally," while it specifically prohibited activities focused on exposing the "dangers and evils of communism."[6]

By the spring of 1933, the idea of creating an inclusive umbrella organization of youth groups was percolating in the mind of German-born New Yorker[7] Viola Ilma, founder and editor of *Modern Youth Magazine: The Voice of the Younger Generation*. Established when she was only 21 years old, this magazine was intended to energize those in Ilma's cohort whom she believed were listlessly drifting amidst the storm of the Depression without prospects to put to work what they had gone to college to learn.[8] She had just returned from Europe, where she had seen youth organized, committed to action, and making a difference.[9] She hoped to replicate that sense of purpose in the United States. In her role as editor, she was brought more in touch with the suffering of American youth as she fielded letters from those disaffected by the American Dream. Although her magazine folded after only three months, it was long enough for her to realize that something must be done to help the young people of America, especially since the letters to the editor continued to arrive long after publication was suspended. The relationship between editor and reader, then, was not simply one of disseminating information; it also served as an enlightening educative endeavor for those editors like Ilma who had escaped the worst ravages of the Depression.

After attending an international congress of women in Chicago, she was chosen as a delegate to the World Conference of Youth in Geneva. Back in Europe for the conference, Ilma visited Germany and Italy, where she was heartened to see that the fascists at least recognized the youth problem.[10] Upon her return, she formed the Central Bureau for Young America—choosing herself as president—to organize the first conference to discuss the problems facing American youth. The way Ilma envisioned it, the conference would gather together the leaders of as many youth organizations as possible, they would discuss the problems facing young people, and then they would propose changes to be effectuated by the Bureau, which was to be a permanent organization spearheading a genuine youth movement. That movement, she said, "should depend on emotion rather than rationality in making its appeal. . . . Lots of action, then, and little platform should be the watch-word."[11] The superficiality she assigned to such a movement was counter-productive. Yet there was an even more serious flaw in Ilma's design. That she intended to bring together young people to discuss and then address their needs was widely popular among youth activists; her methods for doing so were not. The authoritarianism she exhibited was ill-matched to youth activists' democratic ideals.

The American Youth Congress (AYC) that was created in 1934 to take the place of Ilma's Bureau was an inclusive and progressive organization. About this there is much agreement.[12] Five hundred delegates from seventy youth and student groups convened on the campus of New York University in 1934, representing 1.5 million young people; by the end of the 1930s, the AYC claimed to represent nearly 5 million young people.[13] Historian Robert Cohen, in summarizing the AYC, has argued that "more than any other organization, the Youth Congress broke down the barriers between the college elite and non-student youth. The Youth Congress served as an advocate for millions of underprivileged young Americans—blue collar workers, blacks, the unemployed, and needy students—who traditionally had been ignored by the political process."[14]

Nevertheless, historians have maintained that from its inception, the AYC was controlled by the Young Communist League because its leaders, acting in concert with socialists, seduced naïve liberals into giving them control.[15] Youth activists at the time, however, saw the AYC as a unified group in which socialists, communists, and liberals worked together to address youth's needs and carry out their will. Many of them charged Ilma with authoritarian impulses favoring fascism[16] and were deeply disturbed that she had met with top Nazi leaders, including Joseph Goebbels, during her visit to Germany.[17]

Even more incriminating than the company she kept were Ilma's own words. A year after the demise of her magazine and in preparation for the gathering of youth representatives, she published a book titled *And Now, Youth!*[18] In it, she explained how Hitler, Stalin, and Mussolini succeeded in achieving their aims in part by utilizing the energy of youth, and thus she cast totalitarianism in a positive light, alienating many would-be youth supporters.[19]

Ilma believed that "the Youth Movement in Germany, Russia, Sweden, and Italy is most vital and alive, and holds the greatest promise of a better future. The youth in America is no less serious in purpose, no less endowed in ability."[20] Such statements alarmed many youth activists—conservative, liberal, and radical, alike—but it was the procedures Ilma adopted to run the first congress that truly frightened them. It has been argued that Ilma was forced out of her leadership position and out of the American Youth Congress altogether through a *coup* orchestrated by the communists. The source of this story is none other than Viola Ilma herself. In her report of the Congress, she described the deviousness of the radicals who forced their rule upon innocent victims. The radicals, she said, disguised themselves as unaffiliated delegates who "were holding hurried consultations . . . changing seats, whispering and breaking up" and "passing in and out" of the meeting with but one purpose in mind: "these radicals were engineering a coup," the purpose of which "was to either gain control of the Congress or break it up."[21] Ilma maintained that the radical "bloc on the floor sprang from several points into immediate and noisy action. People were shouting wildly, demanding the right to elect all officers, change the existing set-up, prepare the agenda, pass on credentials and conduct the Congress."[22] The meeting was adjourned, and when a similar scenario unfolded at the evening session, she said "the agitators promised to conduct no other business but to listen to the speakers if Dr. Nash would vacate the chair and allow them to elect their own chairman."[23] Once they did so, Nash was heckled so much that he was forced to adjourn the meeting, and thus the Central Bureau withdrew its support and decided to meet separately, while the radicals proceeded to invite Norman Thomas and Earl Browder to address them.[24] Ilma claimed that while her group continued to work through the round table sessions[25] as planned, the radical group went on record condemning the Roosevelt Administration.[26] But there is another side to this story.

In 1940, Leslie Gould, a member of the AYC, told his version of how the AYC was created. He conceded that Ilma was a visionary of sorts, crediting her with the idea of bringing youth together; however, he did not think she lived up to her professed concern for youth. In effect, she acted like a dictator who told young people what they needed and tried to control all matters relating to youth.[27] Gould pointed out that she did not consult experienced youth leaders on policies or principles but instead "collected around her a circle of interested intimates. Among them, not one was noted for any previous efforts or achievements in the youth world."[28] He might have also pointed out that while she did not consult youth leaders, she did ask for advice from adults. In a letter to Eleanor Roosevelt in June 1934, Ilma explained that she was "rather anxious to have your constructive advice concerning what you would like to see a Congress such as ours accomplish" and asked Eleanor Roosevelt for the names and addresses of anyone she thought ought to attend.[29] She also wrote to Theodore Roosevelt (President of the National Republican Club), Anne Morgan (President of the American Women's Association),

state governors, Arthur Garfield Hays (ACLU lawyer), Oswald Garrison
Villard (editor of *The Nation*), Henry A. Wallace (Secretary of Agricul-
ture), Chester H. McCall (Assistant Secretary of Commerce), and Claude
G. Bowers (American Ambassador to Spain) for similar recommenda-
tions.[30] One New Deal administrator, Bess Goodykoontz, the Acting
Director of the Bureau of Education, strongly advised the president not
to have any affiliation with Ilma, whom she said was "erratic, although
possibly talented and competent" after meeting her at a conference in
May 1934, and further urged the president not to have any ties to the
Congress, which she said would not be at all inclusive.[31]

When representatives from youth organizations questioned Ilma about
the outside support for the Youth Congress, she was dismissive. And
when they asked about the Central Bureau, she retorted that

> It has personally surprised and somewhat shocked me that all youth
> should be so skeptical of any plans such as the one of the Central
> Bureau. Who is the Bureau? What is the Bureau? Who is financing
> it? The answer is simple. The Central Bureau for Young America
> was at first little more than an idea. . . . It was to be a clearing house
> of information concerning set-up youth organizations in the coun-
> try. The president, secretary, treasurer and office-boy was Viola
> Ilma. My assets were my files of letters from the magazine I edited
> and published, MODERN YOUTH. The Bureau was forced upon me. I
> needed a place to receive mail.[32]

In defending her autocratic control over the Bureau (and thus over
the Congress), Ilma failed to see that this would not be tolerated by
democratic-minded young people.

Her organizational plan proved their suspicions were warranted. In
a letter to Charles Taussig, New Deal youth policymaker, who had expressed some interest in Ilma's effort to unite youth groups, Ilma explained the composition of the Central Bureau for Young America that
was to be replicated in creating a permanent American Youth Congress:

> From the Central Bureau, which is national in its scope, a chairman
> has been appointed in each state, who is directly responsible for the
> operation of the functions of the Central Bureau within said state.
> In each Congressional District, a sub-chairman will be appointed,
> directly responsible to his respective state chairman, and again the
> same system will prevail in each town or township. Each of the
> several chairmen will also have a board of responsible and leading
> adults to be known as the Advisory Board.[33]

Ilma clearly did not intend for the American Youth Congress to be democratically run, nor did she intend for it to be youth-controlled.

A group of concerned youth delegates sought out NYU Professor
of Educational Sociology Harvey Zorbaugh to discuss Ilma's methods
before the conference began. He and Ilma had an arrangement that made
him the *de facto* adult coordinator for the congress.[34] He had agreed to
that position because he believed "this congress would represent the interests and opinions of several million young people in this country who
far from being a 'lost generation' are, to my mind, a generation that are
rapidly making up their minds to do something for themselves."[35] He
had been "intimately in touch with the leaders of all the national youth
groups during the past six months" and from those meetings, came to
believe that "a large number of these (national youth) groups feel that the
administration has not kept in touch with youth's problems and point of
view."[36] He was quick to point out that they were not all radicals, "but
nevertheless there is a growing feeling among all of them, whatever their
political and economic point of view, that the older generation through
the government and otherwise is going to do nothing fundamental for
them and that they must work out their salvation for themselves."[37] It was
because of his close working relationship with the national youth organizations' leaders who, he believed, were representative of American youth
that Zorbaugh decided to break with Ilma two weeks before the conference began over her attempts to keep radical and liberal groups from participating.[38] He urged the delegates to address their concerns to the Admissions Committee—advice they followed only to be rebuffed, leaving
them with no choice but to bring the issue of democratic reorganization
to the floor of the conference the next day.[39] Rather than a conspiracy to
overthrow Ilma, this was an attempt to make sure the leaders of the congress were democratically elected.

The two issues were entwined as far as the delegates were concerned:
In order for democracy to be achieved, Ilma had to be removed from her
position.[40] Arthur Clifford, an AYC delegate in 1934 who wrote about
the creation of the AYC in 1935, explained Ilma's behavior as putting
into practice "the lessons learned from her fascist mentors, suppressing all
democratic rights of free speech and free discussion."[41] These, then, were
not empty charges that had been leveled against Ilma.[42]

Concern about her methods did not stop there. When delegates entered the first meeting, they were handed a packet, which included a list
of American Youth Congress officers and a program of action.[43] It appeared that Ilma expected the delegates to act as a rubber stamp rather
than a deliberative body. Not willing to let democracy be undone, another

packet was surreptitiously handed out by the disillusioned delegates that included an explanation of the previous night's failed attempt to convince Ilma to allow elections from the floor, further explained the undemocratic rules of procedure pre-imposed by the Central Bureau, and called for parliamentary procedure to be followed instead.[44] When the meeting convened, Waldo McNutt, delegate from the Rocky Mountain Council of the YMCA, called for a vote of recognition for the work the Central Bureau had done in organizing the congress and then demanded the delegates' constitutional rights as American citizens be protected in allowing them to elect their own chairman and adopt their own rules.[45] McNutt's motion was seconded and passed unanimously, whereupon new officers were elected. "Thus," Clifford claimed, "on the rock of the American Revolutionary democratic tradition, the American Youth Congress was born."[46]

Ilma maintained at the time that her group had no choice but to withdraw and regroup in nearby Hotel Brevoort to carry on the business of the congress.[47] Gould claims, however, that Ilma left simply because her group lost control through the electoral process and that her claims of a cabal were conjured up because she was "haunted by red bogies since her German excursion."[48] Newspapers at the time labeled the elected group radical, despite the fact that the slate of officers included representative from the National Student Federation of America (NSFA was a liberal organization made up of representatives of student governments from colleges and universities) and YMCA, while the Ilma group was labeled conservative.[49]

Before the elected congress reconvened the next day, the officers invited members from four political parties to come speak to them. The Republicans refused, the Democrats could not be reached, and thus only the Socialists and Communists responded, sending Norman Thomas and Earl Browder, respectively.[50] While it is possible that the left-leaning parties were courting organized youth, it is undeniable that the moderate parties were ignoring them.

James Wechsler participated in the first American Youth Congress. In 1935, he said that "the [American Youth] Congress is the broadest, most heterogeneous youth group in this country today and serves as an excellent link between students and young people generally" and that "it would be a gross distortion to contend that every student, or even a large percentage of those who participated were radicals. They were not; many of them were entirely unsympathetic to or ignorant of left-wing doctrine."[51] In 1953, he recanted, claiming that the first congress had been a communist *coup* and he should know since he was a member of the Young Communist League as of April 1934. He then dismissed allegations that Ilma had any fascist sympathies whatsoever, though, at the time, he said "we were certain (that we had) halted fascism on its own five-yard line."[52] Wechsler offered no further explanation and no evidence to support his latter contention. He reported that communists met as a "faction" to plot events throughout the 1930s and effectively controlled the AYC, which simply became a communist front organization. This reflects his 1953 anti-communist Cold War stance. Interestingly, when liberals met to discuss their positions before attending an AYC National Executive Committee meeting, it was simply referred to as a caucus and good planning; all the while they (the liberals) preferred to refer to the AYC as a popular front organization. Socialists in the AYC and Student League for Industrial Democracy (SLID), meanwhile, were instructed to follow the guidelines established by the Socialist Party, and if there were none to resort to in any given situation, the Young People's Socialist League (YPSL) demanded that its lead be followed.[53] Yipsels—members of the YPSL—were instructed to join "really innocent organizations," such as the AYC and ASU, as a way to increase the influence of socialist activists within those organizations.[54] Party discipline and the discipline of the YPSL were the first priority and the *sine qua non* for any type of negotiations with other radical groups.[55] Members of SLID routinely discussed policy positions with Norman Thomas and other LID leaders before taking a stand on an issue.[56] Young communists, then, if they were taking orders from their organizations, were no different from other activists. Moreover, a well-organized group of loyal socialists along with an even larger contingent of confirmed liberals tempered any communist-desired control over the AYC.[57]

The AYC remained a divided group only for a short time. Despite an invitation to return to the elected congress, Ilma's group finished the conference in isolation. It came up with a platform that called for the creation of a Federal Vocational Advisory Bureau, reformed high school curricula to include sex education, relaxed birth control restrictions, and called for more permissive divorce laws, disarmament, unemployment insurance, old age pensions, and federal works projects and hostels to deal with the transient population.[58] The discussion of the transient issue, in particular, is indicative of the Ilma group's perspective on youth problems and needs. Although the group seemed progressive in calling for increased funding for federal works projects, such funds would go to those projects that already existed in established transient camps. And this, in

Ilma's mind, was not nearly as important as establishing youth hostels to be modeled after those in Europe, which could "help in some measure to cut down vagrancy . . . eliminating the need of riding freight cars and begging."[59] Hostels might offer young people a safe place to sleep, but how transients would come up with the money to pay for such lodging was never discussed. It seemed more important to make a public nuisance invisible than to deal with the reason—unemployment—for transients' existence. This kind of conservatism surprised even some of the adults who attended the Ilma group's round table discussions. Arthur Garfield Hays remarked, after attending those sessions, that "strangely enough, American youth as a whole has seemed more conservative than those who are middle aged or perhaps more definitely centered their interest in personal problems."[60]

Ilma subsequently resigned from the rump organization, presumably because she could not completely control it.[61] Shortly thereafter it disbanded. Ilma began another youth publication, "Voice of Youth," about which one subscriber complained in a letter to the editor that "it lacks reality; it is not close enough to the ground. It has great, big, national, new-deal [sic], approach to the great, big indefinite, problem of YOUTH. I get the impression that you are starting in the clouds somewhere and trying to get down, instead of starting where you are and trying to work on from there."[62] After what she later referred to as her "cyclonic exit from the Youth Congress," Ilma went to work for the National Municipal League studying local government problems and making a survey on youth leadership, which was sponsored by the League.[63] By 1943, she was the executive director of the Young Men's Vocational Foundation and, she proudly remembered later, met with a few Army people on the problem of the teenaged youth.[64] That she was willing to work with the Army to take care of the youth problem speaks volumes regarding how far she strayed from the youth perspective.

The American Youth Congress lasted longer. A continuations committee was formed to carry on the task of organizing a genuine youth movement led by the AYC, which would become an interest group that could influence the American political, economic, and social systems. Although it has been accused of being communist-controlled, the AYC was a true popular front organization that brought together liberals, socialists, and communists, the last of whom were the smallest minority group.[65] Whatever their political affiliations, the members of the National Executive Council unanimously agreed that on all matters of policy, they would make every effort to act by mutual consent and that the final decisions on matters of policy and organization required a two-thirds vote of the national council.[66] Moreover, the National Executive Committee often submitted policy proposals to its member organizations for referenda votes and solicited information and advice from them in preparing the agenda of the annual conferences in yet further attempts to insure that the organization was democratically run.[67]

AYC leaders were not the only ones to be maligned for their efforts on behalf of youth. Professor Zorbaugh's efforts to secure the participation of left-leaning youth (liberals and radicals) earned him condemnation from Charles H. Kenlan, a CCC enrollee who was sent by the director to attend the congress and report back his findings. In his report, he claimed that Zorbaugh was a communist supporter, that NYU was "a fountainhead for the spreading of radical propaganda," and that the elected group was dangerously anti-New Deal.[68] He was particularly outraged that the AYC criticized the CCC as militaristic. This was, indeed, the only negative thing the AYC delegates were recorded to have said about the New Deal and was rather indicative of how young people felt about this *de facto* youth program.[69] Because it was run by the Army, the CCC, according to historian George Rawick who—on this one point—represented youth's perspective well, "was an authoritarian institution in its administrative structure, its administrative practices, and in the general ideological atmosphere which surrounded it."[70] Rather than explaining young people's genuine and broad-based disdain for the CCC,[71] however, Kenlan's report offered blanket support for Ilma's group because she was "more conservative and seemed to deal with some of the real problems concerning youth."[72] Such sentiment is indicative of the prejudice against the AYC, which often stemmed from clear ideological or organizational bias.

Despite the forces marshaled against it, the AYC went to work fulfilling its goals, the first of which was to canvass youth organizations to find out what young people's problems were and their ideas for solving them. To make sure they obtained a cross-section of young people's opinions, the AYC sent questionnaires to any place where young people gathered, including universities, colleges, church organizations, and social groups. That questionnaire stated that the purpose of the AYC was

> To reassert the idealism and the pioneering spirit of our forefathers who established and built this country, and to declare our determination of maintaining and supporting the Constitution of the United States, and to assert our rights to "life, liberty, and the pursuit of happiness." To this end we shall devote our efforts to the

development of democracy in its highest form, to religious and racial tolerance, and to combating the tide of communism, fascism and all narrow and bigoted doctrines contrary to the broad principles of Americanism. We further purpose [*sic*] that the American Youth Congress shall foster and promote consciousness of civic and public affairs, and lend its support to projects which will make youth a constructive force throughout the nation. We believe that only through a properly organized youth can we provide for our future. Containing all shades of opinion, the American Youth Congress takes no stand on current political and administrative questions. It is essential, however, that information on the opinions of youth be gathered.[73]

The strictly anti-partisan questionnaire asked young people if they felt they were afforded the opportunity for employment, whether a federal agency was necessary to create such opportunities, if the education system provided adequate preparation for employment, if they favored the present recovery program, and, finally, if they agreed with the purposes of the AYC as stated in the questionnaire and, if so, if they could be considered a member of the AYC.[74] The responses to this questionnaire were favorable in two respects. First, young people voluntarily identified themselves as members of the AYC. By September 1935, the AYC claimed to represent 1.5 million young people from 850 affiliated organizations.[75] Second, the responses to the questionnaire provided the framework for the planning of the second conference, the purpose of which, the AYC treasurer and Chairman of the Southern Division, William Porter, said was to "work out a program, if possible, to present to the Federal Government, particularly the Youth Bureau in the Department of the Interior."[76] In developing its program, the AYC brought out the common perspective and thus forged closer bonds of unity among youth—"between Jew and Gentile, Catholic and Protestant, Negro and White, native and foreign born, as well as between the youth of America and of other lands, and between youth and adults of the working and middle classes," and in doing so, the AYC became "a champion of all minorities."[77] The AYC thereby developed a program designed by young people—addressing their needs—to bring to the attention of Washington officials as well as to the entire youth population of America.

Eleanor Roosevelt had already become honorary chair of the AYC Advisory Board, and Porter was looking for a written statement from FDR regarding the New Deal's efforts to develop a program for youth.

Porter, speaking for the AYC, wanted to know where young people stood in FDR's policymaking paradigm. He objected to adult-sponsored policies, like those of Dr. John Studebaker, Commissioner of the Office of Education, who wished to act as liaison between the Administration and young people. It was not only the content of such plans that irked Porter and the young people he represented, but Studebaker's conception of his role as a benefactor who would communicate to them the federal government's plans concerning youth. Young people wanted to have a say in the development of those plans. In addition, Porter singled out Bernarr Macfadden's program of physical training activities as inadequate at best. Instead, he said, any youth program, "in order to have their support, must come from the young people," arguing that this would strengthen the support of the Administration among the next generation.[78]

By this point, youth leaders had begun to regularly request meetings with New Deal officials to discuss youth policy, gaining entrée into the world of adult New Deal politics. This access was augmented by the AYC's ability to exert political influence, which increased concomitantly with its breadth of membership. At its third congress in July 1936, the AYC brought together 674 organizations representing 23 anti-war, anti-fascist, and civil rights organizations; 23 fraternal organizations; 54 church organizations; 42 educational organizations; 11 unemployed organizations; 30 political organizations; 48 settlement house organizations; 148 social, cultural or sports organizations; 52 student organizations; 90 AFL trade unions, 50 YM-YWCA groups; 18 industrial, professional, or business groups; 5 farm organizations, 15 economic organizations, 30 independent trade union organizations, and 35 other organizations.[79] With such extensive support, the AYC obliged New Dealers to include young people in policymaking decisions. This would not only serve youth's needs; it would allow young people to begin molding the political system to their democratic vision.

The AYC was an umbrella organization that allowed any youth group to affiliate, while the American Student Union (ASU) was more narrowly representative of liberal, socialist, and communist students' collective desire to create a popular front organization in 1935. Compared to the AYC, the ASU had more factional disputes to overcome in order for such student groups to merge into a cohesive organization.

During the Third Period, when communists were supposed to be, as per Josef Stalin's pronouncements, locked in an ideological and political war with the "social fascists," the Young Communist League (YCL) began to make contact with the Young People's Socialist League (YPSL). In

1932, young communists had appealed to young socialists to enter into united action on behalf of striking miners in Harlan County, Kentucky, and had followed that with solidarity calls on behalf of Reed Harris and the issues of free speech and academic freedom. They were currently calling for united action to help the Scottsboro Boys. To many, it made sense to establish a more formal, permanent union in order to better execute such efforts of united action on college campuses. While the YCL was rebuffed by YPSL leaders, rank and file socialists had gone on record in favor of such a policy within their circle meetings.[80] This predates the Communist Party's official decision to adopt the popular front strategy by three full years.[81] By then the YCL was sending open letters to Yipsels (members of the YPSL), addressing them as "comrades" and asking that they set aside their differences in favor of a united front against fascism.[82] For the communists, the only thing that stood in the way of united action was the socialists' insistence on working with dissident groups, such as the Trotskyites and Lovestonites, and their demand that the YCL do so, as well.[83] Yet, while communists were motivated to root out Trotskyist elements in youth organizations, it was, they believed, more important to side with the American students in support of their needs than to focus on Trotskyists. In explaining this priority to YCLers, Ruth Watt, YCL Secretary, said that the focus should remain on working to unite students against fascism because only in working on common aims could they hope to mold student opinion.[84]

To overcome this impasse, the communists asked for permission to attend socialist meetings to address the issue of working with such renegades, whom members of the YCL believed, "moved in the direction *not* of revolutionary action, *but in the direction of counter-revolutionary action*," whose sole function was "combating and destroying the communist movement."[85] Yipsels were reminded that the YCL had opened its meetings to the socialists and therefore asked that the same courtesy be reciprocated in order to form a better, more understanding working relationship to foster united action and create a popular front. The socialist leaders, however, steadfastly refused, even organizing a separate petition drive addressing the needs of jobless youth, because, they said, it would "discredit ourselves ... by allying ourselves with you."[86]

The communists continued to try, but were never successful in convincing the YPSL to cooperate or coordinate with the YCL because the YPSL was the youth branch of the Socialist Party and did not want to lose its identity as such.[87] The YPSL's position was that members of the YCL were welcome to join the Socialist Party if they indeed wanted to work together.[88] Only the Trotskyites and Lovestonites were willing to do this. The socialists were, in fact, calling for a liquidation of the communist groups—an unattractive course of action for the communists and a hypocritical demand because the socialists were so protective of their own autonomy. This sectarianism kept radical student groups from allying until 1935 because it was complicated by the existence of other radical student groups created in the early years of the Depression: the NSL and SLID. These two groups were sympathetic to the Communist Party and Socialist Party, respectively, but they were autonomous student organizations and thus did not take orders from those parties. Like the YCL, the NSL began advocating united action before the socialist SLID. The members of SLID, though hesitant, were ultimately less reluctant than the members of YPSL, causing much dissension among socialists. It was not just a matter of overcoming socialist-communist differences, then, to create a united student organization. Disagreement among socialists—often brought on by Trotskyite agitation—had to be allayed as well because, as Daniel Bell has said in his chronicle of socialism in America, "for every two socialists, there are always three political opinions."[89]

By the 1920s, socialists in SLID were less concerned than Yipsels with the historical determinism of Marxist theory and tended to found their socialism less in class conflict and more in ethics as a way to emancipate one's spirit.[90] SLID member Joseph Lash attested that SLIDers' "attitude toward Marxism was a very skeptical one. It was a useful tool of analysis, of intellectual analysis, but one that one used very sparingly—like a seasoning or a drug—if it was in the hands of an expert as a tool of intellectual analysis, it was helpful. If you used it overly much, why, it gave you a distorted view of reality."[91] Yet like many other members of SLID, he was committed to socialism as the only way to gain full employment, remove the threat of war, end fascism, and achieve full and equal civil rights.[92] By the time the Great Depression began, SLID was less interested in ethics and emancipation of the spirit and more interested in politics in order to address these immediate problems.

Yipsels were confounded by the presence of the SLID on campuses because they could neither subordinate it to the YPSL's will nor inculcate SLIDers with a more dogmatic definition of socialism.[93] Yipsels' frustration with the SLID was compounded as they felt socialism was losing further recruiting ground because unattached radicals were increasingly joining the NSL, which consequently was seen as the most fully functioning radical student organization on campus.[94] The YPSL blamed the SLID for this and for leaving socialism hamstrung on the campus.

The NSL first approached the SLID with an offer to unite in order to better tackle student problems in 1933, but was turned down on much the same grounds as the YCL had been turned down by the YPSL.[95] The scenario was repeated in 1934. However, the SLID had already begun coordinating and co-sponsoring events with the NSL, and this paved the way for the outcome the NSL sought. Meanwhile, the problem of socialist resistance still had to be overcome, and though this was a much more serious issue for the creation of the ASU, it affected the AYC as well.

Wechsler was not the only former youth activist to cast the AYC as a communist front organization. Hal Draper, who joined the YPSL in 1932 and remained an active leader in its New York City branch after his graduation from Brooklyn College in 1934, also claimed (in 1967) that the communists created the AYC.[96] To understand why Draper would do this, one must rely not on what he said in 1967, but rather on what he said in the 1930s. Draper had never truly supported the popular front.

In 1934, Draper became the leader of a Trotskyist left-wing faction within the YPSL dedicated to a revolutionary socialist program designed "to seize state power for the working class, as a necessary preliminary to the building of a classless society."[97] As a Trotskyist, he did not want to work with those he saw as his most significant enemy: the communists. At the same time, Draper routinely criticized the YPSL leadership for what he perceived as its lack of militancy.[98] The way Draper saw it, a decision had to be made "whether the socialist movement will follow the path of class struggle, of Marx and Engels; or the path of class co-operation, the path of the old guard."[99] Trotskyists' concern was that working with non-radicals would make socialism a non-revolutionary party, and therefore it would lose out as a party of reform at the same time it became ineffectual as a voice of revolution—it would become "hollowed out" like the Old Guard socialists, neither quite revolutionary nor merely reformist.[100] Speaking for his faction in an open letter to Yipsels, he made his opposition to unity quite clear: "We refuse to give up our own right to criticize the communists."[101] He continued carrying on intra-party debates in local newspapers, which only supplied the Hearst press with unnecessary ammunition, contradicted socialist ethics, and directly violated the Socialist Party's prohibition against such actions, causing much embarrassment for the YPSL Executive Committee of Greater New York, prompting it to adopt a statement that "such unsocialist behavior cannot be tolerated."[102] The local branch of the Socialist Party went even further, instructing the YPSL to drop Hal Draper and others over the age of 21 who had been refused admission to the Socialist Party in an (ultimately unsuccessful) attempt to take direct control over the NY YPSL and thus end the general threat to socialism that this kind of publicity engendered.[103]

Lash was an early proponent of the popular front, though he, too, had some initial socialist misgivings about it. At first, he was most disturbed by the accusation that it was socialists who were to blame for fascism coming to power in Europe. Instead, Lash argued, it was the communists' fault because they had refused to unite with the Social Democratic Party in Germany. This made him wary of the communists' calls for a united action when those calls were sounded. He believed at the time that "a united front against war and Fascism is like an emergency cure designed to keep a patient alive until more fundamental processes can set in."[104] A united front, he said, did not get rid of the root cause of fascism: the exploitative capitalist system. He became convinced of the utility of unity only after a trip to Europe.[105]

Just as the AYC was holding its inaugural conference, Lash attended the International Socialist Student Federation triennial congress in Liège, Belgium. En route to that congress, Lash visited Paris, Antwerp, and a socialist commune outside Liège and thus was introduced to the European socialist movement first-hand. He had gone to Europe hopeful that world socialism would rise up against the fascist threat as the Austrian socialists had done in February 1934. Instead, he was surprised to learn the socialists preferred to model their efforts after the French example: the popular front.[106] The European socialists he mingled with, he believed, were less militant than the American socialists, and it shocked him that they questioned his deprecatory view of Franklin Roosevelt and the New Deal while holding the American Socialist Party in low esteem.[107] He reported back to his American socialist comrades that the European socialist press looked favorably on the non-aggression pact Stalin had signed with France in June 1935 as a "signal to communists everywhere that trafficking with bourgeois governments had become legitimate."[108] The French socialists' and communists' move toward cooperation required some rethinking on both their parts. The communists stopped viewing the socialists as social-fascists, while the socialists, Lash said, "were groping toward new programs that might attract the middle class as well as the workers—the 'mixed economy,'" thereby "reining in their economic demands. Some socialist groups . . . sought the public control and ownership of just enough of the economic domain to enable socialist governments to deal with unemployment and underconsumption."[109] While this plan was still under official attack in the Comintern, Lash was won over, rationalizing this change in course as an adaptation of Lenin's New

Economic Policy.[110] Thus, when the Executive Committee met at the culmination of the congress and endorsed united action with communist student groups, Lash was a firm supporter of that policy.[111]

Upon his return to the United States, though, he still faced socialist opposition to such a program. Gravely concerned about the factionalism that raged within the Socialist Party, Lash grew increasing impatient with the opposition forces because, as he saw it, they represented a threat that could tear the socialist movement apart at the very time it should be uniting with other radical groups.[112] Student socialists agreed to joint action with the communists, but they were not yet ready to join together in a popular front organization. That was as far as they would go at this point, and Lash had little choice but to follow that lead. Once the popular front became an established fact, however, he enlisted as its staunchest defender.

Young communists exerted a concerted effort in convincing socialists to join with them to confront issues facing young Americans. It was comparatively much less difficult to convince young liberals, who joined with both groups of radicals because they found they had much in common. This was because, as Daniel Bell pointed out, "a student generation that feared its education would be wasted, all sought hope in going left."[113] Wechsler hoped that liberals who joined with radicals in seeking to deter fascism and its bent toward war would necessarily have to consider its roots in capitalism. The radicals, he said, were obligated to "lead him (the liberal) through that process of enlightenment."[114] However, he went on to say that "on the other hand, if we are wrong, then let him prove us to be so by engaging in joint activity. If capitalism can be restored to health, reaction stifled and war averted within his order, then let us find that out together by combating the symptoms."[115] The popular front, then, was to be a way for young radicals and liberals to face the issues that threatened all of them alike and work out solutions in unison.[116]

What allowed the ASU to come into existence was the radicals' and liberals' shared anti-war stance.[117] As early as 1931, socialists were concerned about the probability of a future war.[118] By 1933, the CCNY administration refused to allow *The Campus* to conduct a poll of student sentiment because the anti-war feeling was so pervasive that the results, the administration believed, would provide the media with more ammunition to use against the college, which was already branded as a hotbed of radicalism.[119] The liberal editor wrote an open letter to the students pointing out that this was yet another example of the administration's determination to silence the student body's collective voice.[120] The NSFA also expressed concern over the coming war danger and, like the radical groups, found much to be wary of in light of the Nye Commission Investigation. It was Ernest R. Bryan, a liberal member of the NSFA, who explained to students that "the munitions maker knows no country, feels no patriotism; his love of country is an appetite for profit," and thus these "war zealots" induced "our government . . . to build up the armaments" of this nation, creating a situation whereby "disarmament efforts are nullified, cooperative efforts for peace are defeated and expenditures for armaments in all the nations of the world are increased."[121] The NSFA decided that the best way to counteract the movement toward war implicit in such policies was to mobilize public opinion to reduce armaments "and a continuous educational campaign on the doings and misdoings of the 'dealers in death.'" Speaking on behalf of the NSFA, Ernest Bryan further explained that "We must . . . work for collective action, for arms reduction and not limitation; build up more trade and thus speed recovery in every country; and substitute friendship and confidence for suspicion in international relations."[122] Student Christian Associations around the country were also mobilized to support students' anti-war activities as part of a year-round peace program because they believed that "students can and must assert their convictions in resisting any tendencies to involve this country in war."[123]

Liberals did not have to be induced to support leftist students' anti-war activities; they were already committed to such an agenda. Eric Sevareid, a CBS journalist who graduated from the University of Minnesota in 1935, remembered that liberals "read with eagerness the new books purporting to expose the munitions racket and accepted all their implications. We cheered Senator Nye in his fight for the Neutrality Act long and loudly."[124] Peace activists hoped that while trying to remove the causes of war, they would be able to hold off the next war long enough so that the veteran-controlled Congress could be replaced by a younger generation without actual experience in or remembrance of war and thus, perhaps, bring about a political resolution to the war danger, a prospect that liberals found very attractive.[125] It was because of the intensity of radicals' and liberals' mutual disdain for war that historian Eileen Eagan identified peace as the ASU's "most successful issue."[126]

American youth's antipathy to war found common ground with youth abroad when Oxford Union undergraduates voted 275 to 153 on February 9, 1933 to uphold a resolution that "this house will in no circumstances fight for King and Country."[127] As this Oxford Oath spread through British universities, it was also introduced in the United States, where students adopted it as: "We pledge not to support the government of the United States in any war it may conduct." This brought ire from adults claiming this was an un-American activity. Lash and Wechsler, in a book written for the express purpose of identifying "the problem of youth and war,"[128] explained that the oath-takers had a different perspective:

> Are those who adhere to the Oxford Pledge "unpatriotic"? The answer depends on the dictionary employed. If we accept the Bible of the Daughters of the American Revolution or similar horsewomen of the republic, the charge is undoubtedly valid. The pledge is a denial of blind faith; it suggests the fallibility of government—a crime committed by the most respectable people in an election year. . . . Whether this strategy is treason depends, again, upon whether allegiance to chaos is a higher form of patriotism. . . . Are we disloyal? It is alleged that endorsement of the Oxford Oath gives comfort to foreign nations. . . . All the facts foreshadow an opposite response.[129]

They insisted that young people had to be prepared to take a stand against war before it began so that they would be on guard against the forces of propaganda that would try to make war hysteria irresistible. If they waited until war broke out to oppose it, they would be labeled as cowards. In that event, "Patriotism becomes the path of least resistance as well as the last resort of scoundrels; intransigence, whether successful or merited, is the difficult road."[130] When properly understood, Lash explained, "it is a deep going love of our country which is embodied in the Oxford Pledge. We believe that the greatest catastrophe that can befall our nation is war"[131] because "another war would destroy everything worthwhile in American civilization—its young manhood, its resources, its culture."[132]

Much is often made of the wording of the Americanized version of the Oxford Pledge to corroborate the notion that organized youth were manipulated by young communist functionaries, who refused to support an "imperialist war," but who, at the same time, reserved the right to go to war to promote a communist revolution and/or defend the Soviet Union.[133] Draper later posited that "the difference was deliberate. It was formulated here by student leaders who, both socialist and communist, regarded themselves as Marxists and did not want to make the pledge a statement of absolute pacifism—a viewpoint which was virtually non-existent among the communist leaders of the NSL and infrequent in the leadership of the SLID nationally or locally."[134] Radical leaders at the time, however, noted that there was no intention to join with the Russian Army, "and only a Hearst foreign expert could view the U.S.S.R. as a threat to peace at a time when reliable observers see fascist maneuvers constantly aimed at her borders."[135] Lash maintained that "the Oxford pledge is not dogmatic nor prophetic—it is an immediate practical affirmation in light of a specific war danger."[136]

On the question of whether or not students should differentiate between aggressive and defensive war, SLID rejected the distinction altogether, claiming that this was "a dodge whereby capitalist nations induce their people to wage their wars" and went on to remind students that "*Every nation in the World War claimed it was fighting a defensive war.*"[137] The issue was not what kind of war the next war would be; the issue was whether or not there would be another war. The Oxford Pledge demonstrated students' unwillingness to participate in the event of war. The wording was a viable substitute for the British usage of "king and country." More conservative-leaning students had just as much say in the wording as did the radicals, and thus it appealed to both sides of the political spectrum.[138] Lash remembered that there was no compromise worked out about the wording of the pledge. And later, in 1936, when the communists wanted to alter the pledge to include a qualifying statement supporting collective security, the socialists would not agree to it.[139] The Oxford Pledge, then, was adopted as a means to avoid all war.

Whatever radical youth leaders may have intended, students supported the Oxford Pledge in large numbers. For the vast majority of young people, it did not really matter whether the next war would result from revolution or imperialism because it would undoubtedly be a harbinger of ensuing chaos. Communists and pacifists alike believed it would simply be a repetition of World War I, which must be avoided at all costs.[140]

As early as 1933, the NSL and SLID worked together to encourage widespread student participation in anti-war activities, paving the way for their joint sponsorship of the first National Student Strike Against War in 1934.[141] At Columbia University in 1933, for example, students declared war on war in a public demonstration.[142] Faculty members publicly supported this action, and in a *Spectator* poll, 42 percent of them said they would not bear arms under any conditions.[143] By 1934, the demonstrations expanded into an anti-war week.[144] Ardent pacifists, however, were concerned by this point that although a substantial number of faculty members supported their decision to walk out of classes in the anti-war strike, the majority was, as Wechsler described, "falling into the same calm, almost deliberate acceptance of the approaching war which characterized the University of 1917."[145] Meanwhile, in a poll conducted

Figure 1. Strike Against War poster, 1935.

among Columbia students, one-third said they would not bear arms under any circumstances, and one-half indicated that they would rather go to prison than fight an unjust war.[146] Adults were advised by newspaper editors at the time not to take young people's anti-war stance seriously, and this, Eagan has contended, outraged young people, who became even more committed to peace.[147] The annual strike against war is a testament to the anti-war commitment of young people who perceived a growing movement toward war and thus increasingly saw themselves as a pre-war generation.[148] Activists were determined to mobilize students for peace, and they struck a chord when they pointedly asked: "Shall we be another war generation? That decision rests with us; we, together with the peoples of other nations, can—and must—determine our own fate."[149]

The 1934 National Student Strike Against War was held on April 13 with an estimated 25,000 students participating. According to Lash, this event was "a dress rehearsal for what we would do in a war crisis."[150] Such actions as the planting of white crosses at Smith College and the burning of William Randolph Hearst in effigy at the University of Chicago gained national publicity and thus allowed the anti-war message to reach an even larger audience of sympathetic students.[151] At Amherst, a SLID member led students in a parade in which he carried a placard made by the NSL as they marched to Smith College, where they participated in a joint Amherst-Smith demonstration.[152] The NSL and SLID were uniting youth and thus coming closer together themselves.

Throughout 1934, the NSL and SLID also co-sponsored anti-ROTC demonstrations. The mobilization of youth against the ROTC rested on the activist students' reasoning that "William James once cited the import of discovering a moral equivalent for war. That equivalent must be found in the movement against war."[153] The occasion for much of the anti-ROTC demonstrations was the Supreme Court case *Hamilton v. Regents of the University of California*. The decision, finally handed down in December 1934, upheld compulsory military training on college campuses. In response, Lash and Wechsler said that

> whatever the judicial logic, precedent or plausibility involved, the decision was momentous for peace advocates. They became finally convinced that military training now—or conscription later— could not be defeated in the courts. The broader arena of social action remained. It was that realization which, perhaps more than any other, brought together the student Christian movement and liberal and radical groups in a collective front for peace.[154]

Lash and Wechsler cast the decision's rationale as anti-American. When the justices agreed that "every student owes the reciprocal duty, according to this capacity, to support and defend his government against all enemies," Lash and Wechsler found this uncomfortably similar to Hitler's assertion in *Mein Kampf* that "our young people have to be stoical. When one neglects to teach youth to suffer without compliant, one should not be astonished, during the critical hours of battle, that the combatant is unable to undergo the hardships of the front."[155] ROTC, they believed, was a menace to world peace because it helped create an atmosphere where militarism was acceptable.[156]

Even moderate groups like the National Student Federation of America were opposed to ROTC. By 1936, its newsletter came out in public support of the Nye-Kvale Bill to make ROTC voluntary, and decrying the expulsion of students in Iowa, Maryland, California, Ohio, Missouri, Kansas, West Virginia, and Maine for their conscientious refusal to submit to compulsory military training.[157] It sponsored an editorial-writing contest to encourage students to write letters to their local newspapers in support of the Nye-Kvale Bill and even called on students to join the War Resisters League.[158] The NSFA, at the same time that it claimed ROTC was turning college campuses into miniature West Points, began to collect stories about hazing involved in ROTC training and reported such incidences to the War Department.[159] The NSFA newsletter picked up the story of one such situation detailed in *Pennsylvania State Collegian* whereby students who did not perform well in shooting range practice were forced to run the gauntlet of 75 cartridge belt-wielding peers who swung at them as they passed.[160] Its press release asked Secretary of War George H. Dern to investigate this and other such incidents. Such occurrences help explain why Sevareid said that liberals "learned to look upon the whole proceeding [of compulsory ROTC training] as a harsh interference with our liberty and a humiliating affront to our personal dignity."[161] He, like many other liberal students, campaigned against the ROTC and used his role as editor of the college newspaper to support anti-war efforts. Sevareid said that

> Very few of us were conscientious objectors to war in the true, religious sense. We had no thought of working for a violent overthrow of the government itself either by removing its internal military defense or by encouraging its defeat by a foreign power. We believed that "preparedness," as the history of warring countries proved, was

no guarantee of peace—that it would be, in fact, a force for easier involvement. We refused to believe that *any* people in the world desired war, with us or with their neighbors. In any case, modern war was a product of the collapsing capitalistic system and the collision of its imperialisms and was encouraged and desired only by the professional military, financiers, and munitions makers, who were associated in a kind of loose but real conspiracy against the innocent people of every land. The whole effort, the whole meaning of our own lives in our time must be to improve the material and spiritual condition of man in society, and war was the negation of all this.[162]

Students at CCNY were urged by *The Campus* editor to mobilize for peace in 1935 as the only way to avoid being sacrificed on the field of battle in a future war: "Don't go to the library during the free hour. Your studies will be of little use to you after you've been ground up by shrapnel. Don't hang around the alcoves or eat your lunch. The titanic struggle to avert a war which would mean agony and death to you and those near you demands your support."[163]

Wechsler's outrage against the ROTC was manifest not only in his belief that it bred a culture of war for which young men would be sacrificed in order to save the House of Morgan's profits, but also in the unjustified situation whereby "thousands of students (were) being forced to curtail their education, whole schools (were) being shut down as 'economic' measures, (while) appropriations for the corps was rising."[164] The needs of the War Department should not trump the needs of young people, he and others believed.

Moreover, ROTC represented a direct threat to the anti-war movement. Citing examples at Michigan State College and Pennsylvania State University, Wechsler and Lash noted that "violence has flared at numerous anti-war meetings through the intervention of R.O.T.C. men."[165] Ralph Brax, in his study of student activism, recounted numerous instances of such behavior, which was sanctioned by college administrators who reacted negatively to the anti-war strike. Indeed, administrators were more likely to take disciplinary action against the peaceful anti-war demonstrators than the violent interveners.[166] At Johns Hopkins University, ROTC members launched a barrage of eggs, overripe tomatoes, and fish heads at the peacefully assembled student strikers, and one student opponent opened a fire hose on them, resulting in a near riot. A strike supporter wrote to the editor of the campus newspaper explaining that "we are glad" about the way the strike turned out "because it offers convincing, indeed irrefutable evidence to the Administration that it has unconsciously catered to a group of vandalistic imbeciles whose lack of knowledge is only surpassed by their disrespect for the rights of others."[167] ROTC was, then, sometimes used as another tool to suppress young people from speaking up for what they wanted.[168] It was not successful. Between 1930 and 1935, there were more than one hundred anti-war conferences and symposiums held on college campuses across the nation.[169]

By 1935, anti-militarist sentiment was pervasive on college campuses. At CCNY, as part of the demonstrations supporting the annual strike, a poll of 1,795 students was conducted that revealed the depth of that sentiment on a number of anti-war resolutions, the results of which were published in *The Campus (see accompanying table)*.[170] It was not only CCNY students who were against war. In 1935, the *Literary Digest* polled 65,000 students, 68 percent of whom felt the United States should stay out of another war, 81 percent said they would not fight if the United States was the aggressor nation, and 90 percent said they favored government control of munitions manufacturers.[171] The *Daily Herald* at Brown University conducted an even more extensive survey of 65 colleges in 27 states and found that 39 percent of respondents refused to participate in any future war, and only 33 percent said they would fight if the United States was invaded.[172]

	Yes	No	Not Voting
We pledge ourselves not to support the United States in any war it may conduct.	1,544	186	65
We petition Congress to abolish all forms of military training (ROTC) in the high schools and colleges; and to abolish the C.M.T.C.	1,644	111	40
We protest militarization of the youth in the C.C.C. camps and we denounce the campaign of the jingo press to inculcate the militaristic spirit among the youth of the country	1,738	25	32
We petition Congress to divert all military funds for increased educational and recreational activities	1,628	121	46

	Yes	No	Not Voting
We protest the Supreme Court decision upholding compulsory military training in the land grant colleges	1,694	53	48
We petition Congress to reject all Alien and Sedition laws pending before them, which would deny free discussion, let loose a deportation terror, make bona fide trade unions illegal, etc.	1,675	66	54
We favor repeal of all federal espionage and all state syndicalism laws and the release of all persons imprisoned thereunder	1,559	115	121
We are against all forms of oppression of national and racial minorities in the United States and its possessions—including Mexicans, Negroes, Jews, Japanese, Puerto Ricans, and Filipinos	1,740	15	40
We favor the withdrawal of all United States troops in China, Cuba, the Philippines, and Puerto Rico	1,612	115	68
We give our full support to the boycott of all goods from Germany, Italy, and other fascist countries	1,610	117	68
We favor the freeing of all those imprisoned in fascist countries for their militant opposition to war and fascism	1,653	61	81
We demand the reinstatement of all students of the college expelled for anti-war and anti-fascist activities	1,605	117	73

The shared animus toward war on the part of both the socialists and the communists helped to bring these opposing groups together in joint activity, and, in doing so, they discovered that they had a common interest in other issues as well. It is because of this that the SLID and NSL, along with the Intercollegiate Disarmament Council, YMCA, YWCA, and the National Council of Student Christian Associations sponsored a three-day National Conference on Students in Politics held in Washington, D.C. in December 1933. Delegates deliberated the major issues facing students, namely how to participate in politics as a means to create a peaceful world. To that end, they debated the merits of the National Recovery Act, tariffs, fascism, inflation, and military service. Lending legitimacy to the discussion was the participation on the advisory board of Charles Beard, John Dewey, Morris R. Cohen, Reinhold Niebuhr, Norman Thomas, and New York Senator Robert Wagner, some of whom also agreed to chair the round table discussions.[173] The NSL, in its call for participation in this conference, clearly saw this as a step toward the creation of a united student organization, for which "the reasons for its existence are inescapable; its possibilities are manifold."[174] They summoned students to form committees dedicated to such an organization so that when it was formally established, it would be truly representative of the student body.[175] These all served as necessary precursors to the merger of the NSL and SLID in forming the ASU in December 1935; however, SLID leaders were still reluctant to merge.

In February 1934, Lash, the editor of SLID's newspaper *The Student Outlook*, wrote an editorial attempting to explain the conundrum facing SLID members coming out of the recent conference they had co-sponsored with the NSL and other groups. "Conservatives," he claimed, wanted "unity on the basis of *no* program" while communists wanted "amalgamation despite the certainty of a future schism," neither of which was attractive to SLID leaders.[176] This, Lash said, was "not because it wished to perpetuate the present factionalism, or because of organizational pride, but because it desired to see a student movement that was genuinely radical and truly united."[177] It was the socialists who did not want to work with the liberals, whom they referred to as conservatives or—in the case of the National Student Federation of America—reactionaries, and who also refused to side too closely with the communists. It was the socialists' commitment to the popular front, then, that was weak in the beginning, and, later, it would be the socialists who first opted to leave it.[178] Lash did not publicly favor amalgamation at this point, but he recommended that SLID continue to co-sponsor anti-war activities in order to avert war.[179] The NSL renewed its unity offer to SLID in December 1934 for the third time, calling for joint chapter meetings so that the differences in program and approach could be discussed on every campus.[180]

In April 1935, the NSL and SLID once again co-sponsored what was becoming an annual strike against war; this time, however, it was expanded into the National Strike Against War and Fascism because student organizers of the anti-war movement recognized fascism as the most se-rious threat to world peace,[181] and while Columbia University President Butler expressed hope in March 1935 that Hitler would lead Germany in a return to the League of Nations in order to avert growing tension in Europe, students believed the elimination of fascism was a prerequisite for peace.[182] SLID leaders were very clear on this connection:"Fascism breeds war and the fight against war must be the fight against Fascism."[183] SLID, true to its socialist roots, went further, saying that "capitalism, Fascism, war are inextricably interwoven" because "the search for profits brings na-tions into conflict.... When profits are imperiled by an economic crisis, capitalists resort to Fascism. When Fascism is unable to satisfy the eco-nomic needs of the masses who turned to it for succor, Fascism then turns to war."[184] SLID led students in a boycott of German goods as a demonstration of their anti-fascist sentiment.[185]

It was the war issue that finally convinced SLID members to join to-gether with the communists and liberals. In doing so, SLID leaders did not relinquish their radical long-term goals, but they did choose to focus on short-term objectives—the most important of which was avoiding war. SLID members were less dogmatic than Yipsels and wanted to build up a mass movement of young people. In doing so, SLID's socialist ide-ology may have become diluted, but it brought SLID more in line with other groups of young people, laying the foundation for amalgamation.[186] Lash defensively maintained, however, that SLIDers were, if anything, more socialist than the Yipsels because, while the Yipsels pontificated their socialist ideology, the SLIDers were demonstrating and organiz-ing the masses of students to help bring about fundamental change in America, showing that "there's a great deal of difference between ideo-logical pronouncements that sound revolutionary and genuine militancy of spirit."[187] Meanwhile, liberals, according to Sevareid, "knew the mo-ment the Nazis burned the books that fascism wanted war. We knew it in our bones."[188] And, he said, they "remained desperately anxious to keep America out of it, to preserve at least one oasis of sanity in an insane world.... Fascism meant war, but instead of accepting war as inevitable, the thing to do was to stop fascism this side of war."[189] The desire to avert war brought SLID in line with the mainstream youth perspective and al-lowed it to work together with various other groups.[190] Lash explained that while SLID members adjusted to the realities of American politics, the "custodians of the true faith," as the Yipsels liked to think of them-selves, believed the SLID members' socialism was becoming corrupted, causing constant friction in the socialist camp.[191] The YPSL grew increasingly isolated as the SLID edged closer to uniting with the NSL and liberal groups.

Representatives from the NSL and SLID, along with others from the National Council of Methodist Youth, the AYC, the American League Against War and Fascism, and the Inter Seminary Movement joined together to form the Central Strike Committee in order to plan the 1935 anti-war strike. Students were to leave class at 11 AM on April 12 to protest against war and fascism as they had the year before. Most of the demonstrations were peaceful gatherings, such as convocations and prayer meetings. However, in 1935, the purposes for the strike were enlarged: students were also showing their condemnation of armament appropriations, the Hearst press for supporting war,[192] maneuvers of the U.S. Pacific fleet they believed were provoking Japan, and what they saw as the attempt to turn workers at CCC Camps into Army reserve units. In addition, they pushed for the abolishment of the ROTC, supported the World Student Congress as a way to increase international cooperation, and reaffirmed their commitment to the Oxford Pledge.[193] In a radio speech before the strike was held, Lash urged students to strike against a war that would destroy his generation "in a holocaust of shrapnel, gas and barbarism" just as the Great War had done to the previous generation.[194] He pointedly asked President Roosevelt, "At whom are we to shoot these rifles we are learning to handle in our R.O.T.C.'s? When we have learned these drill formations, over what foreign fields do you propose to march us?"[195] And then he intoned students' demands: "We say abolish the R.O.T.C.! Build schools, not battleships!"[196] The official call for student support was addressed to "fellow classmates" and reminded them in no uncertain terms that "Our lives are at stake. We have no alternative. Strike against war!"[197] An alternate version of the strike call included an image of military men representing France, England, the U.S.A., Germany, Japan, and Italy, all sharpening their swords in preparation for war as a stark visual warning of the urgency entailed in the strike.[198]

Participation in the second strike against war increased dramatically; 175,000 students from at least 150 colleges took part.[199] The first strike had largely been a New York City affair, but thanks to youth activists' expert use of the national press, this second strike reached across the country. In New York City, 30,000 students struck, while at least 10,000 students struck in Philadelphia, Boston, Chicago, Washington D.C., and Los Angeles. It also reached beyond the urban centers and into the backwoods of the country. At Phillips University (a small Christian college) in

Oklahoma, for example, 200 students, representing 50 percent of the students enrolled, participated, along with the entire student body of Reed College in Oregon.[200] Leftist activists organized the strike, but it was the student body that supported it.

Adults decried youthful activism as naiveté. Activists, however, knew full well the limited use of the strike as a means to avert war. As early as 1933, SLID warned that "our strike must not be considered the be-all and end-all of the anti-war movement. In fact, it is only the beginning."[201] Lash and Wechsler were more specific:

> We have confessed guilt: the strike does not eternally safeguard peace. It is, however, the most potent instrument that students and workers can employ to postpone, prevent and influence a specific war situation. . . . The strike's immediate end is to curtail war preparations, defeat "disaffection" bills, combat compulsory military training and false neutrality measures which hasten war, duties which are the heaviest ones of the present. Accomplishment of these aims will at least delay the outbreak of war."[202]

The strike was literally conceived as a preparatory drill demonstrating what students would do in the event of a declaration of war; adult policy-makers, they warned, should take heed.

With joint action well established, Wechsler lent his voice to the chorus calling for an NSL-SLID union. In June 1935, he reinforced the NSL's position that the only way to create a truly unified student movement was to create an all-inclusive organization that could win the trust, respect, and cooperation of every segment of the student population. Such an organization, he said, must be truly representative of its followers to be successful, and thus the NSL, "without hesitancy or reserve . . . joined hands with any group or individual genuinely devoted to (the) immediate struggle against a war which may break out at any hour."[203] The only way to overcome the reaction that had already set in against the student anti-war activities was for the NSL and SLID to come together so that they did not appear to be working against each other.[204] And while he, too, hoped that one day students would "believe the ultimate roots of war lie in our declining profit economy," he was willing to focus on students' immediate needs—foremost among which was to avoid becoming cannon fodder.[205]

It was only after their successful coordination of the second anti-war strike that the national executive committees of the NSL and SLID met and formulated plans[206] for the creation of the American Student Union, a non-partisan organization the stated purpose of which was to struggle against war and fascism, fight for academic freedom, and break down racial discrimination.[207] The coordinating committee then issued a call to all high schools and colleges for delegates to the first national convention of the ASU to be held in Columbus, Ohio in December 1935.

In the meantime, the two groups once again coordinated efforts with other youth groups to organize peace demonstrations to commemorate Armistice Day under the slogan "an eleventh hour demonstration against war."[208] A delegation of eighteen youth representatives was granted an audience with President Roosevelt in November 1935 during which FDR read a written statement encouraging students to face the war question in a sacrificial mood, spoke vaguely about how the United States had foregone imperialism with the adoption of the Good Neighbor Policy, and then thanked them for visiting since he wanted to know what was happening on the college campuses. The students were not allowed to ask any questions before they were summarily dismissed. They left disillusioned by the manner in which the meeting was conducted. SLID representative George Edwards remarked that even Tom Neblett, liberal leader of the NSFA, was discouraged and growing more cynical.[209] FDR still saw these students as individuals, not as representatives of an important constituency. That only changed once the students came together in the ASU.

In forming the ASU, the members of the NSL and SLID voted to dissolve their organizations. While the NSL vote was open and unanimous, the SLID meeting was closed, and although a majority (97) voted in favor, seven voted against and eight abstained.[210] Dissension among the Socialists rankled, creating a precarious sense of unity.

The delegates to the first ASU conference voted approval of the Oxford Pledge as an expression of youth activists' anti-war convictions that also served as a focal point around which young people who wished to maintain peace could coalesce.[211] While it served as a platform and a recruiting tool for the ASU, it also gave opponents a reason to attack the new organization. New York State Senator Joseph D. Nunan used students' adherence to the Oxford Pledge to rally support behind his loyalty oath bill in the New York legislature.[212] The assumption that young people who espoused the Oxford Pledge were not good Americans continued to be hotly contested. Lash claimed that "the Oxford pledge represents the patriotic conviction that another war would destroy everything worthwhile in American civilization—its young manhood, its resources, its culture, all of which suffer in war. . . . War is so destructive a thing, so utterly devoid of purpose and value, that a system and a government by the very act of bringing us into war loses all claims to our allegiance."[213]

Although he was accused of being a Stalinist puppet for his endorsement of the peace program of the ASU, Lash maintained that the program in general and the Oxford Pledge, in particular, was neither "dogmatic nor prophetic—it is an immediate practical affirmation in light of a specific war danger."[214]

Lash not only defended the ASU peace platform against rightist political opponents; he defended it against attacks coming from the left, as well. When the SLID decided to join with the NSL in forming the ASU, the members of the YPSL could not have been more delighted to be rid of a competitor socialist group and soon saw an even greater benefit to this new situation. The YPSL agreed to work with the communists indirectly through the ASU. Yipsels were told to join the ASU while also maintaining their independent YPSL activities on campus to supplement the ASU's activities.[215] In the best case scenario, the YPSL might thereby gain influence in the ASU;[216] at the very least it was guaranteed a secure place as the main socialist group on campus. Although the socialists joined with the communists in forming the popular front, this did not mean they were all working together in unified harmony. Indeed, the factionalism continued, but, in the early years, it was more an internecine feud among socialists than a socialist-communist struggle.[217]

Left-wing groups, like the Trotskyists, continued to be an obstacle in creating genuine unity. The socialists, as a whole, had moved left, but Trotskyists thought they should move even further left. Professing the Troskyite position, Hal Draper had resisted every effort to create and maintain a popular front coalition because it undercut true Marxism: the communists had moved too far to the right, especially after 1935, and thus the popular front would drag socialists in the opposite direction than the one it should be headed.[218]

Having failed in his effort to prevent the creation of the ASU, Draper took to sabotaging it from within. He claimed that the popular front was all part of a communist plot: The YCL, in particular, was sabotaging the revolutionary potential of the socialists' work in the ASU by courting the liberals.[219] True socialists, he believed, should not be fooled by such deception. The YCL countered that it was the Trotskyites who were the danger. In an open letter to members of the NY YPSL, the YCL warned that

> the role of the Trotyskites during this crisis in your organization is one that every YPSLer must be cognizant of. . . . Many of them have come into the YPSL (after having been discredited and driven out of all other organizations) for the sole purpose of destroying it,

and in reality have become the most effective instruments of the old guard, supplying them with lies and slander against the communists, the Soviet Union, and the united front.[220]

As a member of the ASU National Executive Committee, by virtue of his leadership position in the influential New York YPSL, Draper attacked the preparations for the 1936 anti-war strike activities in the *American Socialist Monthly* as watered down bourgeois displays that disowned any relationship to socialist action or ideology. Socialists, he claimed, duped into supporting such benign activities as peace assemblies in high schools for which students would not even have to walk out of classes, were betraying their commitment to radicalism and thus becoming stooges of the communists.[221] Draper further claimed that the communists in the ASU were only going along with the Oxford Pledge because it was essential to the creation of the organization, but that they did not really support it.

It was socialist leader Joseph Lash who came to the YCL's defense against Draper in explaining the organic unity of the ASU. Lash railed against Draper's claim that "the ASU under YCL pressure is pursuing an opportunist line," accusing him of "scandal-mongering" by casting unfounded aspersions on the YCL.[222] Instead of attacking the communists, Lash said that Draper should inform himself of the socialist approach to the student movement,

> This is not that there will be inevitable polarization in the student population, but that the majority of students can be united around a program of immediate demands which they believe can be obtained under capitalism, but which Socialists believe will involve them finally in the struggle against capitalism and for Socialism. Draper's main concern is to shun allies who may later desert us; my main concern is to set students in motion to the point where they must make the decision between capitalism and socialism.[223]

Lash starkly iterated the only two options for socialists: Work together with communists and liberals or the "continuance of a policy such as is implied by Draper [which] will only hamper the work of the ASU and isolate the YPSL."[224] It was only grudgingly that Trotskyists like Draper worked with popular front organizations, and then it was only because of a shared antipathy toward war.[225] Consequently, the executive director of the Chicago chapter of the ASU labeled the Trotskyists as the number one enemy of the ASU.[226]

Lash took to the Socialist Party press to respond to Draper's attack.

He defended the less-than-militant activities in the high schools, where, he said, radicalism was weaker as a matter of practicality. He pointedly reminded Draper that it had been socialists who had raised objections to the Oxford Pledge, and then he launched into a counterattack. Draper, he explained, was trying to destroy the recent merger between the socialists and communists.[227] In order to prove Draper's allegations false, Lash sent letters of explanation to youth leaders accompanied by both Draper's article and his response, along with ASU leaflets, editorials from college newspapers, the official call for the strike, and the bulletin sent out from the ASU National Executive Committee to ASU chapters, all of which emphasized the Oxford Pledge.[228] Many of those youth leaders responded in a show of support for Lash's position. The leader of the Student Christian Movement in New England intimated, in his response to Lash's letter, that Draper's diatribe was part of a concerted effort on the part of the YPSL to discredit the ASU, and, like Lash, he "was sick and tired of the splitting tactics" and promised that "sabotaging from foetal theoreticians is not going to be tolerated."[229] Bob Newman, chairman of the Committee for Peace and Freedom in Boston, thanked Lash for unmasking Draper, and the "lefter than left clique" for what they really were: anti-communists.[230] Newman agreed with Lash that the communists were sincere in their support of the popular front, pointing out that "the YCL has been anything but opportunist in ... New England," while "the Trotskyites ... are proving more and more of a damnable set of trouble makers."[231] Despite the fissures in the socialist camp, the socialists, communists, and liberals had finally come together, and Lash (at this point) was committed to maintaining that unity.

The make-up of the ASU's National Executive Committee (NEC) exemplifies just how much of an equitable alliance this group was: of the thirty members of the NEC, eleven were SLID members, nine were NSL members, and ten were unaffiliated liberals. Although Wechsler, representing the YCL, was chosen as the Director of Publications and thus became the editor of the ASU's newsletter *The Student Advocate*, Lash, a SLID member, was selected to be the National Secretary, Molly Yard, "a nonconformist socialist" was elected treasurer, and George Edwards, a socialist, was chosen as National Chairman.[232]

Looking back on this merger, Wechsler said that

the communists stationed me in the ASU on the assumption that I would zealously carry out the communist line there. But I soon found myself far more interested in promoting the popular front idea than in performing factional communist assignments. I was sure Joe Lash and I could prove something to the world by working together harmoniously. He felt the same way about it. . . . I had the general feeling that the communists and socialists, pacifists and Quakers, single-taxers and dedicated civil libertarians were on the side of the angels in the conflict against the mighty battalions of reaction, and that it was pointless for us to quarrel among ourselves so much of the time.[233]

For the popular front to come to fruition, Wechsler could not have been alone in feeling this way. Nor was it a uniquely communist policy to propose ideologues for positions of importance in youth organizations. For example, when George Edwards resigned from the ASU in order to go to work for the United Automobile Workers, the National Student Committee of the YPSL insisted that he be replaced by a member of YPSL rather than dissident socialist.[234] Moreover, of the 427 delegates from 135 colleges, universities, and high schools coming from 18 states, representing as many as 200,000 students, who met in Columbus, Ohio in 1935, most of them must have shared Wechsler's sentiments about the utility of a united organization.[235] Of those delegates, 141 were representatives from the NSL, 116 were from SLID, and the majority (170) were unaffiliated with either organization.[236] Most of these unaffiliated members, Lash later maintained, were genuinely independent liberals and not radicals in disguise.[237]

Lash, in introducing the ASU to Eleanor Roosevelt, simplified its program as an attempt to "enlist students in a movement for peace, freedom and security."[238] He and the other leaders of the ASU envisioned the organization as a broad-based advocacy group, not as a radical vanguard. Despite its reputation in the Hearst press as a subversive, conspiratorial organization, this was not the case. What young radicals said at the time seemed revolutionary, and this impression allowed their opposition to pretend that they were.[239] If anything, rank and file ASU members complained that there was not enough of a take-charge attitude among the leadership who seemed to base their decisions not on ideology, but rather on practical considerations of how to win more student support.[240] It was leftist socialists, especially, who attacked it on such grounds. To join the ASU, a member need only agree to one or more of the following ideals: democratic student government and school press; equality of educational opportunity regardless of race, creed, or color; modern schools with a modern curriculum; opportunities for increased social, cultural, and athletic activities; close cooperation among students, teachers, administrators, and community members; financial and medical aid to needy students; American schools and American government as an active force for peace; character development and good scholarship, and youth leadership, which "means alert citizens for an advancing democracy."[241] Many of these platform planks were moderate, indeed.

After the strong electoral showing of Norman Thomas in 1932, Lash had believed that "socialism was on the march and braced with an enthusiastic influx of young radicals from the colleges would, we were sure, emerge from the Roosevelt interregnum, as the major challenger in 1936."[242] He did not know then that FDR was preparing legislation "that would transform American society and make the socialist movement an irrelevancy" and would not have listened if anyone had told him so because, he realized later, "it would take a long time and many deeds before we were ready to listen again, really listen, to someone who was not a socialist."[243] In reality, it was not a long time at all. By 1937, Lash had resigned his membership in the Socialist Party in order to become a full time New Deal supporter. By that point, Irving Howe attests, the Socialist Party had collapsed, "a victim of both severe external pressures and an inner quarrelsomeness that can't easily be distinguished from a drive to self-destruction."[244]

In trying to explain the failure of socialism in America, sympathetic observers, like sociologist Daniel Bell, claim that socialists were in the world, but not of the world[245]—that, in their dedication to Marxism, they wore, to use Bell's phrase, "a set of ideological blinders" that prevented them from understanding American society.[246] And yet they failed to bring about a Marxist revolution. Socialists, then, are chastised for being too Marxist (and thus un-American) at the same time they were not Marxist enough (and, presumably, then, too American). From an alternative perspective, though, American Marxists in the 1930s (whether they followed the Socialist Party, Communist Party, or no party at all) succeeded in overcoming America's traditional antipathy toward radicalism, making some real policy gains that augured well for the future of socialism, and then abandoned their commitment to revolution to conform to American beliefs and values.[247]

Many leftist youth activists later became ardent New Deal liberals.[248] The path to liberalism was marked by young activists' participation in popular front organizations—the AYC and the ASU—where they learned to compromise and better appreciate how the democratic process works. Increasingly recognized as political interest groups, they were brought more into the New Deal coalition. Despite their critical assessment of New Deal policies for youth, they often became more (rather than less) committed to the American political system because of their experiences working with New Deal officials. Young radicals hoped to use these popular front organizations to bring about the economic and political restructuring their ideological beliefs called for, all the while making America a more democratic society. In participating in the democratic process, however, they began to shy away from efforts and arguments to dismantle capitalism.

The course young radical activists took was not unique. It was, Richard Pells has argued, the path Depression era intellectuals followed as they chased after their radical dreams "to create a new spirit of community and cooperation throughout the land, and to help inspire genuine political and cultural revolution that would transform the lives of every American."[249] Young radicals, who thought of themselves as the next generation's intelligentsia, were heavily influenced by the rhetoric of John Dewey, Reinhold Niebuhr, and Sidney Hook, as well as the left-leaning analyses they read in *The New Republic*, *The Nation*, and *The New Masses*, as these magazines embraced the radical zeitgeist. *The Nation* and *The New Masses*, both published in New York City, were widely available to youth leaders, such as Joseph Lash. Lash, who studied philosophy at CCNY under the guidance of Morris Cohen and then pursued a graduate degree in literature at Columbia, imbibed the radical vision of a better tomorrow. He, Irving Howe, and other young radicals had joined the Socialist Party because their "imaginations had been fired by the vision of a new world."[250] Like most young radicals, he read the works of Richard Wright, John Dos Passos, Dashiell Hammet, and William Faulkner. Their works, according to Pells, represented "at bottom, this urge to do more than merely restructure institutions (which) reflected a profound loss of faith in the American dream and an effort by intellectuals to discover some new value system that might fill the void."[251] They, like Lash and Wechsler, turned to Marxism. And, like the intellectuals, once these young radicals committed themselves to the popular front, "in effect, they ceased to be rebels, alienated by and in resistance to American society; instead, they behaved like men anxious to fit in and conform" and "by flirting with the idea of government-as-broker, they inadvertently confessed their acceptance of more conventional attitudes about American institutions."[252] By the end of the decade, external events pushed radical intellectuals into a defense of American values that would pave their way to a consensus alliance with the state after World War II.[253] The same thing happened to Lash, Wechsler, and so many other young radicals. Their change of heart, however, does not negate the sincerity of their previously held radical ideas.

By 1935, youth activists who supported the popular front were already softening their radicalism so that they could work with people to their right within their organizations and in government to bring about change in America. Nevertheless, they remained committed to a vision of a peaceful world. Unlike New Dealers, who seemed to shift focus from domestic to foreign policy agendas over the course of the Depression decade, young people's vision of a democratic, equal society rested fully on the ability to avoid international situations that would lead to war. When war broke out anyway, it tested both their commitment to popular front organizations and the democratic process.

5

Playing Politics and Making Policy
Institutionalizing a Vision from New York to Washington

That the New Deal attempted to solve the "youth problem" through constructive programs is indicative of the Administration's recognition of the particular needs of people aged 18–25. Yet the narrow design of those programs demonstrated that the New Deal did not understand the problems facing youth, and this obligated activist youth to continually push for more. Ernest K. Lindley, a journalist for the *New York Herald Tribune*, and his wife, Betty, who were hired by New Deal policymaker Charles Taussig to write the official history of the most significant New Deal youth program—the National Youth Administration (NYA)—argued in 1938 that as "destructive as enforced idleness may be at any age, it is likely to be most devastating to youth." They feared that without relief programs, youth "may be a deadweight on the nation for a half century to come."[1] The Lindleys asserted that the emphasis of New Deal youth programs should not be on moral righteousness or a social duty to help young people, as it was for some of those involved in the development of youth policy, but rather on alleviating an economic strain and potential threat to the social order. Yet implicit in these programs was the acknowledgement that young people were society's hope for the future. In a speech entitled "Youth Today Is Tomorrow's Nation," Eleanor Roosevelt declared "my generation has a responsibility for today's youth which it cannot escape."[2] It was because youth policymakers, such as Eleanor Roosevelt, were concerned about young people's futures and not just about the future of America, that young activists believed they could work with

124

New Dealers to construct programs that embodied their vision of a free, equal, and democratic American society. While they promoted a broader scope for the NYA and were quite willing to work within its structure to achieve their goals, they saw the NYA as a stopgap measure and thus advocated a permanent program to ensure full employment and educational opportunities to all young people as described in the American Youth Act they developed. Thus, activist youth recognized both the promise and the inadequacy of New Deal youth policy, and as political players, they sought to gain as much as they could for their constituents.

Youth did not define their "problem" narrowly; Franklin Roosevelt's Administration, however, did. Harry Hopkins aptly represented the Administration's position: what youth needed, as did so many Americans, was relief from the economic hardships of the Depression. New Deal historian William Leuchtenburg has argued that "Hopkins' approach— which would get more men to work right away—had the greater appeal" to FDR, in particular, who rarely conceptualized in anything more than economic terms in the early years of the New Deal.[3] True, many problems could be at least partially solved with economic prosperity, unemployment chief among them. But this could offer no long-term safeguards against the future precarious position of youth, who insisted that the educational system had to be reformed to meet their needs. Rather than train elite young businessmen as captains of industry, for example, high school and college curricula should provide vocational training for the masses of young people. Charles Taussig, Chairman of the National Advisory Committee of the NYA, said, in sympathy with many young people, that "with all the progress in our educational technique, much of it is still based on a world which no longer exists and which has never existed for the younger generation."[4] This assessment merged neatly with young people's perception of the educational system as outdated and overly influenced by conservative advocates of the status quo. Youth leaders maintained that the future of democracy and the future of education were inextricably interwoven.[5] Meaningful educational opportunities, they maintained, were the first step to preventing fascism. Thinking in terms of their future (as well as future generations of youth), rather than only of immediate needs, young people were also adamant in their call for peace. Their annual strike against war stood as a reminder of the covenant signed—and ignored—by sixty-three nations to discard war as an instrument of national policy.[6] The three key issues, then, around which youth rallied in trying to shape New Deal policy, were economic relief, educational reform, and peace. To them, any viable youth policy had to fully address all three issues.

The New Deal's youth policies were explicitly designed to address the demand for economic relief. At first, the needs of the family and society overrode those intrinsic to youth. Work relief was acceptable because it meant additional family income; thus, youth could contribute to family sustenance, as had previously sanctioned child labor. Civilian Conservation Corps (CCC) camps were popular in this regard; they provided supplemental income for families because young men who entered the CCC were obligated to send home 85 cents of their one-dollar-a-day pay.[7] This arrangement was problematic. Not only was the pay scale insufficient, but the CCC was required to take enrollees from the relief rolls, and the money earned was deducted from the family's relief allowance. Families were financially no better off when their sons joined the CCC, which served only 2 percent of unemployed youth.[8] Moreover, as the American Youth Congress (AYC) pointed out, the CCC was unpopular among youth because the Army ran the camps.[9]

The military regimentation and propaganda pervading the camps were anathema to young people's pacifist sensibilities.[10] The editor of the *Columbia Spectator* worried about the "gangs, gambling, racket monopolies, and strong arm tactics" that flourished in many of the camps, where boys were taken out of their neighborhoods, separated from their families, and lived in male-only isolation. He was even more concerned about the potential these camps presented for systematizing fascism.[11] Assistant Secretary of War Harry Woodring said that "the organization of over 300,000 men in more than 1500 Civilian Conservation Corps camps was the first real test of the Army's plans for war mobilization under the national Defense Act."[12] And in explaining that "the C.C.C. mobilization is thus more than a great military achievement; it is a dress rehearsal of the Army's ability to intervene, under constitutional authority in combating the depression," he corroborated many young people's worst fears.[13] A student journalist sounded the alarm that "a Hitler or a Mussolini could scarcely have struck a more genuinely Fascist note."[14] The American press and public failed to note the corollaries between the CCC and fascist youth movements; youth activists cataloged them meticulously. Despite a Gallup Poll conducted in August 1938 that indicated 75 percent of Americans were in favor of military training in the camps and a subsequent poll in October 1939 that showed 90 percent approval, American youth organizations consistently resisted compulsory military training and saw the CCC as a threat to both democracy and peace.[15]

Youth objected to the CCC on ideological as well as economic grounds. The education offered each CCC boy was pervaded by the military ethos at the same time that it was pitifully meager, amounting to a governmental expenditure of only fifty cents per boy per year.[16] Further, a study done of youth programs in 1941 for the American Youth Commission emphasized that the work experience to be gained in a CCC camp was of minimal value since the future of conservation work was bleak and the program took boys out of the cities where their future employment was likely to be found.[17] While some adults might find the potential rehabilitative environment of the CCC camps attractive as a place where delinquency could be squashed and some appreciatively pointed out that it did provide work relief for nearly 2.5 million youth between its creation in March 1933 and its termination in 1942,[18] the CCC did not represent an adequate youth program as far as young people and New Deal youth policymakers were concerned. Its creation did, however, pave the way for more constructive youth programs, administered at first by the Federal Emergency Relief Administration (FERA)[19] and later expanded under the NYA.

FDR was not the prime mover behind policies for youth.[20] Instead, he allowed the priorities of his relief administrators and the public to set his youth agenda from 1933 to 1934.[21] Thus, the NYA's creation rested upon the efforts of youth advocates both within and outside the Administration. Various youth organizations pressured FDR to do something more for youth. A. W. Vandeman, writing on behalf of the Pennsylvania Youth Movement, argued for a government-supported program "whereby the youth can develop a program of intensified civic training and practical service to their country . . . to answer the Communistic, Fascist and Nazi philosophy."[22] Both Ambassador to Germany William Dodd and Edward A. Filene, department store owner and chairman of the Massachusetts State Recovery Board, wrote to FDR in a similar vein.[23] The key difference was that young people—like Vandeman—thought this program should be devised by young people, themselves.

Dodd and Filene sounded a familiar alarm. They, along with New Dealers such as Charles Taussig, were instrumental in convincing FDR that youth needed to be schooled in democratic ideals at the same time that they were offered relief in order to stave off foreign ideologies that could be planted in the despair and idleness of Depression-laden youth.[24] It was important to retain youth's allegiance to and confidence in American government. Thus, New Deal youth programs were thoroughly infused with democratic ideals. Meanwhile, young people believed that they were the ones who were going to make the political system more democratic, both by their inclusion in policymaking and the inclusiveness of the policies they made.

The American Youth Commission, a group of prominent citizens brought together by the American Council on Education to consider the needs of young people, met in 1936. The purpose for the conference, the chairman noted, was to deal not only with the emergency situation, but with long-range problems, as well.[25] Rainey, in his report to the conference attendees on the problems facing American youth, put the situation in stark numerical terms: There were approximately 20.1 million young people in America between the ages of 18 and 24, of whom 4 million were in schools and colleges; 500,000 were working part-time; 7.6 million were employed on non-work relief jobs; 2.8 million were married women who were neither employed nor in school. That left 5.2 million youths out of school and unemployed, which represented approximately one-half of the total number of unemployed people in 1935.[26] The only acceptable solution, he said, was a national plan to provide a job for all so that there would be no out-of-school unemployed youth under the age of 21[27] wandering ominously through what Taussig referred to as a depression-made no-man's land.[28] Youth activists heartily agreed.

Like Rainey, Eleanor Roosevelt also believed that youth had a responsibility to become good citizens. At the same time, though, the government had a responsibility to the younger generation. She insisted that those in power must be willing to listen to and address youth's concerns and problems. The youth organizations were a manifestation of youth's attempted involvement in the democratic process. They, therefore, were not only applauded by Eleanor Roosevelt, but could count her as an active supporter. She, Taussig, and Aubrey Williams were the New Dealers most involved in the development of youth policy.

When pressures emanating from a number of directions finally convinced FDR to develop a program specifically for youth in 1934, he assigned the task to Hopkins, who then delegated the responsibility to his lieutenant at the FERA, Aubrey Williams, advising him to invite and encourage the participation of young people and their organizations.[29] Like Hopkins, Williams was concerned with economic recovery, but as a trained social worker, he also saw the educational and social reform potential in a comprehensive youth program. The Williams Plan that was unveiled in November 1934 called for work projects for needy youths as well as classes in vocational education and democratic ideals, to be funded jointly by federal appropriations and private corporations. Williams justified his plan by explaining "it is a primary obligation of government that the skills and morale of these young people shall not be lost to the future."[30] The Williams Plan was both too little and too much; not enough youth would be served (only 730,000), and it would cost too much (more than $6 million per month).[31]

Before the Williams Plan was announced, John A. Lang, President of the National Student Federation of America (NSFA), submitted for consideration a "federal youth service plan" many of whose characteristics were reflected in the Williams Plan. Lang's plan, like Williams's, involved the cooperation of private corporations in funding and the use of advisory committees that included youth leaders to decide policy. It, too, reflected the need for a comprehensive, rather than ad hoc, solution to youth unemployment.[32]

This was not the only proposal to be considered. Responding to the request of Senator David Walsh (D-MA), the Department of Labor devised its own plan for youth in the fall of 1934. Secretary of Labor Frances Perkins delegated this responsibility to Katharine Lenroot, head of the Children's Bureau. The plan, submitted on April 5, 1935, was a collaborative effort among Hopkins, Lenroot, and Perkins.[33] The only significant difference between the Department of Labor's plan and the Williams Plan was that the former recommended that student aid be provided under the auspices of the U.S. Office of Education (USOE) while the latter placed the entire program within the FERA. In effect, this exacerbated the relationship between the New Dealers and the USOE, whose administrators jealously guarded their jurisdiction on educational matters and held fast to decentralized, state-run education.[34] The USOE simultaneously publicized its own plan, which conservatively called for an adaptation of the FERA college student aid plan and the CCC program to provide aid to schools, whereby local school districts could maintain control over curriculum and provide relief to at least 2 million unemployed young people engaged 42 hours a week in work, education, and recreation combined or in education, alone.[35]

The American Youth Congress, which, from its inception, had been advocating a federal youth program, did not look favorably upon the possibility of USOE administration over youth policy. In March 1935, before USOE Commissioner John Studebaker unveiled his plan, William Porter, AYC treasurer, wrote to the President's secretary explaining that he had discussed AYC proposals with Studebaker, but had concluded, "frankly ... he is not the man to present to young people the program of the Federal Government.... He seemed to think he could work it through his County Chairman, which sounds good in theory, but that is exactly what Young America is tired of doing."[36] Furthermore, he was put off by Studebaker's unwillingness to work with youth leaders and argued "that any program sponsored by young people in order to have their support must come from young people," who would not bear Studebaker's "condescending attitude."[37]

The AYC's position that youth should be involved in youth policy development ultimately garnered FDR's support. He decided "that much good may result from the efforts of young people to think through the problems which confront them" and would "be glad to see a copy of any program which [the AYC] works out."[38] Less than a week later, the President's secretary defended the publicity given to the USOE proposal by claiming that "the object . . . [had] been to discover the popular reactions to it."[39] That accomplished, FDR could effectively ignore the USOE plan, much to the relief of the AYC leaders.

Upon Perkins's recommendation, FDR established a committee to work out the differences among the various plans. The group consisted of non-governmental officials and youth supporters, including Charles Taussig, Eleanor Roosevelt, David Sarnoff of RCA, and Owen Young of GE. At this juncture, youth's indirect influence was felt. Taussig and Eleanor Roosevelt had both been meeting with youth leaders informally and were well versed in youth's interpretation of their needs. Youth leaders were invited to meetings where the outline of the NYA was devised.[40] FDR remained conspicuously aloof from the entire process of formulating youth policy. Taussig requested his input but was told "Impossible to arrange appointment. Go right ahead working out concrete plan."[41] In true Roosevelt fashion, FDR then turned all four contending plans over to Hopkins (who, in similar fashion turned the task over to Williams) to develop a plan integrating the best features of each. In the final proposal, which closely resembled the Taussig group's plan, lays the origin of the NYA. It called for a national youth division of the Works Progress Administration (newly formed from the now defunct FERA) to provide aid for youth in and out of school, at the approximate cost of $50 million annually.[42]

Just before the official creation of the NYA by Executive Order 7086 proclaimed on June 26, 1935,[43] the President's secretary sent a confidential memorandum to Commissioner Studebaker informing him of a conference scheduled between John Lang and Harry Hopkins. The purpose of the conference, he explained, was "to get this whole movement with its ramifications brought to the point where some concrete proposal can be submitted to the President,"[44] signaling a last minute attempt to ensure youth's approval of New Deal youth policy. Young Americans' abiding support proved difficult to attain considering that the NYA was given an appropriation of $50 million, or less than $10 per idle youth.[45]

The NYA, in its design, was an economic relief agency. But because of its decentralized administration, it did develop in some areas as a social reform agency mostly because its administrators perceived it as such and because young people took advantage of such opportunities to move the NYA in that direction. At the very first meeting of the NYA National Advisory Committee, Thomas Neblett of the National Student Federation of America (NSFA) warned that young people did not want the NYA to be simply a relief organization. At the very least, it needed to provide education and vocational training and should be turned into a permanent National Youth Service.[46] The New Dealers most responsible for its existence and thus those most interested in shaping its vision— Williams, Taussig, and Eleanor Roosevelt—agreed. Taussig boldly told the president the day after he created the NYA that "the Horatio Alger opportunities for youth are gone, and it will be necessary for the government, for a long time to come, to assist youth in finding their new place in our national life."[47] While youth leaders and some policymakers shared this vision, there were many adults both inside and outside the New Deal Administration who did not.

Because the NYA was a decentralized agency with Directors in every state who oversaw projects responding to localized needs, the NYA was not a federal takeover of state-administered education, as some feared, but rather a response to the needs of youth, which was no longer simply a matter of local concern.[48] If not the NYA itself, some other sort of permanent federal youth agency based on the NYA idea was necessary to meet the needs of the millions of youth as yet untouched and those to come in the future.[49] The NYA not only looked toward that future by providing economic and educational programs; it also sought to correct the past by insisting on equal opportunity. It was to be both a public works program and a means for socioeconomic development.[50] Clearly, however, FDR did not see the NYA as an enduring agency of social reform, evidenced by his lack of support for a permanent youth agency or, in its absence, a consolidated youth agency that would bring together the NYA and CCC.

Even before the NYA was created, youth advocates clamored for its permanency. Alex Gaal, Jr., a self-proclaimed national officer of student leaders "representing a multitude of energetic youths," joined other youth leaders in urging the establishment of the proposed Division of Youth Service because "no greater service could be offered to the young people of America!"[51] Some adults agreed. In November 1935, the National Committee on Research in Secondary Education called for the creation of a single, permanent youth agency to be administered on the NYA model.[52] That model provided part-time work at prevailing local wages on projects that were created with three goals in mind. First, the work had to be real work, not leaf-raking make-work. Second, it should develop the employability of young people by giving them experience in fields in which they were interested and capable. Third, the work should be of definite benefit to the community and preferably to the youth of the community.[53] This model provided young people with job skills training at the same time that the salary earned could offset the financial difficulties for those who wanted to remain in school.

Youth leaders insisted that any youth program should reflect youth's needs and that successful policies necessitated youth's participation in the policy-making process. AYC leader William Hinckley was particularly unsettled by the appointment of members to the NYA National Advisory Committee by the president rather than their election to such position by youth because, he said, "this method of procedure bears a closer resemblance to the political philosophy of Tammany Hall than to that of Thomas Jefferson."[54] Thomas Neblett, President of the NSFA, approached Charles Taussig in September 1935 on this matter, citing the joint proposal from twenty youth groups, which said that if the spirit of cooperation between the Administration and youth groups was to be maintained, then youth members had to be admitted to the NYA National Advisory Committee as well as hired in administrative positions to oversee the implementation of the NYA; Taussig expressed his "vigorous support on this immediately."[55]

He wrote to both Eleanor Roosevelt and FDR in January 1936 with a proposition for choosing youth to fill such roles. He suggested a national essay contest, the winners of which were to be appointed to the National Advisory Committee of the NYA. With his wife's prodding, the President not only approved such a plan but went on to say that he was "in hearty accord ... that we should encourage youth to express itself of matters of education, business and government" and that he "observed that youths' lack of practical experience is frequently compensated by their idealism and sense of justice."[56] Although Williams and Taussig had granted approval of such a plan, Studebaker effectively stalled it. The Commissioner of Education sent the President's secretary a confidential note stating that, in his opinion, the NSFA knew nothing of Neblett's plan and that if the President should reply favorably and the NSFA subsequently did not support the plan, it would cause embarrassment for the President.[57]

Indeed, Neblett's plan had provoked a controversy within the NSFA. Some members objected to the notion inherent in the plan that a good essay writer would necessarily make a good youth representative, while others took that idea one step further, pointing out that since the reward was a presidential appointment to the advisory board, the essay would be, by nature, sycophantic. Another concern was that one person's effort to crystallize the youth problem was antithetical to youth organizations' efforts to reach a consensus.[58] Neblett was pressured to quietly rescind his plan as impractical in a letter to FDR while at the same time acknowledging the president's welcomed desire to appoint youth leaders and suggesting he cull candidates from a list provided to NYA executives by youth organizations.[59] The whole plan raised the suspicion of some American Student Union members that perhaps the NSFA was becoming too close to the Administration. Neblett became even more suspect when he tried to engineer a coup to oust Joseph Cadden (both the NSFA Secretary and the AYC Executive Secretary) from his leadership position as a first step toward getting the NSFA to reverse its critical stance against the NYA and adopt a friendlier attitude toward the Administration instead.[60]

In contrast, the AYC had already been more successful in this endeavor; in response to its demands, representatives of the AYC were already on the National Advisory Committee of the NYA.[61] And state youth directors were strongly urged by the Deputy Executive Director, Richard Brown, to include students in the planning of the Student Aid program of the NYA. Specifically, they were to be given a voice in the planning and conducting of state conferences that would determine the Student Aid program for the coming year. They should contribute to the planning of suitable projects and the development of creating on-the-job training opportunities at the same time they studied the effectiveness of the program and played a role in the administering of the program—all necessary prerequisites for the program to be deemed truly successful by the young people it served.[62]

Youth organizations, in addition to gaining youth appointments to the National Advisory Committee, were also effective in having adult members removed who did not sufficiently understand youth's needs. FDR, impressed by Bernarr Macfadden's community calisthenics and cooperative sports programs, personally insisted that he be appointed to the Advisory Committee.[63] However, Macfadden resigned in December 1938 because he claimed that his "repeated efforts [in] reference to the building of additional man power [that] will be most tragically needed in the future if we got in trouble with any of the war glorifying nations [had been] fruitless."[64] Taussig wrote to the President explaining that Macfadden had shown no interest in any of the actual work of the National Youth Administration and therefore urged him to accept Macfadden's resignation.[65] In a letter to Eleanor Roosevelt, dated the same day, Taussig explained that "as you probably know, there has been quite some criticism from youth of Bernarr Macfadden being a member of the National Advisory Committee. I feel that it would be well for the President to accept his resignation."[66] Eleanor Roosevelt then had this letter forwarded to FDR so that he would know the true reason Macfadden's resignation should be accepted; he did not understand youth's problems from youth's perspective and was therefore rendered incompetent to influence youth policy.

Taussig also took this opportunity to bring to FDR's attention the Committee's position that it did not have a sufficient number of youth members. FDR's reply signaled his agreement that the composition of the National Advisory Committee should be a fair representation of all those directly concerned in the operation of this program.[67] The inclusion of youth was a perennial issue that Taussig continued to champion throughout the decade. Two years later Taussig was still pressing FDR to appoint additional youth members to the Committee. At that point, the President replied that he did not want to contend with any more "headaches" and told Taussig to "keep on going the way you are."[68] Taussig, insisting that three additional young people be approved for membership on the Committee, drew Roosevelt's rebuff that the Advisory Council on Defense's prediction of a prospective personnel shortage in the spring was a much more pressing issue than the makeup of the Advisory Committee.[69] By 1938, then, youth policy was subordinated to defense needs.

As early as April 1936, the National Advisory Committee of the NYA recognized the limited mandate given to the NYA and recommended that its activities be extended to U.S. territories, particularly Puerto Rico,[70] as demanded by seven thousand young Puerto Ricans.[71] But the Committee went even further than simply objecting to its geographic constraints. It professed "the belief that an extension of the activities of the National Youth Administration is justified in the direction of an enlargement of the functions of the Administration beyond relief."[72] The members of the Committee, who worked closely and sympathetically with various youth organizations, recognized the NYA's broader social reform potential.[73]

The National Youth Administration provided relief but also effectively reformed education, at least for its duration (1935–1943). To do so, youth leaders and policymakers had to go beyond its limited mandate. Palmer O. Johnson and Oswald L. Harvey, in their staff study of the NYA concluded that "in actual operation the National Youth Administration . . . transcended the immediate problem of relief and . . . ventured, with considerable success, into educational and employment fields which might have been deemed entirely outside of its province."[74]

Youth organizations readily recognized the potential for the NYA to do more. With the looming termination of the NYA's one-year appropriations in 1936, youth organizations began to petition the president in earnest to either continue the NYA or, even better, institute a permanent organization in its place to provide education, training, and employment to young people. The AYC, ASU, Young Women's Christian Association, and Young Men's Christian Association sprang into action.[75] But even lesser known organizations like the Borough Park Community Council came out in favor of such a plan, too.[76]

At its second annual conference in 1936, the American Student Union delegates passed a resolution insisting on more direct youth participation in formulating youth policy at the same time that it called for increased pressure on the Administration to expand the NYA and to rescind proposed cuts. The Chapter Guide distributed to ASU chapters urged them to pass resolutions demanding more aid, while the ASU planned a NYA protest demonstration in 1937 that was supported by the NSFA, AYC, and the Ys. Members viewed this as only the beginning of the protests against the NYA.[77] Intending to rouse public attention to the NYA's inadequacy in meeting youth's needs, the ASU called a conference of leading educators and youth leaders to meet in December to consider the future of student aid, and aid to youth generally—taking up the issues of the amount needed, methods of administration, and the need for the American Youth Act, as well as the formation of NYA associations through which NYA workers could come together to consider the problems they faced and solutions to them.[78]

Both the ASU and the AYC leaders feared the possibility that young NYA workers would be viewed simply as a cheap labor source for the capitalist economy. Hinckley, concerned about the "sweatshop rates," claimed that "the National Youth Administration may be described briefly as containing a fair proportion of the most vicious characteristics of child labor, peonage, and the yellow-dog contract. It will still further undermine an already low standard of living and create artificial distinction

between young and old, student and worker."[79] The Marxist roots of the
socialist and communist members of the two organizations, together with
the liberals' general antipathy toward exploitation, underlay their demand
for a union to represent NYA workers. Youth activists remembered well
the coalminers of Harlan County. The NYA Workers Union, created as
a result of their agitation, met regularly with the NYA Administrators to
discuss workers' grievances and recommendations for improvements in
the NYA training program as yet another avenue through which to shape
policy.[80] The Union also acted as a liaison with organized labor and was
successful in garnering adult labor unions' support for the continuation
of the NYA in a coalition-building maneuver to increase political influence.[81]

In addition to idealistic notions about helping disadvantaged youth and
economic imperatives to alleviate unemployment, New Deal politicians
quickly recognized another benefit of the inclusion of youth as policymakers: Youth leaders could be useful in creating Administration support among youth organizations and the younger generation, in general.
With that end in mind, Taussig advised the President to conduct his interview with the *Student Mirror* (the NSFA publication) before October
1936 so that it could be included in the special edition devoted to the
upcoming presidential election, which would be "tremendously useful
in the campaign," especially because the NSFA, he believed, would soon
declare itself for the President publicly.[82] Young people, in turn, knew
the political capital they could muster. As Hinckley, then AYC National
Chairman, pointed out in 1936, there were five million young men and
women who came of voting age in the previous four years, and there
would only be more in the future, and therefore "the candidates for President want us: they want our strength."[83] Political parties could ignore
youth, he warned, only at their own peril. Taussig realized this point,
too. "It has been my observation," he said, "that the employment of men,
women and youth on socially useful projects has materially helped them
in identifying themselves with their government and with the common
effort of the people of the United States" and that this "identification of
the individual with the national or community purpose of the (NYA)
program transcends in importance even the relief elements of the projects."[84]

As their working relationship with adult policymakers grew closer,
youth leaders were invited to attend numerous social occasions at the
White House in addition to being permitted both public and private
audiences with the President, most often secured through the combined

efforts of Williams, Taussig, and Eleanor Roosevelt. Indeed, by 1939, Joseph Lash had become a nearly permanent fixture at White House functions. Such meetings were seen as mutually beneficial: Young people could voice their concerns in the highest echelons of political power while the President could reach out to innumerable constituents through the favorable impressions he made upon young people.[85]

Youth used such access to further their agenda: enlarging the mandate of the NYA and their top priority—pressing for passage of the American Youth Act. In doing so, it should be noted, they were working within and contributing to the American democratic process, rather than fomenting revolution. The Youth Act was to provide vocational guidance, vocational training, and employment opportunities for all needy youth between the ages of sixteen and twenty-five and to create increased educational opportunities for high school, college, and post-graduate students.[86] While vocational training in job skills would be the hallmark of the secondary school program, the college program was to support academic projects. All projects were to benefit the larger community in some way, and none of them could have a direct or indirect military character.[87] It was to be administered and controlled by youth employment commissions, one-third of whose membership would be elected youth representatives from youth organizations, one-third elected by labor groups, and one-third elected to represent local social service, educational, and/or consumer organizations.[88]

At its 1935 annual conference, which brought together representatives from 104 college and university student councils, the NSFA identified its main goals as pushing for the passage of the American Youth Act and the Nye-Kvale Bill, which would have made ROTC training optional.[89] The NYA, though it started to address youth's needs, did not do enough.[90] By February 1936, the NSFA was urging students to pressure their schools' faculty and administration as well as local politicians to support the Youth Act instead.[91]

In its very first newsletter, the ASU published in stark terms a full-page side-by-side comparison of the NYA and American Youth Act. While the NYA provided for only 500,000 youth, the Youth Act would provide for all: five million unemployed, one million homeless, and several million needy students. The wage differentials were even more striking: NYA workers and graduate students received $15 per month, while high school aid ranged between $2–6 per month. Under the American Youth Act, young workers would receive $15 per week, graduate students would receive $25 per month with an additional $3 per dependent for both

Figure 2. Official Report of the American Youth Congress, publicizing the Declaration of American Youth, issued July 4, 1936. The Declaration served as the ideological framework not only for the official report of the AYC's annual meeting, but the American Youth Act, drafted by young activists to replace stop-gap New Deal programs they deemed insufficient to meet youth's needs.

graduate and undergraduate students, and high school aid would be set at a minimum of $15 per month. Whereas adults controlled the NYA, the American Youth Act would be administered by equal representation of youth, labor, social service, and educational organizations. The $50 million appropriation for NYA, set to expire in June 1936, would be replaced by an uncapped monetary amount to be taken from the Federal Treasury with increased taxes on inheritances, gifts, and individual and corporation incomes of $5,000 a year or over, if necessary, to offset costs.[92] The Act was, the ASU intoned, "the first realistic, bold attempt to meet the crisis of this 'lost generation.'"[93] The ASU took this message directly to the college campuses, launching a speaking tour that allowed ASU leaders to debate the merits of the two programs, which, once reported in the college press, then reached an even larger audience of students.[94] College newspapers printed the full text of the Youth Act in an attempt to sway students with its comprehensiveness and simplicity.[95] Socialists in the Young People's Socialist League wasted no time on the NYA, instead throwing its support behind the American Youth Act, as well.[96] The YPSL saw the Act's economic leveling provisions as a way to bring large numbers of young people unaffiliated with socialism in any way into the class struggle.[97]

Meanwhile, the AYC marshaled significant support at the national level for the Youth Act. As William Hinckley pointed out, the NYA was "hopelessly inadequate" because of the "total lack of democracy in its administration and its threat at the already declining wage standards" as well as the fact that its appropriations could only help a fraction of needy youth.[98] Extension of the NYA and increased appropriations were still not enough. In 1937, when Aubrey Williams announced that the NYA student aid program was reaching 10 percent of college students nationwide in what was supposed to be a celebratory news release, to youth that meant that 90 percent of college students were receiving no such aid, further demonstrating its inadequacy.[99]

Not only did Eleanor Roosevelt and Taussig support the American Youth Act,[100] but members of Congress did as well, thanks, in part, to the lobbying efforts of young activists. It was introduced into Congress every year from 1936 to 1940, except 1939, and reached full committee hearings twice.[101] In 1935, the AYC published a pamphlet, "Youth Speaks for Itself," that outlined the provisions of the Act and gave practical advice for how young people could get it passed. Copies were distributed to all its affiliated groups. In addition to writing their own congressmen and senators, young people were encouraged to write or wire Representative Vincent L. Palmisano (D-MD) and Senator David I. Walsh (D-MA), urging the Committee on Education in the House and Committee on Education and Labor in the Senate to hold immediate joint hearings on the Act. At the same time they worked as individuals to pressure congressmen, they were to get official endorsements of the Act from organizations, including trade unions, student councils, clubs, Y's, settlement houses, churches, and city councils to compound their lobbying efforts.[102] The AYC also called on regional youth congresses to contact specific members of the congressional committees. To mobilize more general support, the AYC decided the radio could be employed to provide broader publicity, and so they filled airtime with congressional speeches supporting the Act.[103] By January 1936—six months after the creation of the NYA—the AYC was already pressuring FDR for a statement outlining what he intended to do to assure the passage of the American Youth Act.[104]

Their lobbying efforts met with some success, but the problem youth leaders could not overcome, in the end, was the perception that supporting the NYA and the American Youth Act were mutually exclusive propositions. Advocates for the Youth Act put FDR and the New Deal Administrators in a difficult position: How could they support such a measure without calling into question their own established program? When the National Council of the AYC met in Washington that same month, Eleanor Roosevelt attended and agreed to answer questions. When asked what should be done to relieve the distress of the more than five million unemployed youth, she candidly admitted the inadequacy of the NYA in replying, "You don't have to tell me that the Youth Administration doesn't touch the whole problem. I know that."[105] Even someone like Eleanor Roosevelt, who supported the merits of the Youth Act, became defensive when the NYA was characterized as accomplishing too little.

In seeking support for the Youth Act elsewhere, youth leaders were faced with the same either/or predicament. When the AYC first approached labor leaders, they were often rebuffed. To gain their support, Hinckley pointed out that rank and file members of the American Federation of Labor supported the Act and that the NYA, by training youth for industrial jobs, was providing a future competitive labor source for organized labor.[106] In campaigning for the Youth Act, he was, in effect, campaigning against the NYA. To get organized labor's support for the American Youth Act, youth activists also had to overcome the arguments of New Deal policymakers, like Charles Taussig, who pressed for organized labor's support for the NYA by championing its short-term benefit to workers: It temporarily removed a competitive labor market by keeping young people in school longer.[107] Ideally, Taussig envisioned a future where every boy and girl could extend his or her education by four or five years, removed from job competition, while preparing for what he called "enlightened citizenship."[108] To gain organized labor's support for the Youth Act, it would have to be more beneficial to adult workers than the NYA. As part of its lobbying effort, the AYC sent representatives to attend the AFL Convention,[109] while Hinckley intended to meet with William Green and John L. Lewis during the youth pilgrimage to

Washington in December 1936 and with Phillip Murray in January.[110] His meetings met with some success. By November 1937, the American Youth Act had the complete approval of Lewis and therefore of the Congress of Industrial Organizations, though the AFL tended to favor the more conservative policies of the NYA.[111]

To publicize their support for the passage of the American Youth Act, which had become its top priority by 1936, the AYC organized a pilgrimage of several thousand young people to Washington, D.C. to petition both the president and the Congress. Preceding that pilgrimage was a Youth Act Month during which the AYC called on youth groups to publicize the American Youth Act. A manual was drawn up outlining suggestions that ranged from town hall meetings, essay contests on the theme of "why I want the American Youth Act passed," to radio broadcasts. It even included a song about the Act titled "Listen, Young America" and a "playlet" called "Dear Senator" in which three youth representatives shot down the objections to the Act expressed by two ultra-conservative senators. The climax scene showed the youth representatives leading the senators to a window where, outside, 2,000 representatives of youth organizations had assembled on the pilgrimage.[112]

As part of that pilgrimage, William Hinckley (AYC president) requested a time to meet with the President to discuss the need for the American Youth Act.[113] The President's secretary did not think this matter warranted the President's personal attention, and so he forwarded it to Hopkins at the NYA, who had already been contacted by telegram by Hinckley, who asked that he help him secure a meeting with the President. In response, Hopkins urged the secretary to schedule a time for the youth delegates to meet with the President.[114] Hinckley had, by this point, learned how to navigate Washington politics. In 1937, he regularly sent signed petitions supporting the passage of the American Youth Act to the President, which were forwarded to the NYA.[115] NYA Director Aubrey Williams was becoming, next to Eleanor Roosevelt, the most important contact for youth leaders. Indeed, Williams often drafted FDR's responses to youth leaders' communiqués. When Hinckley wrote to the President about the upcoming Third American Youth Congress, for example, Williams responded (under FDR's signature) that young people's acceptance of the responsibilities of citizenship were welcomed, and, in speaking for the Administration, Williams further added that "there is real hope in the fact that young people themselves are coming together to seek, through cooperative endeavor, a solution to [their] problems."[116]

Youth leaders regularly requested meetings with any Washington politician or policymaker they thought might help further their cause. Aubrey Williams, Eleanor Roosevelt, Charles Taussig, and FDR were the ones with whom they most often sought to meet to press their agenda. These adults were also invited to youth's conferences, symposiums, and meetings in order to demonstrate the democratic nature of youth organizations and enlist support for their positions. But they were not the only ones whose political support was courted. Even lower-level policymakers, such as Gardner Jackson at the Agricultural Adjustment Administration, were invited to attend National Council meetings of the AYC.[117] By this point, the AYC had added another position to its National Council: Legislative Director, whose job was to coordinate lobbying efforts. In that role, Abbott Simon familiarized himself with New Deal administrators (even addressing his letters to "Pat," as Gardner Jackson was known among friends and colleagues) and began soliciting information in order for the AYC to play policymaking roles in other areas, such as those concerning rural farm youth.[118] The more access they obtained the more influence they could wield.

In March 1936, nearly 1,200 students made the trip to Washington, D.C. again—this time to observe the three-day Senate committee hearings on the American Youth Act. Celeste Strack, ASU leader responsible for organizing at the high school level, said in her testimony that

> young people feel that it is of crucial importance, particularly at this time, that youth be equipped for the manifold social, economic, and political problems that face them within the American democracy at the present time. They are not being prepared to do it. Merely having the school buildings in which to carry on education is not enough to provide equal opportunity, and, for this reason, we urge that the American Youth Act be reported back out of this committee, in response, not to my pleas as an individual, but to the plea of many organizations, in answer to the plea and needs of the 10,000,000 youths of high school age in America, of whom only 40% are enrolled in school.[119]

Leaving Washington, youth leaders expected the bill to be pigeonholed, yet, James Wechsler noted, "so encouraging were the hearings, so indicative of our future tasks and possibilities, so vast the response [that] we have made a beginning more notable than we could have anticipated."[120] With increased AYC lobbying efforts in the next session of Congress concomitant with an increase in youth's participation in the AYC, he believed success was inevitable.

To garner more youth support for the Act, the National Council of the AYC proposed to print a pamphlet on the hearings; however, it did not have the funds in its coffers to do so.[121] Gil Green, a National Council member and leader of the Young Communist League, came to the rescue by pledging that his organization would pay in advance for the cost of printing 25,000 copies of the 16-page pamphlet that would sell for one penny.[122] Thus garnering full-fledged liberal, socialist, and communist support, the Youth Act represented the Popular Front in action on a measure that truly unified youth.

Hinckley counted the hearings a success on another front: He believed it was the show of force that youth had made during the committee hearings that convinced the Administration to extend a 50 percent increase in funding for the NYA when the future of the NYA had been in doubt before the hearings began.[123] Accruing political support for any youth policy stacked the political deck in favor of young people.

Just as support for the Act was growing, however, Thomas Neblett, NSFA President, was causing trouble again. He had spoken in support of the American Youth Act before the Senate Committee, and then one week later—while the committee was discussing the merits of the bill— he sent a letter to 800 student council leaders and NSFA members, saying that he no longer supported the American Youth Act. He said he did not think it went far enough to ensure a healthy future for youth. He envisioned a permanent Federal Youth Service to provide not only economic, but health and recreational benefits to young people. James Wechsler was outraged. He believed that Neblett had done a great disservice to the potential success of the American Youth Act by advocating something in its stead, and lambasted him publicly for his failure to represent the NSFA platform. He even went so far as to say that Neblett had become nothing but a governmental stooge.[124] Wechsler intimated that this was nothing but self-aggrandizement in an effort for Neblett to secure himself a job within the New Deal administration once his tenure as NSFA President expired upon graduation one month later.[125]

Delegates to the third annual conference of the AYC in 1936 adopted a Declaration of Rights of American Youth commemorating the 160th anniversary of the signing of the American Declaration of Independence. Young people's assessment of the current state of America as well as their prescription for the future was clearly spelled out:

Today our lives are threatened by war; our liberties threatened by reactionary legislation; and our right to happiness remains illusory in a world of insecurity.... We declare that our generation is rightfully entitled to a useful, creative, and happy life, the guarantees of which are: full educational opportunities, steady employment at adequate wages, security in time of need, civil rights, religious freedom, and peace.... We are determined to realize in actuality the ideals of a free America. We demand not only the maintenance but the extension of our elementary rights of free speech, press, and assemblage.... We consider full academic freedom essential to progress and enlightenment. We strongly oppose Fascism, with its accompanying demagogy, as a complete negation of our right to liberty.[126]

And lest anyone question their loyalty—perhaps those who had missed the opening of the conference, which had begun with those assembled singing "America"—the 1,323 delegates from 1,007 organizations representing 1.65 million young people in 29 states reaffirmed their constructive critique of America to be the height of patriotism by declaring: "We look at this country of ours. We love it dearly; we are its flesh and marrow.... Because we know it so well, we know that it could be a haven of peace, security, and abundance for all.... With confidence we look forward to a better life, a larger liberty and freedom."[127] In his report to the AYC, National Chairman Hinckley reminded the assembled delegates of their special place in the American polity. "We are," he said, "those to whom the future of America belongs. We are those who will—who must—fashion this future. But we cannot live in tomorrow. We have come here these two days to deal with the present. For what we do today will determine the kind of future that is ours. Out of this Congress will come the voice and plans of young America."[128] The other main order of business at the conference was developing the coming year's platform by agreeing on resolutions. The first and most important one, which identified the passage of the American Youth Act its primary goal, was passed unanimously. The AYC pledged itself to not only getting the Act introduced in Congress, but in state legislatures, as well.[129] In this the AYC members saw some initial success as both the California and Minnesota legislatures began discussing the American Youth Act within three months.[130]

In the coming months of the election campaign, youth activists were to pointedly ask every candidate for any political office what they intended to do regarding the American Youth Act. This brought attention to the Act while at the same time it created a catalogue of the Act's supporters so that youth could more effectively target their lobbying efforts. Hinckley supplied a response to those, particularly those in the Liberty League, who opposed the $3.5 billion per year cost of the program the American Youth Act would set up by pointing out that the government spent that same amount on juvenile crime the previous year, implying that the money would be better spent on education and vocational programs than on penitentiaries and court costs.[131] He also reminded adult lawmakers that young people would prefer that the money appropriated for defense, which prepared their future for war, be spent on preparing their future for work and peace, and "our right to life."[132]

Hinckley sent letters on behalf of the AYC to all the presidential candidates that year asking a series of questions, the first of which was whether or not the candidate believed the American Youth Act was an indispensable item in their legislative program. The letter also asked where the candidate stood on the militarization of the CCC camps, the Nye-Kvale Bill[133] to abolish compulsory ROTC training, the Wagner-Costigan anti-lynching bill, juvenile delinquency, expansion of the NYA, and workers' right to organize.[134] As of October, when the President was preparing for his interview with the NSFA, he still had not replied to Hinckley, though the other candidates—Alf Landon, Norman Thomas, and Earl Browder—had. Hinckley reassured the President that the AYC had no partisan bias and only wanted to present each party's platform positions on matters that concerned youth so that young people could make informed choices in the future.[135] While Roosevelt may not have been concerned with courting youth's electoral support at this point, others took note of the several hundred thousand first-time voters aged 21–24 in the 1936 election. Charles Taussig was enlisted to aid Roosevelt's reelection campaign through the Roosevelt Youth Club Movement in a nonpartisan get-out-the-vote effort.[136]

The ASU held political symposiums throughout the country during the election campaign to present different political points of view and conducted straw votes as an initiation of students into the realm of politics.[137] Such activities reaffirmed the broad political spectrum represented in the ASU, as thousands did not vote for the socialist or communist candidates. Yet, because all four candidates garnered significant support, the results should have also assuaged the fears of New Deal critics who saw NYA aid as nothing more than political scholarships or bribes corrupting the political system.[138]

The AYC intended to launch a national petition campaign to collect one million signatures, culminating in another pilgrimage to Washington to take place on inauguration day. The ASU fully supported this endeavor and pledged to devote its attention to mobilizing students for the pilgrimage in the months leading up to it.[139] Pending enactment of the American Youth Act, youth organizations were to demand the following amendments to the NYA: increased appropriations for relief projects so that wages could be raised to prevailing trade union wages, inclusion of youths aged 16 and 17, and a prohibition of discrimination against African-American and foreign-born youth.[140] Thus, while they worked toward their goal of getting the American Youth Act passed, they remained active on other fronts trying to win concessions for youth.

To the same end, youth organizations—especially the ASU—also operated within the political system of the college campus. But it did not limit itself to myopic support of the Youth Act. By the fall of 1936, the ASU adopted a new policy to alleviate some of the students' financial distress that was also in line with radicals' economic ideas. It advocated the creation of college cooperatives in housing, food, and books. Pilot programs had already proven successful: At the University of North Carolina, 2,000 out of 2,500 students were members of the local cooperative; at Berkeley, the largest apartment house was owned by a student cooperative; at a Texas college, students were provided food and housing for ten dollars a month; and Harvard's cooperative bookstore did nearly $900,000 worth of business in 1935.[141] Cooperatives were to be run on a not-for-profit basis, and though they would bring popular support to the ASU, the National Executive Committee warned that they were not to be set up "to satiate any thirst for glory," and they were not to compete with functioning ones already established.[142] Moreover, they were to operate on a democratic basis, with every effort made to enlist the aid of campus leaders including fraternity house managers, church groups, Y leaders, and members of student government. Expertise could thus be commandeered as the ASU became more integrated in campus affairs, and students took more of an active role in the functioning of their educational experience. Students, in effect, would be running the campus to a much larger extent for their own benefit. The ASU was concerned with the development of student self-government at the high-school level as well, and began in 1936 to put together a plan to institute such a system.[143]

The AYC adopted a comprehensive view of what exactly democratic education entailed at its Model Congress held in Milwaukee in 1937, arguing that there should be democracy of opportunity, content, and control.[144] Educational opportunities must be open to all youth regardless of race, income, or geographical location. Curricula should be geared to providing young people with the means by which to participate effectively and fully in American society. Democratically chosen school boards representing education, labor, and youth organizations should oversee educational institutions where student governments were given autonomy, and teachers and students should be assured complete academic freedom.[145] Young policymakers thus worked simultaneously on several political fronts in the local, state, and national arenas.

In 1937, Congressman Jerry Voorhis (D-CA) and Senator Ernest Lundeen (Farmer-Labor Party-MN) sponsored the Youth Act. Upon his wife's advice, FDR met with Voorhis in 1937,[146] but this was really because of the lobbying efforts of William Hinckley[147] of the AYC who had suggested that course of action. The AYC ran that year's annual conference as a Model Congress, which found widespread support in New Deal circles. FDR said that

> it is indeed gratifying to see in this congress still another evidence of the growing interest which young people are showing in the affairs of government. It is encouraging and reassuring to know that the future of our democracy rests in the hands of a generation which is alive to the responsibilities which democratic government involves and well versed in its mechanics. . . . This is no time for complacency or indifference; it is a time when vigorous and intelligent participation in the solution of our common problems is needed from every citizen in our democracy. The American Youth Congress has become an important instrument in achieving this end and, as such, has the good will and best wishes of all who are concerned with the future of American democracy.[148]

The AYC saw the Model Congress as an exercise in democratic citizenship. Hinckley tried to flatter the President into attending this Model Congress of young senators and representatives by referring to him as "one of the greatest exponents of the democratic ideal."[149]

While young people were pressuring Congress and the President to do something more for youth from a minimum of expanding the NYA to the more amenable passage of the American Youth Act, adult organizations, such as the American Youth Commission, were still studying the "youth problem." The American Youth Commission was set up by the American Council on Education in 1935 in order to ascertain youth's needs and then develop a comprehensive program for the care and education of youth.[150] After two years of investigative study, the Commission identified employment, education, equal opportunity, recreation, and health as the most important "youth problems," yet it had developed no program to combat those problems.[151] The Commission did not finish its report until 1938,[152] by which time FDR's attention had been diverted from domestic policies concerning youth to events abroad. Had the Commission—made up of sixteen adults representing government, business, labor, and college administrators, many of whom were hostile to activist youth—included youth leaders or talked to the leaders of youth organizations, it certainly would have had little excuse to be so slow-moving.

FDR's ad hoc Advisory Committee on Education, created in September 1936, received the American Youth Commission's interim report. Hinckley quickly contacted the committee's Chairman, Dr. Floyd Reeves, upon the publication of the report, to bring the omission of youth participation to his attention, asking him to provide the AYC with copies of the report and all other materials put out by the committee and further asking if it might be possible for the AYC to present some of its views on the subject.[153] Shortly thereafter, Hinckley provided Reeves with the program of the AYC in order "to place before the committee the proposals of young people themselves relating to legislative and other action in the field of education,"[154] which Reeves then circulated among the committee members.[155] Hinckley and Reeves developed a symbiotic relationship whereby Reeves sent the AYC copies of the committee's reports, and Hinckley continued to provide Reeves with updates on the AYC program and policies. By 1938, Hinckley was able to call on Reeves to testify on behalf of the American Youth Act. In addition, Hinckley circulated the Committee's report among the members of the Education Commission of the AYC so that it could start a national campaign for the adoption of the committee's recommendations, which ended up being very much in line with the American Youth Act, another indication of his lobbying success.[156]

While pushing for more far-reaching policies, young policymakers had to continually shore up support for existing programs so as not to lose political momentum in what could be a conservative political riptide. In 1937, that brought them head-to-head with the limits of the New Deal. In seeking to slash government spending in 1937, FDR cut NYA funding, intending to spend only $40 million of the $75 million congressional allotment. In New York City alone this represented a 20 percent cut for high school students, 40 percent cut for college students, and 100 percent cut for graduate students.[157] In response, the AYC and ASU launched protest action.[158] The ASU called on every chapter to "drown out the tories—the conservative and reactionary groups—masquerading as budget balancers," by coming together in a nationwide demonstration sponsored by every campus organization.[159] Before the demonstration was held on October 14, 1937, the ASU chapters were to conduct a survey of students to ascertain the need for the NYA, which would then be used to pressure the New Deal Administration. Key to this was the cooperation of college presidents, for whom NYA cuts would be a real problem, as enrollment would surely decline. The ASU chapters were also expected to coordinate activities with other local colleges, high schools, NYA unions, and non-student groups. Results of the demonstrations were then supposed to flood the desks of Aubrey Williams and FDR through a telegram-sending and letter-writing campaign, while delegations of students visited state NYA Administrators and local congressmen. The ASU National Office had already coordinated with the NSFA, YMCA, and YWCA, and, together, the leaders of these organizations wrote letters to college presidents, editors of college newspapers, and Washington politicians, while the AYC contacted state NYA directors and governors.[160]

The protests achieved results: A conference of NYA officials, congressmen, progressive educators, and student leaders was held Dec 6, 1937,[161] and in April 1938, the Administration announced that it would be spending $75 million on NYA programs as part of its recovery program, in large measure as a response to the political backlash caused by the Roosevelt Recession.

Threatening to cut the NYA program was significant because of the wide reach of the NYA; by 1940 there were NYA projects in 2,900 of the 3,072 counties in the continental United States.[162] In rallying support behind the NYA, its advocates attacked the CCC as a way to maintain its portion of the New Deal pie—a position that brought them more in line with youth activists' contempt for the CCC. The NYA program remained much more cost-effective than the better-known CCC program. It cost the federal government only one-thirtieth the amount necessary to keep a youth in high school, one-tenth as much to keep a college student matriculated full time, and one-fifth as much to keep out-of-school young people enrolled in NYA programs as it did to send a boy to a CCC camp, while it cost the federal government one-fourth as much to operate the NYA Resident Centers as it did to run the CCC camps.[163] To put it another way, the cost of the NYA program as a whole was less than the cost of one battleship.[164] The NYA was preserved, in part, by such cost-saving logic. But in pitting one youth policy against another (and no matter how ill-equipped the CCC was to serve youth's needs, it was perceived by many politicians as a youth policy), this tactic had the effect of decreasing support for any broader program as envisioned by the American Youth Act. Nevertheless, youth leaders continued to push for its passage.

In 1938, the AYC organized yet another pilgrimage to Washington, the stated purpose of which was to bring attention to youth's need for jobs and education. Hinckley hoped a delegation of youth leaders could be admitted to a private meeting with FDR and the directors of the NYA, CCC, and WPA. Eleanor Roosevelt added her own pressure upon the President with a penciled notation on a letter from Hinckley that she forwarded to FDR asking him to consider meeting with the youth representatives.[165] Five students were granted that meeting with FDR.

By this time, Hinckley even began requesting appointments with James Roosevelt, the President's son, and invited him to attend conferences on youth as a way to gain access and influence in the Administration.[166] In March 1938, at Hinckley's suggestion, James Roosevelt testified on the current needs of young America before the Senate Committee on Education and Labor then debating the American Youth Act, which had already been introduced in the House and was supported by all the major youth organizations and youth serving agencies.[167] Hinckley's political influence had grown substantially. Indeed, Senator Joshua Lee (D-OK) relied on Hinckley to arrange the schedule of witnesses to testify in favor of the Act.[168]

In 1939, the AYC, as a result of its close working relationship with members of Congress, decided to work, in consultation with six senators and two representatives, to simplify the provisions of the American Youth Act as much as possible before its reintroduction.[169] It also decided to begin a regular newsletter to send to member organizations summarizing the provisions of bills of interest to youth currently being debated on Capitol Hill in an effort to keep young people informed about what the government was doing, along with a Youth Legislative Calendar so that young people could keep track of pending legislation.[170] Young people were called on to support, among other things, labor rights under the Wagner Act; appropriations for housing under the Wagner-Steagall Act; federal aid extended to farmers; an amendment to the Social Security Act extending benefits to migratory, agricultural, and domestic workers; expansion of WPA; as well as extension of the NYA and placement of it on a permanent basis.[171]

The AYC held another Model Congress of Youth in July 1939, inviting national youth groups to elect five "senators" each as delegates and local youth groups to elect one "representative" for every fifty members of their organization. In order to reach out to even more young people, the AYC decreed that a youth organization did not even need to be affiliated with the AYC to participate in this Model Congress.[172] The panel discussions at the Congress explored how organizations and the AYC could prepare youth for citizenship in American democracy by promoting interfaith and interracial understanding; participation in politics and government; opportunities for education; recreation, sports, and cultural activities; opportunity and security for rural youth; opportunity and security for urban youth; peace action; and better health and clean living. In the face of fascist advances, the AYC proclaimed, "*Youth Must Build Democracy Today!*" And, to do that, it explained, "democracy must strengthen its foundations of racial and religious understanding, rivet its framework of freedom, and reinforce its pillars of opportunity for all."[173] By participating in this Model Congress, young people could participate in the democratic process at the same time they decided how they could make America more democratic.

The AYC was completely devoted to its lobbying efforts for the American Youth Act. The ASU was supportive of those efforts, but by 1938 its attention was more focused on the democratic reconstruction of the education system in America.[174] Its fourth national convention was primarily devoted to creating what ASU National Executive Secretary Joseph Lash called "the university we want to study in," which, he said, "must be a student-centered democracy or it is nothing."[175] To that end, the resolutions adopted called for academic freedom, equality of opportunity regardless of race or class, a revised curriculum that reflected current problems and needs, and a reorganization of the administrative structure whereby students and faculty as well as farmers and laborers were co-equal members on Boards of Trustees to counteract the prevailing presence of business and finance representatives. It was necessary for these previously excluded groups to have a recognized voice in developing policies that governed the educational institution as stakeholders of that institution. The ASU also called for federal aid to education through NYA projects and federal appropriations for buildings, equipment, and supplies.

As Lash explained, "the area in which the student can make the greatest contribution toward strengthening a hard-pressed democracy is within the educational system itself."[176] In a post-Munich world, the educational system became a battleground where fascism could be held at bay. One of the signals of fascist takeover, Lash argued, was the debasement of the university where free thought was pushed aside for government control. Lash warned: "Democracy today is in jeopardy. Education cannot ignore this danger, for the survival of education as we know it is bound up with the fate of democracy. . . . In the struggle between democracy and fascism, education cannot remain neutral."[177] In his annual report to the ASU convention, which was endorsed by the 625 delegates representing 183 institutions, Lash clarified the connection between the future of the educational system and the future of democracy by explaining: "Fascism gains a hearing as democracy fails to serve human needs."[178]

The current educational system was failing to meet students' needs. Its curriculum focused on creating among the student body a very small number of scholars, while the majority of students never assimilated the subject matter because it was not important to them. Lash therefore called for more individualized treatment of students. The discussion in ASU national convention committees explored a few alternative programs offered to students that spoke to their needs and interests: At Bennington College, there were no required courses, and students spent seven weeks during the winter interregnum working in fields related to their interest; at Princeton University, students were offered a course called the School of Public International Affairs in which they studied and discussed current issues including, for example, English farm systems, cotton tenancy, neutrality, and the Negro problem; at Sarah Lawrence, there were no exams, no marks, and no required courses, allowing students to develop their own educational path with the aid of a faculty mentor; at Swarthmore, an honors program allowed students to develop their own curriculum; at Antioch, the Cooperative Plan was offered, which allowed students to alternate between studying and working at regular jobs. The deficiencies of these programs—especially the difficulty of finding meaningful work and the fact that they were often only available to a small percentage of college students—were duly noted, but they were nevertheless held up as examples of college programs that provided more individualized treatment of students, catering to their needs and desires and thus representing curricular democratization. The guiding purpose of colleges and universities, as well as high schools, the ASU was saying, should be to provide education for life, whereby students obtained a meaningful understanding of their world and were fully prepared to participate in it through work, leisure activities, and political engagement. To that end, Lash pointed out, it was students' "job to win from the university recognition that students have a right to be heard on their own education.

In essence this means student self-government—the right of students to govern their own activities, to be heard on matters of curriculum and administrative policy," by working with administrators through whatever democratic processes existed.[179] Democratizing the educational system would, the ASU believed, go a long way toward democratizing America.

Lash also sought to unite students behind the objectives of the New Deal as a way for students to "unite the campus to play a decisive part in the 1940 elections."[180] This proposition, however, was seen as too partisan for the politically unaffiliated ASU, and it was not included in the resolutions passed. Instead, the delegates, who represented the policymaking body of the ASU, approved a legislative program to be pursued as a way to meet the needs of students. The ASU was to seek federal aid to education, adequate social security legislation, an expansion of the NYA, a federal slum clearance and housing program, a federal health program, defense of the Wagner Act, security of tenure and lower cost of production for the farmer, anti-lynching legislation, and a peace program that would defend democracy.[181] The National Executive Committee, headquartered in New York City, was charged with carrying out that legislative program, while the 300 chapters of the ASU were urged to endorse and actively campaign for progressive political candidates in the lead up to the 1940 election. Upon these activities rested the future of American democracy because, the members resolved, "We must get out the progressive vote and unite the campus as a 'fortress of democracy.'"[182]

The ASU held mock elections, provided absentee ballot services, and in general cemented its ties with the other groups interested in progressive action. This brought the ASU temporarily much closer to the Administration because at the same time that FDR had decided to wage war on Democratic Party conservatives in the 1938 midterm elections, he could look upon the ASU's platform on race, education, and economic policies as more in line with the liberal direction he wanted the Democratic Party to pursue.

FDR greeted the fourth annual convention of the ASU, saying in a letter to Joseph Lash that "the virile strength of an effective democracy will be demonstrated in the United States if educational forces, particularly those on the college level, will accept the challenge which is thrown out to the world today."[183] Of its accomplishments in 1938, the ASU boasted of its commitment to peace in the face of Nazi advances in Europe while, at the same time, it had focused on the midterm elections at home. The results of those elections demonstrated that the crucial struggle would come in 1940. Lash predicted "our experience in 1938 will help to make the ASU the decisive factor on the campus in the 1940 elections."[184] What this also indicated was how entrenched some in the ASU leadership—especially Lash—had become in its partnership with the "progressive candidates" who supported the New Deal.

The New Deal attempted to address the economic difficulties facing youth and supported the general notion of democracy, but it failed to meet youth's third demand, and, in fact, by 1938 the NYA became a youth division of the defense industry.[185] FDR's attention had turned, by then, to foreign policy and the looming war in Europe. The means for transforming the NYA were found through one of its smaller programs—the Resident Centers originally established as camps for unemployed young women and later expanded to include young men, as well. Designed as a way to provide work projects for needy rural youth by congregating them in one locale, by 1938, there were more than 100 NYA Resident Centers established in 22 states employing 4,500 young people.[186] These Resident Centers could, Lewis Lorwin suggested in his report to the American Youth Commission of the American Council of Education in 1941, be readily transformed into compulsory camps of young workers where military training could easily be introduced.[187] He rejected the notion that this smacked of fascism, claiming that the administration of such a universal labor/military service need not be totalitarian in spirit or method because it would, in time, be as accepted as compulsory education.[188] Young people would not stand for this kind of program, which Lorwin admitted was unnecessary anyway because the government could accomplish the same goal by shifting NYA work projects toward defense training programs.[189] That is exactly what the NYA did.

Meanwhile, during that summer of 1938, 500 representatives from around the world met at Vassar College for the 2nd Annual World Youth Congress, which simultaneously served as the annual conference of the AYC, indicating that the issues of domestic policy and foreign policy—especially centered on issues of war and peace—could not be separated in the eyes of the 11 million youth the AYC claimed to then represent. Joseph Cadden, Executive Secretary of the AYC, was selected by *The Parents' Magazine* to receive the 1938 gold medal awarded each year to the young person who has rendered the greatest service to the cause of American youth in his capacity as Chairman of the Committee on Arrangements of the World Youth Congress.[190] Cadden had, the awards committee decided, "made the World Youth Congress an outstanding event in the annals of youth" in that it brought young people from 54 countries together to cordially discuss the problems of unemployment, education, recreation, health, and legislation affecting young people and, "above all, how best to preserve peace and further international understanding in a troubled world."[191] But just as the relationship between the New Deal Administration and youth organizations seemed to have solidified and youth leaders were winning accolades for their political accomplishments, that relationship was torn apart by the war young people had so much hoped to avoid. By 1939, then, the NYA's purpose was not to aid youth but rather to help the nation prepare for war, by providing training for defense workers and through actual war production. Richard Reiman ended his study of the NYA in 1939 because, he argued, after that the NYA was no longer a New Deal reform agency, but rather a defense agency.[192]

On August 21, 1940, the NYA announced that it was relinquishing all control over academic and vocational training to the public school system in an agreement worked out with the U.S. Office of Education.[193] The NYA now was, in fact, what many had wanted it to be all along: a relief work agency.[194] No longer tied to visions of democratic idealism or to practical considerations of youth's educational and occupational needs, the NYA was turned into a defense training program to serve the needs of the Administration because the out-of-school, unemployed youth represented, Lorwin argued, "a great untapped reservoir which should be directed into mechanical pursuits of great value to the nation."[195] Consequently, the NYA, in accordance with the general purposes of the defense program, changed the nature of its work projects.

In just three months, from May to August 1940, the number of clerical projects decreased from 102,000 to 69,000, while the number of mechanical, radio, automotive, and other shops rose from 54,000 to 71,000.[196] That shift brought the NYA a supplemental appropriation of $32.5 million to be used in acquiring better equipment and increasing the number of similar projects from 71,000 to 125,000.[197] One such project was approved in Newburgh, New York in which 400 young people would be housed on a 35-acre site across from Stewart Airfield, where most of the enrollees would work on metal, machine, and welding job orders for West Point, while a select few who had advanced skills training would work on airplanes in a ground aviation mechanics unit.[198] AYC leader Jack McMichael was clear in what this meant for young people: Although the NYA had always provided inadequate aid to youth, now the focus was on increasing appropriations for machinery, equipment, and war-related material—not on youth wages or training for civilian occupations. In turning their backs on the AYC program, he said, "the

American Youth Act (was) buried in the Congress, which (was) too busy with 'defense' to defend *us*."[199]

By 1942, with the United States at war, the graduate student aid program was terminated, and remaining student aid funds were slashed by two-thirds.[200] Williams had agreed to these cuts because he believed the only way to save the NYA was to make it indispensable to America's defense. The problem with this was that while it allowed the NYA to linger on for one more year (it was finally terminated in 1943), in adopting this strategy, Williams lost support from both the ASU and AYC, as well as support from within the NYA, without increasing congressional or administration support.

In the face of the war danger, adults turned their backs on the philosophical justification for the alliance forged between themselves and youth leaders, reverting to an earlier notion of young people as children who should obey their elders. Eleanor Roosevelt was one of the very few who remained committed to the idea of youth as policymakers even as Charles Taussig reluctantly gave up that vision. Their difference of opinion became clear during a series of meetings between youth leaders and youth service agencies the two of them sponsored in the spring of 1940. These meetings were supposed to bring the two groups together to develop a common ground in order to further develop youth policy. Instead of frank discussion and negotiation, what she saw was a concerted effort on the part of the youth service agencies to dominate the youth leaders, using the divide and conquer tactic in threatening to support only those youth groups that pledged allegiance to the adults' visions and policies.[201] In trying to explain her opposition to Taussig, Eleanor Roosevelt said

> I think it is good for us to understand the objectives, to know how young people think and feel, and why they do. It is wrong for us to try to keep them from trying their own experiments and come to their own conclusions, and I think it is especially bad for us to try to use force of mind to do this, further that force in the withholding of financial assistance or threatening to uphold some group or groups.[202]

Eleanor Roosevelt presented the minority view. By this point, Taussig was resigned to the situation and hoped "to be agreeably surprised" when the school system continued the work the NYA had pioneered over the last five years, though in a candid moment he admitted that the NYA had capitulated to "the reactionary forces" of the "school crowd" when the educational aid program was moved from the NYA to the USOE.[203] But even Eleanor Roosevelt eventually put aside her reservations once Taussig assured her that he would make sure more youth members were added as advisors to the NYA, and Williams assured her that this was the best case scenario in the present political climate.[204] Her confidence in Taussig may have been misplaced because it was Taussig who suggested to the President as early as 1938 that the NYA begin a project to provide preliminary training for officers and men of the Merchant Marine, who, as of 1936, were considered military personnel.

The National Advisory Committee of the NYA clearly enunciated the traditional hierarchical relationship between adults and youth that was to be resumed when it said that "the National Advisory Committee emphasizes once more that the problem of youth is in very great measure the individual responsibility of older people: parents, teachers, employers, friends."[205] For youth leaders, who had fought for the right to be considered at least junior members of the policymaking network, this was the ultimate disappointment. For young people, generally, this was especially disconcerting because they were being told that their voice did not matter on issues of war and peace. The National Advisory Committee's statement justified the transformation of the NYA into a defense-training program.[206] Although the members of that committee argued that "the only reason for having a defense program at all is to protect youth and its right to grow up, grow strong, and make its contribution to the country in its own way," this line of thinking contradicted what young people had been saying about the way they wanted to grow up, grow strong, and contribute to the country.[207] Their peace platform was rendered irrelevant, and, consequently, as political players, they were being rendered irrelevant, as well. When the committee said, "in one sense, the national defense is primarily the defense not of this generation, but of the next generation," it corroborated what so many young people had been saying: They were the lost generation.[208]

Young people protested the usurpation of the NYA program by the defense industry, but the moment for listening to what young people wanted had passed. The AYC held steadfast to its democratic ideals—in February 1941, its annual congress was organized as a town hall meeting—but, as its chairman Jack McMichael characterized the situation, his cohorts had once again become superfluous because "today folk in high places are showing an unparalleled disregard for American youth and American youth's needs and ideals."[209] Washington policymakers no longer took note of youth's program for jobs, civil liberties, education, or peace. Aubrey Williams, whom youth leaders had counted as one of their strongest allies, especially after he testified before the Senate in favor of the American Youth Act in 1938, now spoke against it.

The proposed cut in NYA appropriations in 1939 led the ASU to urge each chapter "to send at least one representative to the Pilgrimage on Lincoln's Birthday [the Citizenship Institute in February, 1940], together with Student Council and other delegates . . . as a start of a campaign for increased NYA and for the American Youth Act."[210] That year, the NYA was granted an appropriation of $100 million, which was $25 million more than the previous year and a marked achievement because other New Deal programs had been cut, despite the fact that it was less than the $123 million requested. Yet, at the same time, the NYA and CCC were placed under the newly created Federal Security Agency, a further indication of its new role as a defense subsidiary. The administrator of that new agency, Paul V. McNutt, did not see fit to invite youth representatives to meetings concerning the operations of the NYA.[211] Meanwhile, the hearings on the American Youth Act scheduled for May 1940 were cancelled.

In June 1940, his company loaned John Haien, an official at the Chrysler Corporation, to the NYA to aid it in adjusting to its program to meet national defense needs.[212] Not only did he aid NYA leaders in defining worthy work projects by their ability to meet defense needs, but he also inaugurated the possibility of young people, themselves, being defined by their ability to meet defense needs. This was a problem as far as young people were concerned. When Williams provided a list of project workers to Army recruiting officers, the AYC protested vociferously that this was "a gross violation of the purpose of the NYA" and asked him to end efforts "to subordinate NYA to war preparation."[213] The AYC was not convinced by Williams's explanation that lists of NYA project workers were public information that any citizen, including Army recruiting officers, were entitled to view and that there was "not the slightest coercion, either implicit or explicit, in our furnishing such lists to the Army."[214]

Youth's last hope for the NYA was extinguished in March 1942 when Aubrey Williams sent a letter to all state youth administrators ordering that all work projects carried out in cooperation with public agencies primarily for local benefit should be stopped at once because

> all available funds should be concentrated on projects to turn out workers for the war effort—either on industrial production lines or for the Army and Navy. Eligible youth who have not attained the age of 18 should be given work experience and training—in production, so that when they do reach the age of 18 they will be prepared to man war industry machines . . . Close those projects

which are not preparing producers for the war machine and enlarge those that are—at once! I am not unmindful of the adjustments this plan of action will require. I realize that it will mean terminating projects such as school buildings and community services that, while very desirable, are not essential to the war effort. But, I repeat, eliminate those projects that are not turning out war production workers to go into the war effort and the Army or Navy. All else must wait![215]

Williams also dismantled the state-by-state structure of the NYA, retaining only the regional structure, in an attempt to downsize and economize so that the NYA might escape total dissolution.[216] Such efforts were to no avail. When the NYA was finally terminated in 1943 as a cost-saving measure, Taussig held out hope that it was only a temporary suspension, and "that at the proper time its successor will emerge strong and sturdy from the experience we have accumulated during our eight years of existence," but Williams was less optimistic.[217] In a last ditch effort to save the NYA, Williams wrote an article entitled "Betrayal of Youth," in which he blamed Treasury Secretary Morgenthau's cost saving schemes and Studebaker's jurisdictional battles for casting a negative shadow over the NYA. He defended young people's right to work and insisted that society has an obligation to serve youth's needs.[218] But since the National Advisory Committee of the NYA itself had recommended the amalgamation of the NYA and CCC,[219] Williams found no support within the New Deal Administration. Indeed, he could find no newspaper or magazine to publish his piece.[220] Williams had already participated in at least five groups whose purpose was to construct a postwar plan for youth, but after one or two meetings all such efforts dissipated.[221] Aubrey Williams had been one of organized youth's strongest advocates. In addressing the AYC, he had once said:

I am glad that you exist as an organization, and I glory in the high, unequivocal grounds that you have taken on many, as far as I know, all, of the important problems confronting you and likewise confronting this nation. I especially glory in the fact that you have taken such fine and unequivocal stands with regard to no discrimination in race or matters of that character. And also, I glory and congratulate you in the fact that you have taken a position of unequivocal opposition to war . . . and I think that your whole position in calling the attention of the country to the need, the great need, of youth is a very fine thing, and I know that it has already yielded some good results and that it will yield more.[222]

When Williams, who so clearly understood and appreciated both youth's perspective and their efforts to institute their agenda, turned his back on those efforts, youth's tenuous hold on their policymaking position slipped markedly.

And then Eleanor Roosevelt began to advocate the institution of mandatory universal training, based on the CCC model.[223] This plan required young people to volunteer to serve their country. The objective was to get people to work on projects needed in communities across the United States, thereby instilling a sense of democratic responsibility and so she believed this plan would address the needs of both youth and society.[224] Her plan was never implemented, however, because the very nature of compulsory service was antithetical to American ideals of democratic volunteerism that both youth and adults held dear. Those closest to her warned that this plan was not realistic and, in fact, represented ideas foreign to American sensibilities. Many associated universal service with forced labor familiar under totalitarian regimes. That she based it on a CCC model only enhanced this criticism. Joseph Cadden, a member of the AYC, argued against the plan on the basis of its similarity to mandatory military service and accused it of "being subversive to democracy and even more specifically the United States Constitution."[225] Cadden has been vilified for his charges "that the First Lady was involved in 'a Fascist or Nazi scheme' to 'force all young men and women into Nazified labor camps.'"[226] Cadden's language was inflammatory, but it represented youth's perception that such conscription eerily resembled fascist youth movements. Historian Robert Cohen has dismissed Cadden's accusation as evidence of "the Youth Congress' communist-dominated leadership [hurling] wild and scurrilous charges at their former allies" for supporting a "program in which youth would provide voluntary public service for a year."[227] Cohen, thoroughly convinced that Cadden was distorting the program in a fit of "propaganda worthy of Goebbels," missed the essential *mandatory* nature of Eleanor Roosevelt's plan.[228] Curiously enough, for all her democratic idealism regarding youth, Eleanor Roosevelt was not in favor of lowering the voting age to 18, precisely because she thought youth between the ages of 18 and 21 would better serve their country through their mandatory inclusion in the universal service program.[229]

None of these people saw mandatory service as incompatible with democratic ideals concerning citizenship. Yet, for youth, the premise of mandatory service, like military training, was anathema to their needs, which is why youth organizations consistently pilloried both the ROTC and the preparedness policies of FDR. Youth, however, were not wholly devout in their pacifist beliefs. Defense work provided both vocational training and economic relief and was therefore acceptable as a last resort, but it was not laudable.

The adult consensus concerning compulsory training for youth found its ultimate expression in the Selective Training and Service Act "which provide[d] for compulsory training and service in the land or naval forces of the United States for men who are between the ages of 20 and 45."[230] FDR deferred endorsing the recommendation of Congressman Lesinski (D-MI) to push for "compulsory military training for one year for the youth of our nation who are between the ages of 18 and 23, to include premilitary training in the CCC and NYA followed by service in the Army ... until the termination of the War."[231] It is significant to note that FDR did not blatantly repudiate such a plan, but merely deferred discussion.

In spite of presidential abandonment of a youth agenda, the defection of policymaking allies to positions inimical to their needs, and congressional termination of youth programs, there were some advocates unwilling to surrender. Senator Claude Pepper (D-FL), Chairman of the Subcommittee on Wartime Health and Education (of the Committee on Education and Labor, which had recommended the termination of the CCC and the extension of the NYA in 1942), wrote to FDR as late as December 1944 urging the creation of a Commission for Children and Young People in the Office of War Mobilization and Reconversion.[232] It was clear that the "youth problem" continued, and with the end of the war in sight, attention could be refocused on domestic social issues. Secretary Perkins, also concerned about postwar youth policy, arranged through the Children's Bureau for informal conferences of representatives of federal agencies particularly concerned with the problems of young people in the reconversion and postwar period. The purpose of such conferences was the formulation of suggestions on the general character of services and programs needed to meet the training and employment problems of young people in so far as they were different from those of veterans and adult workers.[233] Youth had been continuously lobbying for a permanent agency, but by 1944, they were officially ignored. In a memorandum from the President's secretary, J. Daniels stated that the Student Federalists "sounds like a kids organization run by one of those poisonous world-saving juveniles. I personally prefer juvenile delinquents."[234] With the President's secretary holding such inflammatory prejudice against youth, it is unlikely that their appeals ever reached the President's ears, let alone his desk. In this case, the Student Federalists' request for a statement from FDR "on the meaning of a world organization to American youth" was flatly refused.[235]

In his final report on the NYA upon its termination, Aubrey Williams insisted that "the NYA has given positive proof that young people can perform valuable work of a socially useful character," and therefore he remained hopeful that "the best of the NYA will find its way into future programs of a similar character for young people." Yet he said he hoped and prayed that in the future it would be a better program.[236] Ironically, he had finally accepted the position youth had held all along.

The wedge between youth organizations and their New Deal benefactors that ultimately drove them apart began with the opening signs of opposition that centered on the Administration's foreign policy decisions. The New Deal's focus shifted from domestic to foreign affairs by the end of the Depression decade; youth leaders had never shared such dichotomous thinking. For them, domestic and foreign affairs were inseparable. The Spanish Civil War, in particular, served as a political crucible determining the incompatibility between the New Deal and youth perspectives, goals for America, and methods to achieve those goals. Their strict anti-fascist positions led youth organizations to support the Spanish Loyalists in opposition to American neutrality, yet their anti-war stance led them to insist on American neutrality in the early years of World War II because they feared a repeat of the Great War.

6

The Fight Against Fascism
The Spanish Republicans Find Their Support in New York City

n the early evening hours of July 17, 1936, a military *coup d'état* against the Second Spanish Republic began, which, confronted by leftist opposition, led to a three-year civil war often remembered as the opening salvo of World War II. The coup and the civil war that followed were the result of longstanding tensions in Spanish political culture and society exacerbated by the transformation from feudal monarchical rule into capitalist democracy that polarized Spaniards into regionalists and centralists, anti-clericals and Catholics, landless laborers and *latifundistas*, workers and industrialists.[1] In the end, the industrial bourgeoisie, argues historian Paul Preston, abandoned its political aspirations to create a viable democratic republic and, instead, allied with the landed oligarchy out of fear of the lower classes. This assessment echoed the conclusions drawn by many contemporary young American leftists.[2]

Further concurring with young American leftists' assessment during the Depression, Preston attested seventy years later that ultimate responsibility for turning a floundering coup into a prolonged civil war rests with Benito Mussolini and Adolf Hitler, who began supplying Francisco Franco's forces by the end of July, thus making Spain "the bulwark against the horrors of Hitlerism" for those who sided with the Republicans.[3] Neither Preston nor fellow historian Hugh Thomas ever mentions American popular front youth organizations' positions and policies on Spain; nevertheless, they represent young American activists' view in their discussion of the communists' role in the conflict. Because very few were privy to the true impetus behind and ramifications of Josef Stalin's domestic policies, his policy to aid the Spanish Republicans cast the Communist-organized brigades in particular, as well as the Soviet Union in general, in a beneficent light wherein the communists were defending democratic rights and trade union freedoms against fascist tyranny.[4] As American youth leader James Wechsler noted, "the democracies were letting the Spanish Republic bleed to death. The Russians were pictured as the only true friends of the embattled loyalists."[5] Further, "The struggle against fascism," Preston maintains, "was seen as merely the first step to building a new egalitarian world out of the Depression."[6] Like Preston, young American leftists saw the civil war in Spain as a democratic litmus test. While they raised money and held demonstrations for beleaguered Ethiopians[7] and called for an official American response to the atrocities committed in China,[8] it was the conflict in Spain that captured young activists' attention most completely because, as had happened with the Reed Harris case of a few years before, they could imagine themselves in the Spanish Republicans' shoes because they, too, were fighting for freedom and democracy. Moreover, in fighting to maintain a republican government that represented the people, Spanish Loyalists championed the very thing young activists wished to preserve and enlarge in America. They did not just sympathize with such Spaniards, then—young activists identified with them.

In the hopes of shoring up democracy in Spain, young activists in America revealed the fragility of the Republic at the very beginning of what has become known as the *bienio negro* (black years of 1934–1936)[9] when Spanish politics polarized into rightist groups[10] intent on protecting the newly elected center-right government and overturning the far-reaching reforms instituted from 1931 to 1933, on the one hand, and leftist groups intent on protecting those democratic reforms on the other. While adult policymakers were preoccupied with institutionalizing the New Deal and many Americans supported an isolationist foreign policy,[11] young activists were intensely interested in events in Spain. The situation there seemed to be simply a magnification of the issues they faced at home. The fight for democracy in Spain was, for many, their own fight because for peace and freedom to exist, democracy had to be protected. In light of the Nazis' electoral triumph in Germany, young leftists were extremely wary of any rightist manipulation of democratic processes, and thus they saw in the new Spanish government not a sign that democracy was functioning effectively by including all groups, but a harbinger of the danger to come.

As they were coming together to form their own popular front or-

ganizations to promote equality, individual rights, and democracy to ac-
tualize the promise of the American dream and stave off fascism, which
James Wechsler identified as the most imminent and menacing danger in
1935,[12] youth leaders hoped to accomplish a similar goal in Spain by ac-
tivating the same process. Indeed, Spain became a rallying point for the
creation of the popular front youth organizations in America. As early as
October 1934 the Young Communist League appealed to the socialists
for a joint demonstration at the Spanish Consulate "in behalf of heroic
socialist and communist workers of Spain, who are struggling militantly
against the attempts to reestablish the fascist dictatorship."[13] Events in
Spain proved to be a unifying force for young activist Americans, though
their hopes for a viable popular front in Spain were not as successful.

By 1935 extreme leftist groups in Spain—socialists in particular—
disenchanted with republican democracy, which allowed reforms to be
supplanted by elected rightists, turned against the government and advocated social revolution as the only way to protect the people's rights,
while rightist authoritarian and monarchical groups had always preferred
abolition of the republic, thus exacerbating the precarious nature of the
Spanish government.[14] Organizing a popular front government to stave
off fascism, then, was profoundly difficult[15] and was not accomplished
until September 4, 1936, two months after the civil war had begun, when
a government formed that included Republicans, Communists, and Socialists.[16]

Youth activists' support for the Republicans in Spain developed not
only in the context of democratic values, but in the realities of international hostilities. Like finely tuned instruments, they responded to the
slightest movement toward war often with what seemed to many exaggerated bravado, but only because of the otherwise orchestrated silence
on such issues. In April 1936, the AYC National Council voted to construct its call for the following month's peace action in the milieu of increasing global militarism by acknowledging that

> whether it be in the burning deserts of Africa, the blizzard-torn
> steppes of Mongolia, or the beautiful Rhineland, the God of War
> rules today. Under the guise of defense, alliances and counter-
> alliances are being formed for war. Germany links herself with Japan
> for the common avowed aim of attacking the Soviet Union on the
> east and west. France and England attempt to use the peace senti-
> ment of the masses and the machinery of the League of Nations for
> their own imperialist interest. Italy, speaking through Fascist dictator

Mussolini, threatens to fight until every Ethiopian is annihilated. And our own American industrialists have taken the infamous role of feeding the battling armies of Europe, Asia, and Africa with oil, steel and cotton, ready to repeat the fiasco of 1917 and drag the American people into a war to protect their profits.[17]

Youth activists, then, were fully aware that their pacifist ideals ran counter to military intervention to protect the Spanish Republic. They held on to those pacifist beliefs as long as they could. But, tested by the coup attempt in July 1936, many activists decided that such intervention was justifiable because it was the only way to protect the hope for democracy in Europe. As Joseph Lash remembered, "we were being anti-Fascist and we were being anti-war, and that was something we were going to have to deal with. . . . You had to decide which you were going to be, you couldn't be both."[18] The fear of a Great War reprise was lucidly genuine. The conflict in Spain could not be contained; young activists believed it would necessarily become a global conflict. And it was not merely a matter of dominoes lined up for the fall of democracy and America deciding whether to intervene to stop the process because if the coup was successful, France would be surrounded by fascist dictatorships. France's fellow democracies would simply not be able to remain aloof.

As the coup precipitated civil war, youth-sponsored activities took on a new urgency, and the tensions between pacifism and intervention played out. When the fourth annual strike against war was held in April 1937, *The Campus* editor explained, the more than one million participants in 700 schools nationwide solemnly filed out of their classes because the "bogey of war, so derisively hailed in 1934 [had been] realized in Spain."[19] The official call for the strike, however, was silent on the issue of Spain. This is because the coordination of the strike was the responsibility of the United Student Peace Committee (USPC), an independent group solely focused on the issue of peace. The USPC issued the call in the interest of attracting as many participants as possible, and thus it was generically anti-war. It called for passage of the Nye-Kvale Bill to eliminate compulsory ROTC, opposed the billion dollar war budget, recognized the Oxford Pledge, defended civil rights and academic freedom as a first step toward defeating fascism, and resolved to keep America out of war. And while the call admitted that neutrality legislation might be inadequate to achieve that goal, it averred that "only by the cooperation of the people of the world can permanent peace be established."[20] In addition, the call included a recommendation that students demonstrate their conscientious

intention to work for peace by fasting on the day of the strike. Youth organizations that supported peace, like the ASU and AYC, officially endorsed the call. ASU leaders Wechsler and Lash, however, felt compelled
to "fill in the enormous gaps" of the call encumbered in the omission of
the war in Spain where, they said, "the future of world peace is being decided."[21] In their editorial supporting the strike they were very clear on
their support for intervention in Spain, arguing that

> If, while fascism throws all its resources into Spain, the allies of the
> Spanish government remain inert, the simple and inevitable conse-
> quence will be World War in which the chances of American in-
> volvement are vast. We do not reduce these chances by abetting the
> war-makers. . . . Today, when Hearst and his American cohorts de-
> nounce and defame the Spanish cause, when they cry out in behalf
> of sham neutrality, aid to Spanish democracy is a weapon of peace.
> We contend that Spain must assume a place of critical importance
> in any anti-war movement.[22]

They called on ASU members to remember Spain in all their activities
on the day of the strike in order to win sympathy and aid for the Spanish
people. Specifically, they proposed that while they fasted, ASU members
gather the money they would have spent on food that day to send to the
Spanish government as a fulfillment of their declaration that "We fast that
Spain may eat."[23]

Youth leaders' positions on Spain were not solely based on theoretical
conjecture. They had discovered that, as Assistant Secretary of State Adolf Berle cautioned them, "while it is easy to talk about abstractions,
you eventually must talk to men."[24] Groups of students from Spain were
sponsored by the AYC, and their calls for both ideological solidarity and
material aid found wide support among AYC constituent groups who
were encouraged to give such requests the greatest possible publicity.[25]
Likewise, communiqués from Spanish youth were printed in *The Student
Advocate*, published by the ASU. One such communiqué, from the Federal Union of Spanish Students, explained the situation in Spain in stark
terms, imploring American students to choose to provide active support
to the Republican side. The way the Foreign Affairs Secretary of the
Union explained it, "two worlds have risen up, one against the other: the
somber, decadent past, seeking in vain to prolong its doomed existence;
in face of it, the living, constructive future, the vital force of the Spanish
people, entering upon a new stage in their life of civilization and creative
achievement."[26] In what had already become a familiar cry, he exhorted

American youth to come to the aid of the heroic Spanish students who were "the defenders of democracy" because "it is world peace which is being fought out on the battlefields of Spain."[27] The Union asked for arms, money, and technical and medical supplies for the lawful government of Spain as well as moral support for the "epic struggle of the Spanish people!"[28]

In an effort to provide further firsthand accounts, an American youth delegation went to Spain in the fall of 1936 and then reported back that supporting the Loyalists was the best course of action to preserve democracy there.[29] Such recommendations carried enormous weight in determining AYC policy toward Spain. Yet the organization was bound by its own democratic machinery, and its leaders, no matter how passionate about the issue, could not on their own commit the organization to a policy on Spain. Such policy had to be agreed upon by a majority of representatives at the annual conference and then implemented by the national executive committee. Waiting until the following July seemed fatal, and so the AYC national council implemented a makeshift democratic procedure. It commissioned Joseph Cadden to write a pamphlet outlining the experiences of the youth delegates to Spain, to be distributed as informational material to regional congresses and local groups, which would then decide on what action to take depending on their constituents' response.[30] Leaving such policy decisions in the hands of local groups, the leaders hoped, would guarantee a response to Spain's needs. Their hope was not unfounded as grass-root sympathy for the Spanish Republic was widespread among youth.

Once travel in Spain became too dangerous, aid-for-Spain groups were invited to speak at AYC National Council meetings as a way to determine how to effectively lend support. After the leader of the Association to Save the Children of Spain spoke to AYC leaders, for example, the National Council decided to help with the educational campaign of the Association, but, in keeping with its democratic processes, left the option to raise funds up to the local groups.[31] At the same time, then, that youth leaders lobbied in Washington for greater economic, social, and political freedoms and for equality in the United States, they were also lobbied to support the causes of economic, social, and political freedom abroad.

While the AYC leaders hoped to convince members to support Spain's Republicans, the ASU was more driven to direct action. Two months into the fall 1936 term, the ASU Chapter at City College was already committed to raising $500 in monetary aid and was also spearheading a clothing drive. Open forums were held on campus to discuss the situation in Spain, and on December 1, 1936, the college newspaper, which ran daily articles on Spain, announced that General Franco, Benito Mussolini, and Adolf Hitler would all be burned in effigy two days hence in a public demonstration on Convent Avenue.[32] While the CCNY faculty were divided on the Spanish Civil War and contradictorily advocated both a hands-off policy and direct assistance, CCNY students, encouraged by the ASU, united with NYU students to form Spanish aid groups.[33] To channel its efforts on behalf of the Republic even more effectively, the ASU formed the United Youth Committee to Aid Spanish Democracy in February 1937. The Committee identified educating students about the Spanish Civil War and providing information about the efforts to aid Spain as its priorities.

Later that year, as students were preparing to head home for the Christmas break, they were reminded by the ASU's monthly publication, *The Student Advocate*, that "there are some students who won't be able to breeze home for the holidays—in Spain, the bombs will not bear ribbons, nor the firing cease. The drive for aid to the Spanish government and its heroic supporters must go on. . . . Spanish refugee children neither need nor want Christmas presents; they want food and a roof over their heads which isn't liable to obliteration by aerial explosives."[34] Another article in the same issue of *The Student Advocate* provided a convincing argument for adopting aggressive measures to meet the fascist threat wherever it reared its dangerous head. This article was on the war in China and came on the heels of a November 1937 demonstration in New York City where 250 ASU-ers picketed the Japanese Consulate to protest Japanese aggression.[35]

The article explained that the war in China had reached a second phase. In the first phase, the Japanese had tried to gain full control over the northern provinces in order to exploit the wealth of China for the maintenance of the Japanese Army, crush the Chinese in Shanghai in order to move quickly into Nanking and set up a puppet regime there, and bombard cities in order to break the will of the Chinese to resist. Having failed to achieve these three objectives, the Japanese entered a second phase whereby they were trying to induce China to sign a peace treaty or to force upon China a compromise to allow Japan time to regroup.[36] This, the author claimed, would be the worst mistake of all because "what the Japanese militarists have failed to accomplish thus far, that is, to crush the Chinese . . . by force, would be neatly accomplished by 'peace'"[37] because it would exacerbate the tensions between the Chinese

Communist Party and the Red Army leading the opposition to Japan on the one hand and the Kuomintang elements seeking peace with Japan in order to consolidate their own power and position in China on the other. Such a compromise would not ensure peace and would certainly endanger democracy in China because "the struggle against Japanese imperialism ... closely coincide(s) with the struggle for a democratic and free China."[38] The message was clear: Supporters of democracy and freedom could brook no compromise with the fascists. Taken together, the articles in this one edition of *The Student Advocate* enunciated the leadership's abandonment of pacifism and commitment to intervention. That intervention, though, was based on the group's broad-based agenda to achieve freedom, democracy, and equality. There was precious little leftist theorizing. Unlike the Young Communists, who had been quick to identify the Italian invasion of Ethiopia as a danger to world peace and neutrality as approval of and encouragement to imperialism, the ASU identified Japanese, German, and Italian fascists as dangerous to world peace and neutrality as an ineffective form of appeasement.[39]

In addition to articles published in student newspapers and lecture tours sponsored by youth groups, American students were kept well-informed of what was happening in Spain through frequent updates from volunteers who went to fight. Altogether, 500 American students volunteered to fight for Loyalist Spain from 1936 to 1938, 88 of whom were members of the ASU. At least eight of them died in Spain. Students made up the second largest contingent of the Abraham Lincoln Battalion and the largest white collar group.[40] One former ASU member who reported from the Spanish front was David Cook.

When Cook, a 1935 Columbia University graduate who helped set up the ASU Chapter there, returned home to England, he was unable to find work and therefore decided to go to Spain because, he said, "life in England was too useless a one to be living at such a time as this."[41] His letter to the editors of *The Student Advocate*, printed in full, described his trip to Spain and his battalion's activities there, which he explained as very different from a Red Army because of "the point that we are here to defend democracy, not set up Soviets,"[42] further elevating the positive evaluation of the communists' contributions. Cook related a story imbued with democratic meaning: An officer, who was second in command of the battalion, entered the club-room looking for someone, and was immediately hushed by "rank-and-filers" for interrupting the news, implying that there was no base to the fear of authoritarian military control subverting the goal of defending democracy on the Republicans' side.[43]

The claim that volunteers were not only defending democracy but instituting it themselves in a military situation that normally would rely on authoritarian control found ready acclaim among ASU members. Cook ended his letter by saying that "if I'm to be among those who don't get back, I'll have concentrated so much [life] into the last short space that it will be as good as having lasted for a normal span."[44] If that was not enough to inspire readers to support the heroic efforts of the Loyalists, the letter was immediately followed by a printing of "Song of Spain," by Langston Hughes, a poem in which he laid plain Spain's plight:

> A Bombing plane's
> The song of Spain.
> Bullets like rain's
> The song of Spain.
>   A knife in the back
> And its terror and pain is Spain.[45]

Cook said that he felt the need to do something about the rising tide of fascism by volunteering in Spain; Hughes sought to make that responsibility universal:

>   I must never do that again.
> I must drive the bombers out of Spain.
> I must drive the bombers out of the world.
> I must take the world for my own again—
>   A workers' world
>   Is the song of Spain.[46]

Such sentiment spoke not only to the left who favored prioritizing revolution over the war in Spain,[47] but also to the general view of the ASU and AYC that non-intervention was not a viable option as long as creating a free, equal, democratic, and peaceful world remained the goal.

Wounded just one week after his first letter was received, David Cook spent several weeks recuperating before returning to the front in Spain. By that point, the character of the war had changed, and he felt obliged to inform his American cohorts about the recent developments. For one thing, there were trenches adding "an air of solidity and permanence" and no more advancing over open country, but more than that, he said, "there's a quiet confidence here now. The testing period is over."[48] Cook conveyed excitement for the Republicans' successful defense of Madrid, despite the merging of rightist groups to form the Falange under Franco's leadership on April 19, 1937. The benefit of this was the creation of a

clearly identifiable enemy. That enemy allied with Nazi Germany, whose
Condor Legion bombed Guernica one week later, eliciting a uniform
response of outrage from otherwise disparate Republican groups. The
fight in Spain was clearly against fascism, something around which loyalists could unite. "And," Cook explained, "as soon as one sees this war in
its historical framework one is filled with a feeling of tremendous pride,
as well as a joy and gratification at the privilege of taking part in it."[49]

Emboldened by such rhetoric and the belief that this was a war worth
fighting, some American youth leaders took part in the conflict in Spain,
as well.[50] Joseph Lash was one of them.[51] In 1936, he and James Wechsler
led a student group trip to Europe,[52] and in 1937 they led a similar tour
that included the option for an extended ten-day tour of the Soviet
Union led by Wechsler and his wife.[53] These tours were sponsored by the
travel agency Open Road, and financially subsidized by the ASU. Educational travel was not enough for Lash, and so, in 1937, he returned to
fight in Spain.

Getting there was no small feat. He accompanied Dave Doran, a YCL
member and later War Commissar for the Fifteenth International Brigade, meeting up with six other volunteers from Austria, Germany, and
Lithuania in southern France, dodging the police, and looking for an
opportunity to slip across the border.[54] Once in Spain, he, along with
Doran, joined the Mackenzie-Papineau Battalion and trained for a month
before the Brigade leadership decided Lash could do more for the Loyalists by recruiting support for their cause than by physically fighting against
the rebels.[55] He attended the International Student Congress in Paris and
then returned to Madrid to report on the battle there.[56]

He did not return from Spain hollow and sick from emotional ex-
haustion the way Eric Sevareid remembered American volunteers returning from the front, but he did share their estimation that fascism would
have to be met somewhere pretty soon, and, like them, he had chosen
to confront it in Spain.[57] He was very clear on this point: "the triumph
of fascism in Spain means the strengthening of the international position of fascism. It will increase their arrogance. It will encourage them
in their readiness to go to war."[58] While Lash sympathized with and respected those who advocated peace, he argued that to remain indifferent
to the struggle in Spain, to go along with non-intervention in an effort
to speak for peace, was "not to have the courage to urge on its behalf the
necessary deeds."[59]

Like many students who returned from Spain, he saw it as his task to
win the country, and especially the students, over to the loyalist cause,

which, to him, meant active resistance.[60] When Lash returned to his alma mater, CCNY, in October 1937, *The Campus* gave his talk to students full front-page coverage.[61] His description of the rebel defeat in Madrid encouraged greater support for the Spanish Loyalists. Two more trips to Spain were undertaken in 1938 and 1939, during which attendees met Republican political leaders, effectively committing them whole-heartedly to the Loyalist cause and to proselytizing their position back home. If they could not go to Spain to fight the fascists, they could do so at home. On March 24, 1938, for example, 8,000 college and high school students participated in an anti-fascist rally in New York City.[62] It was, perhaps more than anything else, hearing such first-hand experiences that molded youth organizations' decision to turn from absolute pacifism to collective security.[63] Ideological purity fell to the desire to do something to help the people of Spain.

Lash's sojourn in Spain coincided with the increased role of the Soviet Union in providing aid through communists fighting on behalf of the Loyalists and the popular front. Josef Stalin had been hesitant to become fully involved in Spain.[64] But, when the government fled Madrid in the face of fascist attack in November 1936, it left the Spanish Communist Party to assume the lead in the city's defense, thereby increasing its stature and paving the way for its assumption of control over the war effort.[65] By October 1937, his reluctance had been overcome. Preston explains that "Stalin had decided to supply enough arms to keep the Republic alive, while instructing his agents in Spain to make every effort to ensure that the revolutionary aspects of the struggle were silenced."[66] This set up, from the very beginning, a desire to squash the Trotskyist groups in Spain. The fight for Madrid assured Soviet supremacy in the defense of the Republic because foreign aid was crucial and the Soviet Union was the country providing the vast majority of that aid, thus helping to push the communists to the forefront of the struggle. It was the communists who were most willing to fight against the fascists in Spain.[67] Joseph Lash, because he had come to adopt the position that fighting fascism took priority over promoting peace, therefore promoted the communists' position on collective security long before his socialist peers did.

Nevertheless, by early January 1938, the ASU had dropped the Oxford Pledge and adopted collective security as its foreign policy stance because of the Spanish Civil War.[68] Lash had played a significant role in that policy debate.[69] He explained that fascist aggression introduced a new threat to peace and security that could only be addressed through economic sanctions backed by military force, but that meant "a bigger navy, a bigger army, a more effective M-Day plan. For unless they are effective, they are useless against the aggressor. Those are the consequences of a policy of collective security, if one envisages it honestly and courageously. In other words one cannot maintain the fight against American war preparation simultaneously with urging that same government to participate in an international front against fascism."[70]

This stance was a direct contradiction to what he and Wechsler had written just one year before in *War Our Heritage*. In that analysis, he had argued against increased military budgets to support a larger navy, which, he said then, was only used to support "the doctrines of an aggressive imperialism, requiring naval prestige, affirming the 'command of the seas' principle and planning with a view to forcible protection of American interests abroad and military defense of trade routes."[71] He had warned that "the M-Day plans mean if we go to war, military dictatorship in the U.S." and he closed by cautioning his readers: "there does not seem to me that there is any gain for world peace or democracy or justice if German fascism is overthrown only to establish fascism in the U.S."[72] Rejecting collective security, he argued then, was not the same thing as accepting isolationism because he fully supported aid to Loyalist Spain. "What we are urging," he summarized, "is that the fight against fascist aggression not be carried on in such a way as to deliver our movement [toward peace] into the hands of the government which we know to be imperialist. We must place no reliance upon the government . . . which is preparing for war," and he suggested that his readers "remember that this war is not our war, that this government which is preparing for war is not our government."[73] It was after writing this that Lash first went to Spain. He then changed his position. Some might argue that this was because he was obligated to support the policy line of the organization he led, but in reality it was because his views changed. What changed his mind was the war in Spain. Like many of his cohort, he came to realize that the only way to save democracy in Spain and elsewhere was to literally, militarily, and not just theoretically defend it.

At a United Student Peace Committee[74] meeting in February 1938, Lash sought to convince other organizations to support the collective security policy of the ASU, but to no avail. Although the members of the committee presented no viable alternative, as far as Lash was concerned, they refused to accept the ASU position.[75] For Lash, the marked changed in the international situation meant that youth organizations could no longer hold dress rehearsals for what students would do in the event of war by walking out of class. The time for dress rehearsals was over. "The curtain is going up," he said, "and it is very unfortunate that some of them are being caught with their pants down."[76] Not only had the time for such preparations passed, but the idea that students could act as a catalyst for a general strike to stop any movement toward war, he decided, was a shibboleth since there was no organized effort to carry out such a strike. Historically, he argued, any such effort had always led to a retreat in which it petered out or an advance toward the revolutionary seizure of state power—an option that he did not see the pacifists or isolationists planning to undertake.[77] What he had that other youth activists lacked, he believed, was not only a firm view of international affairs, but a concrete plan for how to achieve the youth organizations' goals of preserving democracy, equality, and freedom: collective security against the fascist powers.

Organized youth extrapolated from the events in Spain to form a more coherent stance on the broader scope of international events. Adopting more of a global perspective, the AYC decided to forego its annual conference in 1938 in order to host the World Youth Congress held at Vassar College, where the American delegation included representatives from 60 national organizations. In its statement, the U.S. delegation paid tribute to the interconnectedness of its domestic and foreign policy positions by noting that "each day's developments make more and more clear the fact that our own situation is profoundly affected by what happens elsewhere in the world" because "when destruction, impoverishment, and starvation afflict other areas, we cannot, no matter how hard we may try, escape impairment of our own economic well-being [and] when freedom is destroyed over increasing areas elsewhere, our ideals of individual liberty, our most cherished political and social institutions are jeopardized."[78]

Youth organizations from 48 nations sent a total of 500 representatives to the World Congress. Sixteen Latin American nations were represented, precluding European domination for the first time ever, and when coupled with the African and Asian delegations, non-European representatives made up a clear majority of conference attendees.[79] The World Youth Congress was ideologically inclusive, but, even so, organized Catholicism refused to participate because of its position on the Spanish Civil War.[80] This worried AYC Legislative Director Abbott Simon, who wrote to New Deal Administrator Gardner Jackson before the conference opened asking if there was any indication of a break in Catholic ranks on Spain and, more generally, if there were any new developments concerning conservatives' position.[81] He hoped to avoid factionalism in the AYC, but the Spanish Civil War proved to be much too divisive an issue. Catholics and conservatives refused to intervene on behalf of the Loyalists. Socialists, who—at first—were reluctant to join the popular front government to defend the Republic, were now clamoring for full American involvement in Spain.[82]

The commission reports issued by the Congress were in line with those of the ASU and AYC, which were, like the Congress itself, not dominated by the far left, in part because of their self-conscious inclusionary efforts of the previous year whereby they had reached out to liberals and moderates.[83] Although every issue was viewed through the lens of what the official report identified as the "catastrophic deterioration in international morality and by the growth in the forces making for war," the basic premise remained constant: that in order to bring about a new world order based on justice, "the emphasis was laid on democracy as a safeguard of peace."[84] The report went on to explain that democracy acts as a "great unifying factor making for solidarity among all people," while "as a system it places international affairs under the control of the people and provides a guarantee that overwhelming opposition may be raised to the force of aggression."[85] When delegates "generally agreed that permanent peace required not only justice between nations, but also social justice among peoples," this spoke not only to anti-colonial struggles in Africa and Asia, but to the platform of equality, freedom, democracy, and peace the ASU and AYC espoused.[86]

Specific foreign policy initiatives were put forth at the Congress in order to deal with the conflicts in Europe and Asia. Delegates called for the separation of the Covenant of the League of Nations from the Treaty of Versailles,[87] approval of the Kellogg-Briand Pact renouncing war, application of the Nine Power Treaty confirming the sovereignty of China, nationalization of the arms industry, and international control over trade in military weapons. More important, though, was the declaration that the only way to prevent war at this point was through collective action that differentiated between the aggressor and victim nations, allowing the quarantining of the war makers while aid could flow to the war victims.[88] The official report noted that the efficacy of collective security was called into doubt by a small minority of delegates for various reasons: It was incompatible with the existence of imperialism, it was a new form of power alliance, it was an attempt to maintain the status quo. These objections were outvoted by the vast majority who saw collective security as the popular front writ large since it amounted to a voluntary association open to all who agreed with the basic premise and thus were placed on equal footing and, even more convincing to the assembled delegates,

it was seen as the only way to "check the present drift to war and produce those conditions of stability in which peaceful changes could be
effected."[89] In adopting collective security, they had come through what
Assistant Secretary of State Berle had called in his address at New York
City's Randall's Stadium, opening the Congress, "the agony of inde-
cision prevailing today" resulting from the desire to live free from fear
"amid thickening mists of terror."[90] Berle noted that the voice of youth
should be listened to because it speaks to the future and can give hope to
the present: "by it is carried the word which builds a bridge from the old
order to the new; which can set in motion forces to undo the mistakes of
the past; which can state without fear the needs of a world which must be
reborn."[91] Youth were, Berle said, "in the valley of the shadow of death"
because as the world organized into armed camps, it was their generation
that was "marked for that inglorious slaughter of body and spirit which
modern war means."[92]

Once they approved of intervention in conflict through collective
security, delegates then turned their attention to immediate problems
where acts or threats of aggression were being carried out: China, Spain,
Czechoslovakia, Austria, and Ethiopia. An embargo against Japan and a
boycott of all Japanese goods[93] was called for, as well as loans to China
to help it buy arms for its defense. Delegates condemned the imminent
occupation and annexation of Austria, opposed the recognition of Italian sovereignty over Ethiopia, and called on Great Britain to join France
and the Soviet Union in a collective plan for Czechoslovakia's defense.
But, it was to Spain that the delegates directed most of their attention.[94]

Pointing out that the Spanish people were victims of German and
Italian attack, the delegates "showed that the success of this new attack
would constitute a threat to Democracy elsewhere and to the security
of other law-abiding states in Europe."[95] They seemed to recognize the
likely ineffectiveness of their first resolution that called on the League of
Nations "to recognize the aggression in Spain and deal with the aggressors accordingly" because the second resolution affirmed that "the right
of a legitimate government in international law to buy arms should be
restored to the Spanish Government."[96] Only two delegates supported
the continuation of non-intervention in Spain, but even they made a
point of noting that the non-intervention policy should be made effective by the withdrawal of *all* foreign assistance and called on the League
to oversee the removal of Italian and German assistance to Franco. More
concrete suggestions were also offered to aid the victims of aggression
in Spain and China that included the organizing of mass meetings to

demonstrate moral support and solidarity with the victims, establishing children's camps for refugees from war districts, founding international hospitals, sending food and medical supplies to victims of war and securing convoys for their transportation, and cooperating in all ways with international and national agencies aiding refugees, to which end they should bring pressure upon governments to open their gates to victims of war and oppression, provide educational and employment opportunities for them, and help them adjust to their new environment.[97]

Their discussion of conflict, war, and international relations was not separate from their discussion of youth's needs and aspirations, which were pronounced identical everywhere: to enjoy security, leisure, and health, and to mold their lives in a free and progressive atmosphere.[98] The world they envisioned could only be realized if the goals they proffered for themselves and all other youth were achieved. "What is needed today," the official report said, "is an improvement in the material situation of youth which will help in giving them that confidence and hope in life which is a guarantee of peace and liberty in the world" because "in order to save peace" they must also "find the necessary cures which will end the economic difficulties that trouble the world today."[99] Coming back to the point, delegates were exhorted to recognize the international role of the youth movement:

> Today, when the world is dominated by the threat of war, the youth of all lands must affirm their unity in building a world of peace through international cooperation and social justice. This can only be accomplished through the strengthening of the democratic system, placing a great responsibility on youth to train themselves in voluntary and democratic organizations so that they develop into free citizens capable of playing their part in the world today.[100]

The Congress culminated with the delegates pledging their support for the Vassar Peace Pact, which condemned wars of aggression while advocating collective security to bring such acts of aggression to an end. It also called for aid to beleaguered peoples and self-determination.

In an article for *The Nation*, James Wechsler, who by this time had left the Young Communist League,[101] attempted to capture in words what the Congress meant to youth. Reminiscent of his former revolutionary rhetoric, he called it "a conclave of veterans of present and future wars," but in his description of the attendees, he was more subdued, commenting that "often they seemed like victims of a fatal disease, assembled to find some momentary relief and to assert their joy at having survived thus far."[102] Their wariness, he explained, was "like a football team trailing in the final quarter, they kept one eye on the battlefield, another on the clock; they knew that time was running out, they groped for a last-minute formula, they tried to subdue the slowly emerging consciousness of defeat."[103] By now, pessimistic about youth's ability to avert war, Wechsler nevertheless saw genuine value in such conferences because they "best provide instruments for the rediscovery of lost international loyalties, offer some refuge from the prison of inflamed nationalism, hasten an adventure in international education, challenge the stealthy pessimism infecting the non-fascist world."[104] In short, they urged youth to collective action.

When the American delegates left Vassar, they quickly set about implementing their resolutions. The AYC China Aid Campaign launched a series of activities from tag sales to bowl-of-rice balls, lantern parties to mass meetings and rallies, in order to raise $30,000 to cover the cost of 25 mobile hospital units as a Christmas gift for the youth of China.[105] In light of the "Shame of Munich," the AYC sought to carry out its mandate to aid refugees from war and oppression by calling on President Roosevelt to maintain the terms of the Palestine Mandate to allow continued Jewish immigration of the Sudeten German refugees.[106] Next to a sign calling for an end to the embargo against the Spanish Loyalists, in 1939, CCNY ASU members erected crosses to commemorate the deaths of two teachers and two students killed fighting for the Loyalists.[107]

Even though he attended a peace rally in September 1938, Lash had by then become a full supporter of American intervention in foreign wars.[108] What Lash failed to appreciate was members' commitment to peace, which, they believed, could not be maintained if collective security became general policy. It was because of that commitment to peace that the Armistice Day demonstrations of 1938 were carried out in an effort, as their organizers said, to "rally the moral and peace loving forces in the United States, determined to place our Nation first in peace and first in the service of humanity" against the imminent world war.[109]

The AYC was less circumspect in its peace advocacy than the ASU, as shown by its preparations for the Armistice Day demonstrations. Its leadership called for meetings, parades, broadcasts, and any other form of public display against the Munich Pact, which sacrificed the real needs of the people for the political desires of their leaders.[110] The AYC insisted that a world conference—not a European conference—be held to discuss the fate of oppressed people everywhere, but pointedly reminded its members that youth in China and Spain would not be able to participate in such a conference. Part of the proceeds of the Armistice Day demonstrations, it was therefore decided, were to be devoted to "the alleviation of distress in China, the establishment of mobile medical units, food for children, and the construction of refugee homes and schools."[111] The AYC was, Lash would argue, still dedicated to its past policies instead of following new policies to avoid the future war in Europe.

In preparation for the fourth annual ASU conference in December 1938, the theme of which was "Keep Democracy Working by Keeping It Moving Forward," Joseph Lash wrote a seventeen-page pamphlet directed at "the student in the post-Munich world"[112] to explain how youth organizations were misreading the current situation. In Lash's estimation, "Hitler would have backed down before the united resistance of the western democracies, the Soviet Union, and the condemnation of the civilized world," at Munich in September, in which case "both peace and Czechoslovakia could have been saved." But instead of adopting collective security, the western democracies chose non-intervention, as they had regarding Ethiopia in 1935 and Spain in 1936.[113] In his view, France and Great Britain had chosen "cooperation with Hitler in aggression" rather than "cooperation with the USSR in defense of international law and morality," and he likened the agreement to Metternich's Holy Alliance, characterizing it as "a plan against western democracy."[114] He railed against the reactionaries' refusal to adopt "collective struggle for peace and democracy" in a broad-based anti-fascist front, to him, a natural outgrowth of the popular front.[115] Lash urged a repeal of the Neutrality Acts in the forthcoming session of the U.S. Congress so that America could distinguish between victim and aggressor and thereby align itself with the international forces for peace and democracy.[116] To that end, the United States should also embargo Japan, open up trade with the Spanish Loyalists, and carry out the Good Neighbor Policy in Latin America.

Following Lash's lead, at its annual convention in December 1938, the ASU called for "vigorous American leadership [to] unite the peoples of the world against fascist aggression."[117] The minutes from that convention make it clear that the delegates overwhelmingly favored the peace policy adopted by the ASU. In a vote of 434 in favor and only 9 against, they supported a resolution to lift the embargo against the legitimate government of Spain and secure the enactment of an embargo against aggressor nations.[118] Delegates also favored (by a vote of 440–11) supporting the Good Neighbor Policy and the development of democracy in Latin America. The discussion of disarmament, however, was so heated it had to be tabled to allow delegates time to think through the positions proffered. Molly Yard, Chairman of the session, read the proposed policy developed by the National Executive Committee that opposed unilateral American disarmament. Objecting to this position, Oliver Stone, a delegate from Wesleyan University, proposed, instead, that the ASU's policy should be to urge the U.S. government to renew its advocacy of global, multilateral disarmament. Otherwise, he argued, the ASU would be adopting a position that said the only way to check aggression was by joining the arms race inaugurated by Great Britain's rearmament policy.[119] The discussion quickly turned into an ideological battle of collective security versus isolationism versus national defense, wrapped up in a floor fight concerning policymaking procedure.

Stone (who chaired a session supportive of the Good Neighbor Policy at the Conference) argued that national defense was not synonymous with isolationism and that it is inextricably bound with foreign policy. He opposed collective security and thus was against an arms buildup because it would only support such a policy. Lash countered that in order to defend the United States, the Navy had to be prepared to engage an enemy long before it got within striking distance of American shores. He went on to explain how aiding victim nations and embargoing aggressor nations would not involve the United States in war, but, he noted, "failure to check aggression allows the latter (aggressors) to expand to a point where aggression immediately threatens the United States."[120] The crux of the issue, though, was that, as Stone pointed out, it was up to the Convention to decide what the ASU policy would be—that it had to be debated and hashed out and not turned over to the National Executive Committee as the proposed resolution suggested. Lash sidestepped that issue and instead kept the focus of debate on collective security and away from questions of democratic procedure.

Jay Allen spoke about his experiences in Spain and he discussed the "tragedy of the embargo," which meant that "non-intervention is intervention" because the U.S. was allowing the Italians and Germans to support the spread of fascism in Spain.[121] He also brought the situation home to Americans in a way that had not yet been explicitly raised. Leftist youth had been arguing since 1936 that the defense of Spain was, in reality, a defense of democracy and thus a defense of American values. Allen argued that it was a defense of America itself because, just as in 1823 when the Monroe Doctrine was issued,

Spain was and is a springboard to South America. *Then* the British proposed that we formulate what has come to be known as the Monroe Doctrine, to prevent the powers of the Holy Alliance from attempting to reestablish Spanish domination in the New World as a prelude to their own expansion in the West. *Now* Britain asks us to maintain an embargo on the free people of Spain, the last obstacle between the New Holy Alliance and the South America they covet.[122]

The crucial link in this argument was Allen's foresight that the popular front coming to power in Chile would be undermined by the Germans and Italians just as had happened in Spain.[123] The official report of the convention does not indicate that the delegates ever revisited the question of disarmament. Leaders like Lash and Yard left the conference thinking their positions had been wholly supported, but that was not entirely the case.[124]

Lash's experience in Spain and Yard's travels in China had led them to support collective security. They were committed to that policy as the only way to stave off the fascist threat. Yet, this change in policy from pacifism to collective security had been adopted by the ASU with reservations. Many members supported collective security in Spain, but did not support it as a general policy, as Lash and Yard did. Despite his misgivings over the lack of commitment to collective security, Lash remained active in the ASU and AYC.

Rather than advocating a repeal of the Neutrality Act, as Lash demanded, the leadership of the AYC, by January 19, 1939, made a public pronouncement in support of a revision of the Act that would forbid aid from going to any nation that invaded another nation and/or broke an international treaty.[125] While this stance did not ensure aid to beleaguered nations as Lash would have liked, it at least prevented aid from going to the aggressors. Despite his efforts to win over supporters for collective security and intervention, the AYC remained intent on avoiding war.[126]

Even after all of Spain had fallen under Franco's control, American youth leaders were still intent on aiding the people of Spain. The ASU pledged all donations from the third annual Peace Ball held Friday, April 28, 1939 to the Spanish Refugee Relief Campaign.[127] The refugees, as journalist Eric Sevareid remembered them, were sorely in need of such aid as they "crossed the frontier [into France] and were herded into stinking camps, treated like unwanted animals," but American attention focused more on rescuing Americans still in Spain.[128] Those American volunteers and Spanish refugees were, Sevareid explained, "the first casualties of war I had ever seen, the first men who were victims of fascism in their bodies.... They did not talk the language of Tom Paine; they muttered and swore a subdued bitterness" because "this was what the struggle, which began with ideas, came to in the end."[129] Sevareid, like many youth, came to see anti-fascist activities up to that time, which had taken place as "a contest by typewriter and tongue," as "a faint and mocking battle of shadows. Through many nights ... one listened to the stories of what was happening in the central fortress of the fascists. You could not disbelieve—and you could not quite believe."[130] Yet the truth could not be denied. War was coming; he was sure of that after his visit to Germany, where he saw the steady movement of soldiers and claimed that "you had only to experience the *spirit* of the reich, and you knew there was no way to halt and to go about the peaceful business of men."[131] Lash agreed.

AYC policy was again influenced (as it had been vis-à-vis Spain) by the input from youth activists who traveled to Europe. Abbott Simon went to Europe as an American representative to the World Youth Congress in 1939, after which he tried to help refugees leave Czechoslovakia. His "Report on Prague" detailed the disappearance of anti-Nazi youth movement leaders in the Sudetenland and reported that many Czechs were trying to get to Poland, from where they hoped to get visas to go to Britain. He warned, however, that their flight would do little good since, he said, German army officers leaving Prague had told him that the heavy artillery and tank corps were on their way to the Polish frontier.[132] Munich was a clear failure.[133]

As late as June 1939, Lash was trying to maintain the popular front as a way to steer policy toward an effective program of collective security.[134] If opposing political groups within the student population could be convinced to support collective security, then, by extension, so could such groupings in the U.S. Congress and beyond. He therefore defended a local chapter's right to come out publicly against any ideology after an ASU chapter at a teachers' college in Chicago issued a proclamation condemning both fascism and communism, though he also explained that he thought it was an unwise course of action "because it tends to confuse, split, and divide forces that should be united."[135] The problem with such declarations, he noted, was that they led to demands that anyone who adhered to such suspect ideologies be expelled from official posts, and then there would be a witch hunt to determine who else might be an adherent, the net result of which "would be to paralyze and wreck our organization."[136] He saw this effort to root out communists as the cause of the

Minnesota Farmer Labor Party's demise and wanted to avoid such events from occurring within the ASU.[137] Lash chose to emphasize the consequence of removing communists (the demise of the ASU), rather than the reason for not doing so: that the ASU was a popular front organization that necessarily included communist organizations as well as socialist and liberal organizations. His commitment to the popular front by this point, then, was contingent on its benefice to the ASU, in general, and as a vehicle to promote collective security, in particular.

Setting its agenda for the coming year, the AYC resolved at its July 1939 annual congress[138] to oppose all forms of dictatorship—communist, fascist, Nazi, or any other type—and pledged to work for freedom of speech for all persons regardless of race, creed, religion, or political label as a safeguard for promoting democracy.[139] In addition, the delegates voted to continue pushing for the passage of the American Youth Act, the inclusion of young workers in the Fair Labor and Standards Act, and the establishment of an annual Youth Tolerance Week to promote interfaith understanding and respect. In preparation for the national election the following year, they also promised to organize a get-out-the-vote campaign.[140] This congress, then, maintained the commitment to freedom, democracy, and peace the AYC had been advocating since its inception.[141]

Whether or not to support Neutrality Act revision was also taken up at this congress.[142] On the one hand were Lash's supporters who argued that the current policy aided those who had violated international treaties and had become aggressors. They argued that U.S. trade with such nations violated international morality and constituted a danger to the safety of the United States since the aggressors that grew stronger with each conquest would eventually challenge the independence of the western hemisphere. On the other hand, those who wanted to keep the United States out of war said the only way to do that, given the present circumstances, was for the United States to concentrate on domestic issues and reduce armaments. Resolutions supporting the revision of the Neutrality Acts were overwhelmingly adopted. Adults who had been invited to attend this congress were impressed not only by youth's idealism, but their dedication to democracy as a way to tackle the problems of the day.[143] Particularly singled out for praise was the AYC's Creed adopted by the delegates that year as their statement of purpose. In doing so, each member pledged: "I dedicate myself to the service of my country and mankind. I will uphold the American ideal, which is the democratic way of life. I will help assure its bounty to all races, creeds, and colors." The Creed ended with the Pledge of Allegiance.[144] But this congress was also the one that brought up the issue of whether or not the AYC was a communist-front organization.

Murray Plavner, a press agent and onetime AYC member, was the first to seriously raise this issue when he published a pamphlet titled "Is the American Youth Congress a Communist Front: Here Are the Facts, Its History, What It Is, How It Works." In it, he said that "a Communist United-Front organization can be identified in the following manner: There is always a plank against Fascism, BUT NEVER AGAINST COMMUNISM."[145] The American Youth Act, he claimed, was a communist policy not only because it would call on adult wage earners to subsidize the cost of employing young people, but because the CPUSA passed a resolution supporting its passage. According to Plavner, allowing communist members and communist organizations (among which, he said, was the ASU) to affiliate was ipso facto evidence of communist control. He railed against the dissemination of communist literature at AYC conferences, though the only evidence he provided was Earl Browder's Statement of Support for the AYC in which he congratulated the AYC for its commitment to freedom, peace, progress, and democracy.[146]

Plavner, along with Alfred M. Lilienthal, who had earned a law degree from Columbia University the year before and would by 1942 go to work for the State Department, attended the AYC Congress in July 1939, and it was they who insisted that the Congress condemn communism as well as fascism and Nazism and oust the adherents of such ideologies from the AYC. General uproar ensued, but when the votes were cast, the Lilienthal resolution was overwhelmingly defeated. Amidst shouts of "all patriots follow me," he and eleven others left the hall. The other 1,450 delegates and observers remained.[147] Plavner's claims of communist control remained unproven; nevertheless, red-baiting of youth activists intensified through the summer and fall of 1939 as a result of organized youth's response to the outbreak of war in Europe.

The members' inclusive vision of democracy was once again substantiated when a resolution to deny the right of participation in the congress to anyone labeled communist, fascist, or Nazi was defeated. It was subsequently revealed by the Credentials Committee that the sponsor of that resolution, Alfred M. Lilienthal, Jr., and twelve other delegates who had supported his resolution were, as Joseph Lash indicated, solely and obviously intent on disrupting the congress since the organizations they purported to represent were discovered to be non-existent or could not be located at the address provided.[148] The popular front lived on despite the fracturing that had occurred a year before as a result of the debate over aid to Spain.[149]

The closing ceremony of the congress was an address by Mayor LaGuardia in Flushing Meadows at the World's Fair's Court of Peace. This setting was metaphorically fitting: young people's efforts to ensure peace in the coming year were, indeed, put on trial. Pacifists accused collective security advocates of aiding the warmonger enemy, while those who supported active resistance to fascism accused peace activists of bringing about the war they hoped to avoid by appeasing the aggressor. Despite their mutual commitment to other policies and programs, it was the issue of whether or not the United States should intervene in the war in Europe that decided the fate of the movement.

Even though he was no longer in agreement with the AYC's stated foreign policy agenda, Lash continued to be involved in the AYC because he believed the cabinet chosen in 1939, which included Jack McMichael, Joseph Cadden, and Frances Williams—all capable leaders, he said—as well as those he identified as "the opposition," including Jeanne McKay,[150] Harriet Pickens, and himself, was the most representative of any in AYC's history.[151] Moreover, he had been encouraged by the young Communists who expressed uncertainty concerning future policy.[152] He believed that the general agreement to work for civil liberties and improve the standard of living, as well as its commitment to democratic procedure, would allow the AYC to "do a real job in defending the interest of youth."[153] He still hoped that his views—especially those on foreign policy—could hold sway. He and his supporters had convinced the ASU to abandon the Oxford Pledge in the face of strong resistance,[154] and he therefore believed he could convince the AYC majority to support collective security and intervention. Besides, he noted, it would be impossible to build a new youth congress to serve progressive purposes, so the AYC needed to be protected despite its flaws.[155] When events abroad led its members to adopt a different course of action than the one he proposed, however, he, along with other like-minded youth activists, withdrew from the organization, thus leaving the communists and liberals to figure out how to avoid the coming war.

There were still ASU members who believed that the organization should do everything in its power to remain committed to peace by avoiding war. Though they had adopted collective security, they held out the hope that the mere threat of collective security might be enough to stop the fascist aggressors. They preferred cautious optimism. Lash, Yard, Wechsler, and other youth leaders had come to understand, largely through their own personal experiences (Lash's travels in Spain, Yard's travels in China, Wechsler's travels in the U.S.S.R.) that the only way to stop the fascist threat was by putting collective security into action.[156] They preferred realistic pessimism. To them, collective security was not the alliance system in disguise as so many young people feared. These youth leaders believed it was the only way to avoid the global conflict they saw on the horizon; for many youth members, though, collective security could very well hasten the global conflict they hoped to avoid. They agreed on collective security vis-à-vis Spain, but not everyone was as committed to collective security as a general policy. When the socialists realized their position did not hold absolute sway over the popular front organizations they helped establish and led, they opted out. The ones left to navigate the deepening war crises of 1939 were the communists and the liberals. The policy turns engendered by the Nazi–Soviet Pact did not end the popular front organizations. The ASU and AYC were abandoned by their socialist members who had decided during the Spanish Civil War that they had a monopoly on the correct course of action. The popular front in American youth organizations crumbled as a result of the incompatibility of peace and collective security and the defeat of the Spanish Loyalists in April 1939, a crushing blow for the American left, sent groups and individuals reeling further along their disparate ideological paths.

PART III
Disillusion and Dissolution

7

Dissolution
World War II Subverts the Zeitgeist and Youth's Vision for America

On February 10, 1940,[1] American Youth Congress Chairman Jack McMichael[2] addressed a crowd of over 5,100 from the portico of the White House as an introduction to the keynote speaker for the National Citizenship Institute—President Franklin D. Roosevelt. In what he styled a "message to the president," McMichael reminded FDR that "Education, vocational training, employment at a living wage—for all, preservation of the civil liberties proclaimed in the Bill of Rights,—peace—these are our simple aims."[3] And then he pointedly asked the president, "Are we to solve our youth problem by dressing it in uniform and shooting it full of holes?"[4] To the larger public listening via radio broadcast and to those who would read the journalists' depiction of this event, he addressed a third issue, suggesting that

> America should welcome, and should not fear a young generation aware of its own problems, active in advancing the interests of the entire nation. . . . They are here to discuss their problems and to tell you, Mr. President, and the Congress, their needs and desires. America's twenty-one million youth are ready to fight—but determined to do their fighting at home-against indifference, intolerance and greed—for jobs, civil liberties and peace.[5]

Among the listeners that day was AYC member Leslie Gould, who remembered the president adopting a paternalistic tone in his response to the charge implicit in McMichael's speech that the Administration had not done enough for young people, condescendingly admonishing youth

191

activists not to "seek or expect some panacea—some wonderful new law [a reference to the American Youth Act] that will give to everybody who needs it a hand-out or a guarantee of permanent remunerative occupation of your own choosing."[6] The President continued with what has often been referred to as a "verbal spanking" in which he chastised youth activists for passing resolutions concerning the Soviet invasion of Finland[7] that FDR claimed were based on "90 per cent ignorance," therefore amounting to "unadulterated twaddle."[8] The stunned silence that followed marked the end of a decade's worth of effort to get the problems of youth attended to through a symbiotic relationship between young activists and government officials. As internal disputes pitted some youth leaders who agreed with the President's foreign policy against others who tried to hold firm their commitment to avoid war, the AYC and its sister organization, the ASU, lost both their momentum and their focus. The dispute concerning what to do about the war danger led to the end of the popular front and, later, the termination of youth programs, the demise of the youth organizations themselves, and thus the end of youth's vision for America.

The Citizenship Institute was not designed to be the showdown between youth activists and the Administration that it became. Planning for the Institute began at the preceding annual conference the summer before. It was supposed to be an opportunity for young people to learn more about how their government worked by participating in a model congress whose overriding theme centered on responsible citizenship while it offered the youth delegates the opportunity to lobby members of Congress to support the American Youth Act. However, developments in Europe that precipitated World War II interceded in the interim, causing many young activists to readjust their policy positions. By February 1940, some still held steadfast to the hope that American involvement in the war could be avoided and therefore opposed any posturing on the part of the Roosevelt Administration that appeared to move America closer to war while others had decided it was time to join the fight and therefore supported FDR's moves toward intervention.

When the war in Europe began, young Americans neither rose up nor walked out to stop it. Instead, they fretted about whether America would—or should—get involved.[9] Joseph Lash spent the first two weeks after the German invasion of Poland, he said, thinking of nothing else but what the outbreak of war meant for the youth of America.[10] Lash's support for the popular front had waned so much that by this point, however, he had been actively seeking ways to harness the ASU to the Democratic Party.[11]

After leaving the Socialist Party in 1937, Lash shed his radicalism and recast himself a liberal.[12] His initial efforts to secure employment with the Roosevelt camp were shunned by New Dealers who, he presumed, wanted to avoid the stigma of being affiliated with him.[13] He offered to work through the Young Democrats or Good Neighbor Leagues and began to organize a National Student Assembly during the 1939 spring holidays to support a third term for Roosevelt's ideas or for the president himself, if he decided to run, but ultimately deferred to official party decisions on how best to proceed.[14] He had decided that the only way to avoid the cycle that had led from Versailles to the present war was for the people and "the people's governments" to make the peace, "and for that reason," he concluded, "continuation of the New Deal is more important than ever" because it represented "the greatest hope that U.S. influence will be for a just, a generous, a more lasting peace."[15] Further—and demonstrating just how far he had strayed from the ASU's critical stance vis-à-vis the FDR Administration—he hoped that the ASU would be the force to mold student opinion along these lines.[16] Lash now set out to convince the students of America to support not only FDR and the New Deal, but intervention in the war as well. Once he had come to this conclusion, Lash never wavered as to the course of action he thought should be followed. Other youth leaders were not so sure.[17]

Among the ASU leadership there was discussion about what goal collective security served. YCLer Herbert (Bert) Witt, the Secretary of the New York District and National Executive Committee member, maintained that the moment for collective security had passed—that such an effort should have been made instead of the Munich Pact, but now such a policy only isolated the Soviet Union, thus making this a war against the one place on Earth that, however flawed the reality, at least professed a belief in giving power to the people. Isolationism led to appeasement, so that, too, was not a viable option. Given the reality of the situation, the only way to bring about the kind of world young people wanted was to combat fascism generally. But, the United States should stay out of the war, he argued, because choosing the lesser of two evils by aiding Chamberlain and Daladier in order to defeat Hitler was still choosing an evil over a good.[18]

Ten days later, after the Soviets had entered Poland on September 17, 1939 fulfilling the Nazi-Soviet Pact's agreement to partition Poland between the two nations, a "message to the students of America" from

British student organizations was issued from Lash's office, which laid clear his support for intervention. Students were told that

> This war is the only means open by which we can resist the spread of Nazism, defend democracy and preserve the independence and friendship of all peoples. . . . We appeal to you to understand why we, as democratic students, are ready to take up arms and to risk our lives in this struggle; and we hope that we shall have the sympathy and goodwill of the students and people of the United States. Resistance to Nazism is not a European problem alone, but a responsibility of the world.[19]

Publishing this letter and distributing it to ASU local chapters was Lash's way of explaining his own position in opposition to that advocated by Witt, but it was also an effort to transform the upcoming Armistice Day demonstrations into rallies in favor of lifting the arms embargo and replacing it with cash and carry provisions.[20] Three days later, Lash wrote to FDR disingenuously explaining that while young people wished to remain at peace, they "wholehearted approved" of the proposed Cash and Carry policy.[21] He was quick to point out that American youth held Chamberlain and Daladier responsible for the destruction of "the collective organization of peace" that had created a "Frankenstein" in the form of Nazi aggression that the people of the world would now have to destroy, and he offered FDR the assurance of "our continued faith in your leadership at this dark hour."[22] It was this letter that began the unraveling process of the popular front. Lash was no longer advocating a policy within the ASU; he was presenting his position as ASU policy.

When ASU leaders convened the next National Executive Committee meeting four days later to discuss Armistice Day demonstrations, Witt raised an objection to Lash's letter to FDR because it did not say anything about the defense of democracy at home. He also said that the implication that aid to Britain and France would defeat Hitler was misleading, especially because the defeat of Hitler did not necessarily mean the defeat of Chamberlain and Daladier. Witt, supported by two other Executive Committee members, maintained that Lash's letter, along with his recent memoranda to district secretaries, represented a change in the stated ASU peace program.[23] Molly Yard, who came to Lash's defense, claimed that the letter discussed only one specific policy (the revision of the Neutrality Act) and therefore was not a statement of the ASU peace program and that Lash had the right to send out memoranda as this was part of his job.[24] Lash tried to divert the discussion with a counterattack, saying that "there are certain people who have changed their position since the NEC meeting,"[25] and that "if you have lost your confidence in me, and no longer trust my interpretation of the ASU program, I will have to resign."[26] Trying to bring the discussion back to the point, Witt explained that the real question was whether America should be kept out of the war or give all aid short of war to Britain and France, which, in practice, meant giving aid to Chamberlain and Daladier. As another member pointed out, this was a problem because Americans seriously underestimated the nature of British imperialism.[27] Supporting Lash, another member stated that the defeat of Hitler must take precedence over all other considerations. And back and forth they went. Lash, in defending his position, referred to the ASU as "the leading organized liberal student group," a telling admission of what he hoped the ASU would be, not necessarily what it was. In response to Lash's contention that democracy needed to be safeguarded and the only way to do that was to fight fascism, another member, Jack Kamaiko, made the point that the British government, under Chamberlain's leadership, was fighting Hitler, not fascism.[28] Yard then brought out the party issue. She said that

> the problem the YCL'ers have to face is this: There is confusion on the campus about peace, but the feeling on the whole is that the situation is the same today as it has always been. Poland has been invaded, and England and France are defending Poland. We still stand for aid to victims of aggression and their allies. If we deny this, students will say the ASU is communist-dominated and is doing this only because of the Soviet Union. . . . And we must remember that to most people there is a distinction between Chamberlain and Hitler.[29]

Witt quickly pointed out that "it is not so easy to say that there is a division between Communists and non-Communists. Many of the people in the United States who are not Communists have the same position as the latter. America has a duty to the people of England, France, and Germany, and therefore should lend aid to neither the governments of Britain, or France, or Germany. . . . Chamberlain is not fighting against fascism."[30]

Aside from the interpretation of the ASU peace policy, the other issue here, Lash said, was "whether we are to allow the staff complete freedom in terms of their characterization of the war,"[31] to which "Witt suggested that we make it known to ASU members that there is not complete unanimity in the ASU on the interpretation of the war."[32] Witt's recommendation was not adopted, as Lash insisted there should be no statement on the character of the war and that the staff should be as tact-ful as possible in order to keep the unity in the ASU.[33] Witt, it seems, was putting into practice the methods used thus far in the ASU: to dis-cuss policy positions openly and honestly. Lash, it seems, wanted to avoid any such open discussion in order to avoid confusing students, whom he wanted to come out in full support of FDR's policies.[34]

In the end, the NEC members agreed that the Armistice Day program emphasize that neutrality revision was only one part of keeping America out of war and that the foundation of American security rested upon the defense of people's liberties. Moreover, they decided to add to the pro-gram literature a slogan: "Hitler and Chamberlain have made the war; the people must make the peace."[35]

Lash was not the only youth leader who had chosen to throw his support wholeheartedly behind Roosevelt. William Hinckley resigned as Chairman of the AYC in July 1939, and by October of that year he was, like Lash, soliciting Democratic Party leaders for help procuring a position working for the government.[36] In particular, he was interested in finding a way to contribute to the Democrats' efforts in the 1940 cam-paign and to be of service to the New Deal. He had determined even before he left the AYC that "the only hope for modern civilization is a New Deal victory in 1940."[37] To that end, he provided lists of young people, who, like him, were interested in attending an Institute of Gov-ernment sponsored by officials within the Democratic National Commit-tee.[38] And still others found gainful government employment. Both Molly Yard and Mary Jeanne McKay, former NSFA President, went to work for the NYA in 1940, not as young trainees, but as salaried adults. McKay was employed as a consultant for the completion of a special survey that she hoped would be a stepping stone in her career to more regular political work.[39] Historian Richard Pells explains that the move from radicalism "into a desperate defense of conventional politics and piecemeal reform" over the course of the decade was, for many, the result of "the accu-mulated impact of domestic frustrations and foreign crises."[40] For Lash, Hinckley, Yard, and McKay this was certainly true.

Yet not all young radicals became such stalwart supporters of FDR. A former socialist comrade wrote a letter to Lash (and other former and current members of the Socialist Party) in October 1939, indicating his assessment of both the domestic and foreign situations. George Edwards, who, after serving in the ASU, left to work at an automobile factory for a few months before becoming an organizer for the UAW, saw dictatorship

as the primary evil cursing people around the world, and he, supporting the continuation of a popular front, believed there were many like-
minded people to be found in the Socialist Party, Communist Party, and
the New Deal. "I hope Hitler does not win this war," he said, and "next
in line I hope Chamberlain and Daladier don't. I also hope Stalin doesn't.
I think a stalemate in Europe constitutes the best hope for salvation and
I think the best hope for labor, democracy and any social progress in the
United States is reached by trying to keep this country out."[41] He thought
that neutrality revision would only draw Americans deeper into the war.[42]
Thus it was not just Lash's political opponents who disagreed with him;
Edwards represented the opposition Lash faced among those individuals
with whom he had been, until now, in ideological accord.

In response to Edwards, Lash laid out more clearly than any ASU
proclamation his thoughts on foreign and domestic policy. Concerning
the Soviet Union, he said that democracy had not yet been achieved, but
he hoped that control over both economic and political organs would
one day pass to the people, and that is why, despite aversion to Stalin, he
believed it "the duty of all socialists to defend the USSR."[43] He admitted
that he was reconsidering his previously critical attitude toward the New
Deal and proffered that the Socialist Party had no future in America. On
the issue of war, he maintained his support for lifting the arms embargo
because "there is less danger of U.S. involvement if Hitler is stopped than
if he is winning."[44] He mentioned his subpoena to appear before the Dies
Committee,[45] which he said "will be a fitting epilogue to my work in the
student movement which I am determined to leave this Xmas."[46]

Mary Jeanne McKay had also been preparing to leave the youth movement for some time. Before she did so, McKay issued "A Message on
Peace" in the fall of 1939 to the members of the NSFA in which she reminded them that "we cannot shirk our responsibility" in the event that
America entered the war in Europe.[47] While she recognized that "young
Americans did not want to go to war," she also thought that "Peace and
Justice must somehow become synonymous" as she guardedly tried to
push the NSFA toward a policy of preparedness for intervention in that
war.[48] Nevertheless, the resolutions passed at its 15th annual congress in
December 1939 reinforced its members' commitment to avoid war, while
the NSFA also resolved to continue its affiliation with the AYC.[49] The
NSFA, as the umbrella group for elected student government representatives across the country, voiced the liberal stance within the youth movement, which was at this point still determined to avoid U.S. involvement
in the war in Europe.

Figure 3. Agnes Reynolds and Joseph Lash, ASU leaders, before the House Un-
American Activities Committee (the Dies Committee), 1939.

As indicated by the NSFA plank to remain affiliated with the AYC,
another issue besides the war abroad commanded youth's attention. By
this point, thanks in large part to the convening of the Dies Committee,
the role of the communists in youth organizations had become the focal
point for any discussion of youth in America. Even youth supporters
were determined to get to the bottom of this matter. In response to New
Dealer Charles Taussig's questions concerning correspondence between
the AYC and the Communist Party, Joseph Cadden, AYC Executive Secretary, not only obliged with a list of communiqués, but also pointed out
that neither he, nor any other leader, had ever tried to conceal such correspondence.[50] The AYC routinely sent letters to the Communist Party
when organizing symposiums, annual conventions, and conferences because, he said, "in accord with the policy of the American Youth Congress to help young people become informed on important public issues,"
statements were solicited from the national committees of all political parties and though the AYC routinely received form letters from the Com-

Figure 4. AYC leaders Jack R. McMichael, William W. Hinckley, and Joseph Cadden before the House Un-American Activities Committee (the Dies Committee), 1939.

munist Party, there were many more such communications from the Republican and Democratic Parties.[51] Any effort to discredit the AYC based on such communications, he said, was therefore utterly groundless.[52] Yet those efforts continued unabated and the media spotlight trained on the aspersions that were cast on the patriotic integrity of AYC members.

William Hinckley appeared before the Dies Committee on November 30, 1939.[53] Because he was no longer a member of the AYC, he requested that Joseph Cadden and Jack McMichael be permitted to sit with him to explain the organization's current program. According to the report submitted to the AYC leadership about the hearings, the three of them explained the history of the AYC and also had its constitution and creed read into the record,[54] along with budget reports and explanations of local work. All three refuted the charges that the AYC was undemocratic in nature and that it was dominated by one group.[55] Turning the

table on the Representatives, they read an AYC resolution[56] condemning the Dies Committee as a threat to American democracy.[57] The other
matter of business at the AYC cabinet meeting in which the Dies Committee Hearings had been discussed, revolved around preparations for the
Citizenship Institute to be held in February 1940 about which the only
concern was that more people had expressed an interest in attending than
they had anticipated, so more calls had to be printed.[58] Although members of the Dies Committee tried to cast the AYC as a vanguard of young
radicals, intent on destroying America, the organization enjoyed growing
support among youth.

Even Viola Ilma, who had left the organization immediately after its
inception in 1934, claiming that undemocratic forces were conspiring
against her, came to its defense in 1939. She sent a letter to both the
Dies Committee and Eleanor Roosevelt explaining that she had become
"firmly convinced through serious study of the Youth Congress that the
major break in 1934 was due to my undemocratic procedure as chairman
and that the majority of youth feared undemocratic procedure much
more than they feared the few Communists present." She added that if the
virulently anti-AYC red-baiter Murray Plavner should testify before the
Committee, she wanted her chance to set the record straight.[59]

Refusing to be sidetracked by the accusations emanating from the Dies
Committee, the youth organizations continued with business as usual,
focusing their attention on both the domestic challenges to youth's live-
lihood and the deteriorating international situation that imperiled their
lives. At the fifth ASU convention in December 1939, an advertisement
in the program read "Neither to Finland nor to France, we yanks ain't
comin."[60] At that convention, a proposed referendum on the question of
Russian aggression against Finland was rejected by a vote of 286 to 28,
as was a resolution condemning Russia's attack on Finland by a vote of
322 to 29.[61] The convention did adopt—in near unanimity—a resolution
condemning financial cuts to social welfare legislation and another condemning additional financial support for armaments, while at the same
time passing resolutions supporting the Congress of Industrial Organizations' legislative program and efforts to strengthen the Wagner Act. The
ASU also took up the issue of the Dies Committee, which members
deemed a "national menace."[62] YCLer Bert Witt was elected national
secretary of the ASU, replacing Lash, who had decided not to seek re-
election.[63] Six months later, in reflecting on what he thought went wrong
at that conference, Lash took responsibility for the failure to lead the ASU
in the direction he had wanted it to go. He said the communists took over

the leadership because "I wasn't able to formulate an alternative resolution that was satisfactory. And all of us—the non-Communist left, so
to speak, have been unable to develop a positive program. The reasons
were twofold: the war was developing in a rather unexpected way, and
the New Deal had gone into retreat."[64] Just before they resigned from the
ASU, Lash, Yard, and ASU College Secretary Agnes Reynolds issued an
open letter to ASU members in which they called on liberals to become
involved in the ASU to "save it" from communist domination.[65] Their
effort was unsuccessful in part because "the debate within the ASU," as
historian Eileen Eagan maintains, "reflected the failure of the advocates
of collective security to win over the masses of the students. Although
students were sympathetic to Finland, they were, on the whole, still far
from supporting any American intervention abroad and fearful of taking a position that might lead to that involvement."[66] Despite leaving his
leadership position in the ASU and despite the Dies Committee's allegations of it being communist-controlled, Lash remained active in the
AYC, having been reelected to his leadership role there in July 1939 for
the coming year.

While the ASU splintered, the AYC was developing the program for
the Citizenship Institute. The AYC Cabinet realized two months before
the Institute took place that many more people and groups were planning
to go to Washington than had been anticipated. Not only were local AYC
councils, like the New York City group, planning to send large delegations, but rural groups were as well. In light of this, the Cabinet decided
that while citizenship remained the focus of the Institute, the session
on economic security should deal more with rural issues in order to reflect the interests of the assembled delegates. It was also suggested that in
light of the war in Europe, the likelihood of increased military and naval
appropriations for which social welfare budgets would likely be slashed,
should also be discussed. The program decided upon without objection
was to meet the needs of local groups as much as possible while keeping
the emphasis on citizenship. McMichael, the AYC Chairman, reiterated
the need to be responsive to the member groups.[67] Lash, having just experienced what he referred to as a communist takeover of the ASU, was
skeptical of McMichael's motivations, and so he brought the issues that
weakened the ASU into the AYC.

In January 1940 Lash said he wanted to know what McMichael
planned to say in his report to the AYC members on the "State of Youth,"
and to have that report submitted beforehand to the cabinet for approval.
Lash claimed this was to ensure the content reflected the majority's view

and to make sure that democracy was not subverted.[68] Belatedly realizing that McMichael did express the majority view within the AYC Cabinet, Lash then contrarily insisted that there be a wide range of viewpoints included.[69] Lash ignored the oxymoronic nature of asking the duly elected chairman to submit his report for pre-approval, which would have made the chairman a mouthpiece of the Cabinet's majority view and not the representative leader of the American Youth Congress. Joe Cadden laughingly asked if Lash thought McMichael should submit all his speeches and statements to the cabinet for approval since Lash had certainly not followed this procedure as head of the ASU.[70]

After Lash left the meeting, there was an hour-long discussion about who should speak on behalf of the AYC at the peace session of the upcoming Town Meeting of Youth. The bulk of the debate centered on whether or not Lash should be one of the speakers to discuss aid to Britain. In the end, he was chosen to be on the platform to speak along with two other members about paths to peace.[71] Blanch Kirsch was filling in for Mary Jeanne McKay of the NSFA during this meeting and reported back to McKay on what happened there. She claimed that Cadden and McMichael were "controlling" the meeting. Yet, in her communiqué, she admitted that "a few mistakes were made by us: not to get chairmen of differing points of view ... [and] ask when the cabinet members are going to know who the speakers are definitely. This is in order to have some check on whether Lash will speak."[72] She also sent a copy of her unofficial report to Lash so that they could better coordinate their efforts at the next meeting. Thus, while Lash was accusing McMichael and others of conspiring for a bloc take-over of the AYC, it seems that Lash and his supporters were doing that very same thing. Omitted from McKay's report was the mention of the statement that the upcoming Citizenship Institute to be held in February was to be a place where all AYC members could come to express their ideas and opinions, but that it was not to be a discussion of policy since policy was formed at the annual AYC congress. "No one," the official minutes reported, "will be permitted to bring in policy through the backdoor by attempting to slip it through a progressive suggestion."[73] At this point, the basis for the ongoing debate between Lash and his supporters on the one hand, and McMichael and his supporters on the other, had shifted from policy to procedure, though each believed the proper procedure would protect their preferred policies.

While the disagreements between radical and (newly) liberal leaders burgeoned into open discord, not everyone chastised the radicals. One adult, who spoke in support of the AYC at the Institute, was Attorney

General Robert H. Jackson, who was among three officials to participate at the opening Friday night session titled the "Lincoln Memorial Meeting." He pointed out the hypocrisy of the Republican Party, which refused to send a representative to the Institute because it was associated with radicalism. This, Jackson claimed, was a denial of the Party's roots. He quoted from an attack on Lincoln's anti-slavery remarks, "which reared the cry of 'socialism, and communism and . . . the most ultra doctrines," finding it hypocritical for Republicans to try to don "Lincoln's garments now [since they] refused to associate with any of you youth because some of you are now labeled radicals."[74] Many of the assembled youth agreed with Jackson's positive assessment of radicalism and likewise criticized the more moderate view.

In his opening remarks to the delegates of the Citizenship Institute, Jack McMichael clearly enunciated the link between domestic and foreign policy. He claimed that while some clamored for economy by slashing funding for social welfare measures, many of those same people advocated intervention in foreign affairs. In stark terms, he said,

> it is impossible, they say, to save America from poor housing, from inadequate medical care, to save the 16 year old tenant girl sitting there from being evicted from her home. "We will forget about these problems" they say. But they add, "We can save the world." And so we find economy advocated when it comes to dealing with the vital needs of our people but we find spending advocated when it comes to building battleships and preparing for war.[75]

It was up to young people involved in the AYC, dedicated to justice at home and abroad, McMichael said, to address this issue:

> We can and we will democratically solve the problems of economic insecurity and jobs . . . It has been proposed that we deny the Bill of Rights to certain young American citizens in our midst. We would like to make a suggestion to the Dies Committee to take an interest in extending the Bill of Rights to the ten million Negro Americans. If they are investigating un-Americanism they might be interested in investigating the Ku Klux Klan.[76]

Before discussing anything else, the delegates were presented with a recommendation from the Cabinet regarding procedure that was quickly seconded and passed unanimously. The motion said that there would be no resolutions because this was to be a "great town meeting for American young people. Everyone here is to share with each other a discussion of the real problems facing youth. Young people, you are to speak. You are to listen. You are to learn from fellow American youth."[77] This was the motion agreed upon after Lash left the January Cabinet meeting. Its purpose was to thwart any attempt to change AYC policies and positions before the annual congress to be held five months hence, and to reiterate the deliberative purpose of the Institute. To that end, there were panelists for each of the topic areas, who offered their reports, and then there was general discussion from the floor.

The panel of the first session on Jobs and Training was made up of adults—most of whom were government administrators—to discuss the problem of unemployment. There was widespread support expressed for the American Youth Act, which remained the cornerstone of youth's program for the future. Saturday night, the delegates were invited to a showing of "The Grapes of Wrath," followed by an inter-faith service Sunday morning, and then a session on civil liberties Sunday afternoon that focused on discrimination against African-Americans and the Dies Committee's trampling of civil liberties. One of the issues discussed during this session was "name-calling, red scares, and alien baiting," providing delegates an opportunity to discuss individual cases of prejudice. The last session of the Institute was held Sunday night and discussed "What War Means to American Youth," which was followed by a question and answer session with Eleanor Roosevelt.

Jack McMichael again addressed the delegates—4,765 young people— in the Labor Department Auditorium, opening that last session, reminding them that "we are met here to discuss the problem which has brought you here perhaps as much as any other problem. It is a life and death problem for all of us,"[78] referring, of course, to the war in Europe. The first speaker was Abbott Simon, recently returned from Europe where he served as U.S. representative to the World Youth Congress. In his address, Simon spoke of the slaughtering of a generation that would take place during the current war and the pledge to the youth of the world at Vassar in 1938 "to work together at all costs for genuine peace and social justice," which, he said, was to be accomplished "by slowing down the war machine. . . . Our interests are the same as those of the youth of Europe. We want peace. We don't want the slaughter of lives, of bodies, of spirits."[79] The stance he encouraged was to further the aims of the AYC that were adopted in July 1939 and reaffirmed in February 1940: to keep America out of war, to help China, to preserve and extend democracy at home, and to collaborate with the youth of the world in the movement for peace.[80]

Once the formal speeches ended, Eleanor Roosevelt took the micro-
phone for an hour-long question and answer forum.[81] She could have
been reading from an AYC pamphlet when she said that "the best way
of preventing us from being drawn into the war is to go on working on
our own problems, trying to solve them, trying to keep our civil liberty,
trying to show . . . that a democratic nation can through the processes of
democracy solve its own problems."[82] And when an AYC delegate asked
her if she thought a congress truly representative of American youth
should be willing to pass a resolution condemning the Russian invasion
of Finland, she responded, "No, I don't think you should go on record
for anything you don't believe in."[83] She ended the forum by congratulating the assembled delegates for their fairness and willingness to listen
to other points of view.[84]

Eleanor Roosevelt continued to work with AYC leaders despite the
hostility they faced as a result of the Dies Committee hearings. She hosted
a tea for twenty-nine members of the National Assembly of the AYC
on February 12, 1940, the last day of the Citizenship Institute. She even
suggested to FDR that he meet with twenty-five representatives for two
or three hours in April 1940 for a White House Conference on Youth
Problems, to which he agreed.[85] Two months later, she told a newspaper
reporter that she would go on working with the AYC even if there
were communists in it because she believed the members of the AYC
put partisanship aside in order to promote the interests of youth[86] and
she counseled Joseph Lash not to try to remove the Young Communist
League from the AYC,[87] and even defended the Citizenship Institute. Despite what she deemed a successful Citizenship Institute, the animosity
it brought to the fore among its leaders ultimately led to the dissolution
of the AYC.

A closed Cabinet Meeting of the AYC eleven days after the Institute
started out as a routine meeting. Members discussed the plan to print petitions for the American Youth Act as well as a pamphlet containing Cadden's report on jobs and a summary of the American Youth Act, Frances
Williams' report on civil liberties, a recent radio address, and the proceedings of the National Citizenship Institute, at which point Lash went on
record against the printing of Cadden's and Williams' reports,[88] sparking
a general discussion of the Institute itself. Clearly, strong emotions were
simmering just below the surface. The first to speak was AYC Vice President Louise Meyerovitz. Lambasting a resolution against sending aid to
Finland issued by the New York City Council at its pre-Institute meeting, which was the impetus behind FDR's censure, she explained the

issue for the cabinet members: "The question I place before you, does an individual, because he happens to be an officer of a local or national group have the right to speak on national policy without consulting the cabinet or through referendum? Does a local group have the right to take independent action which is contrary to the wishes of the national congress?"[89] Cadden asked for clarification on who made such statements, and while this was being sorted out, Lash jumped in with his own description of the Institute.

In Lash's estimation, "the Institute turned out to be a demonstration against the administration. It was organized in order to go down and tell the president off. I know the leadership is not naïve and I feel that the leadership did not tell us what was going to happen in Washington."[90] He wanted Cadden to answer a charge brought up in *The New York Times* that he had not included Finnish youth in a recent communiqué to members of the World Youth Congress, intimating that Cadden was somehow behind the New York branch's resolution against sending aid to Finland. He then launched into a defense of Eleanor Roosevelt, asking if she had been informed in advance that the Institute would take on a political character before coming around to the main issue, as he saw it. He thought

> the experience of the pilgrimage raises some very basic facts about the future of the youth congress. Unless the leadership can devise methods by which it guarantees that a meeting of the young congress represents American youth, we will merely have duplication of what happened in Washington. We have the responsibility to see that a cross section of American youth come to our meetings and speak up at our meetings.[91]

Cadden categorically refuted Lash's charges. He said he had not sent the communiqué to Finnish youth because it was sent to the 54 nations where the AYC had at least one single contact. He explained that the youth groups in Finland had not been allowed to send representatives to World Youth Congress meetings, and thus there was no organization to which to send such material. He then addressed Lash's characterization of the Institute, saying that it was not organized "to tell the president off" and that

> the policy toward the president has remained unchanged. We have always been concerned with a legislative program and not with a personality or party.[92] When the president sent the budget to Con-

gress, the cabinet adopted a policy toward it, opposing the reductions he proposed. It is my opinion that the reaction to the president's speech was normal and spontaneous. The question about
Mrs. Roosevelt hardly needs an answer. We have always told Mrs.
Roosevelt what our feelings are very frank. She knew in advance
about the arrangements for the Institute and has since then expressed herself, both in speeches and in her column, about the
success of the Institute.[93] As for the speeches of the officers please
point out anything I said which is contrary to Youth Congress
policy. The speech was written based on AYC policy entirely.[94]

As for the resolution passed in New York, delegates there had gone
against AYC policy so it was therefore not binding even for the New
York City Council. Moreover, he said that when the president quoted
from those resolutions, and the press subsequently reported those resolutions as AYC policy, such stories "were not accurate and that this [is what]
caused a great deal of the misunderstanding that followed."[95]

At this point Jean Horie, representative from the New York City
Council, who was accused of sponsoring the resolution in question, explained that "the resolution finally presented at the Y meeting was to get
an expression of opinion by the group. The New York City Council is
autonomous."[96] And this was the crux of the matter. Lash maintained that
the local affiliates were not autonomous, and that they had to submit to
the national leadership, which was the opposite of what he had argued
in June 1939. In Horie's opinion, the AYC—an umbrella group—was
a confederation of autonomous organizations.[97] As the opposing sides of
this issue solidified, Lash finally said what he really wanted to say all along:
"What I think is worrying us is our confidence in the Congress itself. My
dissatisfaction is that safeguards must be taken that the Congress will not
be used as a political instrument of the Communists."[98] The discussion
was quickly steered back to the issue of whether or not a local organization could act independently of the Youth Congress, to which Cadden
said that this was a new question and one to be considered. Finally a motion was introduced to submit a report on the New York City Council
meeting of February 3, 1940, the occasion for the resolution in question,
and that then the cabinet would be better able to decide its position on
local autonomy on the basis of that report. This motion carried unanimously.[99]

That subsequent report clearly spelled out what had happened in New
York prior to the Institute. It said that the meeting of approximately 1,000

young people was held as preparation for the pilgrimage to Washington. Though the New York Council of the AYC called the meeting, it was not an official meeting of that organization, and thus it was decided that no resolutions should be passed. However, to provide some order for the meeting and to serve as a guide for the discussion of youth problems, three statements (including the one that was adopted as the resolution condemning aid to Finland) were drawn up by the Executive Board of the New York City Council. Horie, in delivering this report, added that "the Executive Board of the New York City Council of the American Youth Congress regrets the misconceptions created by the press about the meeting . . . and wishes to announce that the New York City Council of the American Youth Congress has not yet adopted policy on the controversial questions contained in press reports, particularly on the question of loans to Finland."[100]

She also sought to make clear the relationship between the NYC Council and the AYC, saying that the national organization bore no responsibility for the program or policy of regional councils, quoting, in the NYC Council's defense, from the AYC Constitution adopted in July 1939:

> The American Youth Congress is established as a non-profit, educational association which shall serve as a cooperating center and clearing house for all youth organizations, youth-serving agencies, local, state, and regional youth councils or assemblies, and organizations desiring to promote the welfare of youth. The basis of cooperation with the American Youth Congress shall be a desire to participate in any one or more activities or projects undertaken by the Congress and to utilize its services.[101]

She then drew from the 1938 proceedings of the NYC Council's own conference, in which it was recognized as "the official New York State body of the American Youth Congress but retains its autonomy with regard to program and policy."[102]

The discussion among the Cabinet members that followed indicates that the Cabinet was mollified by Horie's explanation and perhaps by her reminder of the nature of the relationship between the AYC and its affiliated organizations, as well. In the end, a resolution was unanimously passed whereby the Cabinet noted its regret for the ill-advised action taken by the NYC Council since the Institute was not a policy-making body, reiterating that AYC policy was only determined at the national congresses.[103] Lash was among the eleven AYC leaders who voted for this resolution. The charge that there was a group acting in concert to sabotage the AYC seemed to have been laid to rest. Discussion then turned to more routine matters, such as the relationship between the AYC and labor's Non-Partisan League's recent hearings on the National Youth Administration. However, the issue was not really laid to rest. For that to happen, the relationship between the local councils and the national organization would have to be taken up at the next annual congress, to be held in July.

The ramifications of the February Institute and the aspersions cast upon youth organizations by the Dies Committee began to quickly coalesce. Aubrey Williams had announced, without explanation, that the NYA workers assigned to perform clerical work in the AYC New York office were being reassigned. To quiet rumors that this was punishment for what had happened at the Citizenship Institute, Cadden dispatched a delegate to meet with Williams to find out the reason for this action, cautioning that the appropriate angle to get information was to stress the important training the NYA workers were getting at the AYC offices.[104] It was clear, though, that while Eleanor Roosevelt was willing to continue to support the AYC,[105] other New Deal officials were not. Indeed, it was politically necessary for FDR to sever his Administration's ties to the youth movement once its leaders had been denounced as communists, especially in an election year. His speech at the Institute signaled that change in course.

As government officials increasingly retracted their support, the AYC attempted to carry on its work. The Peace Commission—a subcommittee of the AYC Cabinet—met on April 17, 1940, just eight days after German troops invaded Denmark and Norway, to prepare the pre-convention material for delegates to the July Congress. While the assembled youth did not make specific mention of the German advances, they took note of the changed international situation in devoting more than five hours of the upcoming congress to the issue of war and peace. The commission chose four areas to focus that discussion. The first was devoted to the Far East. Among the questions to be taken up included whether to embargo Japan, how to prevent a Munich in China, what Russia's role in China was, what the internal relationships were within China in order to address whether or not China was democratic, and what Britain's role in the Far East was. For the session on Europe, the questions to be discussed included whether Britain and France were fighting for democratic, religious, and civil protections of small nations; whether the Soviet Union was a neutral nation or an ally of Germany; whether the Soviet Union was an imperialist country; what the relationship was between Spain, Munich, and the Soviet-German Pact to the present war; why the Finnish War occurred; and why there was no fighting on the western front. The third session was to discuss America's role in the current war. The questions to frame the discussion in that session included what would happen to the United States if the allies won; what would happen to the United States if Germany won; where America's economic interests lay; what effect loans, credits, and cash and carry had on farmers and unions; what kind of neutrality should be pursued; what effect the war would have on civil liberties; whether the United States should stay out of the war or get into it; the relation of foreign policy to domestic policies; whether or not Roosevelt's policy was a peace policy; what the role of labor in the war was; what the role of youth in the war was; and a general discussion of the 1940 elections. The last session was to take up the issue of refugees.[106] The July congress, then, was to engender a comprehensive discussion of the entwined nature of foreign and domestic policies.

Because of the media attacks against the AYC, Mary Jeanne McKay proposed that the organization submit an official statement to clarify its position on the Soviet Union and its foreign policy. But this was no impromptu proposal. McKay introduced this measure as a pre-planned strategy developed by Joseph Lash and his like-minded peers in the Cabinet as a way to try to manipulate AYC policy to adopt their pro-Roosevelt position. This maneuver had been discussed for two months prior to the meeting.[107] Recognizing the serious implications the proposed statement entailed, discussion about it was tabled and put on the agenda for a special Cabinet meeting to be held on May 4, 1940. Those who could not attend the meeting were encouraged to write letters explaining their position on the measure. One member from California warned that any statement saying that the AYC must be free of all political domination implies that there is political domination, which was refuted, even before the Dies Committee. Another member pointed out that "nothing would please our enemies more than to have our work obstructed by red-baiting and other forms of confusing important issues" and therefore suggested the statement be tabled so the Cabinet could focus on doing its work. Putting the AYC on the defensive was a bad idea, said another, who also pointed out that the AYC was lowering itself to the level of the name-callers. He went on to say that any such statement condemning the Soviet Union's invasion of Finland would also have to condemn all forms of imperialism, including that undertaken by Italy and Germany, as well as Britain's policy in Ireland, India, and Palestine.[108]

The open discussion that followed centered on the issue of whether or not this statement amounted to a new policy, which the Cabinet was not authorized to make, or a clarification of existing policy, which the Cabinet was obligated to carry out. Joseph Cadden accused Joseph Lash, Mary Jeanne McKay, and Molly Yard of orchestrating this measure and sending it around the country to member organizations as a way to plant the seed of confusion and distrust for the Cabinet in the minds of those who received it. He added that the AYC should be focusing on carrying out its program, not calling special meetings to discuss this statement, which, he said, should have been ruled out of order from the beginning and should now be tabled.[109] This was the confrontation the previous year's disagreements had set the stage for.

Lash defended his actions saying that he thought the statement could help the AYC. He admitted that the Cabinet had the job of defining policy in terms of current events, but said that his impression was that the Cabinet had already reversed AYC policy established at the previous congress. In July 1939, he said, the AYC was in support of the New Deal, collective security and the condemnation of aggression, but by this point (May 1940), it had become isolationist and anti-Roosevelt. Getting to the heart of the matter, Lash said that whether one supported the statement or not would depend on the interpretation of the framers' motivation for writing it. He claimed that the aim was to unify the AYC by stating its position on this one issue so that it could get on with its work and not be plagued by the continued discussion of the role of communists in the AYC sure to resurface otherwise, inhibiting the effectiveness of the up-coming congress. Lash pointed out that "the failure to establish its position clearly with regard to the communists has time and again affected the Congress in its work with the public," indicating that Lash was really concerned with how the AYC was viewed rather than its role as a place where all youth—including communists—could participate on matters affecting them.[110]

Some argued that the anti-Soviet statement introduced by McKay represented a new policy. In October 1939, the AYC's policy (determined at the previous July congress) not to take a position on the war in Europe was reaffirmed. Therefore, issuing a statement that condemned the Soviet Union placed the AYC on record against the Soviet Union and, by default, on the side of the Allies. Furthermore, when Murray Plavner had tried to insert a condemnation of the Soviet Union, in particular, and communism, in general, it was voted down. Thus, adopting a statement hostile to the Soviet Union would, indeed, go against the AYC's policies determined through democratic practice. It would make the AYC a partisan organization in support of the Roosevelt Administration. Frances Williams stated this clearly: "Since when," she asked, "do we declare our non-partisanship by slandering one group within the congress?" She said that the NSFA did not think the statement necessary, a clear affront to McKay, a fellow NSFA leader.[111] Some members of the Cabinet agreed with Cadden that issuing such a statement aimed at certain groups (and not all groups) was a Machiavellian tactic to cause friction in the AYC. It was not just the content of the statement, then, but the statement itself, as a procedural issue that had to be taken into account.

When discussion finally ended, a motion was made to table the statement so that it could be discussed democratically at the Congress, since it was the only body empowered to establish AYC policy. That motion carried 17–5.[112] The effects of this vote were immediate. Louise Meyerovitz, representing Young Judea, voted against tabling the statement and when that position lost, she then read a letter informing the Cabinet that Young Judea thereby resigned from the AYC because the latter refused to adopt the statement condemning the Soviet Union.[113] Meyerovitz, though she had led the argument in favor of the statement, pointedly said that she was not resigning from the AYC and that she had not recommended the withdrawal of her group. Another group that resigned, but still sent observers to the Lake Geneva congress in July 1940, was Unitarian Youth. Rescinding support for the AYC was not completed in wholesale fashion; however, groups resigning when their position did not carry the day accelerated as events abroad unfolded.

Lash later admitted that the reason why the communists came to the fore in the AYC was because isolationist groups that had not agreed with the collective security policy toward Spain withdrew, and though small in number, this set the precedent for an even larger number of groups to withdraw when the AYC adopted the policy of non-intervention in the European war after the invasion of Poland. As seasoned veterans of the AYC, like Lash, resigned their roles, it became difficult, he said, to keep "leadership and responsibility, particularly in the local councils, from going by default to young Communists, who though they are devoted and high-minded must seek to influence the Congress for the narrow purposes of their party."[114] As the socialists withdrew from the popular front organization,[115] then, it was left to the communists and liberals to figure out policy and program.

When Lash resigned his membership in the ASU in 1940, it had been eight years since he had been a student; he was 30 years old. For an organization to truly be a student- or youth-led organization, he could, therefore, not, in good conscience, continue to be the leader. Yet, his interest in youth affairs remained, which is why, he said, he had remained active in the AYC. The issue of what place people who no longer belonged to a youth organization were to play in the AYC leadership structure was brought up one month before the sixth annual AYC congress of July 1940. A cabinet subcommittee appointed to study what other organizations did in such a situation, recommended that those who were no longer technically young, but who maintained an active interest in youth affairs from the time they were young, be given a vote at the congress. This motion carried.[116]

While the schism between radical and liberal leaders widened into the abyss of dissolution for the popular front youth organizations, anti-war activity continued unabated. The Youth Committee Against War planned for a strike against war to be held in April 1940, reminding young Americans of the peril they faced as more than half the world's people were already engaged in combat, and the danger of American intervention continued to increase.[117] April was especially auspicious for such anti-war activity, the YCAW said, because it was the month that America had entered every war it had fought thus far.[118] Even after Germany invaded the low countries on May 10, 1940, the YCAW remained adamantly committed to U.S. neutrality.[119]

With Lash no longer at its helm, the ASU also continued its anti-war stance, holding a Peace Rally at Columbia University on May 9, 1940.[120] To stem the movement toward disintegration, a vote was held four days later to establish a small permanent committee responsible for all statements and publicity published in the name of the ASU, require a summary of Executive proceedings to be read at each membership meeting, and require regular financial reports. In addition, members were encouraged to vote for their representative to the Executive Committee with an eye to assuring a truly representative ASU.[121] Youth were encouraged to attend an anti-war mobilization in Washington, D.C. in June 1940[122] that coincided with the sobering news of the Franco-German Armistice on June 22, 1940. It was against this backdrop of international events that youth assembled for the July 1940 congress, which would also witness Lash's last-ditch effort to set the course for the AYC, in particular, and for the youth movement, in general.

As planned, the theme of that congress was "Youth Defends America," which was especially fitting because many Americans had grown increasingly concerned about security after the fall of France. In his keynote speech, McMichael catalogued the AYC's activities throughout the previous year designed to carry out its agenda (created in July 1939) to maintain peace and promote democracy. He noted the unforeseen obstacles that had occurred over the course of that year, such as the war in Europe and the creation of the Dies Committee, but optimistically reported that young people remained committed to peace and continued to pressure Congress to pass the American Youth Act.[123] Acknowledging the attempts to break up the Congress, he asked the delegates to reaffirm their steadfast devotion to democratic institutions and procedures since, "Democracy helped get a larger N.Y.A.; democracy can keep us out of war. . . . Youth will continue to strive for the solution of the country's problems by asking and working for more democracy, not less!"[124] "Peace," he said, "is still the best defense of American democracy."[125] Youth's health, housing, education, and employment needs were all discussed at this congress, but the longest plenary session—extending to six hours—discussed issues of war and peace.

The opening resolution for that session, introduced by Malcolm Cotton Dobbs, the Executive Secretary of the League of Young Southerners, maintained that "the first line of defense of our country is a free, unregimented and happy youth, guaranteed the right to education, vocational training and jobs," and he therefore called for passage of the American Youth Act.[126] Roy Lancaster, representing the United Mine Workers, expressed support for the Dobbs resolution because it "spoke out clearly on the rights of labor, on the rights of young people . . . against conscription and regimentation."[127] Lash opposed the resolution because, he said, it was not "up to date on current developments in the world;" the only way to stop Hitler's advance was to provide "unequivocal support for aiding England."[128] He argued that any discussion of defense was inextricably linked to a question of England's survival. Lash's friend at the International Student Service, Irwin Ross, defended the position of both Lash and President Roosevelt and in a testament to how far some had strayed from youth's position on fundamental issues, added that he thought it might be a good idea for there to be a compulsory youth training program.[129]

At this point in the discussion, National Negro Congress youth leader Louis Burnham recounted the AYC's consistent stand to fight, defend, and die for American democracy. He stated his belief that the FDR Administration was taking steps toward war and thus supported the Dobbs resolution for opposing such a course of action. He then singled out Aubrey Williams for condemnation because of his attitude toward lynching and the poll tax, which Williams had referred to as "child's play" at an NAACP convention.[130] Louis Moroze, of the Albany Jewish Youth Congress, "classed England and Germany as one in their sell-outs of the Jewish people in Spain, Poland and Czechoslovakia."[131] Despite disparate views regarding whether or not the United States should become more involved in the war, then, youth continued to conflate issues of freedom and democracy abroad with those closer to home.

In support of Lash's position, Mary Jeanne McKay, NSFA leader, spoke against the Dobbs resolution because it mentioned nothing about the possibility of invasion. YWCA representative Harriet Pickens voiced her position favoring aid to England, but not conscription, which then led to a general discussion of whether or not England was really a democracy. Another YWCA representative voiced fears that if the Dobbs resolution were not adopted, then the same course that led to war in 1917 would be repeated. It was only at this point that a communist, Max Weiss, spoke.

Weiss, the YCL National Chairman, agreed with the concerns about a Hitler-dominated Europe, but insisted that the British government was fighting for imperialist aims and not just to stop German aggression. In order to safeguard American peace and security, he urged collaboration with the Soviet Union. As a counterpoint, Bert Witt, another communist, spoke in favor of the Dobbs resolution not because it offered defense of a geographical area, but because it promoted jobs, freedom, and a way to avoid war. The communist contribution to the discussion ended there.

A motion was then proposed to close the discussion with just two more speakers for and against the proposed resolution because it was believed that most points had been covered. Lash defended the President's actions and admitted that the British government was "not all it should be," but nevertheless advocated siding with it because "sometimes you must go into battle on terrain that is not of your own choosing," indicating that he believed avoiding American entry into the war was an impossibility.[132]

In support of the Dobbs Resolution, Milner Dunn, of the Young Peoples Christian Union of the Universalist Church expressed an extremist view that "the Roosevelt Administration was bringing fascism to the U.S." while the Dobbs resolution represented the best Christian tenets.[133] Joseph Cadden was left to defend the resolution in more pragmatic terms, which echoed isolationists' arguments against intervention, though neither Cadden nor other AYC members wished to make common cause with the America First Committee. Affirming that there was no one who wished to see a Hitler-dominated Europe, he said the point was to decide the best way to defeat Hitler and all he stood for and that the best way to do that was to avoid the patterns of the last war.[134] A vote was called, and the Dobbs resolution passed 384–19. Resolutions were then overwhelmingly passed with little debate to aid the people of China, boycott Japanese goods, and condemn colonial rule to end the session.

The session on education called for the passage of the American Youth Act as the AYC's major objective, the report on the Civil Liberties Commission vowed to continue its support for passage of the anti-lynching bill and the anti-poll tax bill as well as a general condemnation against war hysteria and talk of a fifth column, and the jobs commission called for expansion of the NYA and WPA to help curb unemployment.[135]

The only other time the issue of communism was raised at the Congress was during the discussion of whether or not to reaffirm the 1939 stance of "democracy v. dictatorship." Again there was an attempt to put the AYC on record saying it was against dictatorship, regardless of whether it was carried out by communists, fascists, Nazis, or any other group. While some argued that a generic anti-dictatorship plank was sufficient, others insisted that the AYC clarify its position on communism. YCL spokesman Carl Ross stated that he thought the AYC should be wary of condemning a nation (the Soviet Union) that was at peace, that he thought the Soviet Union represented the best hope for democracy, and that the delegates had no reason to fear a Soviet invasion. But he recognized that many Americans and, indeed, many youth delegates, favored the inclusion of the word "communist" in such a declaration, and therefore his group would abstain from voting on the resolution. He said he did not want to cloud the issue: The AYC stood against dictatorship.[136] The 1939 position was overwhelmingly reaffirmed. Joseph Lash, in a letter to the editor of the *New York Times*, explained that many people, like himself, who voted against the resolution to condemn Russia, did so not because they believed Russia was a democratic paradise, but because it did not make sense to lump together Germany, Italy, and Russia. England was, he further explained, trying to wean the Soviet Union to an anti-Hitler orientation and thus those who supported aid to Britain could not permit gratuitous criticisms.[137] Moreover, he continued, "If Hitler menaces American interests, as I believe he does, then it likewise is to our advantage to hope for a break between Stalin and Hitler."[138] He ended his letter by praising, once again, the representative leadership of the AYC, which, he said, reduced the influence of the communists to a degree proportionate to their small numbers.[139]

After the congress, anti-war activities, sponsored by both the AYC and ASU, continued. When Germany invaded Belgium, the Netherlands, and Luxembourg in May 1940, the ASU had vowed that "1940 shall not be 1917!"[140] As explained by the ASU, Americans would not be duped into entering the war in Europe as they had been in 1917 because "the issue for America is sharp and simple: WAR OR PEACE. And we the people of America choose peace."[141] To carry out that policy, a Rally for Peace at New York City's Randall's Island was held on August 4, 1940.[142] AYC leaders continued to lobby politicians in Washington, even observing the House Military Affairs Committee hearings on the Burke-Wadsworth (conscription) Bill to ascertain whether its letter-writing and petitioning campaign against military conscription had any effect on the Senators.[143] They were happy to report that it had directly resulted in the divided opinion of the Congressmen.[144] The AYC also spearheaded a new campaign, introduced at the 1940 Congress, called Emergency Peace Mobilization to encourage any and all anti-war activities across the nation.[145] Cadden was especially delighted with this development because, historically, AYC activity had slackened during the summer months.[146] J. Carrell Morris, of the Christian Youth Council of North America, reported that Christian groups throughout the country supported the Emergency Peace Mobilization activities.[147] While the youth organizations focused on keeping America out of war throughout the rest of the summer, Lash focused on the upcoming presidential election. By the fall, it was his sole focus.

Lash did not attend the September AYC Cabinet meeting because he was busy organizing on behalf of President Roosevelt.[148] Four days after that meeting, Lash arranged for a group of students, who were the vanguard of a new movement called the College Clubs for Roosevelt Movement, to interview Senator Norris. The purpose of this group was to organize Roosevelt clubs on campuses across the nation in order to get out the vote, educate the people on campus regarding the aims of the Democratic Party, and to do the leg work of the Presidential campaign.[149] To that end, Lash attempted to create a National Independent Youth Committee affiliated with the Committee of Independent Voters, but in order to build up such an organization, he culled membership from the ASU, sending letters to his former colleagues, urging them to join forces with him in support of Roosevelt.[150]

By October 1940, Lash was working full time for the Roosevelt reelection campaign, handing out "Youth for Roosevelt" buttons, setting up an independent liberal youth organization, and trying to entice

ASU chapters to join his group.[151] He claimed that he left the ASU because he was "in complete disagreement with its new policies."[152] One of those policies with which he likely disagreed was the 200–2 vote against FDR.[153] Other groups, like the YPSL, even more virulently opposed Roosevelt's war-supporting measures, calling for "a day of national mourning" on 16 October 1940, the day FDR proclaimed as Registration Day for military conscription.[154]

Lash, in his support for the President, turned his back on the AYC, of which he had been a leader just three months before. He clearly enunciated his pro-Roosevelt position in a letter to the editor of the *New York Times* in which he railed against the First Voters League for its pro-Willkie advertisement. The advertisement accused members of the Roosevelt Administration of encouraging appeasement through their aid to the AYC, an organization that opposed military preparedness, advocated isolation, and refused to condemn the Russian invasion of Finland.[155] The intent to damage the Democrats by identifying Lash with the unpopular views of the AYC, he said, was a desperate attempt to hoodwink Americans, which was especially grievous since he claimed that young people believed "that their lives are safer in the hands of" Roosevelt because, after all, the "New Deal has been Youth's Deal," and FDR represented "democracy's last hope."[156] Lash's support of Roosevelt was based on both his advocacy of New Deal programs and on his understanding of international events: He thought the most significant threat to American democracy came from abroad. There were still many members of the ASU and AYC, however, who believed it was domestic politics and policies that represented the most significant threat to American democracy.[157] Lash had shared that view as late as September 1939, when he said that "by keeping America out of war and by safeguarding American democracy we will assure that America will be a force for just and lasting peace."[158]

While the AYC was calling on youth representatives to meet with Congressmen to discuss the problems facing youth—in particular, the cuts in the NYA budget, the inadequacies of the vocational training program of the U.S. Office of Education, and decreased minimum wage—Lash was handing out buttons that said "The New Deal Is Youth's Deal."[159] When AYC leaders met with Congressmen to discuss the effects of the Administration's policies on youth, they also decried the attempt to silence dissenters and maintained the AYC's intent for youth to vote to defend democracy on election day.[160] While Lash wholeheartedly supported Roosevelt's third term, the AYC called on young voters to use the following criteria as "youth's yardstick for the 1940 election: Do the candidates measure up to the American Youth Congress program?"[161] To that end, the candidate should oppose any policy that would bring America into war in Europe and/or allow it to intervene in Latin America or the Far East. In addition, the candidate should support bills that would extend democracy and improve living standards, including, of course, the American Youth Act.[162]

Although he had not attended a Cabinet meeting in months and was, in fact, organizing a youth movement outside the parameters of the AYC, and despite his objections to what he referred to as the one-sided nature of the upcoming Town Hall Meeting, Lash insisted on speaking at the January 1941 Cabinet meeting in favor of Lend-Lease.[163] Failing to convince the Cabinet to support Lend-Lease, Lash came away from that meeting even more embittered. He particularly resented the fact that Jack McMichael would speak on the topic of "Youth and the Nation" at the Town Hall Meeting without mentioning the minority view of those—like Lash—who disagreed with the majority position. He voiced his displeasure to the Cabinet members as well as to the broader public by subsequently writing a letter to the editor of the *New York Herald Tribune*.[164] He accused Joseph Cadden of trying to merge the AYC with other groups without consulting the AYC leadership, which, as was explained very clearly to him, not the case at all.[165] The rift between Lash and other AYC leaders was widening.

The Town Hall meeting in Washington, D.C. in February 1941 brought the AYC back to the original issue that prompted the creation of national youth organizations at the beginning of the Depression decade—youth's First Amendment rights. In this case, it was a denial of the right to assemble. The AYC had asked permission to use the Labor Department Auditorium as it had the year before during its Citizenship Institute because it was one of the few places in the city that was large enough to accommodate the young delegates that was also open to a non-segregated audience. Much had changed in the intervening year, though. AYC leader Frances Williams was first told that a non-governmental group could only use the space if it was sponsored by a government agency. The previous year, the AYC had been sponsored by the NYA, but Aubrey Williams could no longer be counted as an AYC supporter after the disagreement about whether or not NYA workers names and addresses should have been released to Army recruiters.[166] The AYC therefore approached John Studebaker, head of the U.S. Office of Education, who agreed to sponsor the event, only to then be over-ruled by John Carmody, of the

Federal Works Administration.[167] The AYC joined with the National Federation for Constitutional Liberties to object to this decision. A letter-writing and petition campaign was immediately undertaken because, as the AYC leaflet explained, "the way to keep free speech is to speak."[168] Ultimately, the AYC secured a venue, but the deliberate obstruction its leaders faced in doing so indicated how far apart the AYC and FDR Administration had grown.

Jack McMichael's remarks to the Town Hall Meeting addressed the issue of how much had changed in one year. No administration official addressed the delegates in 1941, and the only ones who attended their sessions, he jested, were disguised members of the F.B.I. The change, he stressed, did not reside "in the ranks of ordinary American youth who came to Washington last year on behalf of jobs, civil liberties, and peace and who have come again this year with the same program and aims."[169] It was the government's position that had changed and so he decried its policies that had turned the National Youth Administration into a national defense agency, and he criticized its lack of support for the American Youth Act.[170] Singled out for particular castigation, in this regard, was Aubrey Williams who, in order to preserve NYA funding, called for the defeat of the American Youth Act and thus, McMichael said, "cuts himself off from the rank and file of American youth and American workers."[171] In the final analysis, he said, 95 percent of Americans still wanted neutrality and were against Lend-Lease not only because it destroyed American neutrality but also because the drift toward war threatened to destroy American democratic liberties, as political and racial minorities continued to be targets of discrimination and prejudice. To combat that, the vast majority of American youth, he claimed, citing a Gallup poll, stood strongly behind the AYC's program for jobs, peace, and civil liberties.[172]

Regardless of the hostility it received from the Administration, following the Town Hall Meeting, the AYC National Assembly met to discuss the agenda for the next congress. Joseph Cadden suggested that the next congress should focus on methods for carrying out the AYC program, but no further details were ironed out because, as another delegate explained and the experience of the previous year attested, no one knew what part the United States would be playing in the war five months hence, so flexibility would be necessary until the AYC could determine governmental policy and react appropriately toward it.[173] Most of this meeting was therefore devoted to a discussion of a "fellowship appeal to world youth," which sought to maintain the solidarity of youth from around the world established by the world youth congresses. In its proclamation, though, the AYC stressed its commitment to both American ideals and the spirit of international cooperation and understanding, saying that "thus we proclaim our loyalty to our country and to the high ideals of the world fellowship and the right to asylum for which our people, since 1776, have fought. Thus we say that no matter what the enemies of youth may attempt, our international brotherhood shall survive, our goals shall be triumphant."[174] In the spirit of brotherhood, the AYC sponsored a Bill, introduced by Representative Vito Marcantonio (American Labor Party-NY) in March 1941, to prohibit racial discrimination.[175]

Lash continued to work outside the AYC to support the Administration's foreign policies, which, according to his personal credo, was the only way to safeguard democracy. He still maintained his socialist belief that political democracy must be accompanied by economic democracy if every man and woman was to enjoy life, liberty, and the pursuit of happiness. The "menace of totalitarian control from right or left," however, led him to believe social justice could only be assured through the New Deal, but for that to happen, Hitler must be defeated.[176] In April 1941, he had become the spokesman for a new group, Students in Defense of Democracy (SDD). In its newsletter, he criticized the AYC's proposed anti-war strike because "to strike against aid to England is to help Hitler" and said that young people mistakenly believed that the issue of war and peace could be decided by peace advocates, when, instead, the question was being decided by the very nature of fascism.[177] He again argued that the only way to stop Hitler, and presumably create a future peace, was to support Lend-Lease as well as convoy supply ships to Europe, which the SDD had just voted to support.[178] The ASU saw this as yet another step toward American entry into the war. Further, the ASU cast the SDD as so identified with the FDR Administration that it could not be called a youth organization at all.[179]

It was the issue of aid to Britain that finally convinced Lash and two other Cabinet members to leave the AYC in May 1941. According to Lash, the resignations came as a result of the undemocratic nature of the AYC, which, he said, in vague red-baiting terms, was no longer representative of American youth and no longer adhered to the democratic process. This indictment, however, rested on the AYC's refusal to adopt one policy: aid to Britain. To support his case against the AYC leadership, he claimed that the February Town Meeting of Youth in Washington was engineered by underhanded tactics into a three-day demonstration against such aid, thus presenting only one point of view and refusing the minority the right to present its case.[180] Yet Lash had been chosen by the Cabinet to provide the rationale for aid to Britain. His position had simply not been adopted. This was because, Lash complained, "opposition leaders [like himself] were booed and scarcely listened to until the leadership itself, alarmed at the bad effects the spectacle of intolerance and closed-mindedness was having, adjured the audience to listen quietly."[181] Lash failed to see the contradiction: It was the delegates themselves who refused to listen to him, not the leadership.

While Lash claimed his views represented a majority of youth, who, like the majority of Americans, wanted to aid Britain, he offered no proof that this was true. Indeed, he had to omit information from his letter of resignation that contradicted his understanding of the issue. In the original draft of the resignation letter, which he sent to Louise Morley, John Darnell, Jeanne McKay, and Harriet Pickens, all of whom, he hoped, would join him in a joint resignation, he included the results of a recent poll of student opinion conducted at Yale and Harvard. Although it showed that only 19 percent of Yale respondents and 14.7 percent of Harvard respondents favored strict neutrality, it also showed that only 39 percent of Yale respondents and 44 percent of Harvard respondents favored all aid to England to ensure victory, including war, if it became necessary.[182] Morley pointed out, in a handwritten comment on the draft, that the Harvard and Yale polls did not prove that the AYC's position was unrepresentative of youth, in general, and not even of those youth who had participated in this specific poll; this information was therefore stricken from the letter.[183]

The AYC leadership was following the policies decided upon at the previous Congress and reaffirmed at every major gathering since. The only evidence Lash offered against the AYC to support his charge was that it had refused to adopt his (minority) position—a position he had been unable to convince the majority to support at the July Congress, the Armistice Day demonstrations, the February Town Hall Meeting, or the April Strike Against War. He did admit that he had stayed in the AYC even though his position was no longer policy because he, and the other members of the minority view, hoped to ultimately prevail. Failing this, they withdrew from the organization.[184]

Communists had sided with many of the liberals, pacifists, and isolationists against aid to Britain. When their position changed, as a result of the German invasion of the Soviet Union in June 1941 just two months later, they faced the same struggle Lash had faced: trying to convince the majority to support their position. To that end, Carl Ross outlined, in a report to the National Committee of the YCL, the communists' plan. The first priority was to avoid sectarianism because, he said, "the glaring search-light of the new conditions [require] national unity in the defense of America."[185] Communists should be willing to work with any organization that supported aid to Britain and was willing to extend that aid to the Soviet Union, including the Student Defenders of Democracy and the Clearing House for Youth established by Joseph Lash. He warned, though, "that any tendency by Communists to monopolize the anti-Hitler movement would only justify and strengthen [the] fears and tendencies" of the masses to distrust the communists, so "young Communists must be always prepared to work on the basis of widest mutual interdependence with all youth regardless of any past differences or their attitude toward our program, provided we agree on the *one single issue* that confronts us all—defense of America against Hitler and the friends of Hitler."[186] He reminded YCL members that, after all, they shared many similar views and positions with their former opponents, including opposition to Jim Crowism, the desire for greater representation of youth in labor and political organizations, and opposition to the changes made in the NYA program. Thus common ground should be easily attained.[187] Once young communists made the defeat of Hitler and Hitlerism the paramount goal, they advocated the necessity of unity regardless of class outlook or position.[188]

Joseph Lash refused, as General Secretary of the International Student Service, to bow "to the deluge of proposals for the restoration of the Popular Front" because, he said, "the Youth Congress and its kindred groups are unreliable allies."[189] Those kindred groups were the communists, who, he said, had not only convinced the AYC to adopt isolation after the Nazi-Soviet Pact and collective security after the German invasion of the Soviet Union, but had "prevailed upon" socialists to create the organization in 1934.[190] He explained that the socialists and liberals were not duped; they believed "the group working most loyally and unselfishly for democratic purposes would gain the adherence of the majority," and "we had no doubt that group would be ours."[191] But that did not happen, and "the Communists walked off with the organization" in 1939.[192] In his explanation for this, he said that "in the period '37, '38, when the Socialists left the ASU [and AYC], it was difficult to distinguish between Communists and democrats. It was not so much that democrats had become Communists as that Communists had become democrats."[193] Lash, though he implies that the communists' support of democracy was merely a ploy, also inadvertently admits that it was the socialists and their liberal supporters who pulled out of the youth organizations when they no longer carried the majority, and this is what, in the long run, caused the demise of the popular front organizations that had been the voice for activist youth.

Those who left the movement, however, justified their actions by claiming the communists had orchestrated a coup. An unsigned addendum to a confidential report for the American Youth Commission filed by Molly Yard claimed that the ASU had been taken over by the young communists, and the author lamented that "it might have been wiser to dodge the issue of Soviet aggression at all costs, even after it had been thrust upon us by not only the YCL but by history."[194] However, when the AYC followed just that course of action, it, too, was condemned. An anonymous analysis written of the 1940 AYC Congress at Lake Geneva, Wisconsin, concluded that by that point the AYC was no longer a representative organization because delegates from only 244 organizations attended, compared to the 500 that had been represented at the previous congress. The analysis also claimed that the overwhelming majority of progressive, non-communist youth organizations were now operating outside the AYC.[195] Yet the NSFA and YWCA, stalwart liberal organizations, remained. What was missing was the Socialist contingent that had resigned in the interim.[196] The report listed known communist-controlled or communist-led organizations, claiming that the communists could therefore count on 18 of 33 votes in the Cabinet.[197] In identifying YCLers, the report dubiously explained that "those listed under 'Young Communist League' have accepted the YCL leadership completely on every count, whether card holders or not."[198] Among those so-identified were Jack McMichael, Joseph Cadden, Powell, Frances Williams, and Abbott Simon.[199] The report went on to identify Joseph Lash as "the leader of those few oppositionists who wanted to, or thought they could, work within the AYC framework. The degree of support he received (19 votes on the most important issue, national defense) indicates what his chances are."[200] The report did not say why the socialist organizations thought they could no longer work within the AYC framework nor did it explain how Lash could convince 19 members to go along with him if 18 supposedly took orders from the YCL.

Later, when he reflected on the shift in AYC policy more philosophically, Lash came up with an explanation that was not so dependent on a sense of communist malevolence. He reasoned that because young people, especially students, were caught up in a world wracked by social and economic catastrophe, they were searching for a *weltanschauung*—a worldview—that would offer an explanation for the present state of affairs as well as a proscription for the inevitable creation of a new world.[201] "They wanted," he said, "a fighting faith which girdles the globe with themselves as militant crusaders."[202] They wanted something to believe in and fight for—a "world revolutionary fellowship," which, for so many young people during the Great Depression, rested on faith in the Soviet Union.[203] No criticism of the Soviet Union could be contemplated because of its centrality to their worldview. That was why, Lash explained, young people were willing to overlook the Soviet invasion of Finland. Even though he understood the logic, he said he found it naïve at best and dangerous at worst. The Soviet Union was not above reproach and criticism, and, he maintained, "a faith which refuses to examine the objective evidence which calls it into question, will crash all the harder later on."[204]

Much attention has been given to the changes in communist positions, especially in the period between the signing of the Nazi-Soviet Pact in August 1939 and the German invasion of the Soviet Union in June 1941, to prove that communists in America were following the official communist line as determined in Moscow. While that played a part in determining official Communist Party policy, and to a lesser degree, YCL policy, it does not *ipso facto* mean that was what determined ASU or AYC policy because these organizations were not arms of the Communist Party machinery. For the communists in those organizations to influence policy, they had to convince non-communist members to go along with their analysis of the current situation and their prescriptions for what should be done. That was much more easily accomplished when the socialists withdrew from the popular front organizations, which was already underway in 1938—before the Nazi-Soviet Pact.[205]

All of the major youth groups changed their peace policy positions at some point during the Depression decade; the fulcrum on which that decision to change rested was based on each group's understanding of the best way to avoid war. For Yipsels, it was keeping out of collective security agreements because alliances with the imperialists damaged the possibility of class revolution; for liberals, it was joining collective security agreements, but only after war in Europe broke out and America's involvement seemed inevitable; for communists, it was joining collective security agreements, but only after the Soviet Union was invaded and the last best hope for avoiding global conflagration was extinguished. Radical youth who decided to support the war did so on the basis of when they believed not doing so would damage, rather than help, their quest for

freedom, equality, and democracy. For some, that decision came about
when Poland was invaded; for others, it was when the Soviet Union was
invaded.

Socialists, like communists and liberals, determined their policy positions based, in part, on ideology, but also as a reaction to the current
political situation. The most rigid ideologues who insisted that ideological
purity take precedence over practical considerations for advancing their
program—like the Trotskyists—were sidelined in the youth organizations. Those who had learned to compromise to advance their position
were able to convince others to support their agenda. This made them
able politicians, not evil Machiavellians intent on making the United
States a satellite of the Soviet Union. Communists—like the socialists
and liberals—sincerely hoped for democracy, equality, and freedom. They
worked with—not against—other young activists to create the vision
they saw for America. As historian of the student movement Ralph Brax
cautioned, "one should resist the temptation of assuming that anything
that corresponds to Soviet policy automatically contradicts the views and
interests of other people on the left."[206] Socialists, however, decided that
they could no longer work with the communists and thus abandoned the
organizations dedicated to creating the society they sought.

The socialists pulled out of the popular front by 1939; their liberal-
minded colleagues—the Lash bloc—pulled out by the spring of 1941.
Reflecting on this development, Lash later wrote that the "tragedy was
that the leftward movement of young people had no way of expressing
itself once the socialist Party moved toward sectarianism."[207] That splin-
tering led to the demise of the American Student Union, which held its
last convention in December 1941 and the American Youth Congress,
which held its last convention in July 1941, though it continued a quasi-
existence through the first half of 1942.[208] Organized youth failed to
maintain the popular front and had failed to achieve their primary objective: peace. And as the organizations they created dissolved, activist youth
lost not just their voice, but their vehicle for expressing their vision of
and for America.

Conclusion

During the Cold War many aspersions were cast upon young, left-leaning activists of the 1930s, often made by former young radicals themselves. That should not eclipse what they believed, the policies they pursued, and the goals they sought at the time. Looking at the 1930s through the perspective of activist youth allows for a greater understanding of the decade as a time of uncertainty when anything seemed possible: the end of capitalism in America, the rejuvenation of free enterprise; the spread of fascism, true political freedom; world peace, world war. During the decade, no one knew how it would all play out. Youth wanted to make sure they had a voice in the ultimate outcome because they believed their perspective was valid and because they wanted to make America live up to its promises. The 1930s, they therefore believed, was the opportune time to remake America politically, economically, and socially.

It was activist, left-leaning youth who first recognized the potential for drastic change in America, seizing upon the desperation of Harlan County, Kentucky, coalminers in 1932 as the personification of economic deprivation. Rallying to the coalminers' cause, young idealistic college students set out from New York City only to be met by the cruel reality of coal country's brand of law and order. Regrouping, the organizers of the trek used the experience to establish youth-led organizations on the college campus, the most notable of which was the National Student League (NSL). The NSL and other student groups, like the Student League for Industrial Democracy (SLID), found fertile ground on academic quadrangles, especially those located in New York City, where they hoped to plant their roots for radical change. Their concern for Reed Harris's academic freedom at Columbia University, emerging just one week after the Harlan County trip, found a ready audience among students chafing against the authoritarianism of college administrators. Their demands for more economic opportunity were thus coupled with demands for more freedom and democracy.

Extrapolating from their personal experiences, supporters of the left-leaning groups began to expand their vision of what America should be from the college campus to the larger society and from New York City to the nation, all the while catalyzing a confluence between the local and national situations. The plight of the Scottsboro Boys highlighted the discrepancy between professed loyalty to freedom and equality and the reality of racism in America, unmasking the kind of hypocrisy they would not tolerate. In agitating for the Scottsboro Boys' acquittal, they were fighting once again against the larger issues of discrimination and prejudice. This case allowed them a national platform upon which to base their calls for freedom, democracy, and equality. Yet the tenor of those calls was also determined by more immediate cases of prejudice, like those suffered by CCNY track star Welford Wilson. This constant pull between local and national events kept young activists' ideology grounded upon pragmatic solutions at the same time they would brook no compromise with what they believed to be not only morally righteous positions, but those founded upon quintessential American ideals.

In order to bring about the changes they desired, youth activists realized they would have to become political players and the only way to do that was to create larger, inclusive youth organizations to act as political lobbying groups. Such a conclusion coincided with the rising menace of fascism abroad, prompting youth to come together in forming popular front organizations where liberals, socialists, and communists worked together to promote peace as a way to ensure political, economic, and social freedom and equality. The resulting American Youth Congress, created in 1934, and American Student Union, established in 1935, were youth-led organizations that immediately began pressuring the New Deal Administration to do more for young people, basing their argument upon the premise that doing so would allow America to live up to its promise. It is true that membership in youth organizations represented only a small fraction of young people in the United States, but, as Joseph Lash argued, this is not a fair gauge of their influence because they became a motivating force in a wider coalition that recognized the great dangers confronting the country and the world.[1] The synergistic outcome for activist youth was a fully formed worldview that sought to safeguard freedom, equality, democracy, and peace.

Pressuring Congress for more appropriations for the National Youth Administration, making sure that agency provided equal opportunity for all young people through a democratic organizational structure, and lobbying for a more inclusive American Youth Act brought youth leaders into the American political mainstream. Yet at the same time, the AYC and ASU were actively promoting peace through radical methods, like the Student Strike Against War. The Janus-faced nature of working with the Administration on domestic policy, but maintaining a particularly critical stance toward its foreign policy meant the youth organizations acted independently in what they believed to be youth's best interest, but it also meant that the relationship between the organizations and the Roosevelt Administration remained fraught with tension.

That tension heightened during the Spanish Civil War. Seen by youth as a portent of the world war to come, they actively protested the war itself; but, at the same time, this was a war against fascism fought by the beleaguered Loyalists who, like young Americans themselves, were fighting for freedom, democracy, and equality. The Spanish Civil War, then, catalyzed the breakup of the youth's popular front organizations as young people split ranks based on which ideal they prioritized as a necessary precondition for the others: peace on the one hand and freedom, democracy, and equality on the other. The policy impasse between the advocates of collective security and the advocates of pacifism led many socialists to withdraw from the ASU and AYC. With unity broken, the weakened organizations were left to face a world quickly dissolving into war.

In 1939, the dimensions of the fascist threat to world peace were reconfigured around the Nazi-Soviet Pact and the subsequent German invasion of Poland and Soviet invasion of Finland. The difficulties in creating peace increased exponentially. As the war in Europe gained momentum with the Nazi invasion of Scandinavia and the low countries in April–May 1940, and the fall of France in June 1940, it exacerbated tensions within the youth organizations. Many withdrew from the ASU and AYC because of what they perceived as the imminence of a war from which the United States could not remain aloof. Continuing to pursue peace seemed futile. For others, there had never been a more auspicious time for dedication to peace. Once the Soviet Union—what many believed to be the last hold out for peace—was invaded, the possibility of avoiding world war crumbled, as did the youth organizations themselves.

At the same time they were confronted with the fascist threat abroad, youth activists were attacked by the red-baiting House Un-American Activities Committee, chaired by Texas Democratic Congressman Martin Dies. Youth organizations' reputations as communist safe havens, coupled with those organizations' criticism of FDR's foreign policy, caused a breach in the relationship between the young activists and New Deal administrators that severely damaged their ability to affect policy. As some youth leaders became increasingly supportive of American interventionism, other youth leaders found themselves advocating a program favored by isolationists. Liberals withdrew from the ASU and AYC in order to support America's burgeoning war effort, further fragmenting the organizations that quickly dissolved after December 7, 1941.

The demise of the youth organizations does not dispel their significance. The vision of and for America those organizations advocated expressed the desire of a generation of young people ravaged by Depression to create a better world—one in which America lived up to its ideals of freedom, democracy, and equality. Even as some former youth leaders went to work for the FDR Administration[2] and the FDR Administration turned its back on youth programs,[3] youth's vision lived on.[4]

Some former youth leaders, such as Joseph Lash and James Wechsler, went to war.[5] That war, Eric Sevareid said, "was for us not merely a crisis in our physical lives but an intellectual and moral purgatory."[6] And although "it would be possible, no doubt, and in an accepted tradition, to write of this university period with the humorous superiority of tolerant adulthood, to regard it as a natural manifestation of naïve idealism of youth," Sevareid explained, "it would be easier, but it would be an error of judgment" because "we had a definite effect upon our times."[7]

In like fashion, the times affected those young people. The events of the Depression decade spurred youth to action. It was their understanding of what each event meant for freedom, democracy, equality, and peace that determined their actions. It was not just their actions, then, but the understanding that girded them that helps bring to light the problems and possibilities of the 1930s.

Notes

Abbreviations Used in the Notes

AW   Aubrey Williams Papers, Franklin D. Roosevelt Library, Hyde Park, New York

CCNY   Cohen Library, City College of New York Archives

CT   Charles Taussig Papers, Franklin D. Roosevelt Library, Hyde Park, New York

DP   Democratic Party, Women's Division Papers, National Committee Papers, Franklin D. Roosevelt Library, Hyde Park, New York

ER   Eleanor Roosevelt Papers, Franklin D. Roosevelt Library, Hyde Park, New York

ERPC   Eleanor Roosevelt Pamphlet Collection, Franklin D. Roosevelt Library, Hyde Park, New York

JM   Jack McMichael Papers, Tamiment Library, New York University

JPL   Joseph P. Lash Papers, Franklin D. Roosevelt Library, Hyde Park, New York

JW   James Wechsler Papers, University Archives / Columbiana Library, Columbia University

PC   Tamiment Library Pamphlet Collection, New York University

POF   President's Official File, Franklin D. Roosevelt Library, Hyde Park, New York

PPF	President's Personal File, Franklin D. Roosevelt Library, Hyde Park, New York
RH	Reed Harris Papers, University Archives / Columbiana Library, Columbia University
YPSL	Young People's Socialist League Papers, Tamiment Library, New York University

Introduction

1. Paula Fass, *The Damned and the Beautiful: American Youth in the 1920s* (New York: Oxford University Press, 1977), 346.

2. Ibid., 329.

3. The National Student Federation of America was established in 1925, marking a significant moment when a small subset of youth came together. The *New Student*, published by the National Student Forum, even hoped to spark a genuine youth movement; however, even a strong conviction to be informed and involved in larger matters quickly evaporated, Fass argues, as "the *New Student*'s political push quickly relapsed into the fashionable emphasis on cultural philistinism and the issue of freedom of expression." Fass, *The Damned and the Beautiful*, 337.

4. Joseph Lash, "Two Lives" (Unpublished Autobiography, Chapter 3), 11, JPL Box 78.

5. Ibid.; James Wechsler, *Revolt on the Campus* (Seattle: University of Washington Press, 1973). Paula Fass talks about an "ethos of hostility toward the faculty" in the 1920s, which helped college students make the campus their own, which plays a part in the youth of the 1930s operating outside parameters controlled by adults. Fass, *The Beautiful and the Damned*, 180.

6. See Fass, *The Damned and the Beautiful*, Chapter 8. In the 1920s, activism tended to be reactive whereas in the 1930s it started out as reactive and quickly transformed into proactive efforts to shape future policies and the larger social, political, and economic systems.

7. Beverly Beyette, "NOW Chief Molly Yard Was 'Born a Feminist,'" *Los Angeles Times*, July 21, 1987, http://articles.latimes.com/1987-07-21/news/vw-5159_1_molly-yard.

8. See Lash, "Two Lives" (Unpublished Autobiography, "A Trip to Europe"), 26, JPL Box 78

9. Richard Pells, *Radical Visions and American Dreams: Culture and Social Thought in the Depression Years* (New York: Harper & Row, 1973), 131.

10. Lash, "Two Lives" (Unpublished Autobiography), JPL Box 78.

11. William Hinckley to Gardiner Jackson, February 13, 1937, Gardner Jackson Papers, Box 5; at a National Council meeting on January 16, 1936, 12 of 14 attendees were based in New York. Only Waldo McNutt and Molly Yard were not. National Council Meeting Minutes, January 15, 1936, JPL, Box 29.

12. Report of the 6th American Youth Congress, JPL, Box 23.

13. Joseph Lash to FDR, July 2, 1936, POF 58.

14. Robert Cohen, *When the Old Left Was Young: Student Radicals and America's First Mass Student Movement, 1929–1941* (New York: Oxford University Press, 1993), xviii.

1. The Effects of the Crash: The Youth Problem from New York City to Harlan County, Kentucky, and Back Again

1. April 4, 1935, POF 58.

2. James Wechsler, *Revolt on the Campus* (Seattle: University of Washington Press, 1935), 101.

3. Hal Draper, "The Student Movement of the Thirties: A Political History," *As We Saw the Thirties: Essays on Social and Political Movements of a Decade* (Chicago: University of Illinois Press, 1967), 166; Wechsler, *Revolt on the Campus*, 91–108; Michael Henry Miller, "The American Student Movement," 1931–1941: A Historical Analysis" (PhD diss., Florida State University, 1981), 28–30. Significantly, Miller points out that the 80 students who participated in the trip "claimed to be communists." Miller, "The American Student Movement," 95–96.

4. The expulsion, protests, and ultimate outcome of this incident is fully discussed in Chapter 2.

5. Wechsler, *Revolt on the Campus*, 99.

6. Rob F. Hall, "Kentucky Makes Radicals," *Student Review*, May 1932, JPL Box 29.

7. Ibid.

8. See, for example, *The Campus*, December 14, 1931, CCNY.

9. *The Campus*, March 4, 1932, CCNY. Included among the 175 professors who signed the protest were Rex Tugwell, Franz Boas, and Carliss Lamont of Columbia University.

10. *The Campus*, December 4, 1931, CCNY.

11. Hall, "Kentucky Makes Radicals," JPL Box 29.

12. Ibid.

13. *The Campus*, September 28, 1931, CCNY.

14. Wechsler, *Revolt on the Campus*, 99.

15. Ralph Brax, *The First Student Movement* (Port Washington, N.Y.: Kennikat Press, 1981), 21.

16. Wechsler, *Revolt on the Campus*, 101.

17. Ibid.

18. Hall, "Kentucky Makes Radicals," JPL Box 29.

19. Ibid.

20. Senator Edward Costigan (D-CO) chaired a subcommittee of the Committee on Manufacturers that later conducted official hearings on the situation in Harlan County.

21. Hall, "Kentucky Makes Radicals," JPL Box 29.
22. Ibid.
23. Wechsler, *Revolt on the Campus*, 107.
24. Hall, "Kentucky Makes Radicals," JPL Box 29.
25. Ibid.
26. Ibid.
27. Joseph P. Lash, "Autobiography," JPL Box 27.
28. Brax, *The First Student Movement*, 22.
29. Brax, *The First Student Movement*, 14.
30. Michael B. Smith, "Autobiography," JPL Box 21.
31. Ibid.
32. Ibid.
33. Norman Ball, "Autobiography," JPL Box 21.
34. Leslie Gould, *American Youth Today* (New York: Random House, 1940), 165.
35. Student League for Industrial Democracy Leaflet, 1933, YPSL, Box 1.
36. Eleanor Roosevelt message concerning youth, n.d. ER File 3033; Betty Lindley and Ernest K. Lindley, *A New Deal for Youth: The Story of the National Youth Administration* (New York: Viking Press, 1938), 7.
37. *Youngville, USA* (New York: American Youth Congress, 1937), 4–5, DP Box 275.
38. Eleanor Roosevelt, untitled, 1936, ER File 3033.
39. Lindley and Lindley, *A New Deal for Youth*, 8. There are no official unemployment statistics for young people. The 1930 census did not break down unemployment by age. According to the 1940 U.S. census, of the people aged 18–24, 54.4 percent white women, 55.1 percent nonwhite women, 16.9 percent white men, and 11.6 percent nonwhite men were unemployed. Retrieved from http://www2.census.gov/prod2/decennial/documents/41236810p1_TOC.pdf.
40. Lindley and Lindley, 8.
41. Ibid., 7.
42. Jacques, "Society's Crime," *Voice of Youth*, March 1936, CT Box 89.
43. Ibid.; YPSL Convention Handbook, 1939, YPSL, Box 1.
44. James Wechsler, *The Age of Suspicion* (New York: Donald I. Fine, Inc., 1953), 36.
45. Draper, "The Student Movement of the Thirties," 155.
46. Joseph Lash and James Wechsler, *War Our Heritage* (New York: International Publishers, 1936), 50.
47. Wechsler, *The Age of Suspicion*, 36.
48. Ibid.
49. Ralph S. Brax, *The First Student Movement*, 105.
50. Robert Morss Lovett, Introduction to Wechsler, *Revolt on the Campus*, xiii.
51. Brax, *The First Student Movement*, 62.

52. *Youngville, USA*, 7.

53. W. D. Coley to Franklin D. Roosevelt, October 5, 1935, POF 58.

54. *Youngville, USA*, 8; American Youth Commission of the American Council on Education, "Preliminary Inquiry on What is the Youth Problem?" January 1936, Vertical File: Youth, FDR Library.

55. Brax, *The First Student Movement*, 62.

56. "Dormitories Affected by Depression," *Columbia Spectator*, February 17, 1931, Microform and Periodicals Collection, Columbia University.

57. Robert Cohen, *When the Old Left Was Young: Student Radicals and America's First Mass Student Movement, 1929–1941* (New York: Oxford University Press, 1993), 15.

58. Eleanor Roosevelt, *The Autobiography of Eleanor Roosevelt* (New York: Harper & Brothers, 1961), 208. Joseph Lash pointed out that Eleanor Roosevelt's concern was the exception as young people and their needs were largely ignored. See Joseph Lash, "Two Lives" (Notes for Unpublished Autobiography), JPL Box 33.

59. See Joseph Lash, *Eleanor and Franklin: The Story of their Relationship, Based on Eleanor Roosevelt's Private Papers* (New York: Norton, 1971) and Blanche Wiesen Cook, *Eleanor Roosevelt, Volume I: 1884–1933* (New York: Viking, 1992).

60. Eleanor Roosevelt, *It Seems to Me* (New York: Norton, 1949), 133.

61. Eleanor Roosevelt, "Kindergarten Age," radio broadcast from Warm Springs, Ga., November 25, 1934, ER File 3026.

62. Eleanor Roosevelt, untitled, *Future*, May 1944, ER File 3050.

63. *Youngville, USA*, 16.

64. Eleanor Roosevelt, "Young People and Unemployment," *Columbia Syndicate*, May 3, 1935, ER File 3031.

65. Labor leaders tended to see young people as a competitive labor force, which drove down wages and represented a potential labor force replacement for unemployed adult workers. It was only later in the decade, after much effort exerted by youth leaders, that an alliance of sorts was worked out between youth organizations and labor leaders.

66. Eleanor Roosevelt, "Questions on Topics Affecting Education," *Progressive Education*, October 1937, ER File 3034.

67. Eleanor Roosevelt, "What Do We Want as an Education for Our Girls," *Woman's Journal*, November 1947, ER File 3053.

68. *Youngville, USA*, 11.

69. See Lewis L. Lorwin, *Youth Work Programs: Problems and Policies* (Washington, D.C.: American Council on Education, 1941), Chapter 2, and Lindley and Lindley, foreword by Charles Taussig.

70. Harry L. Hopkins to Franklin D. Roosevelt, May 7, 1935, POF 58b.

71. Draper, "The Student Movement of the Thirties," 156.

72. Charles Taussig, "Youth Comes of Age," March 2, 1936, CT Box 83.

73. YPSL Convention Handbook, 1939, YPSL, Box 1.

74. Brax, *The First Student Movement*, 61.

75. Wechsler, *The Age of Suspicion*, 58.

76. Ibid., 62.

77. Cohen, *When the Old Left Was Young*, n.64, 355.

78. Howard Maclay, "Radicalism in the Thirties: The Trotskyist View" in *As We Saw the Thirties*, 8.

79. See, for example, Cohen, *When the Old Left Was Young*, 40–41.

80. Cohen, *When the Old Left Was Young*, 318.

81. George P. Rawick, "The New Deal and Youth: The Civilian Conservation Corps, the National Youth Administration, and the American Youth Congress" (PhD. Diss., University of Wisconsin, 1957), 296.

82. Statement adopted by the Executive Committee of YPSL of Great New York, November 21, 1934, YPSL, Box 1.

83. Student League for Industrial Democracy leaflet, 1933, YPSL, Box 1.

84. Wechsler, *Revolt on the Campus*, x.

85. Ibid., vii.

86. Fass, *The Damned and the Beautiful*, 338.

87. Altbach, *Student Politics in America*, 45.

88. To confuse matters more, the NSL claimed the LID as its parent organization, not the CPUSA. In any event, the NSL was established as a rival of SLID, which it saw as too timid and not sufficiently Socialist. See Miller, "The American Student Movement of the Depression," 19, 57; Draper, "The Student Movement of the Thirties," in *As We Saw the Thirties*, 165; Wechsler, *Revolt on the Campus*, 94.

89. See Earl Browder, "The American Communist Party in the Thirties," in *As We Saw the Thirties.*

90. YCL leaflet, n.d., JPL Box 24.

91. Wechsler, *The Age of Suspicion*, 80.

92. Historians of the youth movement have tended to take Wechsler's words uttered in 1953 at face value rather than place them in the context of that time. That Wechsler believed the negative things he said about communism in 1953 is undoubted; yet, that does not negate the opposite—positive—view he had of communism in the 1930s and its validity for understanding youth's perspective of the Depression decade. See Wechsler, *The Age of Suspicion.*

93. This was a decision Wechsler came to after meeting with the *Nation* managing editor Bob Bendiner, who encouraged him to break with the YCL in order to have the freedom to voice his own opinion in the editorial column he would subsequently begin writing for the *Nation*. Wechsler, *The Age of Suspicion*, 128.

94. Wechsler, *The Age of Suspicion*, 124.

95. Cohen, *When the Old Left Was Young*, 36.

96. Draper, "The Student Movement of the Thirties" in *As We Saw the Thirties*, 166.

97. Gould, *American Youth Today*, 47–48.

98. *Youngville, USA*, 6–7.

99. Eagan, *Class, Culture and the Classroom*, 21.

100. Maxine Davis, *The Lost Generation: A Portrait of American Youth Today* (New York: Macmillan, 1936), 251–56.

101. The call for more control was aimed at the federal government, not at parents. This both stemmed from, and contributed to, what many saw as a breakdown of the American family that only intensified the seriousness of the "youth problem."

102. Edward Browning, Jr. to Franklin D. Roosevelt, 1934, POF 58.

103. Charles Taussig, "Youth Comes of Age," March 2, 1936, CT Box 83.

104. Wechsler *Revolt on the Campus*, 39–40.

105. Gould, *American Youth Today*, 51–52.

106. Altbach, *Student Politics in America*, 79.

2. The Reed Harris Affair: Youth Claim Their Rights and Freedoms at Columbia University and Beyond

1. James Wechsler, *Revolt on the Campus* (Seattle: University of Washington Press, 1935), 51.

2. Paula Fass, *The Damned and the Beautiful: American Youth in the 1920s* (New York: Oxford University Press, 1977), 328–29.

3. Robert Cohen, *When the Old Left Was Young: Student Radicals and America's First Mass Student Movement, 1929–1941* (New York: Oxford University Press, 1993), 55–56. Also, see Paula Fass, *The Damned and the Beautiful*.

4. James Wechsler, *The Age of Suspicion* (New York: Donald I. Fine, Inc., 1953), 23.

5. "Columbia University Strikes," *The Student Review: Official Organ, National Student League*, May 1932, JPL Box 29. Harris is representative of 1930s college editors, many of whom professed a radical perspective. This is in stark contrast to the 1920s when football was, along with fraternity activities, the center of campus social life, which editors did not consider criticizing. ROTC was often criticized on college campuses in the 1920s, but not so much because it was a military preparedness program, but because it was compulsory, and thus infringed on students' freedom of choice. Neither editors nor the wider student body in the 1920s called for eradication of the program. See Fass, *The Damned and the Beautiful*.

6. Ibid.

7. Ibid.

8. "Dining Service Directors Declared Incompetent," *Columbia Spectator*, March 30, 1931, Microform and Periodicals Collection, Columbia University.

9. "Columbia University Strikes," *The Student Review*, May 1932, JPL Box 29.

10. Reed Harris to Dean Hawkes, April 1, 1932, RH Box 378.

11. This was a perennial issue at Columbia. Four years later, the *Spectator* reported that students had contracted food poisoning after eating there.

See "Students Taken Sick After Dining Hall Meal; Administration Assailed,"
February 12, 1936, *Columbia Spectator*, Microform and Periodicals Collection,
Columbia University.

12. Reed Harris to Dean Hawkes, April 1, 1932, RH Box 378.

13. Ibid.

14. *Columbia Spectator*, September 28, 1961, RH Box 130, Folder 13.

15. Reed Harris to Dean Hawkes, April 1, 1932, RH Box 378.

16. Nicholas Murray Butler to John G. Saxe, April 9, 1932, RH Box 378.

17. Nicholas Murray Butler, "Talks with Undergraduates: President Butler
Writes on the Distinction Between Government and Liberty in an Article
Written for Spectator," *Columbia Spectator*, March 23, 1931, Microform and
Periodicals Collection, Columbia University.

18. See Fass, *The Damned and the Beautiful*.

19. Wechsler, *Revolt on the Campus*, 74.

20. Ibid, 67.

21. Ron Blum, *Columbia Magazine*, November 1983, JW Box 328; James
Wechsler, *Revolt on the Campus* (Seattle: University of Washington Press, 1935),
65, 68.

22. "End Trustee Domination," *The Student Outlook: The Intercollegiate Socialist Review*, May 1934, JPL Box 30.

23. Reed Harris, "Campus Tammany," *The Student Outlook*, May 1934, JPL
Box 30; "Harris Attacks Secret Societies, Calls Nacoms Campus Tammany,"
Columbia Spectator, May 1, 1933, Microform and Periodicals Collections, Co-
lumbia University.

24. "Columbia University Strikes," *The Student Review*, May 1932, JPL Box 29.

25. Ibid.

26. Ibid.

27. John G. Saxe to Nicholas Murray Butler, April 12, 1932, RH Box 378.

28. "Columbia University Strikes," *The Student Review*, May 1932, JPL Box 29.

29. Wechsler, *Revolt on the Campus*, 117.

30. John G. Saxe to Nicholas Murray Butler, April 14, 1932, RH Box 378.

31. Wechsler became a member of the Young Communist League just
before graduating from Columbia in 1934; he left the organization in 1937.

32. Wechsler, *Revolt on the Campus*, 410.

33. Cohen, *When the Old Left Was Young*, 63; "Columbia University Strikes,"
The Student Review, May 1932, JPL Box 29.

34. See pictures in *Evening Graphic*, April 6, 1932, RH Box 130.

35. Dr. Adam Leroy Jones to Nicholas Murray Butler, April 12, 1932, RH
Box 378.

36. *Ibid*.

37. "Free Speech at Columbia," *The Nation* 20 April 1932, RH Box 130.

38. Ibid.

39. Wechsler, *Revolt on the Campus*, 118.

40. Ibid., 120; Philip G. Altbach, *Student Politics in America: A Historical Analysis* (New York: McGraw-Hill Book Company, 1974), 60.

41. Reed Harris, "University Disease" in *The Student Review*, October 1932, RH Box 130. Columbia University, however, did not expel any future editors. Instead, those like Wechsler, who pushed too hard against the administration, would find their paper suspended from publication for days at a time. See JW Box 328.

42. Fass, *The Damned and the Beautiful*, 339–42.

43. *The Campus*, October 20, 1930, CCNY Archives.

44. Robinson was a 1904 graduate of CCNY, former faculty member, and, before his appointment as president of the college in 1927, Dean of the Business School.

45. Joseph Lash, "Two Lives" (Unpublished Autobiography, Chapter 3), 5, JPL Box 78; Joseph Lash, "Meet the Stuffed Shirt," *Revolt: The Intercollegiate Socialist Review*, December 1932, JPL Box 30.

46. *The Campus*, December 3, 1930, CCNY.

47. *The Campus*, January 7, 1930 and January 9, 1930, CCNY.

48. Wechsler, *Revolt on the Campus*, 382.

49. *The Campus*, February 25, 1931, CCNY.

50. Ibid.

51. *The Campus*, March 13, 1931, CCNY.

52. *The Campus*, April 6, 1932, CCNY.

53. *The Campus*, April 8, 1932, CCNY.

54. Ibid.

55. *The Campus*, October 7, 1932, CCNY.

56. Ralph S. Brax, *The First Student Movement: Student Activism in the United States During the 1930s* (Port Washington, N.Y.: Kennikat Press, 1981), 24–25.

57. *The Campus*, October 28, 1932, CCNY.

58. *The Campus*, February 19, 1933; 21 February 1933; and 10 March 1933 CCNY.

59. *The Campus*, December 5, 1932, CCNY.

60. *The Campus*, December 9, 1932, CCNY.

61. Ibid.

62. Cohen, *When the Old Left Was Young*, 108.

63. Wechsler, *Revolt on the Campus*, 385.

64. Ibid., 386.

65. "Henderson Appointment Ended; Conflicting Explanations Issued," *Columbia Spectator*, April 5, 1933, Microform and Periodicals Collection, Columbia University.

66. Wechsler, *Revolt on the Campus*, 422.

67. See Wechsler, *Revolt on the Campus*, 422, and Brax, *The First Student Movement*, 25.

68. Reed Harris, n.d., Demonstrations Collection Box 124, University Archives/Columbiana Library.

69. "1,000 Engage in Near Riot at Henderson Mass Protest," *Columbia Spectator,* May 11, 1933, Microform and Periodicals Collection, Columbia University; Brax, *The First Student Movement*, 26.

70. *The Campus*, May 24, 1932, CCNY.

71. See James Wechsler, *Revolt on the Campus*; Celeste Strack, "Expulsions at California," *The Student Review*, February 1934, JPL Box 29; Brax, *The First Student Movement*, 46.

72. James Wechsler, "Editors and Cocktails," *The Student Review*, February 1934, JPL Box 29.

73. Cohen, *When the Old Left Was Young*, xv. Also see Chapter 5 where Cohen discusses this in more depth and the Appendix where Cohen lists examples of FBI records kept on student activists.

74. "Senate Passes Student Oath Bill Ignoring Recent Vassar Opposition," *State College News*, March 2, 1935, retrieved on July 15, 2009 from www.library .albany.edu/speccoll/findaids/issues/1935_03_08.pdf.

75. "50 Delegates Depart for Albany," *Columbia Spectator*, March 7, 1935; "Student Groups Plan to Oppose Nunan Measure," March 2, 1936, Microform and Periodicals Collection, Columbia University.

76. "Fight the Nunan Bill," *The Campus*, February 27, 1935, CCNY.

77. "Fascist Forces," *The Campus*, March 5, 1935, CCNY.

78. Robert Gerald Spivack, "Autobiography," n.d., JPL Box 21.

79. Ibid.

80. E. Ray Scott to Franklin D. Roosevelt, n.d., POF 58b.

81. Eleanor Roosevelt, "Dear Mrs. Roosevelt," *Democratic Digest*, August–September 1939, ER Box 3036.

82. Ibid.

83. Bill Hagen to Franklin D. Roosevelt, April 17, 1939, POF 58.

84. "End Trustee Domination," *The Student Outlook*, May 1934, JPL Box 30.

85. Robert Gerald Spivack, "Autobiography," n.d., JPL Box 21.

86. Altbach, *Student Politics in America*, 43.

87. Ibid., 73.

88. Ibid., 73–74.

89. Michael Henry Miller, "The American Student Movement of the Depression, 1931–1941: A Historical Analysis" (PhD diss., Florida State University, 1981), 57.

90. Brax, *The First Student Movement*, 13.

91. "Thomas Leading in Poll After First Day's Vote," *Columbia Spectator*, October 18, 1932, Microform and Periodicals Collection, Columbia University.

92. Wechsler, *The Age of Suspicion*, 40.

93. Cohen, *When the Old Left Was Young*, 75.

94. Ibid., 78.

95. Wechsler, *Revolt on the Campus*, 454.

96. Wechsler, *The Age of Suspicion*, 29.

97. James Wechsler, in particular, wrote on several occasions that his youth-

ful radicalism caused him much discomfort later on, saying in his introduction to the 1973 edition of *Revolt on the Campus* that he had been "dogmatic" and "self-righteously wrong in my assessment of some wholly decent men who happened to differ with the conventional radical wisdom of that time." See Wechsler, *Revolt on the Campus*, ix and introduction for the booklet commemorating the 25th reunion of Columbia University Class of 1935, May 1960, JW Box 328.

98. Wechsler, *Revolt on the Campus*, vii.

99. Altbach, *Student Politics in America*, 50.

100. Miller, "The American Student Movement of the Depression," 166–67.

101. Altbach, *Student Politics in America*, 85.

102. Ibid., 40.

103. Ibid., 83.

104. "Student Groups Plan to Oppose Nunan Measure," *Columbia Spectator*, March 2, 1936, Microform and Periodicals Collection, Columbia University.

105. Miller, "The American Student Movement of the Depression," 69–72.

106. Altbach, *Student Politics in America*, 102. The close relationship between the youth organization's leaders and the FDR Administration will be fully discussed in Part II, particularly in Chapter 5.

107. *The Campus*, May 24, 1935, CCNY.

108. "Committee Proves Robinson Charges," *The Campus*, January 14, 1935, CCNY.

109. "Robinson Under Fire," *The Campus*, January 6, 1936, CCNY.

110. *The Campus*, October 16, 1936, CCNY.

111. *The Campus*, December 16, 1938, CCNY.

112. *Columbia Spectator*, November 12, 1935, RH Box 130.

113. *Columbia Spectator*, September 28, 1961, RH Box 130.

114. Wechsler, *The Age of Suspicion*, 39–40.

115. Leo M. Friedman, "Reviewer Calls Harris' Book Biting Commentary on Colleges," *Columbia Spectator*, September 20, 1932, Microform and Periodicals Collection, Columbia University.

116. Ron Blum, *Columbia Magazine*, November 1983, JW Box 328. James Wechsler insisted on an investigation by a group of eleven editors, dubbed the Freedom Committee, to determine if McCarthy had violated his freedom of the press and then brought a libel suit for $1.525 million against Walter Winchell who, relying on the McCarthy hearings, repeated—in print—McCarthy's charge that Wechsler was pro-communism.

117. Wechsler's experience under fire during the McCarthy hearings inspired him to write *The Age of Suspicion*.

118. "Outdoor Meetings Banned at Columbia," *The New York Times*, October 4, 1932, Demonstrations Collection, Box 124 University Archives / Columbiana Library.

119. Demonstrations Collection, Box 124 University Archives / Columbiana Library.

120. "Complete Text of Statement on Dining Hall Investigation," *Columbia Spectator*, September 30, 1932, Microform and Periodicals Collection, Columbia University.

121. *Columbia Spectator*, September 30, 1932, Microform and Periodicals Collection, Columbia University.

122. "Butler Denies Outside Radicals Freedom of Speech on Campus," *Columbia Spectator*, February 25, 1938; "Opposition to Heidelberg Festival Mounts on Campus as University Accepts Nazi Bid to Send Delegate," *Columbia Spectator*, March 2, 1936, Microform and Periodicals Collection, Columbia University.

123. Editorial, *Columbia Spectator*, 1982, RH Box 130.

124. Leo M. Friedman, "Reviewer Calls Harris' Book Biting Commentary on Colleges," *Columbia Spectator*, Microform and Periodicals Collection, Columbia University.

3. The Scottsboro Boys: Demands for Equality from the Deep South to New York City

1. James A. Miller has argued that the Scottsboro case defined American racial discourse from the first trial in 1931 through the 2007 Duke University rape case. See James A. Miller, *Remembering Scottsboro: The Legacy of an Infamous Trial* (Princeton: Princeton University Press, 2009). It was because of the attention given to this case by the International Labor Defense—the legal arm of the Communist Party—that the Scottsboro Boys' names became familiar throughout the nation and remained a lead story throughout the decade. Legal historian Mark Weiner's analysis explores the connections between the Communist Party and black civil rights. See Mark Weiner, *Black Trials: Citizenship from the Beginnings of Slavery to the End of Caste* (New York: Vintage Books, 2004), 256, 247.

2. "They Shall Not Die!" *The Student Review: Official Organ, National Student League*, October 1932, RH Box 130. There is some question about the validity of the NSL's remarks. Dan Carter and Adam Fairclough confirm that a brass band was, indeed, present and that a local Ford dealer arranged musical entertainment for the crowd of thousands. See Dan Carter, *Scottsboro: A Tragedy of the American South* (Baton Rouge: Louisiana State University Press, 1979), 40–41; Adam Fairclough, *Better Day Coming: Blacks and Equality, 1890–2000* (New York: Penguin, 2002), 135. James Acker confirms that the band played "There'll be a Hot Time in the Old Town Tonight." See James Acker, *Scottsboro and Its Legacy: The Cases That Challenged American Legal and Social Justice* (New York: Praeger, 2007), 26. While the NSL may have exaggerated some in its depiction of this "show trial," its description of the situation in Alabama is corroborated by historians who refer to the event as a "legal lynching." The first trial was presided over by Judge Alfred E. Hawkins. He was determined, according to Weiner, "that the trials be more than kangaroo proceedings, though perhaps

not much more; between his own prejudices, his poor judicial handling of the case, and his apparent desire to see the defendants convicted—as well as the extraordinary popular pressures aimed at discouraging potential defense attorneys." In his assessment, the first trial was nothing more than a legal charade and the self-congratulatory attitude of those who celebrated the fact that the boys had not been lynched rang hollow. Weiner, *Black Trials,* 253. James Goodman has pointed out that even those southerners who opposed lynching did not necessarily do so from an appreciation of blacks' right to due process or, more fundamentally, their right to life, but, rather, from their assessment that lynching generated more violence and lawlessness than it deterred. James Goodman, *Stories of Scottsboro* (New York: Vintage Books, 1994), 16. While most white Alabamans were proud that the law had been allowed to take its course, many white liberals agreed to some degree with the Communist Party's explanation that "the façade of judge and jury" had replaced "the rope as the primary instrument of capitalist oppression." Goodman, *Stories of Scottsboro*, 26, 29–31. Haywood Patterson's third trial and Clarence Norris's second, presided over by William Callahan, in particular, represented southern justice as legalized racism whereby, Goodman argues, "Callahan had been named not to judge but to impose the majority's will"—an assessment shared by Samuel Leibowitz, the Scottsboro Boys' attorney, most northerners, and even some prominent Alabamans. Goodman, *Stories of Scottsboro*, 209. For a discussion of Callahan's conduct during those trials, see Goodman, *Stories of Scottsboro*, 209–29. Weiner has argued that the line between law of the courts and mob rule was only beginning to appear when the Scottboro Boys went on trial and that "through most of the South, it hardly existed at all." Weiner, *Black Trials*, 250. Weiner argues that "rather than killing blacks upon the cross of a tree, a white jury or judge could send a black man to a lifetime of backbreaking labor in one of the notorious gulags that dotted the South or . . . put him to death with a surge of electricity or by the gallows" through the process of a "legal lynching." Weiner, *Black Trials*, 252.

3. "They Shall Not Die!" RH Box 130. Such rhetoric was, of course, part of the Marxist analysis whereby the Scottsboro Boys, symbolic of all black southerners, were victims of capitalist exploitation, and thus their case was on the frontlines of the battle between workers and the ruling class. See Weiner, *Black Trials*, 256.

4. "They Shall Not Die!" RH Box 130.

5. Carter, *Scottsboro*, 49. Other historians agree with Carter's assessment. See Weiner, *Black Trials*, 256, and Goodman, *Stories of Scottsboro*, 25, 42.

6. Carter, *Scottsboro*, xi. Although many would argue, as Goodman does, that communists' "charge that the verdicts were the result of class . . . prejudice was preposterous," most would agree with Hollace Ransdall (as Goodman also does) that "the Scottsboro trials, like the Dreyfus affair and the Sacco and Vanzetti case, 'laid bare' the forces moving beneath the surface of the social structure." Goodman, *Stories of Scottsboro*, 42, 50. While many simply see racism

244   Notes to pages 62–63

as the force beneath the surface, the communists argued that racism could not be extricated from class oppression. In any event, the Communist Party's good deeds in support of racial equality supplied a ready reply to criticism of its motives and explained why the Scottsboro Boys should accept the aid of the International Labor Defense: Should drowning men demand reasons for helping hands? See Goodman, *Stories of Scottsboro*, 72. Or, as Haywood Patterson's mother said, and the other boys' parents agreed, "I don't care whether they are Reds, Greens, or Blues, they are the only ones who put up a fight to save these boys and I am with them to the end." Quoted in James Goodman, *Stories of Scottsboro*, 84. Goodman points out that though black membership in the Communist Party remained (to party officials) disappointingly low, most southern blacks approved of what the Communist Party was saying and doing to help the sharecroppers. Most of those sharecroppers were illiterate and indifferent to theoretical analysis, but were nevertheless impressed that "the Communists proposed to do precisely what needed to be done." Goodman, *Stories of Scottsboro*, 76–81.

7. *Youngville, USA* (New York: American Youth Congress, 1937), 20, DP Box 275. Goodman explains the dire circumstances of African-Americans during the Great Depression in stark terms: "Negroes were hungry. They were being thrown out of work in numbers well out of proportion to their share of the population, and the wages of those who kept their jobs were being reduced to levels that made starvation and homelessness inevitable." And, Goodman argues, the black sharecroppers' dependence on the cotton market meant that its collapse caused widespread desperation unequalled among white farmers. Goodman, *Stories of Scottsboro*, 36.

8. New York City college newspapers regularly published articles about conditions around the country, especially the south. An example of this is "Arkansas Sharecroppers Describe Oppressive Conditions in the South," *The Campus*, March 22, 1935, CCNY.

9. Leslie A. Gould, *American Youth Today* (New York: Random House, 1940), 230. This, too, identifies the 1930s youth cohort in opposition to that of the 1920s when issues related to racial injustice—let alone racism as a system of oppression—rarely were reported in the college press. Paula Fass points out that "when the issue did emerge, Northern students self-consciously took a liberal stand, while Southern students, quite as consciously, took the opposite." Paula Fass, *The Damned and the Beautiful: Youth in the 1920s* (New York: Oxford University Press, 1977), 351.

10. *Youngville, USA*, 21, Democratic Party, Women's Division Papers, File 275, FDR Library.

11. Kingsley Davis, *Youth in the Depression* (Chicago: University of Chicago Press, 1935), 7, Vertical File: Youth, FDR Library.

12. Ibid, 8.

13. Ibid.

14. Goodman, *Stories of Scottsboro*, 36.

15. Davis, *Youth in the Depression*, 23.

16. Ibid.

17. To that end, the AYC also supported A. Phillip Randolph's efforts to rid the AFL of racial discrimination and to convince the AFL to take up the cause of racial discrimination against African-American workers. See Proceedings of the National Council Meeting of the AYC, 22 February 1937, JPL Box 23.

18. Mark Weiner has argued that the case of the Scottsboro Boys helped achieve what Reconstruction had not: real, lasting citizenship for African-Americans. Despite the ratification of the 14th and 15th Amendments, African-Americans were denied their citizenship rights, especially their right to due process and equality before the law. He argues that this case—which ultimately assured black rights to serve on juries—brought African-Americans closer to the center of civic life and thus paved the way for the inclusionary racial vision embodied in *Brown v. Board of Education*. It was the Scottsboro Boys' case, he said, that was instrumental in overcoming Jim Crow and thus allowed "the liberal cultural revolution of the era, the assimilation of blacks into American law and national identity" that provided the groundwork for racial equality before the law. See Weiner, *Black Trials*, 243–245.

19. "They Shall Not Die!" RH Box 130.

20. Ibid.; Carter, *Scottsboro*, 50.

21. Miller, *Remembering Scottsboro*, 9.

22. Ralph S. Brax, *The First Student Movement: Student Activism During the United States in the 1930s* (Port Washington, N.Y.: Kennikat Press, 1981), 52.

23. "Student Meeting Weights Expulsions, Scottsboro Cases," *The Campus*, December 14, 1934, CCNY.

24. Gould, *American Youth Today*, 64.

25. Robert Cohen, *When the Old Left Was Young: Student Radicals and America's First Mass Student Movement, 1929–1941* (New York: Oxford University Press, 1993), 210–11; Gould, *American Youth Today*, 77; "Proceedings of the Third American Youth Congress," July 1936, Gardner Jackson Papers, Box 5, FDR Library.

26. David Blunt, "Black and White: Let's End Discrimination in Cleveland," *Voices of Youth*, July 1936, CT Box 89.

27. Ibid.

28. "The Creed of the American Youth Congress," found in Gould, *American Youth*, 289. This creed was adopted in 1939.

29. Racial segregation in housing delegates for AYC conferences remained a perennial issue. In 1941, youth groups sought a meeting with President Roosevelt to discuss the difficulty of finding housing for African-American delegates to the AYC Town Hall Meeting in Washington, D.C. They were rebuffed by the President's secretary, who said that the White House would not get involved in housing issues in Washington, D.C. See Reba Lawren Telegram to President Roosevelt, January 29, 1941; Edwin Watson to J. Russell Young, January 29, 1941, POF 3910, Box 2.

30. Youth activists were quick to respond to racial discrimination. For example, when representatives to the AYC National Council were meeting at a YMCA in Washington, DC in 1937, the African-American delegates were not allowed to eat lunch in the main cafeteria. The group immediately and unanimously passed a resolution deploring the segregationist policy, brought the matter to the attention of the YMCA national office, and demanded that this discrimination be addressed as it negated the basis of the organization's loyalty to the brotherhood of man. See Proceedings of the AYC National Council Meeting, February 22, 1937, JPL Box 23.

31. Alvaine Hollister, "Autobiography," n.d., JPL Box 21.

32. Cohen, *When the Old Left Was Young*, 214.

33. Jack McMichael, from Atlanta, Georgia, was a leader of the National Intercollegiate Christian Council, which comprised the national student groups of the YMCA and the YWCA. McMichael also chaired the Southern Field Council of the YMCA and spent eight months in China in 1938 as a Student Movement Exchange Fellow. He was elected Chairman of the American Youth Congress in 1939.

34. "Murder in the South," *The Campus*, April 6, 1932, CCNY.

35. See, for example, "Peonage and Torture Revealed in Lecture on Southern Negro," *The Spectator*, October 1932, Microform and Periodicals Collection, Columbia University. While northern white college student activists railed against such events, Langston Hughes railed against southern black colleges that remained silent on such issues. Miller, *Remembering Scottsboro*, 57.

36. The AYC catalogued racial abuse against African-Americans around the country in its meeting minutes as a way to both publicly condemn such actions and publicize them as a national problem for their membership. For example, at one National Executive Council meeting, the following civil liberties violations were listed: Tom Mooney, Angelo Herndon, and the Scottsboro Boys were all kept in jail; an African-American student was expelled from Annapolis; Frank Weems of the Southern Tenant Farmers Union in Arkansas mysteriously disappeared; King, Ramsey, and Conner were arrested for alleged criminal activity during the Maritime Strike in Oakland, California in what was said to be a frame-up; Jerome Davis, the president of the American Federation of Teachers for Yale University, was dismissed; and there was general discrimination against African-Americans in Washington, D.C. See: Proceedings of the National Council Meeting, February 22, 1937, JPL Box 23.

37. Memorandum, n.d. JPL Box 29.

38. Ibid.

39. "Philadelphia Hotel Refuses Lodging to Negro Trackman," *The Campus*, May 1, 1935, CCNY.

40. "Student Council Will Probe Jim-Crowism at the College; Protest[s] rise in Wilson Case," *The Campus*, May 7, 1935, CCNY.

41. "Committee Acts to Stamp Out Race Prejudice," *The Campus*, September 9, 1935, CCNY.

42. "Fraternity Refuses to Admit Negro Student to Smoker," *The Campus*, September 27, 1935, CCNY.

43. "Negro Discrimination," *The Campus*, December 20, 1935, CCNY.

44. "Negro Discrimination," *The Campus*, December 20, 1935, CCNY.

45. Such solutions showed how liberal youth activists could be. While Socialist and Communist Party members maintained the only way to end racism was to destroy the capitalist system, youth activists offered more moderate short-term suggestions all the while espousing the same long-term goals of equality and a classless society. Most of them, then, were true democratic socialists.

46. "Proposed Course on Negro Race," *The Campus*, October 20, 1935, CCNY.

47. "Dr. Max Yergan, Negro Educator, May Teach Here," *The Campus*, April 16, 1937; "Negro Wants Equal Chance with Others, Says Yergan," *The Campus*, January 7, 1938, CCNY.

48. Max Yergan, "Negro Wants Equal Chance with Others," *The Campus*, January 7, 1938, CCNY.

49. James Wechsler, *Revolt on the Campus* (Seattle: University of Washington Press, 1935), 212.

50. Ibid.

51. ROTC's segregationist policies mirrored those of the U.S. military. In protesting campus ROTC programs and policies, then, young activists were also challenging the national government's stance on race issues. A similar process would occur on NYA projects and at NYA resident centers where enrollees insisted on racial equality. The NYA enrollees, however, could count on the support of New Dealers, like Aubrey Williams and Charles Taussig, to support their cause.

52. "Student Council to Probe Anti-Negro Bias Case," *The Campus*, April 27, 1936, CCNY.

53. "Turner Scored for Attitude as Anti-Negro," *The Campus*, December 23, 1936, CCNY.

54. Wechsler, *Revolt on the Campus*, 217–18.

55. Cohen, *When the Old Left Was Young*, 208.

56. "Kansas Is a White Man's School," *The Student Advocate*, March 1936, CT Box 85.

57. Letter signed by H. R. Burbaker, Notary Public, July 30, 1935, included with "Kansas is a White Man's School," CT Box 85.

58. George Streator, "Patronizing the Negro Student," *The Student Outlook*, October 1934, JPL Box 30.

59. Ibid.

60. Ibid.

61. John J. Bednarz to Joseph Lash, January 7, 1936, *The Student Advocate*, Volume 1, Tamiment Library, NYU.

62. Joseph Lash, "Are Liberals Immune?" *The Student Advocate*, February 1936, Volume 1, Tamiment Library, NYU.

63. Ibid.

64. Ibid.

65. Ibid.

66. Ibid.

67. Editorial reprinted in *The Student Advocate* February 1937, Tamiment Library, NYU.

68. Ibid.

69. The administration maintained that its discriminatory policies were designed to satisfy student sentiment. The Committee called for a survey of student opinion to determine student sentiment. George Collins, "Liberalism and Negroes," *The Student Advocate*, February 1937, Tamiment Library, NYU.

70. "Call for a Southern Negro Youth Conference," PPF 4266.

71. The Scottsboro trials were often referred to as a legal lynching in which the South's legal system carried out the mob's demand. See, for example, Carter, *Scottsboro*, 115; Goodman, *Stories of Scottsboro*, Chapter 4.

72. "Call for a Southern Negro Youth Conference," PPF 4266.

73. Richard R. Brown to Marvin McIntyre, December 30, 1936, PPF 4266. The documents included a pamphlet issued by the Negro Congress, a report of the Fifty-Sixth Annual Convention of the American Federation of Labor, which included an outline of a resolution proposal from A. Philip Randolph, President of the National Negro Congress, correspondence between the National Negro Congress and Mary McLeod Bethune, Director of the NYA's Division of Negro Affairs, and the only article advertising the conference in an adult publication from the *Washington Tribune*.

74. Memorandum, National Youth Administration Division of Negro Affairs, January 1937, Eleanor Roosevelt Microfilm Collection, Reel 1, FDR Library.

75. Report of the National Conference on the Problems of the Negro and Negro Youth, January 22, 1937, Eleanor Roosevelt Microfilm Collection, Reel 1, FDR Library.

76. FDR called for a "united democracy" in his opening message to the 76th Congress.

77. Report of the Second National Conference on the Problems of the Negro and Negro Youth, January 12–14, 1939, Eleanor Roosevelt Microfilm Collection, Reel 1, FDR Library.

78. Ibid.

79. Ibid.

80. Report of the Second National Conference on the Problems of the Negro and Negro Youth, January 12–14, 1939, Eleanor Roosevelt Microfilm Collection, Reel 1, FDR Library.

81. "School Books Create Racial Prejudice," *Youth Letter*, April 28, 1939, CT Box 85.

82. Executive Order No. 8802, issued June 25, 1941, said that all departments and agencies of the federal government concerned with vocational and training programs for defense production must ensure that such programs are administered without discrimination because of race, creed, color, or national origin.

83. Aubrey Williams to all regional directors and all state youth administrators, July 1, 1941, AW Box 12, FDR Library.

84. Aubrey Williams's unreserved support for racial integration came at a political cost for both himself and the NYA. He was vilified by anti–New Deal groups. Interestingly, the most popular charge leveled against him was for being a "red," and the "evidence" marshaled to support such a charge often involved his insistence on equal pay and equal opportunities regardless of race, demonstrating, once again, the link between racist attitudes and anti-communism. The most common criticism of the NYA was that, under Williams's tutelage, it was introducing and/or reinforcing subversive ideas and that it was staffed by communists. See, John Salmond, *A Southern Rebel: The Life and Times of Aubrey Willis Williams, 1890–1965* (Chapel Hill: University of North Carolina Press, 1983.)

85. Telegram from citizens of Moravia, New York to Aubrey Williams, June 15, 1943, AW Box 6, FDR Library.

86. For a clear discussion of Aubrey Williams's progressive ideas about race and other issues, see the only biography published about him to date: John Salmond, *A Southern Rebel: The Life and Times of Aubrey Willis Williams, 1890–1965* (Chapel Hill: University of North Carolina Press, 1983.)

87. See, for example, Statement of Sherman Forbes, June 16, 1943, AW Box 6, FDR Library.

88. Auburn Chamber of Commerce to James M. Mead and Robert F. Wagner, August 31, 1942 and W. B. Harvard to C. D. Greene, March 2, 1942, AW Box 6, FDR Library.

89. Fass, *The Damned and the Beautiful*, 351–52.

90. Wechsler, *Revolt on the Campus*, 355.

91. "Boycott the Olympics!" *The Campus*, October 9, 1935, CCNY.

92. The interconnectedness of anti-Semitism and racism is clearly shown in the transcripts from the Scottsboro Boys' trials wherein their Jewish lawyer, Samuel Leibowitz, became a target of the prosecution. See Carter, *Scottsboro*, 235.

93. Wechsler, *Revolt on the Campus*, 372.

94. Ibid., 373.

95. Quoted in Goodman, *Stories of Scottsboro*, 133.

96. Goodman, *Stories of Scottsboro*, 151. Leibowitz spoke out publicly against the rampant racism and anti-Semitism he observed. See Goodman, *Stories of Scottsboro*, 153–54. It was largely on the basis of the pervasive anti-Semitism that Leibowitz relinquished his leading role in the defense by September 1935; he believed he had become as much a hindrance to the boys' release as a help.

Although he technically remained the lead defense attorney, he allowed a local lawyer to examine prospective jurors and witnesses, and he cooperated with the Scottsboro Defense Committee, comprising the ILD, NAACP, ACLU, LID, and the Methodist Federation for Social Service under the leadership of a minister Allan Knight Chalmers. See Goodman, *Stories of Scottsboro*, 244–46.

97. "Anonymous Letter Mailed to *The Campus* by Anti-Semite," *The Campus*, December 10, 1937, CCNY. Though this threat was not carried out, it served as a reminder of how minorities—racial and religious—could be targeted at any time.

98. Ibid.

99. William Hinckley, "Youth Seeks Peace, Freedom, and Progress," Chairman's Report, Third American Youth Congress, July 1936, Gardner Jackson Papers, Box 5, FDR Library.

100. "The Young Ask Questions and Mrs. Roosevelt Answers," February 2, 1936, CT Box 81.

101. Most observers now find the truth in Ruby Bates's admission in January 1933 and subsequent testimony in April 1933 that neither she nor Victoria Price had been raped, rather than the original story she testified to in 1931 and to which Victoria Price remained committed throughout her life. Each of the Scottsboro Boys was plagued by their experience in one way or another. None of them were ever acquitted; only Clarence Norris was pardoned—in 1976. Until then, he was a fugitive, having broken parole by going North in 1947. For information about the hardships each of the Scottsboro Boys faced after the 1930s and the tragic deaths of some of them, see Goodman, *Stories of Scottsboro*, 356–89.

102. Dan Carter explains in *Scottsboro* that the Sixth Comintern Congress meeting in Moscow in 1928 had adopted the position that the only solution to the race issue in America was for African-Americans to form a "black republic" of their own. Yet the American CP members saw this "as so much nonsense," and there is very little evidence that they tried to carry out this program. Carter, *Scottsboro*, 64, 169. This is yet another example of how Moscow did not control communism in America and how American communists, even while espousing doctrine emanating from Moscow, had some power to choose which policies to push. James Miller corroborates this position by relating the intra-party disputes over how to effectively mobilize propaganda efforts on behalf of the Scottsboro Boys. Tom Johnson, the district organizer in Chattanooga, refused to go along with the party slogans such as "Demand the confiscation of land from the landlords for the Negro and white croppers" and thus struck at the CP's larger agenda of organizing southern sharecroppers. Miller, *Remembering Scottsboro*, 17–20.

103. Miller, *Remembering Scottsboro*, 47. Haywood Patterson said, "What happened in the Scottsboro case wasn't unusual. What was unusual was that the world heard about it." As quoted in Miller, *Remembering Scottsboro*, 190. See also Weiner, *Black Trials*, 256–59.

104. The relationship of the communists (as represented by the International

Labor Defense) to the Scottsboro trials is a complex one. Dan Carter has shown that the Communist Party used the case for its own propaganda purposes, and he meticulously shows the conflict between the ILD and NAACP that rested on the communists' desire to exploit the case against capitalism. See Carter, *Scottsboro*, Chapter III, Chapter V. The communists' antipathy toward the NAACP—which they saw as a gradualist, reformist organization that shirked its responsibilities by allying with the would-be exploiters and working within the system—was palpable. See, for example, Weiner, *Black* Trials, 259.

105. At the same time, there were those who feared the connections between the communists and such liberal causes as racial equality—not because they doubted the communists' sincerity, but because by allying with liberals to fight against discrimination, they catalyzed the ire of reactionaries, including those in the Ku Klux Klan, who adroitly used the specter of communism to stir up support. Non-communist liberals in the South, like Grover Hall, the influential editor of *Montgomery Advertiser*, feared a resurrected Klan would return to power in such a situation, making the prospect for racial justice even more remote. He did not work against communists, then, because he thought the South was really in danger of going red; he thought of them, instead, as carpetbaggers. See Goodman, *Stories of Scottsboro*, 296–97. Young activists—especially those in the Northeast—had little patience for such analyses. They were increasingly unwilling to turn their backs on those who agreed with their vision of America and were much more willing, therefore, to promote the ideas of the popular front.

106. American Youth Congress Cabinet Meeting Minutes, March 8, 1941, JPL Box 24.

107. Ibid.

108. Ibid.

4. The Popular Front. Strength in Unity: New York City Organizations Come Together in Solidarity

1. A large number of people moved through radical parties during the desperate economic times of the Great Depression. Communist Party turnover in 1932 was 75 percent, and although there were 47,000 new members by1934, only 12,000 of them "stuck," so that "real" membership in the CPUSA is only numbered around 24,000 people: Daniel Bell, *Marxian Socialism in the United States* (Ithaca: Cornell University Press, 1996), 141–42.

2. Selden Rodman, "Why There Is No Youth Movement: An Analysis, a Warning, and a Plea," *The Social Frontier*, May 1935, JPL Box 23.

3. Linton M. Collins to Marvin H. McIntyre, Secretary to the President, June 6, 1934, PPF 614.

4. FDR to Leslie B. Farrington, June 12, 1934, PPF 614.

5. The JCC remained committed to this program throughout the rest of the decade. See Perry Pipkin to FDR, December 16, 1939, PPF 614.

6. Memorandum, W. Caldwell, Chairman of Americanism Committee of the United States Junior Chamber of Commerce to all presidents and secretaries of JCC as well as all members of Americanism Committees of JCC, December 10, 1935, PPF Box 614.

7. Arthur Clifford, "The Truth About the American Youth Congress," 1935, PC Box 1198.

8. Leslie Gould, *American Youth Today* (New York: Random House, 1940), 53.

9. Ibid. Ilma does not seem to have wanted to model an American youth organization *exactly* upon the fascist model. She appreciated the organization, discipline, motivation, and dedication of the German and Italian youth groups. She seems to have overlooked the militaristic nature of those programs and the way the Hitler Youth, in particular, served as a training corps for future SS officials. Thus, she did not talk about regimenting American youth, something for which young Americans would have had little tolerance. She, instead, emphasized the *esprit de corps* developed in the 1920s through the bündische youth. For information about the development of the German youth movement, see H. W. Koch, *The Hitler Youth: Origins and Development 1922–1945* (New York: Cooper Square Press, 2000); Walter Laqueur, *Young Germany: A History of the German Youth Movement* (New Brunswick: Transaction Books, 1962); Peter D. Stachura, *The German Youth Movement, 1900–1945: An Interpretative and Documentary History* (Stirling, Scotland: University of Stirling, 1981); For information about the Hitler Youth program, see Lawrence D. Walker, *Hitler Youth and Catholic Youth, 1933–1936: A Study in Totalitarian Conquest* (Washington, D.C.: Catholic University of America Press, 1970); Gerhard Rempel, *Hitler's Children: The Hitler Youth and the SS* (Chapel Hill: University of North Carolina Press, 1989; Michael S. Steinberg, *Sabers and Brownshirts: The German Students' Path to National Socialism, 1918–1935* (Chicago: University of Chicago Press, 1973). For information about the Italian youth program see Tracy Koon, *Believe, Obey, Fight: Political Socialization of Youth in Fascist Italy, 1922–1943* (Chapel Hill: University of North Carolina Press, 1985).

10. Gould, *American Youth Today*, 54.

11. Viola Ilma to Charles Taussig, January 3, 1934, CT Box 2.

12. Charles Taussig, for example, chose to ignore Ilma's group in favor of the AYC for representing young people. In 1939, he was still organizing luncheons to raise funds for it. See CT Box 2.

13. Michael Henry Miller, "The American Student Movement, 1931–1941: A Historical Analysis" (PhD diss., Florida State University, 1981), 73; Robert Cohen, *When the Old Left Was Young* (New York: Oxford University Press, 1993), 190; Ralph Brax, *The First Student Movement* (Port Washington, N.Y.: Kennikat Press, 1981), 67.

14. Cohen, *When the Old Left Was Young*, 189; Brax, *The First Student Movement*, 69.

15. George Philip Rawick, "The New Deal and Youth: The Civilian Conservation Corps, the National Youth Administration, and the American

Youth Congress" (Ph.D. dissertation: University of Wisconsin–Madison, 1957), 284. The issue of how this organization came to exist represents a clear divide between those who have been influenced by the anti-communist rhetoric of the Cold War and those who were not—that is, those young people in 1934 who actually created the AYC. The most important influence has been that of George Rawick's dissertation, published in 1957. Not only is that dissertation steeped in Cold War rhetoric, but it is also the result of Rawick's Trotsky-ist background. He is therefore doubly antagonistic toward the communists of the 1930s. This dissertation has become the foundation for all subsequent published studies of youth activists in the Depression. No one has seriously questioned Rawick's biases. Underlying the charge of communist control is the belief that communist groups in America were controlled by the Soviet Union through the policy pronouncements of the Comintern. Historians such as Kermit E. McKenzie support such an understanding. See Kermit E. McKen-zie, *Comintern and World Revolution, 1928–1942: The Shaping of Doctrine* (New York: Columbia University Press, 1964). Studies published after the opening of Soviet archives have challenged this notion. See Harvey Klehr and John Earl Haynes, *The Secret World of American Communism* (New Haven: Yale University Press, 1995); Kevin McDermott and Jeremy Agnew, *The Comintern: A History of International Communism from Lenin to Stalin* (New York: St. Marten's Press, 1996).

16. In condemning the AYC as communist-controlled, Ilma has been ab-solved of the charges against her. Those who have written about youth activists during the Depression have argued that Ilma was not even a fascist sympathizer, let alone a fascist or semi-fascist, as some at the time claimed. See, for example, Clifford, "The Truth About the American Youth Congress," 1935. Daniel Bell called Ilma a "well-meaning liberal." Bell, *Marxian Socialism in the United States*, 149.

17. Rawick, "The New Deal and Youth," 285.

18. Report of the First American Youth Congress, published by the Central Bureau for Young America, October 1934, American Youth Congress Vertical File, Box 58-B, FDR Library and CT Box 2.

19. Rawick admitted that "*And Now, Youth!* obviously lends a certain cre-dence to the attack on the young Viola Ilma, for it certainly smacks heavily of the ideology of totalitarianism," yet he refused to condemn her for this. Instead, he dismissed it, saying that "she appeared equally friendly to Hitler, Stalin, Mussolini, and Roosevelt." Rawick, "The New Deal and Youth," 286–87. Historians, relying on Rawick's analysis, have continued to absolve Ilma and castigate the radicals for "taking over" the AYC. For example, Ralph Brax refers to Ilma as a moderate who was outmaneuvered by the communists; Robert Cohen sidesteps the issue by never once mentioning Ilma, all the while defend-ing Rawick's argument that the communists took control of the AYC through Machiavellian means, and Daniel Bell refers to Ilma as a liberal. That is not how youth at the time interpreted the situation.

20. Viola Ilma to Eleanor Roosevelt, March 25, 1933, ER Box 100.

21. Report of the First American Youth Congress, published by the Central Bureau for Young America, October 1934, American Youth Vertical File, 58-B, FDR Library and CT Box 2.

22. Ibid.

23. Ibid.

24. Ibid. Also see Rawick, "The New Deal and Youth," 289–90.

25. All of these roundtable discussions were chaired by adults who exerted wide control over the discussions. See "Program of the First American Youth Congress," CT Box 2.

26. "Program of the First American Youth Congress," CT Box 2.

27. Gould, *American Youth Today*, 54–55.

28. Ibid, 55.

29. Viola Ilma to Eleanor Roosevelt, June 15, 1934, Eleanor Roosevelt Microfilm Collection, Reel 1, FDR Library.

30. "Quotes," n.d., POF 58, Box 3.

31. Memorandum, W. L. M. to Stephen Early, August 14, 1934, POF 158, Box 3, and Telegram, Stephen Early to Harvey Zorbaugh, August 9, 1934, POF 3910, Box 10.

32. Viola Ilma to delegates to the American Youth Congress, August 4, 1934, POF 58, Box 3.

33. Viola Ilma to Charles Taussig, April 1934, CT Box 2.

34. In order for him to hold his summer session course of youth leaders, he needed youth leaders to come to NYU. Ilma provided the leaders; he provided the facilities for the conference. The first American Youth Congress was held on the Washington Square campus of NYU August 15–17, 1934. See Gould, *American Youth Today*, 56.

35. Harvey Zorbaugh to Stephen Early, Secretary to the President, August 9, 1934, POF 58, Box 3.

36. Ibid.

37. Ibid.

38. Rawick, "The New Deal and Youth," 289.

39. Gould, *American Youth Today*, 56–57.

40. Even Rawick admitted that "the opening day of the congress . . . Miss Ilma automatically became chairman, her supporters pointing out that she had gone to much trouble and expense to organize the conference. The YCL-YPSL–led caucus objected. They demanded that a chairman be elected from the floor. Miss Ilma refused to allow this and continued to speak." Rawick, "The New Deal and Youth," 289–90.

41. Clifford, "The Truth About the American Youth Congress," 1935.

42. Michael Henry Miller went even further in claiming in his dissertation that Ilma "visited Nazi Germany to study the Nazi youth movement. Ilma returned to the United States determined to organize America's youth in a similar fashion, and her efforts resulted in the first meeting of the AYC

in 1934." Michael Henry Miller, "The American Student Movement of the Depression, 1931–1941," 73.

43. Gould, *American Youth Today*, 57.

44. Ibid.

45. Ibid, 58 and Rawick, "The New Deal and Youth," 290. The fact that Rawick clearly identifies McNutt as a YMCA delegate contradicts his claim that this was a coup carried out by the YCL and YPSL.

46. Clifford, "The Truth About the American Youth Congress," 1935.

47. Report of the First American Youth Congress published by the Central Bureau for Young America, October 1934, American Youth Vertical File, 58-B, FDR Library and CT Box 2.

48. Gould, *American Youth Today*, 58.

49. Ibid., 59–60. Moreover, if the representative formula devised by Ilma had been adopted, the National Executive Committee of the AYC would have been made up of one representative from each national organization, twenty representatives of unaffiliated youth, the state chairmen, and five governors of the Central Bureau, which would have meant that all but the national organization representatives would have been hand-picked by the Central Bureau. This is especially important because aside from repeating Ilma's claims, Rawick relied most heavily on contemporary newspaper articles, especially from the *New York Times*, to substantiate his argument. He did not have access to manuscript collections. He did interview Viola Ilma, Joseph Lash, and Joseph Cadden. Those interviews, however, are not referenced in the footnotes because, he said, he wanted to protect their privacy. Historians, resting on Rawick's analysis, then, have promulgated this same bias. None of these claims investigated what young participants said at the time. Irving Howe also steadfastly maintained that the popular front was a brilliant masquerade orchestrated by the communists rather than the result of democratic good will. While this may be true in other venues, it is not supported by the documents young activists left behind regarding the AYC. See Howe, *Socialism and America*, 104.

50. Gould, *American Youth Today*, 61.

51. James Wechsler, *Revolt on the Campus* (Seattle: University of Washington Press, 1973), 172, 173.

52. James Wechsler, *The Age of Suspicion* (New York: Donald I. Fine, 1985), 70.

53. Winston Dancis to Members of the Socialist Party, January 26, 1935, YPSL, Box 1.

54. Report of the 17th Annual Convention of the Greater New York Federation of YPSL, February 1, 1936, YPSL, Box 1.

55. Hal Draper to the Yipsels of New York City, 1934, YPSL, Box 1. Yipsels were routinely given orders by the YPSL on the course of action they should pursue within the ASU. See, for example, "Student Bulletin #4," JPL Box 30.

56. Joseph Lash interview with Joel Chernoff, January 5, 1978, JPL Box 78.

57. YCL leader Gil Green was committed to the idea of a broad-based

organization dedicated to addressing the needs of youth and defended his
position of calling together religious and non-religious youth groups for that
purpose in the pages of the communist press. See "Youth Steps Out Fighting
for Jobs Through Collective Action," *Daily Worker*, July 18, 1936, JPL Box 30.

58. Report of the First American Youth Congress, American Youth Congress Vertical File, Box 58-B, FDR Library and CT Box 2.

59. Minutes from roundtable discussion of transients, August 1934, CT Box 2.

60. Ibid.

61. Viola Ilma to Marvin MacIntyre, April 13, 1935, POF 58, Box 3. The
rump organization continued, for a time, moving even further to the right. It
accepted financial backing from Bernarr MacFadden, for example, whose emphasis on physical culture smacked of adult-controlled regimentation of young
people that was incompatible with young people's political actualization as far
as youth activists were concerned.

62. John Millar to the Editor, *Voice of Youth*, December 1935, Olds Papers,
Box 23, FDR Library.

63. Viola Ilma to Eleanor Roosevelt, February 1, 1943, Eleanor Roosevelt
Microfilm Collection, Reel 1, FDR Library.

64. Ibid.

65. Of the forty members of the AYC's National Council—the executive
board that would oversee operations between annual conferences—historian
George Rawick identified only fourteen as members of the YCL or fellow
travelers. Yet he insisted that the AYC was communist-controlled. To explain
the apparent hole in this argument, he claimed in a footnote that "the communists sent in a host of 'faceless people' into such organizations as the American
Youth Congress; with a few exceptions we do not know who they were....
Joseph Lash in the heyday of the popular front period was part of the communist bloc within the youth movement even though it cannot be demonstrated
that he was a member of the Communist Party." Rawick, "The New Deal
and Youth," 296. It could not be demonstrated that Lash was a member of the
Communist Party because he never was; he was a member of the Socialist Party.
Similarly, Rawick says that he cannot prove that Joseph Cadden (Executive
Secretary); Waldo Mcnutt, William Hinckley, and Reverend Jack McMichael
(the three Chairmen from 1934–42); Abbott Simon (the Legislative Secretary);
or Miriam Bogarad and Frances Williams (Administrative Secretaries) were
members of the Communist Party or the Young Communist League, "however, they all consistently followed the Communist Party line through all of its
twists from 1935 to 1942." Rawick, "The New Deal and Youth," 297. Perhaps,
though, the changes in position had more to do with what young people
wanted at any particular moment than with what the communist line was at
that time, especially since Cadden and Simon were self-identified socialists.

66. "Principles of Organization of the American Youth Congress," JPL
Box 23.

67. Minutes of AYC National Executive Committee Meeting, August 6,

1936; Minutes of National Executive Committee Meeting, August 20, 1936; Proceedings of National Council Meeting," February 22, 1937, JPL Box 23.

68. Charles H. Kenlan to J. J. McEntee, August 18, 1934; J. J. McEntee to Louis Howe, August 21, 1934, POF 3910.

69. Even Rawick understood that the CCC did not serve American youth, arguing that "from the point of view of providing an adequate solution to the needs of American youth, the Civilian Conservation Corps was a failure," and therefore "while the congressmen voted *for* the CCC with their hands, twenty percent of the CCC enrollees voted *against* the CCC with their feet" by deserting. Rawick, "The New Deal and Youth," 131, 136.

70. Rawick, "The New Deal and Youth," 380.

71. The CCC became a youth program because of a decision adopted by FDR in May 1935, which obligated enrollees to come from relief rolls. As the Director of Emergency Conservation Work, Robert Fechner, noted, this would necessarily upset the balance of enrollees from each state and would therefore increase the distance between the place of selection and the available work projects. Unemployed men and war veterans (the intended beneficiaries of the CCC program) were unlikely to leave their families to go to work in CCC camps far from home. Young, unmarried men were the ones to enroll in the program, and this only solidified for its adult defenders the necessity of regimentation in the Army-run camps. Robert Fechner to FDR, May 15, 1935, POF 3910.

72. Charles H. Kenlan to J. J. McEntee, August 18, 1934, POF 3910.

73. AYC Questionnaire, 1934, PPF 2282.

74. Ibid.

75. Russell A. McNutt, Acting Chairman National Council of AYC to Col. McIntyre, September 30, 1935, POF 3910.

76. William E. Porter to Louis M. Howe, February 4, 1935, PPF, 2282.

77. Arthur Clifford, "The Truth About the American Youth Congress," 1935.

78. W. E. Porter to FDR, March 7, 1935, POF 3910.

79. "American Youth Congress," 1936, Gardner Jackson Papers, Box 5, FDR Library; AW Box 25, FDR Library.

80. "An Appeal to Members of the YPSL," October 6, 1934, YPSL, Box 1. Norman Thomas was, at this point, advocating cooperation on specific issues, though not a wholesale fusion of socialists and communists. See Irving Howe, *Socialism and America*, 62. The use of the phrase "united front" is cause for confusion. As Comintern policy, the United Front lasted from 1921 to 1928 and thus predates the Third Period. (Although the United Front was first introduced in December 1921, the details were not worked out until the Comintern Congress of 1922.) This was a time when capitalism seemed to be regaining stability in the west after the immediate negative economic effects of World War I had passed. Communist parties, as small groups that had split from the left wing of larger socialist parties, were not mass parties. Thus, in

order for communism to rebuild in such a hostile environment, communists were directed to join progressive organizations as a strategic maneuver, working in concert and uniting from below, whereby they could convert workers to communism. The United Front from above, meanwhile, would be between the leaders of such organizations. Ideally, the communists would be able to co-opt such organizations. See Theodore Draper, *The Roots of American Communism* (New York: Viking Press, 1957), Chapter 19; Albert S. Lindemann, *A History of European Socialism* (New Haven: Yale University Press, 1983), Chapter 7.

81. The Third Period is usually dated from 1928, with the ending of the New Economic Policy and beginning of Stalin's first five year plan, to 1935, with the adoption of the Popular Front policy. Irving Howe, however, dates the Third Period from 1929 to 1933. Howe claimed in 1977, when *Socialism and America* was first published and again in its 1985 reprint, that "there is precious little evidence for this claim" that the Communist Party "was inching toward a Popular Front policy even before Moscow mandated it" because, this analysis, he says, "ignores the reality that for many decades the party functioned as a slavish dependent of Moscow. The initiative for the Popular Front came during the 1935 Seventh World Congress of the Comintern" while "the American CP did not, however, fully articulate the new Popular Front line until the spring of 1936, when its two main leaders, Earl Browder and William Z. Foster, visited Moscow." See Howe, *Socialism and America*, 89.

82. "YCL Appeal to YPSL for United Action," March 20, 1935, YPSL, Box 1.

83. "An Appeal to Members of the YPSL," YPSL, Box 1.

84. Ruth Watt, "Struggle Against Trotskyism in the Student Movement," n.d., JPL Box 30.

85. Ibid.

86. National Executive Committee meeting minutes, April 19–21, 1935, YPSL, Box 1.

87. Report of 17th Annual Convention of the Greater New York Federation of YPSL of America, February 1, 1936, YPSL, Box 1. To complicate matters even further, the YPSL often chafed at the Socialist Party's heavy-handed directives toward it, arguing that the local Socialist Party should listen to the National Executive Committee of the YPSL rather than telling the local YPSL what to do. The Socialist Party believed any attempts at local independent action was tantamount to factionalism. See YPSL NEC meeting minutes April 19–21, 1935, YPSL, Box 1.

88. Statement issued by the National Executive Committee, YPSL of Greater New York, November 21, 1934, YPSL, Box 1.

89. Daniel Bell, *Marxian Socialism in the United States*, 9. The fractious nature of socialism in America, as explained by Frank Warren, results from the fact that "a Socialist Party is not a capitalist party, and it would seem that there are limits beyond which an ideological difference is incompatible with membership in the party." Frank A. Warren, *An Alternate Vision: The Socialist Party in the*

1930s (Bloomington: Indiana University Press, 1974), 115. It is because of this, he argues, that the Socialist Party experiences periodic splits and purges.

90. Joseph Lash, "Two Lives" (Unpublished Autobiography), 8, JPL Box 27.

91. Ibid., 4–5. This line of thought would cause many problems between Lash and the Socialist Party hierarchy later in the decade resulting in him leaving the Socialist Party. Lash maintained that he voluntarily left the organization; Warren contends that he was expelled because he strayed too far from the party line. See Warren, *An Alternate Vision*, 149. This issue will be discussed more fully in Chapters 6 and 7.

92. Ibid., 13.

93. Report of the 17th Annual Convention of the Greater New York Federation of YPSL of America, February 1, 1936, YPSL, Box 1.

94. "Some Questions to New York Yipsels: Organizational Appeal," 1935, YPSL, Box 1.

95. Ruth Steinberg, "The American Student Union," *Voice of Youth*, February 1936, CT Box 89.

96. Hal Draper, "The Student Movement of the Thirties: A Political History," in *As We Saw the Thirties: Essays on Social and Political Movements of a Decade* (Chicago: University of Illinois Press, 1967), 159, 166. Despite the fact that he was the student director of the New York YPSL for several years and thus was intimately involved in the emerging youth movement, he admitted that he "leaned heavily on both Rawick and Wechsler's accounts for the factual framework" for his analysis of that movement. Draper, "The Student Movement of the Thirties," 158, 153.

97. Harold Draper to the Yipsels of New York City, 1934, YPSL, Box 1.

98. "Some Questions to New York Yipsels: Organizational Appeal," 1935; YPSL, Box 1.

99. Open letter to all members of the YPSL of NY, March 1935, YPSL, Box 1.

100. Howe, *Socialism and America*, 44, 55, 83.

101. Hal Draper to the Yipsels of New York City, 1934, YPSL, Box 1.

102. Statement adopted by Executive Committee of YPSL of Greater New York, November 21, 1934, YPSL, Box 1.

103. Many feared that an irrevocable split in the socialist ranks was forming because of the insolence of the New York group. See William E. Bohn to Winston Dancis, January 18, 1935; Ethel Schachner to William E. Bohn, March 26, 1935, YPSL, Box 1. This challenge to the leadership led to the temporary suspension of the NY YPSL until it was reinstated in March 1935. In the end, Draper was not removed. The NY YPSL was temporarily suspended, but reinstated in March 1935 by the YPSL National Executive Committee. This action protected Draper's position, but that was not because of any loyalty to him, but rather as an effort to protect the YPSL from a takeover by the party. The NEC ruled that the New York executive committee could issue its statement, but

the Socialist Party could not take any action against Draper or the others "until their applications for membership in the party have been finally acted upon and the principle upon which their applications were rejected has been acted upon by the highest body;" in the meantime, the New York branch could issue its statement and vote to withdraw support from Draper. YPSL NEC Meeting Minutes, April 19–21, 1935, SPUSA-YPSL Conflict File, YPSL, Box 1; Statement adopted by the N.E.C., 24 March 1935, YPSL, Box 1.

104. See Lash's review of R. Palme Dutt's book, *Fascism and Social Revolution* (New York: International Publishers, 1936); Joseph Lash, "Fascism or Socialism?," *Arise*, 1936, JPL Box 27.

105. Joseph Lash, "Leon Blum; Their Most Dangerous Opponent," 1936, JPL Box 78; Joseph Lash, "Two Lives," 21, JPL Box 27.

106. The French led the way in developing the popular front in Europe. French socialists and communists had joined together in anti-fascist demonstrations in February 1934, leading to closer collaboration in June, followed by the communists' suggestion to include the radicals in March 1935. This led to a formal agreement among the three parties in January 1936. When the leftists won the elections of May 1936, it allowed Léon Blum to form a popular front government in France. See Jackson, *The Popular Front in France*, 36. Jackson's analysis is important not only because it outlines how the popular front developed in France, but also because it challenges previous historiographical arguments. Kermit McKenzie argued, in 1964, that communists supported the formation of popular front governments because doing so gave them an opportunity to hold ministerial posts *before* the communist seizure of power. Jackson shows, however, that the communists occupied no ministerial posts under Blum's government.

107. Joseph Lash, "Two Lives," 26, 30, JPL Box 78.

108. Ibid., 27.

109. Ibid., 29.

110. Ibid., 30.

111. Ibid., 29.

112. Ibid., 33.

113. Bell, *Marxian Socialism in the United States*, 136.

114. Wechsler, *Revolt on the Campus*, 454.

115. Ibid.

116. Ibid., 453.

117. Eileen Eagan, *Class, Culture, and the Classroom: The Student Peace Movement of the 1930s* (Philadelphia: Temple University Press, 1981), 13–14.

118. "Thomas Accepts Probability of Future War," *Columbia Spectator*, March 19, 1931, Microform and Periodicals Collection, Columbia University.

119. Gilbert E. Goodkind, "Campus chooses to Stop War Poll Rather Than Brand College 'Red'" *The Campus*, April 4, 1933, CCNY.

120. Ibid.

121. Ernest R. Bryan, "Rewarding the Munitions Makers," *The Student Mirror*, May 1935, CT Box 85.

122. Ibid.

123. "Major Challenges Facing the Student Christian Movement," n.d., JPL Box 21.

124. Sevareid, *Not So Wild a Dream* (New York: Alfred A. Knopf, 1946), 64. Senator Nye's support for the American Student Union, the annual strike against war, and the Oxford Pledge won him further support among youth activists. Joseph Lash, "Morgan: Wanted for Murder," *The Student Advocate*, February 1936, CT Box 85.

125. Ruth Sarles, "10,000,000 Young Voters for Peace," *The National Student Mirror*, January 1936, CT Box 85.

126. Eagan, *Class, Culture, and the Classroom*, 13–14.

127. Ibid., 58.

128. Contract between International Publishers Co. and Joseph P. Lash and James A. Wechsler, June 26, 1936, JPL Box 27. The book that resulted from this contract was *War Our Heritage*, about which reviewer Crane Brinton said "they (Lash and Wechsler) are young, earnest, and determined to make this a much better world," and though he scoffed at their first chapter "M-Day," in which they satirically describe the college students' mobilization against the declaration of war to come in November 1938, their analysis of the reality of the coming war seems, in hindsight, close to the mark. Crane Brinton, "The Younger Radicals," *The Saturday Review*, n.d, JPL Box 33. *War Our Heritage* symbolically went on sale on 11 November 1936 to commemorate Armistice Day.

129. Lash and Wechsler, *War Our Heritage*, 87–88.

130. Ibid., 89–90.

131. Joseph Lash, "Youth and the War Emergency," n.d., JPL Box 27.

132. Joseph Lash, "The Meaning of the Oxford Pledge," 1937, JPL Box 29.

133. Eagan, *Class, Culture, and the Classroom*, 59; Philip G. Altbach, *Student Politics in America: A Historical Analysis* (New York: McGraw-Hill, 1974), 67; Cohen, *When the Old Left Was Young*, 90.

134. Draper, "The Student Movement," 169.

135. Lash and Wechsler, *War Our Heritage*, 89.

136. Joseph Lash, "The Meaning of the Oxford Pledge," 1937, JPL Box 29.

137. "Why and What Are We Striking For?," *Student Outlook*, April 1933, JPL Box 24.

138. Wechsler, *Revolt on the Campus*, 141.

139. Joseph Lash interview with Joel Chernoff, January 5, 1978, JPL Box 78.

140. Eagan, *Class, Culture, and the Classroom*, 71; "Rally Against War," *The Campus*, April 12, 1935, CCNY.

141. Cohen, *When the Old Left Was Young*, 90–91.

142. "Students to Mass Against War, Faculty Members Spur Pacifists,"

Columbia Spectator, April 6, 1933, Microform and Periodicals Collection, Columbia University.

143. "Faculty Scores Aggressive War," *Columbia Spectator*, April 6, 1933, Microform and Periodicals Collection, Columbia University.

144. "Anti-War Week Initiated Today by Mass Parade," *Columbia Spectator*, April 6, 1934, Microform and Periodicals Collection, Columbia University.

145. James Wechsler, "Open Letter to the Faculty," *Columbia Spectator*, April 11, 1934, Microform and Periodicals Collection, Columbia University.

146. Eagan, *Class, Culture, and the Classroom*, 59.

147. Ibid., 62.

148. See Wechsler, *Revolt on the Campus*, Chapter III: "Pre-War Generation."

149. "A Call to Action," *The Student Review: Official Organ, National Student League*, n.d., JPL Box 29.

150. Joseph Lash to Young Socialists in Student Work, March 30, 1936, JPL Box 21.

151. Eagan, *Class, Culture, and the Classroom*, 116.

152. "Striking Against Imperialism," *The Student Review*, December 1932, JPL Box 29.

153. Lash and Wechsler, *War Our Heritage*, 95.

154. Ibid., 68.

155. Ibid., 68, 71; Joseph Lash, "Not to Fight for King or Country," n.d., JPL Box 33.

156. "Thomas Accepts Probability of Future War," *Columbia Spectator*, March 19, 1931, Microform and Periodicals Collection, Columbia University.

157. Charles B. Hart, "The Nye-Kvale Amendment," *The National Student Mirror*, January 1936, CT Box 85.

158. "Editorial Writing Contest"; "Stop the Next War Now!" *The National Student Mirror*, January 1936, CT Box 85.

159. Charles B. Hart, "The Nye-Kvale Amendment," *The National Student Mirror*, January 1936, CT Box 85.

160. National Student Federation Release, April 3, 1936, C, Box 85.

161. Sevareid, *Not So Wild a Dream*, 59.

162. Ibid., 61.

163. "Mobilize for Peace," *The Campus*, November 8, 1935, CCNY.

164. Wechsler, *Revolt on the Campus*, 137, 140.

165. Lash and Wechsler, *War Our Heritage*, 65.

166. Brax, *The First Student Movement*, 37–40.

167. "Striking Against Imperialist War," *The Student Review*, December 1932, JPL Box 29.

168. "Police Spies Used on Hunter Groups; Activists of Peace Council Watched by Alien Squad to Check Radicalism," May 3, 1935 and "Hunter President Bans Peace Group," May 10, 1935, *The Campus*, CCNY.

169. Brax, *The First Student Movement*, 41.

170. *The Campus*, April 15, 1935, CCNY.

171. Altbach, *Student Politics in America*, 62.

172. Ibid., 63.

173. Conference Call, National Student League, n.d., JPL Box 29.

174. Ibid.

175. Ibid.

176. Joseph Lash, "One Big Student Movement?" *Student Outlook*, February 1934, JPL Box 30.

177. Ibid.

178. This is very different from the demise of the French Popular Front government, which first began to fall apart because the French communists abstained from the vote of confidence in January 1938, leading the socialists to withdraw from the government. Léon Blum's attempt to include the communists in forming another government in March 1938 was unsuccessful because, Jackson argues, the communists believed they would soon be able to form a government of their own without aligning with the socialists and radicals. The subsequent suppression of the general strike in November 1938 signaled the complete dissolution of the Popular Front in France. See Jackson, *The Popular Front in France*, 12, xii.

179. Joseph Lash, "One Big Student Movement?" *Student Outlook*, February 1934, JPL Box 30.

180. "Towards One Student Movement," *Student Review*, December 1934, JPL Box 29.

181. Wechsler argues in *Revolt on the Campus* that it was the fascist threat that acted as a catalyst for the anti-war movement. Though most historians paint Wechsler's arguments as a pro-communist analysis, characterizing it as an anti-fascist analysis is more convincing. See, in particular, Chapter XIII: "The Outlook," *Revolt on the Campus*, 1935, for a discussion of his anti-fascist views.

182. "Butler Returns from Sessions of World Peace," and "3 Views on Fascism Presented at Union; Elimination Favored," *Columbia Spectator*, March 20, 1935, Microform and Periodicals Collection, Columbia University.

183. "Why and What Are We Striking for?," *Student Outlook*, April 1933, JPL Box 24.

184. "Why and What are We Striking for?," *Student Outlook*, April 1933, JPL Box 24.

185. Joseph Lash interview with Joel Chernoff, January 5, 1978, JPL Box 78.

186. Ibid.

187. Ibid.

188. Sevareid, *Not So Wild a Dream*, 64.

189. Ibid., 64–65.

190. In their sustained concern about war and their commitment to peace, young people were quite different from those of the 1920s when apathy suffocated an early interest in peace and internationalism. See Paula Fass, *The Damned and the Beautiful* (New York: Oxford University Press, 1977), 330–31. This is likely because, in the 1920s, the experience of the Great War led to

isolationism in the United States, whereas in the 1930s, the desire to avoid re-peating that war was compounded by the march toward another war evidenced by events in Europe and the Pacific.

191. Joseph Lash interview with Joel Chernoff, January 5, 1978, JPL Box 78.

192. While William Randolph Hearst and his newspaper chain may not have been literally demanding war, Hearst was, according to William E. Dodd, U.S. Ambassador to Germany, "greatly impressed with the genius and friend-liness of the chancellor," after meeting Hitler in 1934, and wanted Dodd to negotiate a deal with Joseph Goebbels to supply the Germany Propaganda Ministry with all the Hearst news service. Dodd even went so far as to call Hearst an ally of Mussolini and Hitler. William E. Dodd to Franklin D. Roose-velt, March 20, 1935, Great Britain/German Diplomatic Files, Box 32, FDR Library. Hearst also produced a newsreel showing the Italian invasion of Ethio-pia in a favorable light.

193. Jean Scott, Chairman of the Central Strike Committee to FDR, April 4, 1935, POF 3910; Bulletin Issued by National Strike Committee, April 1935, JPL Box 29.

194. Joseph Lash, Radio Speech, April 11, 1935, JPL Box 29.

195. Ibid.

196. Ibid.

197. "Strike Against War," April 1935, JPL Box 29.

198. "Fight War!" April 1935, JPL Box 29.

199. Wechsler, *Revolt on the Campus*, 178. In 1936, at least 500,000 stu-dents participated. See Joseph Lash, "500,000 Strike for Peace: An Appraisal," *The Student Advocate*, May 1936, CT Box 85; "Tabulation of Participation in Peace Strike," JPL Box 29. There were over 500 high schools, normal schools, law schools, medical schools, and colleges that participated. In addition, the Amalgamated Clothing Workers Union called for a two-minute work stoppage in sympathy with the students at 11:00 just as the strike began. See Joseph Lash, "American Students Strike Against War," 1936, JPL Box 24.

200. Wechsler, *Revolt on the Campus*, 171–72.

201. "Why and What are We Striking For?," *Student Outlook*, April 1933, JPL Box 24.

202. Lash and Wechsler, *War Our Heritage*, 100.

203. James Wechsler, "Strengthen the Student Front," *Student Review*, June 1935, JPL Box 29.

204. Ibid. See also, Joseph Lash, "Two Lives" (Unpublished Autobiography), 21, JPL Box 27.

205. Wechsler, "Strengthen the Student Front."

206. The national executive committees of each organization voted for amalgamation by September 1935. They then planned to recommend amal-gamation to their respective national conventions, which were to be held simultaneously in Columbus in December, at which time members would vote on whether to dissolve their organization in order to create the ASU. See SLID

Bulletin, September 26, 1933, JPL Box 29. By this point, Norman Thomas and other leaders of the LID had reluctantly given their blessing for amalgamation. See Joseph Lash interview with Joel Chernoff, January 5, 1978, JPL Box 78.

207. Ruth Steinberg, "The American Student Union," *Voice of Youth*, February 1936, CT Box 89.

208. "Armistice Day Proclamation," November 1935, JPL Box 21.

209. George Edwards to Joseph Lash, November 15, 1935, JPL Box 27.

210. Ibid.

211. Joseph Lash, "The Meaning of the Oxford Pledge," n.d., JPL Box 29.

212. Ibid.

213. Ibid.

214. Ibid.; "When Moscow Speaks, Must We Heed Its Voice?," n.d., JPL Box 24.

215. Report of the 17th Annual Convention of the Greater New York Federation of YPSL of America, February 1, 1936, YPSL, Box 1. In their National Membership Drive Handbook, the YPSL explained that being involved in youth organizations would keep the YPSL from being isolated from the general social, cultural, and educational life of the youth in the community; provide opportunities for making young people think of social problems in a serious way; and allow socialist converts to be won. They were given explicit instructions: "In most cases, don't hide your identification as a socialist. Don't flaunt it too much either. Take your socialism as a matter of course. Don't act as if it's very unusual for anyone to be a socialist but as if any young man or woman who really understands society and the interests of the masses of people in this country are socialists" and, lastly, they were warned not to preach too much. See National Membership Drive Handbook, 12, YPSL, Folder 1935.

216. In this, the YPSL enjoyed some success. Lash routinely reported ASU activities to the YPSL National Student Committee. See, for example, Minutes of the National Student Committee, March 18, 1936, JPL Box 30.

217. The residual effects of those struggles continued long after the AYC and ASU were disbanded. It has colored former youth activists' memories of youth organizations, their participation in the youth movement, and the role they played in Depression-era politics. See, for example, Wechsler, *The Age of Suspicion*.

218. Draper claimed that "politically speaking, the socialists and communists crossed each other, going in opposite directions." Draper, "The Student Movement," 166.

219. Joseph Lash to Socialist Comrades, March 30, 1936, JPL Box 21.

220. "YCL Appeal to YPSL for United Action," March 20, 1935, YPSL, Box 1.

221. It was ASU National High School Secretary Celeste Strack, an NSL member, who insisted on the democratic resolution of this issue. She had called on high school delegates to vote on whether they favored a national strike call or a national call for peace actions for high schools. They favored the

latter. Thus, while Draper saw this as anti-revolutionary, most members of the ASU—communists included—saw it as democracy in practice. See Celeste Strack to NEC members, February 18, 1937, JPL Box 21.

222. Joseph Lash, "Two Lives," 33, JPL Box 78.

223. Ibid.

224. Ibid.

225. Hal Draper, "Revolutionary Socialism and War," n.d., JPL Box 30.

226. "We Do Not Build the ASU," n.d., JPL Box 30.

227. Cohen, *When the Old Left Was Young*, 148–50.

228. Joseph Lash to Elisabeth Gilman, Secretary-Treasurer of Christian Social Justice Fund, Inc., April 20, 1936, JPL Box 30.

229. Jeff to Joseph Lash, April 2, 1936, JPL Box 30.

230. Bob Newman to Joseph Lash, n.d., JPL Box 30.

231. Ibid.

232. Brax, *The First Student Movement*, 70; Wechsler, *The Age of Suspicion*, 85.

233. Wechsler, *The Age of Suspicion*, 85–86.

234. Joseph Lash interview with Joel Chernoff, January 5, 1978, JPL Box 78; Minutes of the National Student Committee, April 22, 1937, JPL Box 30.

235. Miller, "The American Student Movement," 62; Cohen, *When the Old Left Was Young*, 140.

236. Cohen, *When the Old Left Was Young*, 140.

237. Lash, "Two Lives" (Unpublished Autobiography), 22, JPL Box 27.

238. Joseph Lash to Eleanor Roosevelt, February 4, 1936, Eleanor Roosevelt Microfilm Collection, Reel 1, FDR Library.

239. Howe, *Socialism and America*, 45.

240. Letters to the editor, *Student Advocate*, JPL Box 21.

241. ASU membership card, n.d., JPL Box 21.

242. Joseph Lash, "Two Lives" (Unpublished Autobiography), 20, JPL Box 78.

243. Ibid.

244. Howe, *Socialism and America*, 49.

245. Irving Howe fundamentally objected to Bell's analysis, arguing that socialists, in order to remain socialists, must not be "of the world" because then they would have to "give up the idea of historical transcendence, the vision of *another* society." See Howe, *Socialism and America*, 35.

246. Bell, *Marxian Socialism in the United States*, xi.

247. In a truly ironic twist, Rawick later quietly contradicted his depiction of youth leaders and organizations as communists bent on conspiratorially manipulating themselves into positions of power to overthrow the American system. Old editions of *Student Advocate* were compiled and published in 1968, for which Rawick wrote the preface. In it, he still maintained that many of the leaders of both the ASU and the *Student Advocate* were members of the Communist Party and the YCL, or were, at the very least, willing to work with such people. (This was a prerequisite, of course, in forming the popular front, though Rawick chose to use this to label people as fellow-travelers.) However,

because the ASU's public image was liberal and pro–New Deal, both it and the pages of the *Student Advocate* were utilized by the New Deal "as propagandists for President Roosevelt's policies." George Rawick, preface to *Student Advocate* (New York: Greenwood Reprint Corporation, 1968), 1. This close working relationship, he said, allowed such organizations to become "conveyor belts that carried young communists and young socialists from these commitments to the official liberalism. The function of the A.S.U. was therefore not that of making communists out of liberals, as has been charged by many, but precisely the opposite. It made liberals out of socialists and communists." Ibid. Although this description accurately depicts what happened to young radical activists and the organizations they led in the 1930s, it has been overshadowed by his dissertation's Cold War rhetoric of eleven years earlier.

248. Chief among such people was Joseph Lash.

249. Richard Pells, *Radical Visions and American Dreams: Culture and Social Thought in the Depression Years* (New York: Harper & Row Publishers, 1973), xii.

250. Howe, *Socialism and America*, 86.

251. Pells, *Radical Visions and American Dreams*, 99.

252. Ibid., 299, 296.

253. Ibid., 345–47, 354, 361.

5. Playing Politics and Making Policy: Institutionalizing a Vision from New York to Washington

1. Betty Lindley and Ernest K. Lindley, *A New Deal for Youth: The Story of the National Youth Administration* (New York: Viking Press, 1938), 12.

2. Eleanor Roosevelt, "Youth Today Is Tomorrow's Nation," Cornell University, February 14, 1935, ER.

3. William E. Leuchtenburg, *Franklin D. Roosevelt and the New Deal* (New York: Harper and Row, 1963), 125.

4. Lindley and Lindley, *A New Deal for Youth*, foreword by Charles Taussig, vii.

5. "The Function of Education in Democracy," Committee on Education Report to the AYC Model Congress, July 1937, President's Advisory Committee on Education, POF, Box 1.

6. Robert Morss Lovett, introduction to James Wechsler, *Revolt on the Campus* (Seattle: University of Washington Press, 1935), xv.

7. A. M. Sirkin, "Youngville, USA," (New York: American Youth Congress, 1937), 25, DP Box 275.

8. "The C.C.C.—Tomorrow's Vigilantes?" *Columbia Spectator*, November 26, 1935, Microform and Periodicals Collection, Columbia University.

9. See George Rawick, "The New Deal and Youth: The Civilian Conservation Corps, the National Youth Administration, and the American Youth Congress" (Ph.D. dissertation: University of Wisconsin–Madison, 1957).

10. Sirkin, "Youngville, USA," 24–25.

11. "The C.C.C.—Tomorrow's Vigilantes?" *Columbia Spectator.*

12. As quoted in Jean Ford, "The C.C.C. Stands Ready," *The Student Outlook*, March 1934, JPL Box 30.

13. Ibid.

14. Ibid.

15. Richard Reiman, *The New Deal and American Youth: Ideas and Ideals in a Depression Decade* (Athens: University of Georgia Press, 1992), 152. While the broader public was likely responding to the growing fascist threat in Europe, young activists remained adamantly opposed to compulsory military training.

16. Sirkin, "Youngville, USA," 25.

17. Lewis L. Lorwin, "Youth Work Programs: Problems and Policies," Prepared for the American Youth Commission (Washington, D.C.: American Council on Education, 1941), 18.

18. Leuchtenburg, *Franklin D. Roosevelt and the New Deal*, 174.

19. The first experimental student aid programs administered by FERA in 1933 were extended in February 1934, and in May 1934 FERA established resident camps and schools for unemployed women. This was meant to supplement the CCC program. They served, too, as prototypes for later NYA programs. See Palmer Johnson and Oswald Harvey, *The National Youth Administration* (Washington, D.C.: United States Government Printing Office, 1938), 7.

20. New Deal historians do see FDR as the primary proponent of the CCC, but this was not a youth program devised in response to youth's demands. See, for example, Paul Conkin, *The New Deal*, 2nd ed. (Arlington Heights, Ill.: Harlan Davidson, 1975).

21. Reiman, *The New Deal and American Youth*, 30.

22. A.W. Vandeman to FDR, September 14, 1934, POF 58B, Box 3.

23. Edward A. Filene to FDR, September 7, 1933, POF 58.

24. Reiman, *The New Deal and American Youth*, 31.

25. Newton D. Baker, American Commission on Education Conference Program, July, 1936, CT Box 1.

26. Homer P. Rainey, "Problems of Employment Among Youth," July 10, 1936, CT Box 1.

27. Ibid.

28. Charles Taussig, Foreword to Betty Lindley and Ernest K. Lindley, *A New Deal for Youth*, ix.

29. Harry Hopkins to all State Emergency Relief Administrations, November 28, 1934, POF 50.

30. "Program for Youth," Hopkins Papers, Box 50, FDR Library.

31. "National Youth Division," Hopkins Papers, Box 50, FDR Library.

32. Reiman, *The New Deal and American Youth*, 102–4.

33. William Lloyd Hurd, "The Origin and Early Development of the National Youth Administration," (M.A. Thesis: University of Oklahoma, 1967), 22; and A.W. Bell memorandum to FDR, July 9, 1937, POF 444D.

34. Memorandum, John Studebaker to Marvin McIntyre, January 24, 1936, POF 444D.

35. Press Release from Department of Interior, Office of Education, April 25, 1935, POF 58B, Box 3.

36. W. E. Porter to Stephen Early, March 7, 1935, PPF 2282.

37. Ibid.

38. Stephen Early to William Porter, March 5, 1935, PPF 2282.

39. Stephen Early to August Heckscher, May 13, 1935, POF 58B, Box 3.

40. Charles Taussig to David Sarnoff, April 18, 1935, CT Box 8.

41. Telegram from M. H. McIntyre to Charles Taussig, April 23, 1935, POF 444D.

42. Carol Weisenberger, *Dollars and Dreams: The National Youth Administration in Texas* (New York: Peter Lang Publishing, 1994), 22.

43. Executive Order 7086, June 26, 1935, Hopkins Papers, Box 24, FDR Library. The NYA, then, was part of the new wave of reform measures referred to as the Second New Deal developed, in part, to build popular support before the 1936 election.

44. M. H. McIntyre to Commissioner Studebaker May 10, 1935, POF 58b, Box 3.

45. What exactly NYA policy was has been open to debate. It has been argued that the NYA was primarily a relief agency whose focus was not on youth, *per se*, but on the economic emergency. This argument rests on FDR's placing the NYA under the WPA, rather than the USOE or Department of Labor. It follows that, as such, FDR never envisioned a permanent youth agency. Ample evidence for this lies in the fact that NYA appropriations relied on annual Congressional approval. See Rawick, "The New Deal and Youth." Others have argued that the NYA was an attempt to provide educational opportunity to the economically disadvantaged (especially minorities and women) and, in so doing, was a social reform agency. See Weisenberger, *Dollars and Dreams*.

46. Thomas Neblett, Remarks to National Advisory Committee of the NYA, April 28, 1936, AW Box 6, FDR Library.

47. Charles Taussig to FDR, June 28, 1935, POF, Box 20.

48. Representative Ross A. Collins (D-MS) to Charles Taussig, December 10, 1936, CT Box 8. Collins was a member of the House Committee on Appropriations and had regular correspondence with Taussig. See CT Box 9.

49. Charles Taussig to Eleanor Roosevelt, November 27, 1936, ER NYA Materials, Microfilm, FDR Library.

50. Lorwin, *Youth Work Programs*, 17.

51. Alex Gaal, Jr. to the President, April 27, 1935, POF 58b, Box 3.

52. Arthur J. Jones to FDR, November 20, 1935, POF 58b, Box 3.

53. Lindley and Lindley, *A New Deal for Youth*, 23.

54. William Hinckley, "Youth Speaks for Itself," 1935, Tamiment Library, NYU.

55. Thomas Neblett to Charles Taussig, September 25, 1935; Charles Taussig

to Thomas Neblett, October 2, 1935; CT Box 8. There is some contention about who came up with the essay-writing plan. The Youth News Service published an article on February 21, 1936 claiming that it was Taussig's plan and that he was trying to use Neblett as a sponsor so that young people would go along with it. CT Box 12.

56. FDR to Thomas Neblett, February 5, 1936, POF 444D.

57. Studebaker Memorandum to Mr. McIntyre, February 5, 1936, POF 444D.

58. Roger Chase to Joseph Lash, February 15, 1936, JPL Box 29.

59. Ibid.

60. Joseph Lash, February 1, 1938, JPL Box 29.

61. Rawick, "The New Deal and Youth," 324. Taussig was particularly interested in working with representatives from youth organizations whatever their political leanings so that they would feel invested in the program and so that the program developed met youth's needs. See Charles Taussig, Foreword to Lindley and Lindley, *A New Deal for Youth*, xi–xiii. Unlike the National Executive Committee, headed by the Assistant Secretary of the Treasury Josephine Roche and composed of departmental officials, The National Advisory Committee, under the chairmanship of Charles W. Taussig, comprised thirty-five representatives from various fields such as labor, business, agriculture, education, and youth. Included among the thirty-five members was Mary McLeod Bethune.

62. Richard Brown to all State Youth Directors, August 15, 1936, Hopkins Papers, Box 24, FDR Library.

63. Confidential Memorandum, M. H. McIntyre to Aubrey Williams, July 16, 1935, POF 444D.

64. Bernarr Macfadden to Charles Taussig, December 12, 1938, POF 444D, Box 19.

65. Charles Taussig to FDR, December 19, 1938, POF 444D, Box 19.

66. Charles Taussig to Eleanor Roosevelt, December 19, 1938, POF 444D, Box 19; Macfadden's rhetoric alone alienated many youth as he talked in militaristic terms that reminded one of fascism. He said during a National Advisory Committee meeting that "life is pretty much a fight" and that "this physical training I believe so much in gives a boy pep and endurance and puts the fight into him, and enables him to go out and dominate the situation." National Advisory Committee Meeting Minutes, August 15, 1935, CT Box 6.

67. FDR to Charles Taussig, December 19, 1938, POF 444D, Box 19.

68. Ibid.

69. Remarks to the National Advisory Committee of NYA, November 9, 1940, PPF: Speeches, File 57.

70. This was subsequently adopted as NYA policy; a Director for NYA in Puerto Rico was included on the list of directors for December 1, 1936, Hopkins Papers, Box 83, FDR Library.

71. Copy of a wire from Union Republican Youth of Puerto Rico to FDR, 1935, POF 58.

72. Statement of the National Advisory Committee of the NYA, April 29, 1936, POF 444D.

73. Lindley and Lindley, *A New Deal for Youth*, xi–xii.

74. Johnson and Harvey, *The National Youth Administration*, 21. Johnson was a Professor of Education at the University of Minnesota, which was the site of the original college federal student aid experiment under the auspices of the Federal Emergency Relief Administration in 1933.

75. Julia D. Gibson, Chairman Public Affairs Committee YWCA to FDR, April 28, 1936, POF 58B, Box 3.

76. Frank Peer Beal, Executive Secretary, to Council Chairmen, June 10, 1936, Olds Papers, Box 23, FDR Library.

77. Minutes of the Administrative Committee of the ASU, October 7, 1937, JPL Box 21.

78. ASU Chapter Guide, October 23, 1937, JPL Box 21.

79. William Hinckley, "Youth Speaks for Itself," 1935, Tamiment Library, NYU.

80. "Appendix A of AYC Activities," n.d., Jackson Gardner Papers, Box 84, FDR Library.

81. Organized labor was at first hostile to young workers, who were seen as a competitive labor force that drove down wages and took what scarce jobs were available. There were some who remained reluctant to support the NYA because, in the long term, it was training young people as skilled workers who, upon leaving the NYA, would be that much more attractive to potential employers. But, for the most part, adult labor union leaders came to support the NYA because it was seen as a way to keep young workers out of regular wage work in the short term. And, if they joined the NYA Workers Union, then they were introduced to the labor union at an early age, which, union leaders hoped, would make them more loyal to the future success of the labor movement as a whole. See Lorwin, "Youth Work Programs: Problems and Policies"; Sirkin, "Youngville, USA," 52; Melvyn Dubovsky and Warren Van Tine, *John L. Lewis: A Biography* (Chicago: University of Chicago Press, 1986).

82. Memorandum, Charles Taussig to FDR, September 16, 1936, POF 444D.

83. William Hinckley, "Youth Seeks Peace, Freedom, and Progress," *Report of the American Youth Congress*, July 1936, Gardner Jackson Papers, Box 5, FDR Library.

84. Charles Taussig, "Youth and Total Defense," October 16, 1940, ER NYA Material Microfilm Collection, FDR Library.

85. See, for example, Charles Taussig to Eleanor Roosevelt, May 4, 1936, ER NYA Materials, Microfilm, FDR Library.

86. Leslie Gould, *American Youth Today* (New York: Random House, 1940), 293; "The American Youth Act," Proceedings of the Third American Youth Congress, July 3–5, 1936, Gardner Jackson Papers, Box 5, FDR Library.

87. "American Youth Act," Proceedings of the Third American Youth Congress, July 3–5, 1936.

88. William Hinckley, "Youth Speaks for Itself," 1935.

89. Joseph Cadden, "The N.S.F.A. Conference," *Voice of Youth*, February 1936, CT Box 89.

90. Joseph Cadden, Editorial, *The National Student Mirror*, November 1935, CT Box 85.

91. "The American Youth Act," *The National Student Mirror*, February 1936, CT Box 85.

92. "Mentionables of American Education," *The Student Advocate*, February 1936, CT Box 85; "The American Youth Act," Proceedings of the Third American Youth Congress, July 3–5, 1936.

93. "Mentionables of American Education," *The Student Advocate*, February 1936.

94. "Youth Urged to Campaign for New Act," *Columbia Spectator*, February 17, 1936, Microform and Periodicals Collection, Columbia University.

95. *The Campus*, May 27, 1936, CCNY.

96. YPSL National Executive Committee Meeting Minutes, October 4–6, 1935, YPSL.

97. "Directives for YPSL Campaign on American Youth Act," March 9, 1936, YPSL.

98. William Hinckley, "Youth Speaks for Itself," 1935.

99. Aubrey Williams, "Student Aid Reaches Ten Percent of National College Enrollment," January 31, 1937, Democratic Party Women's Division Papers, Box 16, FDR Library.

100. Gould, *American Youth Today*, 71.

101. Rawick, "The New Deal and Youth," 328.

102. William Hinckley, "Youth Speaks for Itself," 1935.

103. AYC National Executive Committee Meeting Minutes, January 16, 1936, JPL Box 29.

104. William W. Hinckley to FDR, January 31, 1936, POF 3910.

105. "The Young Ask Questions and Mrs. Roosevelt Answers," February 2, 1936, CT Box 81.

106. William Green to William Hinckley and William Hinckley to William Green as discussed in Minutes from National Council of American Youth Council Meeting, March 26, 1936, JPL Box 23.

107. Charles Taussig, "Address Before the Convention of the American Federation of Labor," October 14, 1935, Eleanor Roosevelt Microfilm Collection, Reel 0275, FDR Library.

108. Charles Taussig, "Youth and Democracy," February 16, 1936, POF 444D, Box 20.

109. National Executive Committee Meeting Minutes, AYC, November 12, 1936, JPL Box 23.

110. National Executive Committee Meeting Minutes, AYC, December 3, 1936, JPL Box 23.

111. John L. Lewis to William Hinckley, November 2, 1937, JPL Box 23.

112. "Plan of Activity for Youth Act Month," JPL Box 23. Later, the WPA produced its own dramatic version of the NYA and the American Youth Act hearings entitled "The Lost Generation," National Executive Committee Meeting Minutes, August 5, 1937, JPL Box 23.

113. William Hinckley to FDR, December 16, 1936, POF 3910.

114. Telegram from William Hinckley to Harry Hopkins, December 22, 1936; Harry Hopkins to Marvin McIntyre, December 22, 1936, POF 3910.

115. Memorandum, Marvin McIntyre to Harry Hopkins, March 30, 1937, POF 3910.

116. FDR to William Hinckley, June 22, 1936, PPF 2282.

117. William Hinckley to Gardner Jackson, February 13, 1937, Gardner Jackson Papers, Box 5, FDR Library.

118. Abbott Simon to Gardner "Pat" Jackson, June 26, 1937, Gardner Jackson Papers, Box 5, FDR Library.

119. Celeste Strack, "Save the Lost Generation!" *The Student Advocate*, April 1936, CT Box 1.

120. James Wechsler, "No Surrender Now," *The Student Advocate*, April 1936, CT Box 1.

121. The AYC was habitually starved for funds; during its National Executive Committee Meeting on June 11, 1936, for example, William Hinckley warned that unless money was immediately forthcoming, the office's telephone would be shut off. The executive committee members relied on affiliated organizations to voluntarily contribute funds to the national office through local fundraising events. It was for this reason that the AYC could only send one delegate (to be chosen at the 3rd Annual Congress in 1936) to attend the World Youth Congress to be held in Geneva; travel costs amounted to $250.

122. National Council, American Youth Congress Meeting Minutes, April 23, 1936, JPL Box 23.

123. William Hinckley, "Youth Seeks Peace, Freedom, and Progress," Report of the American Youth Congress, July 1936.

124. James Wechsler, "No Surrender Now," *The Student Advocate*, April 1936, CT Box 1.

125. Ibid. There was truth to this charge. In 1937, Neblett became a field examiner with the National Labor Relations Board. He resigned that position in 1940 in order to go to work for FDR's campaign. Thomas Neblett to Charles Taussig, September 16, 1940; Thomas Neblett to Franklin D. Roosevelt, Jr., September 16, 1940, CT Box 12.

126. Proceedings of the Third American Youth Congress, July 3–5, 1936, Gardner Jackson Papers, Box 5, FDR Library.

127. Ibid. Also present were 116 observers (those who had not yet affiliated with the AYC) from 106 organizations representing another 2,300,000 young people. Social, cultural, and sports clubs were most heavily represented at the conference, with 151 organizations. The AFL trade unions had the largest number of members (283,070). There were 100 political organizations with 24,475

members and 121 student groups with 76,985 members. The Y's made up 74 of the organizations and represented 143,380 members.

128. Hinckley, "Youth Seeks Peace, Freedom, and Progress," Report of the American Youth Congress, July 1936.

129. National Executive Committee Meeting Minutes, AYC, July 23, 1936, JPL Box 23.

130. National Executive Committee Meeting Minutes, AYC, October 15, 1936, JPL Box 23.

131. Hinckley, "Youth Seeks Peace, Freedom, and Progress," Report of the American Youth Congress, July 1936.

132. Ibid.

133. The AYC was asked to send a representative to testify at the hearings for the Nye-Kvale Bill. Senator Gerald Nye (R-ND) to American Youth Congress as noted in National Council Meeting Minutes, April 9, 1936, JPL Box 23.

134. William Hinckley to FDR, September 21, 1936, POF 3910.

135. William Hinckley to FDR, October 13, 1936, POF 3910.

136. Charles B. Forbes to Charles Taussig, June 19, 1936, CT Box 8. The "nucleus" of this movement for Roosevelt was to be found, Forbes said, in the thousands of college students receiving NYA aid. The Movement was supposed to educate young voters, culminating in a parade ending at Soldier Field in Chicago, where the President would address between one and two hundred thousand young people. Forbes even suggested that Taussig temporarily resign from the NYA during the campaign (resuming his position after the election) so that the NYA could not be officially connected to his efforts on behalf of FDR.

137. Joseph Lash to Paul Reeves, November 10, 1936, JPL Box 30.

138. Ibid.; Letter to the Editor, *New Haven Register*, August 26, 1935, CT Box 80.

139. Minutes of ASU Second National Convention, December 27–30, 1936, JPL Box 24.

140. Proceedings of Third American Youth Congress, July 3–5, 1936, Gardner Jackson Papers, Box 5, FDR Library.

141. "Cooperate on Cooperatives," *A.S.U. Bulletin*, September 1936, JPL Box 21.

142. Ibid.

143. Minutes from ASU Second National Convention, December 27–30, 1936, JPL Box 24.

144. "The Function of Education in Democracy," Committee on Education Report to the AYC Model Congress, July 1937, President's Advisory Committee on Education, Box 1, FDR Library.

145. Ibid. Notably omitted from the AYC's vision of a democratically chosen school board is any capital or business interests.

146. Memorandum from Eleanor Roosevelt to the President, March 4, 1937, POF 444D.

147. Gould, *American Youth Today*, 72.
148. FDR to William Hinckley, June 21, 1937, PPF 2282.
149. William Hinckley to FDR, 1937, PPF 2282.
150. *Activities of the American Youth Commission* (Washington, D.C.: American Council on Education, 1937), 3–5, President's Interdepartmental Committee to Coordinate Health and Welfare Activities, Box 15, FDR Library.
151. Ibid., 12–13.
152. Floyd Reeves to William Hinckley, February 21, 1938, President's Advisory Committee on Education, Box 1, FDR Library.
153. William Hinckley to Floyd Reeves, October 26, 1937, President's Advisory Committee on Education, Box 1, FDR Library.
154. William Hinckley to Floyd Reeves, December 4, 1937, President's Advisory Committee on Education, Box 1, FDR Library.
155. Floyd Reeves to William Hinckley, December 6, 1937, President's Advisory Committee on Education, Box 1, FDR Library.
156. William Hinckley to Paul David, Secretary of President's Advisory Committee, March 15, 1938; Phillip Dobbs, Student Secretary of AYC to Floyd Reeves, March 23, 1938, President's Advisory Committee on Education, Box 1, FDR Library.
157. ASU Chapter Guide, September 28 1937, JPL Box 21.
158. Telegram from AYC of Iowa to FDR, October 14, 1937, POF 3910; National Executive Committee Meeting Minutes, AYC, May 27, 1937, JPL Box 23.
159. ASU Chapter Guide, September 28, 1937, JPL Box 21.
160. Ibid.
161. "Notes on the Nation," *The Student Advocate*, December 1937, CT Box 85.
162. Lorwin, *Youth Work Programs*, 3.
163. Lindley and Lindley, *A New Deal for Youth*, 212.
164. Ibid., 214.
165. William Hinckley to FDR, February 17, 1938; Hinckley to FDR, February 18, 1938; William Hinckley to Eleanor Roosevelt, February 18, 1938; Abbott Simon to FDR, March 5, 1938, Philip Dobbs to FDR, March 4, 1938, POF 444D.
166. William Hinckley to James Roosevelt, 1938, POF 3910.
167. William Hinckley to James Roosevelt, February 23, 1938, POF 444D.
168. William Hinckley to Floyd Reeves, March 1, 1938, President's Advisory Committee on Education, Box 1, FDR Library.
169. American Youth Congress Meeting Minutes, January 19, 1939, ERPC.
170. Ibid.
171. American Youth Congress Meeting Minutes, June 22, 1939, ERPC.
172. Janet Feder, Executive Secretary of AYC to Democratic National Committee, June 27, 1939, Democratic Party Women's Division Papers, Box 275, FDR Library.

173. "Calling the Citizens of Tomorrow to the Congress of Youth; Building Democracy Today," Democratic Party Women's Division Papers, Box 275; CT Box 85.

174. The AYC was also concerned about education. At its Model Congress (4th Annual Congress) in 1937, it adopted a platform in line with the one the ASU pursued: democracy of opportunity, democracy of content, and democracy of administration. See William Hinckley to Floyd Reeves, Chair of the President's Commission on Education, December 6, 1937, JPL Box 23.

175. Joseph Lash, "The University We Want to Study In," Report of Proceedings of Fourth National Convention of the American Student Union, December 27–30, 1938, JPL Box 23.

176. Ibid.

177. Ibid.

178. Ibid.

179. Ibid.

180. Ibid.

181. "Resolution on Legislative and Political Action," Report on Proceedings of Fourth National Convention of American Student Union, December 27–30, 1938, JPL Box 23.

182. Ibid.

183. FDR to Joseph Lash, December 1, 1938, JPL Box 21.

184. "The Student Almanac," Report of the Fourth Annual ASU Conference, December 26–30, 1938, JPL Box 21.

185. Reiman has argued that one of the reasons the NYA was extended in the late 1930s was that FDR was attracted to Williams's reformist ventures in the areas of race, refugee assistance, education, and relief that mirrored the leftward direction FDR took the New Deal after 1938. See Reiman, *The New Deal and American Youth*, 187, and John A. Salmond, *A Southern Rebel: The Life and Times of Aubrey Willis Williams, 1890–1965* (Chapel Hill: University of North Carolina Press, 1983).

186. Lindley and Lindley, *A New Deal for Youth*, 102–3. The Resident Centers were also used as a limited source of aid to Jewish refugees fleeing fascism in Europe. A small number of refugees were enrolled in the NYA training programs. For a discussion of this refugee aid, see Reiman, *The New Deal and American Youth*, 160–70.

187. Lorwin, *Youth Work Programs*, 41.

188. Ibid.

189. Ibid., 44.

190. Press Release from *The Parents' Magazine*, December 20, 1938, DP Box 275.

191. Ibid.

192. See Richard Reiman, *The New Deal and American Youth*.

193. Aubrey Williams and John Studebaker signed an agreement to this

effect on June 27, 1940, itself the result of a long series of negotiations. See Salmond, *A Southern Rebel*, 144–46.

194. Lorwin, *Youth Work Programs*, 65, 118.

195. Ibid., 121.

196. Ibid., 122–23.

197. Ibid., 123.

198. Karl D. Hesley to Eleanor Roosevelt, November 8, 1940, ER NYA Materials, Microfilm, FDR Library.

199. Jack McMichael, "Youth and the Nation," Report to the AYC 1941 Annual Congress, February 7–9, 1941, Vertical File: American Youth Congress, FDR Library.

200. Lorwin, *Youth Work Programs*, 175.

201. Eleanor Roosevelt to Charles Taussig, March 11, 1940, ER NYA Materials, Microfilm Collection, FDR Library.

202. Ibid.

203. Charles Taussig to Eleanor Roosevelt, October 4, 1940; Charles Taussig to Eleanor Roosevelt, October 14, 1940, ER NYA Material, Microfilm Collection, FDR Library.

204. Eleanor Roosevelt to Charles Taussig, September 22, 1940. Four additional youth members were added to the NYA National Advisory Committee in 1941. See S. Born Weston to Eleanor Roosevelt, June 18, 1941, ER NYA Material, Microfilm Collection, FDR Library.

205. "Statement of the National Advisory Committee of the National Youth Administration to the President of the United States," n.d., ER NYA Material, Microfilm Collection, FDR Library.

206. Indeed, Charles Taussig had already decided, in tandem with Aubrey Williams, to launch an all-out propaganda effort to convince young people that the defense training program of the NYA was in their best interest. After the 1940 election, Betty Lindley was to go on the NYA payroll to do another staff study with her husband, Ernest K. Lindley, who was already drafting the book to be titled "Youth and Total Defense" on much the same model as their earlier defense of the NYA, itself, in *A New Deal for Youth*. See Charles Taussig to Eleanor Roosevelt, October 4, 1940, ER NYA Material, Microfilm Collection, FDR Library.

207. "Statement of the National Advisory Committee of the National Youth Administration to the President of the United States," November 9, 1940, ER NYA Material, Microfilm Collection, FDR Library.

208. Ibid.

209. Jack McMichael, "Youth and the Nation," Report to the AYC 1941 Annual Congress, February 7–9, 1941, Vertical File: American Youth Congress, FDR Library.

210. "Student America Organizes for Peace," 5th Annual Convention of ASU December 27–30, 1939, JPL Box 21.

211. Telegram from Paul V. McNutt to Charles Taussig, October 6, 1939, CT Box 9.

212. NYA Press Release, June 12, 1940, CT Box 87.

213. Telegram from AYC to Aubrey Williams, February 8, 1940, NYA Press Release February 8, 1940, CT Box 87.

214. NYA Press Release, February 8, 1940, CT Box 87.

215. NYA Press Release, March 6, 1942, CT Box 87.

216. Aubrey Williams to Hubert Atherton, June 18, 1942, AW Box 12, FDR Library.

217. Charles Taussig to Eleanor Roosevelt, July 29, 1943, CT Box 9.

218. Aubrey Williams, "Betrayal of Youth," November 1942, AW Box 25, FDR Library.

219. On December 9, 1941, Congressman Lyndon B. Johnson introduced a bill in the House of Representatives calling for a merger of the CCC and NYA into a new Civilian Youth Administration, under the Federal Security Agency. Robert Caro argues that the bill (the only one LBJ introduced in his first six years in Congress) was an attempt by LBJ to accrue power through appointment as the new agency's director. See Robert Caro, *Path to Power* (New York: Vintage Books, 1990), 546. In any event, the attempt at consolidation failed, and the CCC was subsequently canceled.

220. See, for example, Bruce Bliven, Editor of *The New Republic* to Aubrey Williams, November 7, 1941, AW Box 25, FDR Library.

221. Aubrey Williams to Charles Taussig, November 17, 1942, CT Box 9.

222. Aubrey Williams, Report to the National Council Meeting of AYC, February 22, 1937, JPL Box 23.

223. Eleanor Roosevelt, "Graduation Address," *Look Magazine*, Des Moines, Iowa, June 1939, ER.

224. Eleanor Roosevelt, "National Service in Democracy," July 23, 1940, and "Where Do We Go From Here?," April 1939, ER.

225. Joseph Cadden to Eleanor Roosevelt, January 6, 1940, ER.

226. Robert Cohen, *When the Old Left Was Young: Student Radicals and America's First Mass Student Movement, 1929–1941* (New York: Oxford University Press, 1993), 320.

227. Ibid., 320.

228. Ibid.; Eleanor Roosevelt, "National Service in Democracy" July 23, 1940, Eleanor Roosevelt Papers; "Where Do We Go From Here?" April 1939, ER. Eleanor Roosevelt's plan predated the passage of the Selective Training and Service Act, which inaugurated the first peacetime conscription of men for military service by 17 months.

229. Eleanor Roosevelt, "Dear Mrs. Roosevelt" *Democratic Digest*, August–September, 1939, ER.

230. FDR to Congressman John Lesinksi, June 13, 1942, POF 444D, Box 19.

231. Ibid.

232. Claude Pepper to FDR, December 21, 1944, POF 58, Box 2.

233. Franklin D. Roosevelt to Claude Pepper, December 28, 1944, POF 58, Box 2.

234. J. Daniels Memorandum to Alice Winegar, November 21, 1944, POF 58, Box 2.

235. Ibid.

236. Aubrey Williams, "Final Report of the National Youth Administration," December 28, 1943, AW Box 15, FDR Library.

6. The Fight Against Fascism: The Spanish Republicans Find Their Support in New York City

1. Paul Preston, *The Spanish Civil War: Reaction, Revolution, and Revenge* (New York: Norton, 2006), 3.

2. Preston, *The Spanish Civil War*, 33.

3. Ibid., 6.

4. Hugh Thomas, *The Spanish Civil War* (New York: The New Library, 2001), 117. Thomas refers to anti-fascism and the popular front as powerful myths that were "almost irresistible to those who both loved peace and liberty and were impatient with old parties."

5. James Wechsler, *The Age of Suspicion* (New York: Donald I. Fine, 1953), 128. In writing this book, Wechsler disavows nearly all of the ideas he espoused as a young communist in the 1930s. The notable exceptions are those concerning Spain. In retrospect, he asks "did it matter decisively that the communists themselves were guilty of sadistic excesses, and even that their revolution was devouring its children? In the long view, which is the rationalization of all oppression, weren't they still on the side of the angels? The questions seemed hard." Lash agreed. When asked later about whether he was aware of the purges and show trials in the Soviet Union and Spain, he said, "The whole movement by the Communist-dominated—particularly as the Russians began to have a greater influence in the Spanish government—the dreadful things that were happening in Catalonia and even in Madrid, purges—one rationalizes to oneself. The anarchists in Catalonia were really breaking up the front and in wartime, you had to have discipline. So you close your eyes to it which one shouldn't have done but I'm just trying to explain my own psychology on the thing . . . I think that there was an awareness that the trials were going on. . . . To me, my own rationalization was that this was a reflection of capitalist encirclement and that you could not expect any kind of liberalization in the Soviet Union until the fascist pressure was lifted." Joseph Lash interview with Joel Chernoff, January 5, 1978, JPL Box 78.

6. Preston, *The Spanish Civil War*, 7.

7. See, for example, *The Campus*, October 4, 1935, CCNY.

8. Activist students were very concerned about the Chinese people. They were also concerned that the United States would not be able to stay out of that war. Lash and Wechsler made the argument in 1936 that war between the

United States and Japan would result not from Japan's imperialist policies, but, rather, from America's desire to protect its market in East Asia. They claimed that the United States was already preparing for war with Japan and "that war will be fought over Chinese markets." Joseph Lash and James Wechsler, *War Our Heritage* (New York: International Publishers, 1936), 81–82; Joseph Lash interview with Joel Chernoff, January 5, 1978, JPL Box 78.

9. Paul Preston refers to this as a time of confrontation and conspiracy as the opposing left and right groups solidified and the planning of the military coup began. See Preston, *The Spanish Civil War*, 66–101.

10. The largest of the rightist groups at the time was the CEDA, Spanish Confederation of Autonomous Rightist Groups, which historian Stanley Payne has described as a Catholic organization whose goal was to create a corporative and conservative Catholic republic. Stanley Payne, *Spain's First Democracy: The Second Republic, 1931–1936* (Madison: University of Wisconsin Press, 1993), 168.

11. In accounting for U.S. policy toward Spain during the Great Depression, Paul Preston has wrapped these two issues together into what he refers to as "New Deal isolationism." Preston, *The Spanish Civil War*, 144.

12. James Wechsler, *Revolt on the Campus* (Seattle: University of Washington Press, 1935), 453.

13. "An Appeal to the Members of the YPSL," October 6, 1934, YPSL, YPSL, Box 1.

14. Indeed, Stanley Payne identifies this as the most important factor in explaining the government's failure to put down the rightist revolt and its defeat in the civil war. Payne argues that the only group wholly committed to republican democracy was the Radicals, and for their willingness to compromise and their lack of doctrine, they were vilified by both the right and the left. Yet, he says, they alone "stood as the principal defenders and practitioners of democratic Republic for all." Payne, *Spain's First Democracy*, 256.

15. This was because Largo Caballero kept the PSOE out of the cabinet in the hopes of creating an exclusively workers' government in its stead. Preston, *The Spanish Civil War*, 163.

16. The Spanish people voted for a popular front government in the February 1936 elections; however, this existed only on the political, and not the governmental, level as the Socialists refused (and were refused) seats in the new administration until September 1936. See Payne, *Spain's First Democracy*, 272–77, 288 and Preston, *The Spanish Civil War*, 163.

17. National Council AYC Meeting Minutes, April 23, 1936, JPL Box 23.

18. Joseph Lash, "Two Lives" (Unpublished Autobiography), 20, JPL Box 27.

19. *The Campus*, April 22, 1937, and April 27, 1937, CCNY.

20. "Strike Against War!" April 22, 1937, CT Box 85.

21. James A. Wechsler and Joseph P. Lash, "April 22nd: We Must Remember Spain," *The Student Advocate*, April 1937, CT Box 5.

22. Ibid. For a discussion of the support of Franco by the Hearst press, see Preston, *The Spanish Civil War*, 144.

23. Ibid. This slogan was used on all ASU publications related to the annual strike. See Meeting Minutes of the United Student Peace Committee, March 16, 1937, JPL Box 27.

24. Address of Adolf A. Berle, Jr., August 15, 1938, Box 141, Berle Papers, FDR Library.

25. AYC National Council Meeting Minutes, October 15, 1936, JPL Box 23.

26. Manuel Tunon, "Appeal from the Spanish Students," *The Student Advocate*, October–November, 1936, CT Box 85.

27. Ibid.

28. Ibid. Maria Gloria was a Spaniard who visited the United States in 1936 on a propaganda tour for the Spanish Republic. After returning to Spain, she opened a refugee camp for Spanish children. In 1939, the Peace Commission of the ASU printed a letter from her (sent through Joseph Lash) that described conditions and the need for additional funds. Such first-hand accounts of the desperate need in Spain were a constant reminder to American youth "lest we forget." Maxine Ture, "Spain Still Marches: Give Aid to a Victim of War," July 11, 1939, JPL Box 23.

29. AYC National Council Meeting Minutes, October 15, 1936, JPL Box 23. Such foreign visitors were asked how it was possible that a democratic country like America could fail to aid the Republic against the Axis dictatorships and how the American government could refuse to sell the legitimate government of Spain the arms needed to defend itself. See Anthony Beevor, *The Battle for Spain: The Spanish Civil War* (New York: Penguin Books, 2006), 240.

30. AYC National Council Meeting Minutes, October 29, 1936, JPL Box 23. This is further proof that the AYC was a democratically run organization and that the communists did not control the AYC.

31. AYC National Council Meeting minutes, March 4, 1937, JPL Box 23.

32. *The Campus*, December 1, 1936, CCNY.

33. *The Campus*, February 26, 1937 and March 9, 1937, CCNY.

34. "Notes to the Nation," *The Student Advocate*, December 1937, CT Box 85.

35. Michael Henry Miller, "The American Student Movement of the Depression, 1931–1941: A Historical Analysis" (PhD diss.: Florida State University, 1981), 136.

36. Chew Tong, "Five Months of War in China," *The Student Advocate*, December 1937, CT Box 85.

37. Ibid.

38. Ibid.

39. "To the Students of America: Mobilize for Peace," Report of the National Conference of the NSL, December 1935, JPL Box 29.

40. Robert Cohen, *When the Old Left Was Young: Student Radicals and America's First Mass Student Movement, 1929–1941* (New York: Oxford University Press, 1993), 156; Eagan, *Class, Culture, and the Classroom* (Philadelphia: Temple University Press, 1981), 176; George Watt, "American Student Union

Memoirs: 50th and 25th National Reunion," retrieved from http://newdeal.feri
.org/sutdents/asu11.htm. Watt's experience in Spain made front-page headlines
in the *A.S.U. Bulletin* when a story was printed of his daring escape from behind enemy lines by swimming the Ebro Riber in order to get back to Loyalist
territory. "A.S.U. Leaders Hit Front Page in Dispatches from Loyalist Spain,"
A.S.U. Bulletin, April 27, 1938, JPL Box 29.

41. David Cook, "From Columbia into Madrid," *The Student Advocate*, April
1937, CT Box 85.

42. Ibid.

43. Ibid.

44. Cook, "From Columbia into Madrid," CT Box 85.

45. Langston Hughes, "Song of Spain," *The Student Advocate*, CT Box 85.

46. Ibid.

47. Paul Preston has argued that "for the anarcho-syndicalist CNT, the more
or less Trotskyist POUM and the left wing of the PSOE, proletarian revolution
was itself the essential precondition for the defeat of fascism" while the view of
"the Communist Party, the right-wing of the Socialist Party and the bourgeois
Republican politicians was that the war must be won first in order to give the
revolution any possibility of triumphing later." Preston, *The Spanish Civil War*,
237.

48. David Cook, "Postscript from Madrid," *The Student Advocate*, May 1937,
CT Box 85.

49. Ibid.

50. As Thomas explained, young American youth felt compelled to fight in
Spain for the Republic because "they saw the Spanish war as a microcosm of
European discontents, a way of fighting fascism" and because doing so "assuaged a longing for action widely felt among the young for whom the civil war
seemed, unlike the war of 1914–18, just." Thomas, *The Spanish Civil War*, 593.

51. Lash enlisted as a volunteer in the Abraham Lincoln Battalion in the
summer of 1937. Wechsler refers to this—aptly in a way—as Lash's pilgrimage
to Spain. Wechsler, *The Age of Suspicion*, 101.

52. There were fifteen students, including Lash and Wechsler. They were in
Paris just after the sit-down strikes in July 1936, attended the Oxford social-
ist student congress, and, as Lash remembered, they championed unity in the
European student movement. They then made a short visit to Moscow, then to
Prague where they met with a leader of the German underground movement,
with a final stop in Austria. There, Lash remembered, their visit to bombed-out
socialist houses brought them nearly to tears. They attended the First World
Youth Congress in Geneva at the end of their trip. Joseph Lash, Notes for "Two
Lives" (Unpublished Autobiography), JPL Box 78.

53. For a description of that tour of the U.S.S.R., see James Wechsler, *The
Age of Suspicion* (New York: Donald I. Fine, 1953), 108–18.

54. Joseph Lash, Notes for "Two Lives" (Unpublished Autobiography), JPL
Box 78.

55. Memorandum, Bill Lawrence, *Seccion Politica de las Brigadas Internaciona-les*, August 31, 1937, JPL Box 27.

56. Joseph Lash, Notes for "Two Lives" (Unpublished Autobiography). Because he was spared from the front lines, Eileen Eagan characterizes Lash's time in Spain as one in which he was accorded "red-carpet treatment." Eagan, *Class, Culture, and the Classroom*, 182. In reporting back to his friends in the ASU National Executive Committee, Lash explained that no unity of the two student internationals (communist and socialist) was achieved at the conference because of the opposition of the Scandinavian, Czech, and French Socialists. Joseph Lash to Molly Yard and Celeste Stack, July 20, 1937, JPL Box 27. For his account of the Battle for Madrid, see Joseph Lash, "Such is the Fortitude of Madrid," n.d., JPL Box 27.

57. Eric Sevareid, *Not So Wild a Dream* (New York: Alfred A. Knopf, 1946), 94.

58. Joseph Lash, "Youth and the War Emergency," n.d., JPL Box 27.

59. Ibid.

60. Eagan, *Class, Culture, and the Classroom*, 181. There is a problem with relying on Eagan's analysis of Lash too heavily: She did not consult the manuscript collection he left behind and many of her statements about him lack citation. One grievous error is that she identifies him as a communist when he was a socialist and, later, an avid New Deal Democrat, which is discussed in Chapter 7.

61. *The Campus*, October 5, 1937, CCNY.

62. Miller, "The American Student Movement of the Depression, 1931–1941," 136.

63. ASU member George Watt later explained the switch from pacifism to collective security: "We should have learned by then never to say 'never.' But it was the rise of fascism which brought us to our senses. We all knew that Hitler was imprisoning and torturing communists, socialists, labor leaders, student leaders and liberals. We knew that he was launching the genocidal destruction of Jews. He had already annexed Austria and was seeking to spread the Nazi venom to all of Europe and the United States. We knew that Mussolini had destroyed all human freedom in Italy and was invading Ethiopia. We could not stand idly by while all this was happening. The American Student Union continued to fight for jobs, for Negro rights, for academic freedom, for labor's right to organize, but the effort to stop fascism became increasingly the most critical struggle of our time." George Watt, "American Student Union Memoirs; 50th and 25th National Reunion," retrieved from http://newdeal.feri.org/students/asu11.htm.

64. While this reluctance is usually explained by Stalin's preoccupation with domestic issues—particularly, the purges and show trials—Paul Preston has offered a different explanation. He argues that "Stalin's dilemma" was brought on by a desire to protect the Soviet Union from the menace of German fascism by seeking western allies, particularly France and Great Britain. If the

Soviet Union became involved in spreading revolution in Spain in the face of the non-intervention policy posture of France and Great Britain, then such collective security hopes of protection would be null and void. Stalin therefore pursued a cautious lukewarm policy of support for the Spanish Loyalists. According to Preston, "Stalin dreaded the prospect of the democracies being driven to line up with the Fascist dictators against Soviet Spain and Soviet Russia." Preston, *The Spanish Civil War*, 146–48, 244.

65. Preston, *The Spanish Civil War*, 166.

66. Ibid., 150.

67. Joseph Lash explained that it had been the Communist Party in Spain that was the first party to realize everything had to be subordinated to winning the war, even going so far as to establish a Party munitions works to aid the development of war industry, which it subsequently turned over to the government. Placing priority on winning the war and thus above ideological positioning won Lash to the communists' cause in Spain. He warned his wife not to take any position hostile to the Young Communist League or the Communist Party because "the Communists are the only worldwide movement that consistently and consciously are working for a socialist society on a worldwide scale" and while he said he would not join the Communist Party, he was already considering resigning from the Socialist Party. Joseph Lash to Nancy Bedford—Jones Lash, July 20, 1937, JPL Box 27.

68. *The Campus*, January 4, 1938, CCNY. Studies on youth in the 1930s have argued in virtual unanimity that the switch from pacifism to collective security was driven by Soviet political expediency—that young Americans were simply following the Communist line. On the contrary, the evidence seems to point more toward their own fear of fascism as the cause of the change. The popular front organizations—which represented millions of American young people—were genuinely concerned about fascism and its threat to freedom and democracy as well as security. Had it only threatened security, young people might have advocated isolationism, but because it was also a threat to freedom and democracy, an alternative response was needed. That response was collective security, which grew out of the experience of working together through the popular front ideology. This was not the old-style Alliance System that led to World War I; it was a time-sensitive response to the matters at hand. Eileen Eagan hints at this argument when she says, in her study of the peace movement of the 1930s that "much of the peace movement's impetus came from events abroad." She later identifies those international events in the chapter dedicated to the Spanish Civil War, which she referred to as "the emotional catalyst and immediate issue for the breakup of the peace forces. Among students it directly resulted in the abandonment of the Oxford Oath as the basis of the peace program of the American Student Union." Eagan, *Class, Culture, and the Classroom*, 103, 169, 180. Interestingly, Wechsler makes the argument in 1953 in *The Age of Suspicion* (which he then reasserts in the new edition of *Revolt on the Campus* in 1972 and new edition of *The Age of Suspicion* in

1985) that he was following the communist line whenever he wrote about the Spanish Civil War during the 1930s. Yet his most substantial works during the time period—*Revolt on the Campus* published in 1935 and *War Our Heritage* published in 1936—were, in significant ways, in opposition to the communist line, which, he admits, got him into trouble with the Communist Party leadership, but in no serious way deterred him from writing his pieces based on his own opinions. That a member of the Young Communist League could publish views antithetical to the communist line indicates how tenuous the hold of that line was over young activists and even more so over young people in general. See Wechsler, *The Age of Suspicion*, 86. Wechsler trips up again when he claims that the Left saw "the early stages of the Spanish conflict [as] a time of hope and excitement, of passions revived and faith rejuvenated." Wechsler, *The Age of Suspicion*, 100. If the Left (by which he means the communists) were following the Soviet line, then there would have been no celebratory anticipation concerning Spain; there would have been reluctant wariness since Stalin did not immediately decide to offer full support to the Spanish Loyalists.

69. Lash claims that it was his experience in Spain that made him advocate dropping the Oxford Pledge in favor of collective security. Joseph Lash interview with Joel Chernoff, January 5, 1978, JPL Box 78.

70. Joseph Lash, "Ten-Minute Remarks of Joseph Lash in Support of Resolution Stating That Support of Oxford Pledge Was Incompatible with Support of Collective Security," n.d., JPL Box 30. M-Day refers to Mobilization Day, the day on which armed forces are mobilized for war.

71. Lash and Wechsler, *War Our Heritage*, 78, 80.

72. Lash, "Ten-Minute Remarks of Joseph Lash in Support of Resolution Stating That Support of Oxford Pledge Was Incompatible with Support of Collective Security."

73. Ibid.

74. The United Student Peace Committee was formed in 1935. It included members of foreign policy associations, the National Intercollegiate Christian Council, National Student Federation of America, AYC, League of Nations Non-Partisan Association, War Resisters League, League Against War and Fascism, University Committee of the Church Boards of Education, and ASU. It became an even larger anti-war umbrella group and was responsible for organizing the annual student strikes for peace.

75. Joseph Lash to Howard Lee, February 16, 1938, JPL Box 27.

76. Ibid.

77. Ibid.

78. "Youth Demands a Peaceful World: Report of the Second World Youth Congress," August 16–23, 1938, Vertical File, World Youth Congress, FDR Library.

79. Ibid.

80. Catholics throughout the world tended to support Franco and the Nationalists because the Catholic Church viewed Article 26 of the Republican

constitution and the reforms carried out in its name as sacrilegious and because the Vatican officially recognized Franco on May 18, 1938, though the Pope and Catholics, generally, had viewed Franco as the savior and defender of the "true Spain" long before that. See Preston, *The Spanish Civil War*, 222; Payne, *Spain's First Democracy*, 81–86; Wechsler, "The Parliament of Youth," JPL Box 27.

81. Abbott Simon to Gardner Jackson, June 26, 1937, Gardner Jackson Papers, Box 5, FDR Library.

82. Lash responded to the accusation that devotion to the Loyalists meant that leftist Americans were anti-religious by explaining that their efforts were on behalf of Spanish democracy and cleared the name of Loyalist Spain on the religion issue by referring to the decree of December 9th, which, he claimed, re-established normal freedom of worship. See Joseph Lash, "Students in the Service of Democracy," Report of the Proceedings of the Fourth National Convention of the American Student Union, December 27–30, 1938, JPL Box 23.

83. James Wechsler discusses the relative ideological make-up of the Congress in "Parliament of Youth," *The Nation*, November 1938, JPL Box 27.

84. "Youth Demands a Peaceful World: Report of the Second World Youth Congress," August 16–23, 1938.

85. Ibid.

86. Ibid.

87. Since the U.S. Senate refused to confirm the Versailles Treaty, separating the Covenant of the League of Nations from that treaty would allow the United States to participate in the League.

88. James Wechsler referred to the "insistent pleas for some framework of collective order" that arose throughout the conference. "Parliament of Youth," *The Nation*, November 1938, JPL Box 27.

89. "Youth Demands a Peaceful World: Report of the Second World Youth Congress," August 16–23, 1938.

90. Address of Adolf A. Berle, Jr., August 15, 1938, Berle Papers Box 141, FDR Library. Eagan argues that although collective security became the new policy, young people were still trying to reconcile this new aggressiveness with their old principles and, at the same time, were trying to compromise with those who feared the drift toward war. Eagan, *Class, Culture, and the Classroom*, 196.

91. Address of Adolf A. Berle, Jr., August 15, 1938.

92. Ibid.

93. At the AYC Conference at Vassar in 1938, delegates made a bonfire in which Japanese silk was burned as a symbol of their opposition to Japanese imperialism and as a dramatic way to try to influence the American government to end trade with Japan. Joseph Lash interview with Joel Chernoff, January 5, 1978, JPL Box 78; Joseph Lash, "Two Lives" (Unpublished Autobiography), 28, JPL Box 27.

94. As Hugh Thomas remarked, "American socialist and liberal intellectuals

took the cause of republican Spain to their hearts as they had never taken any foreign cause, and the anti-fascist (pro-Soviet) organizations already in existence grew in strength." Thomas, *The Spanish Civil War*, 350.

95. "Youth Demands a Peaceful World: Report of the Second World Youth Congress," August 16–23, 1938.

96. Ibid.

97. Ibid.

98. Ibid.

99. Ibid.

100. Ibid.

101. James Wechsler accepted a job as a writer for the *Nation* in 1937. Before taking that position, he discussed his communist affiliation with the managing editor, Bob Bendiner, whom Wechsler identified as a staunch anti-Stalinist. Bendiner told him to sever all ties with the communists so that he would be able to write independent editorials that voiced his own opinion. From Wechsler's own account, he went home and wrote a letter of resignation from the Young Communist League. In that letter, he said that while he "agreed with communist positions on world issues such as Spain and collective security, [he] could not work effectively in an atmosphere which seemed completely intolerant. Moreover, since [he] was now going to work for the *Nation*, [he] wanted to be in a position to think for [himself]." Wechsler, *The Age of Suspicion*, 129–30.

102. James Wechsler, "Parliament of Youth," *The Nation*, November 1938, JPL Box 27.

103. Ibid. The idea of a time running out was further illustrated in an edition of *The Student Advocate* that included an image of a college president handing out sticks of dynamite rather than rolled-up diplomas to graduates. *The Student Advocate*, April 1937, CT Box 85. That same image was used to open *War Our Heritage*, the last page of which showed the same college graduate in a military uniform marching off to war with the grim reaper leading the way. See Joseph Lash and James Wechsler, *War Our Heritage*, 14, 157.

104. Lash and Wechsler, *War Our Heritage*, 14, 157.

105. "Mobile Hospital Units Aim of Nation-Wide China Aid Drive," *Youth*, November 1938, CT Box 20.

106. "Roosevelt, Hull Get WYC Refugee Appeal," *Youth*, November 1938, CT Box 20.

107. Miller, "The American Student Movement," 137. Going even further, the Young People's Peace Lobby called for the resumption of normal unrestricted trade relations with democratic Spain, extension to Spain of commercial credits, and the sending of surplus commodities to war victims in Spain in China. "How to Win Friends and Influence People for Peace," January 1939, JPL Box 23.

108. *The Campus*, September 22, 1938, CCNY.

109. Proclamation of the AYC, December 1938, JPL Box 23.

110. "Armistice Proclamation Scores Munich Pact 'Power Politics'": World Conference Urged," *Youth* published by the American Youth Congress, November 1938, CT Box 20.

111. Ibid.

112. Joseph Lash, *The Student in the Post Munich World* (New York: American Student Union, 1938), 1, JPL Box 21. Eleanor Roosevelt, in defending youth activism in the face of red-baiting efforts to silence it, pointed out, in sympathy with the ASU position, that "no forces can destroy a democracy which meets the needs of its people." Eleanor Roosevelt, "Youth's Contribution in Keeping the Mind of the Nation Young," October 25, 1938, ER Box 3034.

113. Lash, *The Student in the Post Munich World*, 6–8.

114. Ibid., 8.

115. Ibid., 8.

116. Ibid., 12.

117. Joseph Lash, "Students in the Service of Democracy," *Report of the Proceedings of the Fourth National Convention of the American Student Union*, December 27–30, 1938, JPL Box 23.

118. "The World That Will Give Us Peace," College and High School Joint Plenary Session, *Report of the Proceedings of the Fourth National Convention of the American Student Union*, December 27–30, 1938, JPL Box 23.

119. Ibid.

120. Jay Allen, "Situation in Spain," Commission on Peace, December 29, 1938, *Report of the Proceedings Fourth National Convention of the American Student Union*, JPL Box 23.

121. Ibid.

122. Ibid.

123. Ibid.

124. The NSFA, for example, had wanted to aid beleaguered Spain, but feared doing so would drag American into a wider war, which it should not be involved in. It supported aiding democratic movements, but resisted direct American involvement in Spain. Arthur Norwood, Jr. to Rena Burton, November 5, 1936; Rena Burton to Student Editors, 5 November 1936, CT Box 85.

125. "Statement of AYC Resident Board," January 19, 1939, JPL Box 23.

126. Indeed, when asked what she found to be the subject most young people seemed to be discussing as she travelled around the country, Eleanor Roosevelt responded in March 1939 that it was America's foreign policy "particularly as regards the possibility of preventing war." "Questions for Mrs. Roosevelt," *The Democratic Digest*, March 15, 1939, ER Box 3036.

127. ASU flyer, JPL Box 21.

128. Sevareid, *Not So Wild a Dream*, 95.

129. Ibid., 96. George Orwell described his own experience, in contrast, as worth the effort, however ineffectual it had been in avoiding the disaster of the outcome. Writing before the war actually ended, he foresaw any outcome as

devastating for Spain, but, nevertheless, said that "curiously enough the whole experience has left me with not less but more belief in the decency of human beings," and, he said, he was grateful he had not missed it. Orwell, *Homage to Catalonia*, 230.

130. Sevareid, *Not So Wild a Dream*, 96–97.

131. Ibid., 105–6.

132. Abbott Simon, "Report on Prague," May 15, 1939, CT Box 20. Simon remained in Europe as the American delegate to the World Youth Congress for a year.

133. About the Munich Conference, James Wechsler wrote that, "from afar it still looked as though the Soviets were genuinely trying to avert World War II while western statesmen (with the exception of Mr. Roosevelt) floundered, and some hoped that Nazism would fight on the eastern front and leave the west in peace. Both the *Nation* and *New Republic*, while still voicing some uneasiness about the Moscow trials, still looked to Moscow for international comfort—in 1938 . . . only Moscow and Washington seemed to be displaying any resistance to the course of appeasement that led to Munich in September." Wechsler, *The Age of Suspicion*, 137.

134. Lash's continuing efforts to influence AYC policy, which is fully discussed in Chapter 7, is surprising in light of a letter he wrote to an ASU member in May 1939, which said that he had already made the decision to leave the ASU as soon as possible. The ASU member had apparently accused Lash of secretly being a communist because Lash had attended the YCL convention. Lash explained that he did so because he was hoping to get more cooperation from the YCL members, who, he thought, were not doing enough in places like Madison, Berkeley, and Seattle. In defending himself and his decision to leave the ASU, Lash explained that "I am too left. . . . Let me make it clear that the change in the ASU is one that I fully approve, but I believe there are other people who would make better spokesmen for it in the present circumstances." Joseph Lash to Avram, May 19, 1939, JPL Box 23. He repeated this position in February 1940, after he had left the ASU. He said "I did not leave the ASU because of my disagreements with the present trends in its policies, but because of my belief that youth movements should be youth-led if they are to be effective training-grounds for leadership in a democracy and if they are to be sensitive barometers of the aspirations of young people." See Joseph Lash to Mr. Oliver, February 25, 1940, JPL Box 24. It was only later, in writing his (unpublished) memoirs, that Lash revised this story. Later, he would insist that he had left the ASU because of communist machinations as a result of the Nazi-Soviet Pact. See Joseph Lash, "Two Lives" (Unpublished Autobiography), JPL Box 24. Historians, like Robert Cohen, tend to believe the version of the story written in his (unpublished) memoirs rather than that constructed from the documents of the time.

135. Joseph Lash to Richard R. Brown and the American Youth Commission, June 16, 1939, JPL Box 27.

136. Joseph Lash, *The Student in the Post Munich World* (New York: American Student Union, 1938), JPL Box 21.

137. Ibid.

138. The 1939 Congress was also held as a Model Congress where delegates would play the roles of Senators and Representatives in determining AYC policy for the coming year. Joseph Cadden to FDR, March 16, 1939, Eleanor Roosevelt Microfilm Collection, Reel 20, FDR Library.

139. "Youth Congress Closes with Denunciation of Communist, Nazi, Fascist Dictatorships," AYC Press Release, July 5, 1939, Eleanor Roosevelt Microfilm Collection, Reel 1, FDR Library.

140. Ibid.

141. Report of the Proceedings of the Congress of Youth, July 1–5, 1939, JPL Box 23.

142. There were 736 delegates to this congress from 513 organizations representing a total of 4,697,915 young people. There were 112 student groups, 112 labor groups, 93 affiliated bodies, 100 religious organizations, 66 fraternal groups, 52 educational associations, 52 social service groups, 48 peace organizations, 28 civic groups, 25 political organizations, 18 cultural groups, 20 racial/nationality associations, 4 neighborhood groups, and 2 recreational organizations. Of those, 636 were local organizations, and 96 were national groups. The youngest delegate to that congress was 14 years old and the median age was 22. Twenty-two states, the District of Columbia, and Puerto Rico were represented. See Roy Lancaster, Credentials Committee Report, Report of the Proceedings of the Congress of Youth, July 1–5, 1939, JPL Box 23.

143. See Eleanor Roosevelt, "Address to the AYC," Report of the Proceedings of the Congress of Youth, July 1–5, 1939, JPL Box 23; Mrs. Thomas F. McAllister to Janet Feder, July 6, 1939; Mrs. Thomas F. McAllister to Joseph Cadden, July 6, 1939, DP Box 314.

144. Leslie Gould, *American Youth Today* (New York: Random House, 1940), 289. The Creed adopts a very different stance than the Oxford Pledge; however, the Creed was an attempt to explain the purpose of the AYC, while the Oxford Pledge was a statement of peace policy.

145. Murray Plavner, "Is the American Youth Congress a Communist Front: Here are the Facts, Its History, What It Is, How It Works," 1939, CT Box 1. Plavner published the pamphlet himself in New York City. His claim is false; see "Youth Congress Closes with Denunciation of Communist, Nazi, Fascist Dictatorships," AYC Press Release, July 5, 1939, Eleanor Roosevelt Microfilm Collection, Reel 1, FDR Library.

146. Ibid.

147. "Youths Meet," *Time*, July 17, 1939. It was these twelve attendees who were determined to have surreptitiously registered for the conference under false pretenses, purporting to represent organizations that did not exist or that could not be found at the addresses provided to the Credentials Committee.

148. "Youth Congress Closes with Denunciation of Communist, Nazi,

Fascist Dictatorships," AYC Press Release, July 5, 1939, Eleanor Roosevelt Microfilm Collection, Reel 1, FDR Library.

149. That debate resulted in the abandonment of the Oxford Pledge and the adoption of a united front against fascism in Spain. Some members of the ASU National Executive Committee continued to complain about sectarian issues, which involved not just the communists and the socialists, but the pacifists as well, all of whom had developed caucuses within the ASU. These caucuses were seen by some members of the ASU National Executive Committee as counterproductive to the idea of a united student movement. See, for example, Molly Yard to Joseph Lash, November 9, 1937, JPL Box 27.

150. McKay was a leader of the National Student Federation of America; she became its president in 1939; Frances Williams was also a member of the NSFA, a liberal student government organization.

151. Joseph Lash to Roger Daken, n.d., JPL Box 27.

152. Ibid.

153. Ibid.

154. See, for example, ASU Press Release, December 1937, JPL Box 29 and "Student Union Convention Repudiates Oxford Pledge, *Columbia Spectator*, January 6, 1938, Microform and Periodicals Collection, Columbia University.

155. Joseph Lash to Roger Daken, n.d., JPL Box 27.

156. In his diary, Joseph Lash, leaving Cherbourg Harbor on his way home from Spain, wondered whether Europe would be at war by the following summer. He said that "everyone is aghast at the horrible events taking place, and everyone seems bound by invisible chains that prevents them from taking real action. . . . This is the period of wars and revolutions. Horrible catastrophes are building up and the Communists are the only international force with a policy and an iron will to carry out that policy." Joseph Lash, September 9, 1937, JPL Box 27.

7. Dissolution: World War II Subverts the Zeitgeist and Youth's Vision for America

1. AYC news releases stressed that this was in honor of Abraham Lincoln's birthday.

2. Jack McMichael was elected chairman of the AYC in 1939, replacing William W. Hinckley. In the fall of 1939, he attended Union Theological Seminary and later did doctoral work at Columbia University. After his work with youth groups in the 1930s, McMichael became a Reverend in the Methodist Church. He was called to provide testimony before the House Un-American Activities Committee regarding his "communist ties" on July 30–31, 1953. Unlike James Wechsler, McMichael did not try to disown his radical past.

3. Jack McMichael, "Message to the President," February 10, 1940, JPL Box 23; JM.

4. Ibid.

292 Notes to pages 191–93

5. Ibid.

6. Leslie Gould, *American Youth Today* (New York: Random House, 1940), 12; FDR, "Text of President Roosevelt's Address to the Delegates of the American Youth Congress," *New York Times*, February 11, 1940.

7. FDR's comments took this resolution out of context and treated it as the official policy of the AYC when it was not. See AYC Cabinet Meeting Minutes, February 21, 1940, JPL Box 23. This issue is discussed in greater detail later in the chapter. FDR was outraged about the Finland Resolution because it came at the same time he had condemned the Soviet invasion and had just secured Congressional aid for Finland. See Robert Cohen, *When the Old Left Was Young: Student Radicals and America's First Student Movement, 1929–1941* (New York: Oxford University Press, 1993), 290–91.

8. FDR, "Text of President Roosevelt's Address to the Delegates of the American Youth Congress," *New York Times*, February 11, 1940. The public's response to this speech was mixed. Some wrote to the president expressing their agreement with his policy toward both Finland and the AYC while others expressed dismay over his attempt to dictate policy to the AYC and his position on Finland, which, they said, would bring America into war. See letters from citizens to FDR, POF 3910, Box 1.

9. Eileen Eagan has argued that between the outbreak of war in Europe and Pearl Harbor, students remained reluctant to support American involvement. Eileen Eagan, *Class Culture and the Classroom: The Student Peace Movement of the 1930s* (Philadelphia: Temple University Press, 1981), 202.

10. Joseph Lash to Eleanor Roosevelt, September 12, 1939, Eleanor Roosevelt Microfilm Collection, Reel 1, FDR Library.

11. Ruth Watt, former ASU District Office Secretary, recalled just how much of an FDR supporter Lash had become by 1939. She said she remembered walking into the national ASU office in 1939 and Lash saying—and "rather pompously too,—and I quote verbatim for I've never forgotten—'why, I could be the fair-haired boy of the Democrats if I wanted to.'" Ruth Watt to Joseph Lash, December 2, 1952, JPL Box 33. In his undated notes that he intended to use in writing his autobiography, which he hoped to someday publish, Lash wrote that the "ASU became the student arm of the New Deal by self-appointment and as struggle with the right grew keener." He also claimed that "they sought us out." See Joseph Lash, "Growing Up in Wellesley Hills," n.d., JPL Box 33. Lash later referred to himself as "sort of the student brain of the New Deal." Joseph Lash, "Two Lives," 29.

12. Lash later explained this development when he said: "I guess I'm essentially a reformist by nature. . . . I very quickly began to be sympathetic with what the New Deal was trying to do." Joseph Lash interview with Joel Chernoff, January 5, 1978, JPL Box 78. Later, in reflecting on his resignation from the Socialist Party, Lash said that "the Socialist Party had worked itself into a position where its whole being was one of fighting the CP." Joseph Lash, autobiographical sketch, n.d., JPL Box 27.

13. Joseph Lash to May Thompson Evans, September 6, 1939, Democratic Party Women's Division Papers, Box 314, FDR Library.

14. Ibid.

15. Joseph Lash to Eleanor Roosevelt, September 12, 1939, Eleanor Roosevelt Microfilm Collection, Reel 1, FDR Library.

16. Ibid. According to Robert Cohen, the ASU had approximately 5,000 members in 1940. Cohen, *When the Old Left Was Young*, 411–12. The number may have been higher. Cohen cites a letter from Alan Gottlieb to Joseph Lash as the source for the membership tally. However, in that same letter, Gottlieb said the ASU had a maximum of 7,000 members. Alan Gottlieb to Joseph Lash, May 5, 1940, JPL Box 24.

17. The same can be said for American youth, in general, for whom the period between September 1939 and December 1941 was, as Eagan explains, "a time of moral and intellectual anguish." While the debate wore on in America and tension mounted, it was only the perennial hawks and right-wing isolationists who found easy answers. Eagan, *Class, Culture, and the Classroom*, 218.

18. Minutes of ASU Fall Planning Conference, September 8–9, 1939, JPL Box 21.

19. "Message to the Students of America," September 22, 1939, JPL Box 29.

20. AYC National Assembly Meeting Minutes, October 7, 1939, JPL Box 24.

21. Joseph Lash to FDR, September 25, 1939, JPL Box 29.

22. Ibid.

23. Minutes of the Administrative Committee Meeting of the ASU, September 29, 1939, JPL Box 27.

24. Ibid.

25. Lash was launching a veiled attack on communist ASU members whom he believed were following the Soviet line.

26. Minutes of the Administrative Meeting of the ASU, September 29, 1939, JPL Box 27.

27. Ibid.

28. Ibid.

29. Ibid. In supporting Bert Witt's position, another member "urged that in speculating on policy of Russia in the future, we not ignore her consistent efforts for peace in the past, as the most reliable barometer of future peace policy." Minutes, ASU Planning Conference, September 8–9, 1939, JPL Box 21.

30. Minutes of the Administrative Meeting of the ASU, September 29, 1939, JPL Box 27. Confusion about the communists' role in determining youth peace policy abounds, in part, because historians of the youth movement have been intent on explaining the breakup of the youth movement through the lens of the Nazi-Soviet Pact in order for the consequent blame to be placed squarely on the communists. Philip Altbach, for example, erroneously claims that the peace platform of the youth movement was abandoned because "the communists and their allies abandoned [the peace movement] in 1939 and many liberals supported President Roosevelt's preparedness programs." Philip

Altbach, *Student Politics in America: A Historical Analysis* (New York: McGraw-Hill, 1974), 70. Ralph Brax echoes this claim when he says that by 1936 most youth activists were no longer concerned with keeping America out of war. Ralph Brax, *The First Student Movement: Student Activism in the United States During the 1930s* (Port Washington, N.Y.: Kennikat Press, 1981), 78.

31. Minutes of the Administrative Meeting of the ASU, September 29,1939, JPL Box 27. Interestingly, these comments, though included in the minutes, were crossed out some time after they were typed up, perhaps in preparation for dissemination to the chapters.

32. Ibid.

33. Ibid.

34. Other historians do not agree with this assessment. Robert Cohen has argued that this showdown in the ASU leadership was an attempt by the Communists, led by Witt, to pursue the Soviet line and that Lash was correct in his interpretation of the ASU peace program as decided at the last annual ASU convention. See Robert Cohen, *When the Old Left Was Young*, 287–89.

35. Minutes of the Administrative Meeting of the ASU, September 29, 1939, JPL Box 27. Lash agreed to this slogan even though he had objected to it, saying "How are we going to help the people make the peace? Would not failure to lift [the] embargo now be discouraging to [the] people of England and France?"

36. William Hinckley to Mrs. Thomas McAllister, October 2, 1939; Mrs. Thomas McAllister to Mr. Michaelson, Democratic National Committee, October 4, 1939, Democratic Party Women's Division Papers, Box 314; Eleanor Roosevelt to Aubrey Williams, Eleanor Roosevelt Microfilm Collection, Reel 20, FDR Library. In a meeting with Young Democrats, Mrs. Thomas F. McAllister, the Director of the Democratic Party Women's Division, said that she considered Molly Yard "one of them." Agnes Reynolds became a volunteer for the Democratic Party in efforts to re-elect Roosevelt in 1940. Mrs. Thomas McAllister, Democratic Party Women's Division Papers, Box 314, FDR Library.

37. William Hinckley to Mrs. Thomas McAllister, June 9, 1939, Democratic Party Women's Division Papers, Box 314, FDR Library.

38. Ibid.

39. Mary Jeanne McKay to Joseph Lash, 1940, JPL Box 29.

40. Richard Pells, *Radical Visions and American Dreams: Culture and Social Thought in the Depression Years* (New York: Harper & Row Publishers, 1973), 311.

41. George Edwards to Joseph Lash, October 5, 1939, JPL Box 27.

42. Ibid.

43. Joseph Lash to George Edwards, October 19, 1939, JPL Box 27.

44. Ibid.

45. The House Committee on Un-American Activities, known as the Dies Committee after its chairman, Martin Dies (D-TX), was created in 1938 in

response to "the conviction that the crisis of the thirties had been caused by conspiratorial elements whose suppression would quickly restore the nation to a 'normal condition.'" William Leuchtenburg, *Franklin D. Roosevelt and the New Deal* (New York: Harper & Row, 1963), 280. The Committee began hearings in the summer of 1938, and, as Leuchtenburg notes, although its creation resulted from the pressure of antifascist congressmen, it largely ignored the Nazis and instead "made itself a form for allegations of communist infiltration. Dies permitted witnesses to make unsupported charges of the most fantastic character, and rarely accorded the accused the right to reply. In the first few days, witnesses branded as communistic no less than 640 organizations, 483 newspapers, and 280 labor unions." Leuchtenburg, *Franklin D. Roosevelt and the New Deal*, 280.

46. Joseph Lash to George Edwards, October 19, 1939, JPL Box 27.

47. Mary Jeanne McKay, "A Message on Peace," *NSFA Bulletin*, volume xi, no.1, 6 October 1939, CT Box 86.

48. Ibid. The NSFA was considered a liberal organization in the 1930s, and its stances, according to Phillip Altbach, tended to reflect American student opinion. See Altbach, *Student Politics in America*, 83–85. Yet Altbach insists that the communists dominated the AYC and ASU in the late 1930s. The NSFA was not charged with communist domination. It seems, then, that the positions of the AYC and ASU—like the NSFA—were representative of young America, generally.

49. Mary Jeanne McKay, NSFA Press Release, CT Box 86.

50. Joseph Cadden to Charles Taussig, November 201939, CT Box 1; Eleanor Roosevelt Microfilm Collection, Reel 3, FDR Library.

51. Memorandum, Joseph Cadden, November 20, 1939, CT Box 1.

52. Cadden mentioned Plavner's attack, specifically, pointing out that on page 14 of his pamphlet, he purposely omitted the words Democratic and Republican, but left "Socialist, Communist and Farmer Labor Parties" as the only supporters of the Detroit Congress. Joseph Cadden to Charles Taussig, November 20, 1939, CT Box 1. Cadden had earlier sent a letter to Taussig in which he states categorically that the AYC does "not believe in Communism, nor have we ever expressed sympathy for Communism. The Young Communist League participates in the American Youth Congress on the same basis as any other organization. It does so because we bar no group wishing to advance the program agreed upon democratically by all participants. We discriminate against no race, no religion, no political belief." Joseph Cadden to Charles Taussig, December 7, 1938, CT Box 1.

53. Hinckley was supposed to testify at 10 a.m., but was not called until 4:30 p.m. It was this hearing that Eleanor Roosevelt attended as a show of support for youth leaders and the organizations they represented. She refused the offer to sit with the Committee and invited the Youth Congress leaders back to the White House for lunch. The AYC had requested to testify in its own defense as early as fifteen months before. When its request was finally granted, it was given

less than fifteen hours to prepare and travel to Washington, D.C. "Congress Witnesses Expose Dies' Slander," *Youth*, December 1939, JPL Box 28.

54. As reported by the AYC, upon reading the Creed, there was a burst of applause from the audience that the chairman had a difficult time silencing. "Congress Witnesses Expose Dies' Slander," *Youth*, December 1939.

55. AYC Cabinet Meeting Minutes, December 6, 1939, Report on the Dies Committee Hearings, JPL Box 24.

56. An AYC petition castigated the Dies Committee for its attempts to discredit trade unions and other progressive American organizations, misuse of Congressional power, conduct of un-American and unjust hearings that accepted hearsay, slander, and surmise instead of evidence, and provoked "war hysteria with witch-hunting methods," concluding that the Dies Committee should be ended immediately because of it undemocratic nature. AYC National Assembly Meeting Minutes, October 7, 1939, JPL Box 24.

57. AYC Cabinet Meeting Minutes, December 6, 1939, Report on the Dies Committee Hearings, JPL Box 24. The delegates were apparently successful in technically clearing the name of the AYC at the time. A journalist for the *New York Herald Tribune* reported in January 1940 that the AYC was not included as a communist front organization in the report of the Dies Committee. However, the ASU was the second on its list. The author ignored the exoneration of the AYC and, relying on information provided by Murray Plavner, claimed that the ASU was a "transmission belt" of the Communist Party, taking its orders from Moscow. Murray Plavner had written his article on the AYC, not the ASU, but this fact did not seem of any consequence to the author, who went on to describe how astute Stalinist agents had penetrated the group and duped its membership into approving "the bloody Soviet assault on little Finland," in a clear distortion of the resolution that had been passed at the ASU Conference. See "A Test Case," *New York Herald Tribune*, January 5, 1939, JPL Box 21. In their testimony, the AYC leaders called the Dies Committee to task for allowing hearsay to be the foundation of the attacks leveled at the AYC in the Committee's report. In particular, they pointed out, the three men whose testimony said the AYC was a communist front organization had no direct connection to the AYC. When Mr. Whitley tried to defend the committee's report by saying that "they testified under oath. It is not hearsay if they do that," Cadden pointed out that "it is still third and fourth hand information they pass on to you and I call it hearsay," and he got Whitley to admit that there had been no documentary evidence provided. And when committee member Voorhis said "testimony given by former Communists was given, not as members of the Youth congress but to reflect the intent of the communist Party to control the Youth Congress," Cadden replied, "An examination of the intent of the Republican Party will reveal the same thing." Voorhis asked if the members would resent a claim of Republican domination; Cadden said they certainly would, to which Voorhis joked, "I don't blame you." For a transcription of the testimony, see "Congress Witnesses Expose Dies' Slander," *Youth*,

December 1939, JPL Box 28. Despite its ability to counter the attacks against it, the AYC's reputation certainly suffered because of the aspersions cast against it. In particular, it suffered from decreased funding from sponsors who did not wish to have their names connected to the organization anymore because of the suspicions surrounding it. Thus, Eleanor Roosevelt stepped in once again to aid young activists and their organizations by soliciting donations from individuals and advice from officials in coming up with a five year financial plan. See, for example, Eleanor Roosevelt to Bernard Baruch, December 2, 1939, Eleanor Roosevelt Microfilm Collection, Reel 20, FDR Library. Concerning Soviet control over communist parties, Kevin McDermott and Jeremy Agnew pointed out that "influence and control was a two-way game and Moscow did not always have the trump cards." Kevin McDermott and Jeremy Agnew, *The Comintern: A History of International Communism from Lenin to Stalin* (New York: St. Martin's Press, 1997), 56.

58. AYC Cabinet Meeting Minutes, December 6, 1939, JPL Box 24. Plavner also continued his attacks against the ASU and AYC. In January 1940, he introduced a resolution at the delegate assembly of the Teachers Alliance of New York City to ban the "communist-controlled American Student Union" from the four city colleges of New York—City College, Brooklyn College, Hunter, and Queens College. "City to Receive Plea to Outlaw Student Union," *New York Sun*, January 10, 1940, NYU Archives.

59. Viola Ilma to Eleanor Roosevelt, December 6, 1939, Eleanor Roosevelt Microfilm Collection, Reel 1, FDR Library. Ilma came to the AYC's defense even after the Nazi-Soviet Pact and just as Joseph Lash was deciding to leave the ASU.

60. Report on the 5th Annual ASU Congress, December 1939, JPL Box 21.

61. "Student Union Boos Questioner of Russia," *New York Times*, December 31, 1939, JPL Box 21. Lash later said that the outcomes of those votes surprised him. Joseph Lash interview with Joel Chernoff, January 5, 1978, JPL Box 78.

62. "Student Union Boos Questioner of Russia," *New York Times*, December 31, 1939.

63. Discussion of this change in leadership often insinuates that it was the result of communist manipulation when, in fact, Lash was the one who decided to pull out. See Harold Draper, "The Student Movement of the Thirties," in Simon, *As We Saw the Thirties*, 182; Cohen, *When the Old Left Was Young*, 296. In addition to no longer having his ideas hold sway, Lash explained that he was leaving the ASU (and, eventually, the entire youth movement) because he was 30 years old and "every year that goes by while I remain in youth activities makes the transition to another form of work more difficult." As an afterthought, he added, "Youth movements should be led by young people." Joseph Lash to Eleanor Roosevelt, n.d., JPL Box 27.

64. Joseph Lash to Alan Gottlieb, May 5, 1940, JPL Box 24.

65. Joseph Lash, Molly Yard, Agnes Reynolds, "Save the American Student Union," n.d., JPL Box 28.

66. Eagan, *Class, Culture, and the Classroom*, 209.

67. AYC Cabinet Meeting Minutes, December 20, 1939, JPL Box 24. When FDR did recommend decreased appropriations for New Deal programs—the WPA, NYA, and CCC, in particular—the AYC objected because increasing military budgets while cutting social welfare programs did not promote the general welfare. Youth delegates assembling in Washington in what the AYC was advertising as "Mr. Youth Goes to Washington" in a campaign to encourage youth to attend the Citizenship Institute, would therefor ask members of Congress to vote against the budget, vote for increased budgets for those programs, and pass the American Youth Act when they met with them in February. The AYC leadership was therefore already at odds with FDR a month before the Institute began. Joseph Cadden to FDR, January 5, 1940; "Mr. Youth Goes to Washington," JPL Box 24.

68. AYC Cabinet Meeting, January 18, 1940, JPL Box 23.

69. Ibid.

70. Ibid.

71. Blanch Kircsh to Mary Jeanne McKay, Unofficial Report of AYC Cabinet Meeting, January 18, 1940, JPL Box 23.

72. Ibid.

73. AYC Cabinet Meeting Minutes, January 18, 1940, JPL Box 23.

74. Robert H. Jackson, "Jackson Raps 'Indefensible Legacy,'" This Is Youth Speaking: Record of the American Youth Congress National Citizenship Institute, February 9–12, 1940, ERPC.

75. Jack McMichael, "Youth Prevents Democracy's Retreat," This Is Youth Speaking: Record of the American Youth Congress National Citizenship Institute, February 9–12, 1940, ER Pamphlet Collection.

76. Ibid.

77. Jack McMichael, "Adopt Procedure Rules," This Is Youth Speaking: Record of the American Youth Congress National Citizenship Institute, February 9–12, 1940, ERPC.

78. Jack McMichael, "War and America's Youth," This Is Youth Speaking: Record of the American Youth Congress National Citizenship Institute, February 9–12, 1940, ERPC.

79. Abbott Simon, "Slaughter of a Generation," This Is Youth Speaking: Record of the American Youth Congress National Citizenship Institute, February 9–12, 1940, ERPC.

80. "Citizenship in Action," Report of the AYC National Assembly Meeting, February 12, 1940, JPL Box 24.

81. The exchange between Eleanor Roosevelt and the AYC delegates shows that the ties between the Administration and youth were not severed on February 10, 1940, as so many historians suppose. See, for example, Cohen, *When the Old Left Was Young*, 300. Eleanor Roosevelt had served as the liaison between the Administration and youth organizations since 1934. She arranged meetings between youth leaders and New Deal officials, invited youth representatives to

White House events where they were often seated next to such officials, found
funding sources, lobbied congressmen to support youth programs, passed letters
from youth leaders to the appropriate New Deal bureaucrats, and so on. See,
for example, Joseph Lash, *Eleanor and Franklin: The Story of Their Relationship
Based on Eleanor Roosevelt's Private Letters* (New York: New American Library,
1971).

82. Eleanor Roosevelt, "Questions and Answers," This Is Youth Speaking:
Record of the American Youth Congress National Citizenship Institute, February 9–12, 1940, ERPC. The last question she addressed, though, offered another view of America's relationship to the war. When asked specifically what
the Administration was doing to keep America out of war, she said that she did
not think it was ever a good idea to say one would or would not do something
and that "I sometimes tremble when I hear young people say they will not do
certain things without waiting to know what the circumstances are that they
are going to be faced with. I don't see today the slightest reason why we should
go to war and I hope there is not going to be any war and I think it is probable
that one answer is that up to now we have kept ourselves in armaments as well
as in manpower, a strong nation that nobody wishes to attack.... You are sure
you will say the same thing and I hope to goodness the conditions will be such
that you will be able to say the same thing, but I am not going to be a prophet
until I know what I am prophesying about."

83. Gould, *American Youth Today*, 26–27.

84. Eleanor Roosevelt, "Questions and Answers," This Is Youth Speaking:
Record of the American Youth Congress National Citizenship Institute, February 9–12, 1940, ERPC. Contemporary commentators and subsequent historians have not been as generous in their treatment of the Citizenship Institute.
The AYC, in response to this, claimed that "feature writers, columnists, wire
services and Washington correspondents indulged in an orgy of misquotation,
perversion, biased emphases, red baiting and 'herring drawing' that has been
unparalleled in Youth Congress history." See "Citizenship in Action," Report
of the AYC National Assembly Meeting, February 12, 1940, JPL Box 24.
That eleven-page report included more than five pages of analysis of what was
reported in the media compared to what happened at the Institute.

85. Memorandum from M. C. Thompson to General Watson, March 19,
1940, POF 58, Box 4. That meeting was subsequently rescheduled for May 5,
1940 and enlarged to include 47 attendees for a dinner at the White House
followed by a three-hour meeting with FDR. Memorandum, Mrs. Helm to
General Watson, April 24, 1940, POF 3910, Box 1; Eleanor Roosevelt to
Charles Taussig, April 23, 1940, CT Box 1. The minutes from that Conference show that the youth representatives advocated more cooperation between
youth-led and youth-serving organizations to better serve youth's needs. See
Minutes of Conference on Youth Problems, April 29, 1940, CT Box 1.

86. "Mrs. Roosevelt Voices Faith in Youth Congress," *Herald Tribune*,
June 12, 1940, CT Box 81. To dispel complaints against the AYC still being

instigated by Murray Plavner, Eleanor Roosevelt asked Cadden for clarification
of the AYC's position on a number of issues. In response, Cadden pointed
out the factual errors of Plavner's claims as well as the misrepresentations he
fostered. Plavner claimed that the AYC borrowed from a communist pamphlet
written by Max Weiss in developing its Declaration of Rights of American
Youth. This, Cadden pointed out, was impossible given that the Declaration
was written and approved before Weiss wrote and published his piece. Cadden
averred that Weiss simply borrowed from the Declaration in order to garner
more widespread support. Moreover, while Plavner harped on the similari-
ties between the AYC Declaration and the communist pamphlet, no attention is paid to the glaring divergences, not least of which was that "the Youth
Congress in no way advocated the overthrow of capitalism and the essence
of its position is that we must work within the existing framework of legality
and constitutionality for the improvement of the conditions of youth and the
strengthening of the American system of government." He also took aim at
Plavner's accusation that the AYC Creed was a rewrite of communist doctrine
by pointing out that when Bill Hinckley read the Creed to the Dies Committee, the Committee itself was very impressed with it, and he asked, tongue-
in-cheek, "Now if the Dies Committee is being taken in by Communist
doctrines, what is poor America to do?" Joseph Cadden to Eleanor Roosevelt,
April 20, 1940, ER Microfilm Collection, Reel 1, FDR Library.

87. Eleanor Roosevelt to Joseph Lash, May 12, 1940, JPL Box 27. Eleanor
Roosevelt believed that there were many young people who were imbued
with what was also the current communist line. She did not think this proved
inculcation by the communists, but, rather, that it represented a genuine belief
on their part. "Some of it," she said, referring to the affinity for the communist
line, "is the result of our own teaching since the world war that we did not
want to go to war. They do not separate going to war in Europe from defense. . . . We can largely blame ourselves for this attitude." Eleanor Roosevelt to
Mrs. Backer, June 5, 1940, JPL Box 28.

88. Closed Cabinet Meeting Minutes, February 21, 1940, JPL Box 23.
Although there was no recorded explanation of Lash's specific objections to
Cadden's report, it can be surmised that he was upset that Cadden placed the
context of American unemployment in the war-readying economy.

89. Ibid. Lash explained to Cadden privately that he thought Cadden's summary of the President's speech was prejudicial and Lash thought Cadden should
"find less partisan language." Joseph Lash to Joseph Cadden, March 16, 1940,
JPL Box 23.

90. Closed Cabinet Meeting Minutes, February 21, 1940, JPL Box 23.

91. Ibid.

92. Cadden had, as Executive Secretary of the AYC, sent letters to the leaders of all the national parties, asking them to send a representative of their party
to meet with youth during the Citizenship Institute because the goal of the Institute was to get youth in touch with political officials and get political officials

in touch with youth. The Republican Party refused to send a representative to meet with youth. Cadden responded with uncharacteristic vociferousness, sarcastically thanking the Chairman of the Republican National Party for telling "us how to run the American Youth Congress" and pointing out that "shooting at Communists instead of shooting at the problems doesn't kill off the real enemies of American democracy and American youth: unemployment, lack of adequate educational, housing and health facilities, and the threat of war. The four and a half million young people cooperating through the American Youth Congress do not share your lack of faith in the Bill of Rights, which, if you recall, contains no 'ifs' and 'buts' to exclude Communists or any other minority group (such as your own) from the American scene." He then rebuffed the demand to expel communists from the AYC, saying that this would in no way assure jobs to the four million American youth out of work and out of school and that "the experience of other countries leads us to believe it can only result in the elimination of *every* type of dissenter." He maintained that "we are not tied to the political apron strings of any party." Joseph Cadden to John Hamilton, Chairman of the Republican National Committee, February 6, 1940, JPL Box 23.

93. Eleanor Roosevelt was a staunch advocate for young people to freely express themselves without adult interference. She said that New Deal administrators should not discredit anything done by youth-led organizations, nor should they try to dominate or coerce youth organizations to adopt any objective or method. Moreover, she warned, she would not support any attempt by political officials to foster a split in youth forces. This was *after* the Citizenship Institute. See Eleanor Roosevelt to Charles Taussig, March 11, 1940, ER NYA Materials, Microfilm, FDR Library.

94. Closed Cabinet Meeting Minutes, February 21, 1940, JPL Box 23.

95. *Ibid.*

96. *Ibid.*

97. At this point in the discussion, the focus clearly shifted from whether or not a local group could pass a resolution to the nature of the AYC itself.

98. Closed Cabinet Meeting Minutes, February 21, 1940, JPL Box 23.

99. *Ibid.*

100. AYC Cabinet Meeting Minutes March 7, 1940, JPL Box 23.

101. *Ibid.*

102. *Ibid.*

103. *Ibid.*

104. AYC Cabinet Meeting, March 21, 1940, JPL Box 23.

105. Indeed, she wrote an introduction to Leslie Gould's history of the American Youth Congress, *American Youth Today*, published in 1940 even though she thought he was "too unkind to the President" because she still believed that AYC members were "honestly trying to help young people … and … should receive co-operation and understanding." Eleanor Roosevelt, introduction to *American Youth Today*, vii–viii.

106. Peace Commission Minutes, April 17, 1940, JPL Box 23.

107. See correspondence among Joseph Lash, Joseph Cadden, Mary Jeanne McKay, Jim Carey, Sam Ribner, Louise Meyerovitz, March 9–April 5, 1940, JPL Box 24. Lash told Carrell Morris, from the Committee on the United Christian Youth Movement, that he intended to stay in the AYC because he was committed to maintaining its representative membership, even if he represented the minority position. Joseph Lash to J. Carrell Morris, April 22, 1940, JPL Box 24. The response from Morris serves as a reminder that not everyone who opposed collective security did so based on a desire to follow the Soviet line. Morris pointed out that "those of us who are religious pacifists feel that such action would deny the laws of God, which must ultimately prevail despite external indications, and that we are not justified in such methods for the sake of a temporary appearance of peace." J. Carrell Morris to Joseph Lash, June 3, 1940, JPL Box 24.

108. AYC Cabinet Meeting Minutes, May 4, 1940, JPL Box 24.

109. Ibid.

110. Ibid.

111. Ibid. Another member pointed out that if the AYC was going to go on record against the lack of democracy in the Soviet Union, she would insist that it include a statement about the lack of democracy in the South.

112. Ibid.

113. This course of action was predetermined. Joseph Lash had spent the weeks leading up to this meeting counseling AYC Cabinet members to remain in the AYC to "fight it out with the communists" and to try to convince their organizations to remain in the AYC until such time as policy was decided upon. Should that policy refuse to support collective security, only then should the organization withdraw. See Joseph Lash to Alan Gottlieb, May 5, 1940; Louise Meyerovitz to Joseph Lash, April 15, 1940; Bob Spivack to Louise Meyerovitz April 9, 1940, JPL Box 24.

114. Joseph Lash, review of *American Youth Today*, nd, JPL Box 27.

115. "Socialists Leave the Youth Congress," n.d., JPL Box 24. The YPSL had already broken with Lash, Yard, and other ASU leaders because they had voted against a plank to abolish the ROTC in 1939. See *C.C.N.Y. BANNER*, 1939, 1–2, JPL Box 24. Historians have tended to follow George Rawick's lead in describing this process as a purge of the socialists. Rawick claimed that "the Stalinist landlords evicted the ASU's liberal and popular front tenants . . . [including] Lash and the Harvard Liberal Union." Rawick, "The New Deal and Youth," 362.

116. AYC Cabinet Meeting Minutes, June 5, 1940, JPL Box 24. If the communists were truly in control and wished to squash opposition, this motion would have been defeated because the motion allowed non-affiliated youth advocates—like Lash—to continue to vote and potentially affect policy.

117. Among the hundreds of anti-war events that made up the Strike Against War, Senator Nye gave a speech at the University of Michigan, Nor-

man Thomas spoke at Harvard, Archibald MacLeish's "Fall of the City" was broadcast at Dartmouth, and Jeannette Rankin addressed a mass meeting at Montana State University. "Y.C.A.W. in Action," *News Bulletin*, May 1940, JPL Box 23.

118. "Strike Against War," *News Bulletin*, March–April, 1940, JPL Box 23.

119. "Total War Sweeps Europe," *News Bulletin*, May 1940, JPL Box 23.

120. "Join the Peace Rally," May 9, 1940, University Archives / Columbiana Library, Columbia University.

121. ASU Executive Committee to ASU members, May 13, 1940, JPL Box 21.

122. "Call to Washington," 1940, JPL Box 23.

123. Jack McMichael, "More Democracy—Not Less," Report of the 6th American Youth Congress, July 3–7, 1940, JPL Box 23.

124. Ibid.

125. As quoted in Vivien Liebman, "Anti-Conscription Keynote of Youth Congress," *PM*, July 5, 1940, JPL Box 33.

126. Malcolm Cotton Dobbs, "Declaration on National Defense," Report of the 6th American Youth Congress, July 3–7, 1940, JPL Box 23.

127. Report of the 6th American Youth Congress, July 3–7, 1940, JPL Box 23.

128. Ibid. Lash was reported to be "100% for conscription" because he favors the Administration's foreign policy, "is writing a book on President Roosevelt's papers, is friendly with Mrs. Roosevelt, and backs the President completely." Vivien Liebman, "Anti-Conscription Keynote of Youth Congress," *PM*, July 5, 1940, JPL Box 33.

129. Report of the 6th American Youth Congress, July 3–7, 1940, JPL Box 23. Later, in a discussion of a resolution against conscription, Lash indicated just how much he had changed his view on this issue, vowing to vote against the resolution because it made no contingency statement regarding what would happen if the United States was invaded. After some discussion, James Jackson of the Southern Negro Youth Congress, held up the AYC Creed, quoting its promise to "fight now and continually for the preservation and extension of democracy" as proof that Lash's opposition to the resolution was unfounded.

130. Ibid.

131. Ibid.

132. Ibid.

133. Ibid.

134. Ibid. In his summary of this meeting, Joseph Lash commented that "every effort was made to conciliate us [the minority group]." He still hoped to convince Weiss and the others that "you cannot fight appeasement in Europe without seeing that FDR is the strongest barrier to appeasement here." Joseph Lash to Agnes Reynolds, n.d., JPL Box 27.

135. Report of the 6th American Youth Congress, July 3–7, 1940, JPL Box 23.

136. Ibid. If the communists manipulated this congress, as some have supposed, then it seems likely that they would have tried to influence the outcome of this vote.

137. Joseph Lash to Editor, *New York Times*, July 10, 1940, JPL Box 27.

138. Ibid.

139. Ibid.

140. ASU Newsletter, 1940, JPL Box 21.

141. Ibid.

142. Jean Horie to Mrs. Thomas F. McAllister, July 20, 1940, Democratic Party Women's Division Papers, Box 314, FDR Library.

143. Included in that effort was the transmission of a 25-word telegram carrying 4,500 signatures from New York to Senators Wagner and Mead, which took Western Union 6 hours and 15 minutes to translate, thus representing the longest telegram east of the Mississippi in the history of Western Union. This feat, it was noted, got no mention in the media. AYC Cabinet Meeting Minutes, September 1, 1940, JPL Box 23.

144. Joseph Cadden to AYC Cabinet Members, August 7, 1940, JPL Box 23.

145. Frances Williams to AYC Cabinet Members, August 26, 1940, JPL Box 23.

146. AYC Cabinet Meeting Minutes, September 1, 1940, JPL Box 23.

147. Ibid.

148. His support for Roosevelt arose in spite of the retrenchment of New Deal programs and because of the war in Europe. Lash believed that the war would continue and America would have to become involved regardless of who was president, but at least "a New Deal government would be a force for a progressive reorganization of Europe—and the inevitable adjustments here at home will be made with the concern of the common people in mind." Joseph Lash to Alan Gottlieb, May 5, 1940, JPL Box 24.

149. Interview of College Clubs for Roosevelt Movement under direction of Joseph Lash with Senator Norris, September 6, 1940, JPL Box 21.

150. Joseph Lash to Peter Kuh, October 4, 1940, JPL Box 27. In this letter, Lash urged Kuh, head of the Swarthmore Student Union, to push forward with the plan they had discussed with Agnes Reynolds to dissociate from the ASU. Responding to Lash's letter, Kuh explained that such action had already been taken because the ASU had condemned both presidential candidates and had failed to support any candidate (which would have been a violation of the ASU's non-partisan policy), its advocacy of continued isolationism in the face of Britain's great need for aid, its failure to condemn Russia for the invasion of Finland, and the issuance of unsuitable and unscholarly literature even on those issues with which they agreed. Kuh then expressed sympathy with Lash's organization and said that he would do all he could to get a resolution endorsing Roosevelt's third term. Peter Kuh to Joseph Lash, October 6, 1940; Roger Shinn to Joseph Lash, October 10, 1940, JPL Box 27; Joseph Lash to John Kaufman, October 8, 1940, JPL Box 21.

151. Some individuals did follow Lash out of the ASU and into the SDD or his other organization, the National Independent Youth Committee, which was affiliated with the National Committee of Independent voters, who were in full support of Roosevelt's re-election. These included Peter Kuh, Roger Shinn, Harriet Pickens, Louise Meyerovitz, Agnes Reynolds, and Lee Wiggins. See Youth Division of National Committee of Independent Voters for Roosevelt and Wallace Press Release, October 4, 1940, JPL Box 27.

152. Joseph Lash to Ethel Clyde, October 16, 1940, JPL Box 21. The more Lash supported FDR, the more the ASU distanced itself from him. In March 1941, a political cartoon featuring "baby Joe" being coddled by FDR ran in the *Student Advocate*, with the caption "Here's Pal Joey who sold out for Four Grand. A frequent visitor at the White House, Lash is perfectly willing to give up your democracy in order to see a British victory." *The Student Advocate*, March 15, 1941, JPL Box 21.

153. Joseph Lash to Peg Stein, n.d., JPL Box 21.

154. "A Call to a Day of National Mourning" flyer, October 16, 1940, JPL Box 27.

155. Joseph Lash to Editor, *New York Times*, October 31, 1940, JPL Box 27.

156. Joseph Lash to Editor, *New York Times*, n.d., JPL Box 23. Lash's support of Roosevelt and the New Deal was very much in line with the intellectual community's assessment of the period. Richard Pells argues that "after 1939 much of the intellectual community saw the United States—whatever its faults—as the final repository for their hopes and ambitions. In essence, they were transferring their loyalties from one set of symbols to another: from socialism to democracy, from economic justice to political pluralism, from collective action to personal mobility, from the Internationale to the American dream." Pells, *Radical Visions and American Dreams*, 361.

157. See Joseph Lash, untitled, 1940, JPL Box 29.

158. ASU Administrative Committee Meeting Minutes, September 29, 1939, JPL Box 29.

159. Frances Williams to AYC members, October 22, 1940; Joseph Cadden to AYC members, April 17, 1940, JPL Box 23; Joseph Lash to William Comberg, October 17, 1940, JPL Box 27.

160. Joseph Cadden to FDR, October 23, 1940, POF 3910, Box 1; Jack McMichael to AYC members, October 23, 1940, JPL Box 23; "Statement of Committee on Election Rights 1940," October 22, 1940, JPL Box 23; "Youth Votes to Defend Democracy," JPL Box 23.

161. "Youth's Yardstick for the 1940 Election Campaign," JPL Box 23.

162. Ibid.

163. Joseph Lash had become a strong supporter of Lend-Lease. See Joseph Lash, "The American Forum of the Air: Shall We Convoy Materials to Great Britain," April 13, 1941, JPL Box 33. AYC Cabinet Meeting Minutes, January 18, 1941; Joseph Lash to Myrtle Powell, January 28, 1941, JPL Box 24. In his speech, Lash argued that aid to England was in keeping with the AYC's former

policies of aiding Republican Spain and aiding China in its war against Japan. He repeatedly claimed to be speaking for a majority of young Americans, and he said that aid to England represented the three principles that youth united behind: all-inclusive national defense, full support to all peoples everywhere who are resisting aggression, and no acquiescence in a peace dictated by aggressors. Joseph Lash, "Speech in Favor of Lend-Lease Bill," February 1941, JPL Box 24.

164. Joseph Lash to Myrtle Powell, February 1, 1941; Joseph Lash to the Editor of *The Herald Tribune*, February 1, 1941, JPL Box 24.

165. Myrtle Powell to Joseph Lash, February 4, 1941, JPL Box 24.

166. Subsequently, the NYA Art Program began designing army recruiting posters that targeted young people. Charles Taussig, Press Release, August 23, 1941, CT Box 89.

167. AYC Cabinet Meeting Minutes, December 21, 1940, JPL Box 23.

168. "Action Letter," January 11, 1941, JPL Box 24. AYC members believed that in speaking out against the ill treatment of the AYC and by insisting on a venue for their Town Hall Meeting where young people would be able to speak their minds, they were fighting for their right to freedom of speech.

169. Jack McMichael, Speech to the Town Hall Meeting, February 8, 1941, JM.

170. Aubrey Williams had begun the process of turning the National Youth Administration into a defense agency as early as 1937. By 1941, this was the sole justification for continuing aid to the program. In an attempt to justify the continuation of the NYA as a defense agency and to prove that the NYA made young people more committed to the President's defense program, Aubrey Williams commissioned a survey in 1941 of 3,000 NYA enrollees to determine what they could do for their community to strengthen the program of national defense. Only 20 percent of respondents made any suggestion directly connected with defense while 48 percent stressed the importance of the NYA in providing occupational skills for youth, and the remaining 31 percent stressed the general improvement for self, community, or society gained through NYA work. While the survey was cast as displaying youth's eagerness to cooperate in the program of national defense, and therefore solicited a letter of gratitude from President Roosevelt, the results seem to indicate, instead, that young people still viewed the NYA as a program to provide skills in order to counteract widespread unemployment. Only 112 respondents said they would enter military service. See "The Youth Survey," ER NYA Materials, Microfilm, FDR Library. For information about the NYA defense training program, see "Youth, Jobs & Defense," ERPC. Charles Taussig boasted in 1942 that "one NYA youth every minute enters war industries," Press Release, February 12, 1942, CT Box 89.

171. Jack McMichael, Speech to the Town Hall Meeting, February 8, 1941, JM.

172. Ibid.

173. AYC National Assembly Meeting Minutes, February 10, 1941, JPL Box 24.

174. "Fellowship Appeal to World Youth," AYC National Assembly Meeting Minutes, February 10, 1941, JPL Box 24.

175. "Youth Congress Sponsors Bill Prohibiting Discrimination," Press Release, March 8,1941, JPL Box 24.

176. Joseph Lash, "Personal Credo," April 28, 1941, JPL Box 33. Interestingly, despite his arguments against left-wing groups beginning in 1937, and reaching a climax with his anti-communist positions of 1939–41, Lash's socialist beliefs would resurface after the war. In 1946, he wrote a piece in which he argued that the time for nationalization of key industries, wider social controls, and planning had come if social progress was to be made. Without FDR, the Democratic Party had submitted to conservatism; it was no longer the beacon of hope it had once been. Interestingly, he gave no credit to the groups or individuals who had foreseen this in the 1930s. See Joseph Lash, "Where Do Progressives Go from Here," July 25, 1946, JPL Box 29.

177. Joseph Lash, "Youth Congress 'Anti-War' Strike Aimed Wrong; Hitler Real Enemy," SOS, April 18, 1941, JPL Box 27.

178. Ibid. Lash remembered being called "Judas" for his support of Lend-Lease. Joseph Lash interview with Joel Chernoff, January 5, 1978, JPL Box 78.

179. Raymond Friedlander, "Whom Do They Represent," Student Advocate, March 15, 1941, JPL Box 21.

180. This is highly ironic since Lash's cry that his minority view was not being given proper attention echoes Harold Draper's contention in 1937 that the ASU was leaving his group—the YPSL—"out in the cold" along with other minority groups. See, for example, Molly Yard to Joseph Lash, n.d., JPL Box 27.

181. Joseph Lash to Jack McMichael, May 12, 1941, JPL Box 27.

182. Draft letter of resignation to Jack McMichael, JPL Box 24.

183. Ibid.

184. Joseph Lash to Jack McMichael, May 12, 1941, JPL Box 27. In accepting the letter of resignation, Jack McMichael felt compelled to respond to the charges leveled against the AYC. He denied that the AYC was in any way undemocratic, proved, he said, by the fact that Lash's minority view had not become AYC policy. McMichael pointed out the "unpalatability" (to organized American youth) of Lash's "pro-war program," which extended beyond Lend-Lease to convoying and even, eventually, another AEF. He then went on to catalog all the opportunities for Lash's view to be heard, of which he had taken full advantage. He finished his counter-indictment by quoting Lash, himself, who had said after a long discussion of AYC's peace policy, "I wish to thank the delegates for the courtesy they have shown to those of us who represent a minority opinion. We appreciate the fact that we are a minority." Jack McMichael to Joseph Lash, June 19, 1941, JPL Box 24.

185. Carl Ross, "Unity and the Struggle Against Hitler," Clarity, Summer 1941, JPL Box 33.

186. Ibid.

187. Ibid.

188. Ibid.

189. Joseph Lash, "New Directions for Youth," *Threshold*, October 1941, JPL Box 33.

190. Ibid.

191. Ibid.

192. Ibid. Assigning so much authority to the communists is a convenient explanation for what happened; however, as Julian Jackson shows in his study of the popular front and its demise in France, "the obsession with the supposedly ubiquitous role of the communists is quite misplaced: as in June 1936, torn between preserving a revolutionary identity and loyalty to the popular front, they were following events as much as making them." Julian Jackson, *The Popular Front in France Defending Democracy, 1934–1938* (New York: Cambridge University Press, 1988), 109.

193. Joseph Lash, "New Directions for Youth." Eileen Eagan echoes this assessment. See Eagan, *Class, Culture, and the Classroom*, 198.

194. Unpublished confidential addendum to Molly Yard's Memorandum to the American Youth Commission, n.d., JPL Box 24. As early as July 1936, the YPSL National Executive Committee had decided that it would not accept any administrative responsibilities for the American Youth Congress and that it would not allow its members to accept any position on the AYC's national council. The YPSL adopted the position that it would cooperate on issues with which it agreed and its members would act as observers at national council meetings, but otherwise it would distance itself from the AYC. YPSL Resident Board Meeting Minutes, July 23, 1936, JPL Box 23.

195. Those that had withdrawn included the YPSL, YCAW, and Young Judea.

196. Of the thirty-three organizations that did not attend this congress but had attended the previous one, twenty were socialist organizations and many of the remaining thirteen had socialist ties as well as shared membership with the socialist organizations. See "An Analysis of the American Youth Congress Convention at Lake Geneva, Wisconsin, July 3–7, 1940," JPL Box 23.

197. "An Analysis of the American Youth Congress Convention at Lake Geneva, Wisconsin, July 3–7, 1940," JPL Box 23.

198. Ibid. The insinuation here was that communists could not, by definition, be good Americans—a belief shared by Daniel Bell, who called the Communist Party "a garish political group with no real roots in American life." Daniel Bell, *Marxian Socialism in the United States* (Ithaca: Cornell University Press, 1996), 152.

199. "An Analysis of the American Youth Congress Convention at Lake Geneva, Wisconsin, July 3–7, 1940," JPL Box 23.

200. Ibid. Despite saying that the Lash bloc could command majority support, the report claimed that "the Communist Party is still completely in the

saddle" of the AYC. Lash, for his part, when asked what he thought of the new AYC Cabinet elected in 1940, said the same thing he said a year earlier: "the new cabinet chosen today, and which will govern the Congress for the coming year, is the most representative in its history." Lash, Pickens, and McKay, who had all been re-elected, represented a minority view yet he vowed to remain in the AYC because its democratic procedures assured all points of view a fair hearing. He further explained that there was general agreement on such matters as civil liberties, standards of living, and national defense. The AYC would be able to move forward on those issues despite the uncertainty concerning foreign policy "in this 'Brave New World' in which France lies prostrate under Hitler's boot." He closed by saying that Youth Congress must be preserved for it were to be destroyed, "that would only serve the interests of opportunist groups. Nor would it be possible to build a new Young Congress, serving progressive purposes which the majority of the community sanctions." Yet it was Lash who set out to create just such an opposition group outside the parameters of the AYC. Joseph Lash, "Minority Group Claims New Basis for AYC Unity," *PM*, July 8, 1940, JPL Box 27.

201. Joseph Lash to Eleanor Roosevelt, January 3, 1940, Eleanor Roosevelt Microfilm Collection, Reel 1; JPL Box 27. Lash does not treat his own departure from the youth movement in such philosophical terms. An explanation for his decision to leave and the hostility he harbored for the organizations he once led can perhaps be found in Richard Pells's explanation of the impact the Nazi-Soviet Pact had on American intellectuals—a group among which Lash most assiduously hoped to be included. Pells argues that the Pact created a sense of political and personal betrayal through the entire intellectual community. Pells, *Radical Visions and American Dreams*, 347. Pells, too, talks about this search for something larger, though he refers to it as a "search for community." See Pells, *Radical Visions and American Dreams*, Chapter III.

202. Joseph Lash to Eleanor Roosevelt, January 3, 1940, Eleanor Roosevelt Microfilm Collection, Reel 1; JPL Box 27.

203. Ibid.

204. Ibid. Lash recognized young people—himself included—were largely ignorant of the reality of Soviet communism. It was not until after he decided to quit the youth movement that he began to read everything he could about Russia to gain a better understanding of what happened and what was happening there. He, too, had ignored the show trials, heresy hunts against Trotskyism, and an understanding of Stalin's adulation, but now, he said, these things weighed on his conscience. He wondered how Stalin had gotten to power, what social groups he represented that enabled him to stay in power, and whether the despotism in the Soviet Union was a result of Russian backwardness or capitalist encirclement. See Joseph Lash to Monroe Sweetland, January 25, 1940, JPL Box 24.

205. Eagan, *Class, Culture, and the Classroom*, 197; Joseph Lash, "Two Lives," 28, JPL Box 27. Frank Warren closes his study of the American Socialist Party

by asking "just who sacrificed whom for the future?"—a question that can
readily be applied to the dismantling of the popular front at the end of the
Depression decade. Frank A. Warren, *An Alternative Vision: The Socialist Party in
the 1930s* (Bloomington: Indiana University Press, 1974), 190.
206. Brax, *The First Student Movement*, 96.
207. Joseph Lash, Notes for "Growing Up in Wellesley Hills," n.d., JPL Box
33. Lash is representative of what Leon Samson referred to as American infan-
tilism toward socialism: "A socialist spirit in a capitalist system. This is America."
Leon Samson, *The American Mind*, quoted in Warren, *An Alternative Vision*, 61.
208. Rawick, "The New Deal and Youth," 377. Many have argued (beginning with Rawick) that the demise of the youth organizations was the result of
their communist members' strict adherence to following the Soviet line. Thus,
it is argued, the organizations fell apart when Germany invaded the Soviet
Union and the communists began advocating collective security. See, for example, Cohen, *When the Old Left Was Young*, Chapter 9. Yet Eagan, who generally agrees with Cohen, notes that when FDR signed the Selective Training
and Service Act on September 16, 1940, there were no large-scale protests on
college campuses, and this, she says, shows "how far the country and the students had progressed toward war." Eagan, *Class, Culture, and the Classroom*, 221.

Conclusion

1. Joseph Lash, Autobiographical Notes for *Growing Up in Wellesley Hills*,
JPL Box 33.
2. The close relationship between the Roosevelt Administration and some
youth leaders, such as Hinckley and Lash, earned some reprisals from youth
advocates while conservative critics used such relationships to cast aspersions on
FDR, Eleanor Roosevelt, and the New Deal. Westbrook Pegler, for example,
referred to Joe Lash as a "house-pet" of the Roosevelts. Joseph Lash, Autobiographical Sketch, n.d., JPL Box 78.
3. As early as 1937, the NYA had been transformed into a Defense Agency.
Under the Reorganization Act of 1939, the NYA and CCC were merged into
one program under the Federal Security Agency. The CCC was terminated as a
cost-saving measure in 1942; the NYA was likewise terminated in 1943, despite
every effort by Aubrey Williams to save some semblance of the program. Cost-
saving during wartime, inter-departmental disputes within the FDR Administration, and continued red-baiting of both the NYA and Williams ultimately
led to its demise. See Richard Reiman, *The New Deal and American Youth: Ideas
and Ideals in a Depression Decade* (Athens: University of Georgia Press, 1992);
John A. Salmond, *A Southern Rebel: The Life and Times of Aubrey Willis Williams,
1890–1965* (Chapel Hill: University of North Carolina Press, 1983).
4. Senator Hubert Humphrey (D-MN) introduced a bill calling for a
comprehensive Youth Opportunity Program in 1957 that would have reen-
acted the student aid, part-time work philosophy of the NYA along with the

conservation work of the CCC. Memorandum, Office of Senator Hubert H. Humphrey, January 24, 1957, James Roosevelt Papers, Box 502, FDR Library. James Roosevelt was an active supporter of that bill, and as Representative from California's 26th Congressional District since 1954, he re-introduced it on the first day of the 87th Congress (January 3, 1961). He and Humphrey continued to try to get the bill passed through 1963. Many of its provisions were subsequently included in the Higher Education Act of 1965.

5. Wechsler served in the Army in World War II but did not see active combat because he was drafted too late. Lash served in the Pacific Theater.

6. Eric Sevareid, *Not So Wild a Dream* (New York: Alfred A. Knopf, 1946), 51.

7. Ibid., 52.

Bibliography

Manuscript Sources

Located at Columbia University

Columbiana Collection, Butler Library Microfilm Department
James Wechsler Papers, University Archives / Columbiana Library
Reed Harris Papers, University Archives / Columbiana Library
University Archives / Columbiana Library

Located at the Franklin Delano Roosevelt Presidential Library, Hyde Park, New York

Adolf Berle Papers
American Youth Congress Vertical File
Aubrey Williams Papers
Charles Taussig Papers
Democratic Party, Women's Division Papers
Eleanor Roosevelt Papers
Eleanor Roosevelt Pamphlet Collection
Eleanor Roosevelt Microfilm Collection
Gardner Jackson Papers
Harry Hopkins Papers
James Roosevelt Papers
Joseph Lash Papers
Leland Olds Papers
President's Advisory Committee on Education File
President's Interdepartmental Committee to Coordinate Health and Welfare
    Activities File

President's Official Files
President's Personal Files
World Youth Congress Vertical File

Located at New York University
Jack McMichael Papers, Tamiment Library
New York University Archives
Pamphlet Collection, Tamiment Library
Young People's Socialist League Papers, Tamiment Library

Periodicals

The Campus, Cohen Library, City College of New York Archives
Spectator, Microfilm and Periodicals Collection, Columbia University
The Student Advocate, Tamiment Library, New York University Archives

Selected Secondary Sources

Acker, James. *Scottsboro and Its Legacy: The Cases That Challenged American Legal and Social Justice*. New York: Praeger, 2007.
Altbach, Philip G. *Student Politics in America: A Historical Analysis*. New York: McGraw-Hill, 1974.
Beevor, Anthony. *The Battle for Spain: The Spanish Civil War, 1931–1936*. New York: Penguin Books, 2006.
Bell, Daniel. *Marxian Socialism in the United States*. Ithaca, N.Y.: Cornell University Press, 1996.
Boris, Eileen. *Home to Work: Motherhood and the Politics of Industrial Homework in the United States*. New York: Cambridge University Press, 1994.
Brax, Ralph S. *The First Student Movement: Student Activism in the United States During the 1930s*. Port Washington, N.Y.: Kennikat Press, 1981.
Caro, Robert. *Path to Power*. New York: Vintage Books, 1990.
Carter, Dan T. *Scottsboro: A Tragedy of the American South*. Baton Rouge: Louisiana State University Press, 1979.
Cohen, Robert. *When the Old Left Was Young: Student Radicals and America's First Mass Student Movement, 1929–1941*. New York: Oxford University Press, 1993.
Conkin, Paul K. *The New Deal*. 2nd ed. Arlington Heights, Ill.: Harlan Davidson, Inc., 1975.
Cook, Blanche Weisen. *Eleanor Roosevelt*. Vol. 1, *1884–1933*. New York: Viking, 1992.
Davis, Kingsley. *Youth in the Depression*. Chicago: University of Chicago Press, 1935.

Davis, Maxine. *The Lost Generation: A Portrait of American Youth Today*. New York: MacMillan Company, 1936.

Divine, Robert A. *The Reluctant Belligerent: American Entry into World War II*. New York: John Wiley & Sons, 1965.

Draper, Theodore. *The Roots of American Communism*. New York: Viking Press, 1957.

Dubofsky, Melvyn and Warren Van Tine. *John L. Lewis: A Biography*. Chicago: University of Chicago Press, 1986.

Eagan, Eileen. *Class, Culture, and the Classroom: The Student Peace Movement of the 1930s*. Philadelphia: Temple University Press, 1981.

Fairclough, Adam. *Better Day Coming: Blacks and Equality, 1890–2000*. New York: Penguin, 2002.

Fass, Paula S. *The Damned and the Beautiful: American Youth in the 1920's*. New York: Oxford University Press, 1977.

Fearon, Peter. *Kansas in the Great Depression: Work Relief, the Dole, and Rehabilitation*. Columbia: University of Missouri Press, 2007.

Footman, David., ed. *International Communism*. London: Chatto & Windus, 1960.

Goodman, James. *Stories of Scottsboro*. New York: Vintage Books, 1995.

Gordon, Linda. *Pitied But Not Entitled: Single Mothers and the History of Welfare, 1890–1935*. Cambridge: Harvard University Press, 1994.

Gould, Leslie. *American Youth Today*. New York: Random House, 1940.

Hoff-Wilson, Joan and Marjorie Lightman, eds. *Without Precedent: The Life and Career of Eleanor Roosevelt*. Bloomington: Indiana University Press, 1984.

Howe, Irving. *Socialism in America*. New York: Harcourt Brace Jovanovich, 1985.

Hurd, William Lloyd. "The Origin and Early Development of the National Youth Administration." M.A. Thesis, University of Oklahoma, 1967.

Jackson, Julian. *The Popular Front in France Defending Democracy, 1934–1938*. New York: Cambridge University Press, 1988.

Johnson, Palmer and Oswald Harvey. *The National Youth Administration*. Washington, D.C.: United States Printing Office, 1938.

Klehr, Harvey and others. *The Secret World of American Communism*. New Haven: Yale University Press, 1995.

Koch, H.W. *The Hitler Youth: Origins and Development, 1922–1945*. New York: Cooper Square Press, 2000.

Koon, Tracy. *Believe, Obey, Fight: Political Socialization of Youth in Fascist Italy, 1922–1943*. Chapel Hill: University of North Carolina Press, 1985.

Ladd-Taylor, Molly. *Mother-Work: Women, Child Welfare, and the State, 1890–1930*. Chicago: University of Illinois Press, 1994.

Langer, William L. and S. Everett Gleason. *The Challenge to Isolation, 1937–1940*. New York: Harper & Brothers Publishers, 1952.

Laqueur, Walter. *Young Germany: A History of the German Youth Movement*. New Brunswick: Transaction Books, 1962.

Lash, Joseph P. *Eleanor and Franklin: The Story of Their Relationship Based on Elea-nor Roosevelt's Private Papers.* New York: New American Library, 1971.

Lash, Joseph P. and James A. Wechsler. *War Our Heritage.* New York: Interna-tional Publishers, 1936.

Leuchtenburg, William E. *Franklin D. Roosevelt and the New Deal, 1932–1940.* New York: Harper Torchbooks, 1963.

Lindemann, Albert S. *A History of European Socialism.* New Haven: Yale Univer-sity Press, 1983.

Lindenmeyer, Kriste. *"A Right to Childhood:" The U.S. Children's Bureau and Child Welfare, 1912–1946.* Chicago: University of Illinois Press, 1997.

Lindley, Betty and Ernest K. *A New Deal for Youth: The Story of the National Youth Administration.* New York: Viking Press, 1938.

Lorwin, Lewis L. *Youth Work Programs: Problems and Policies.* Washington, D.C.: American Council on Education, 1941.

McDermott, Kevin and Jeremy Agnew. *The Comintern: A History of International Communism from Lenin to Stalin.* New York: St. Martin's Press, 1997.

McJimsey, George. *Harry Hopkins: Ally of the Poor and Defender of Democracy.* Cambridge: Harvard University Press, 1987.

McKenzie, Kermit E. *Comintern and World Revolution, 1928–1942: The Shaping of Doctrine.* New York: Columbia University Press, 1964.

Mennel, Robert M. *Thorns and Thistles: Juvenile Delinquents in the United States, 1825–1940.* Hanover, N.H.: University Press of New England, 1973.

Miller, James A. *Remembering Scottsboro: The Legacy of the Infamous Trial.* Princeton: Princeton University Press, 2009.

Miller, Michael Henry. "The American Student Movement, 1931–1941: A Historical Analysis." PhD diss., Florida State University, 1981.

Orwell, George. *Homage to Catalonia.* New York: Harcourt, 1952.

Payne, Stanley G. *Spain's First Democracy: The Second Republic, 1931–1936.* Madison: University of Wisconsin Press, 1993.

Pells, Richard H. *Radical Visions and American Dreams: Culture and Social Thought in the Depression Years.* New York: Harper & Row, 1973.

Preston, Paul. *The Spanish Civil War: Reaction, Revolution, and Revenge.* New York: Norton, 2006.

Rawick, George Philip. "The New Deal and Youth: The Civilian Conservation Corps, the National Youth Administration, and the American Youth Con-gress." PhD diss., University of Wisconsin–Madison, 1957.

Rees, Tim and Andrew Thorpe, eds. *International Communism and the Com-munist International, 1919–1943.* Manchester: Manchester University Press, 1998.

Reiman, Richard A. *The New Deal and American Youth: Ideas and Ideals in a De-pression Decade.* Athens: University of Georgia Press, 1992.

Rempel, Gerhard. *Hitler's Children: The Hitler Youth and the SS.* Chapel Hill: University of North Carolina Press, 1989.

Roosevelt, Eleanor. *The Autobiography of Eleanor Roosevelt*. New York: Harper & Brothers, 1961.

———. *It Seems to Me*. New York: Norton, 1949.

———. *This I Remember*. New York: Harper & Brothers, 1949.

Rosenbaum, Karen. "Curricular Innovation in Federal Youth Programs: A Comparison of New Deal and War on Poverty Education Efforts." PhD diss., John Hopkins University, 1973.

Salmond, John A. *A Southern Rebel: The Life and Times of Aubrey Willis Williams, 1890–1965*. Chapel Hill: University of North Carolina Press, 1983.

Savareid, Eric. *Not So Wild a Dream*. New York: Alfred A. Knopf, 1946.

Simon, Rita James, ed. *As We Saw the Thirties: Essays on Social and Political Movements of a Decade*. Chicago: University of Illinois Press, 1967.

Skocpol, Theda. *Protecting Soldiers and Mothers: The Political Origins of Social Policy in the United States*. Cambridge: Harvard University Press, 1992.

Stachura, Peter D. *The German Youth Movement, 1900–1945: An Interpretative and Documentary History*. Stirling, Scotland: University of Stirling, 1981. (London: Macmillan, 1984).

Steinberg, Michael S. *Sabers and Brownshirts: The German Students' Path to National Socialism, 1918–1935*. Chicago: University of Chicago Press, 1973.

Thomas, Hugh. *The Spanish Civil War*. New York: Modern Library, 2001.

Walker, Lawrence D. *Hitler Youth and Catholic Youth, 1933–1936: A Study in Totalitarian Conquest*. Washington, D.C.: Catholic University of America Press, 1970.

Warren, Frank A. *An Alternate Vision: The Socialist Party in the 1930s*. Bloomington: Indiana University Press, 1974.

Wechsler, James A. *The Age of Suspicion*. New York: Donald I. Fine, 1953.

———. *Labor Baron: A Portrait of John L. Lewis*. New York: William Morrow and Company, 1944.

———. *Revolt on the Campus*. Seattle: University of Washington Press, 1973.

Weiner, Mark S. *Black Trials: Citizenship from the Beginnings of Slavery to the End of Caste*. New York: Vintage Books, 2004.

Weisenberger, Carol A. *Dollars and Dreams: The National Youth Administration in Texas*. New York: Peter Lang Publishing, Inc., 1994.

Zahavi, Gerald. "'Who's Going to Dance with Somebody Who Calls You a Mainstreeter:' Communism, Culture, and Community in Sheridan Country, Montana, 1918–1934." *Great Plains Quarterly* (Fall 1996).

———. "The 'Trial' of Lee Benson: Communism, White Chauvinism, and the Foundations of the 'New Political History' in the United States." *History and Theory* 42 (October 2003): 332–62.

Zorbaugh, Harvey. *The Gold Coast and the Slum: A Sociological Study of Chicago's Near North Side*. Chicago: University of Chicago Press, 1929.

Index

African Americans: economic issues and, 62–63, 244n7; Scottsboro Boys, 61–83, 242n1, 245n18; and youth organizations, 7. *See also* racial issues

Allen, Jay, 181

Allphin, Herbert, 71

Altbach, Philip G., 54, 293n30, 295n48

American Civil Liberties Union, 45

American Council on Education, 128

American Dream: African Americans and, 63; Harlan County miners' strike and, 23–24; McMichael on, 203; youth organizations and, 10, 37–39

American Federation of Labor (AFL), 67, 140, 245n17

American Federation of Teachers, 58

American Student Union (ASU), 5, 228; and American Youth Act, 146; and AYA, 137–39; and AYC, 97–99; and economic issues, 146; and education, 151–53; and elections, 145; end of, 192, 226; establishment of, 57–58, 85–86, 102–2, 112, 115–16, 118–19; and funding issues, 148–49; ideology of, 6; Lash and, 118–20, 289n134, 297n63, 304n150; and leadership struggles, 194–96, 200–1, 289n134; membership of, 293n16; National Executive Com-

mittee, 75, 119–20, 153; and NYA, 135; and racial issues, 72; and Spanish Civil War, 168–69; values of, 7–8, 73, 120–21; and war debates, 173–74, 176, 179–82, 186–87, 194–96, 200–1, 213, 217

American Youth Act, 137–45, 147, 150–51, 158, 204, 214, 216, 229

American Youth Commission, 128, 147–48

American Youth Congress (AYC), 5, 228, 273n127; and American Youth Act, 139–41, 143, 146; and ASU, 97–99; and auditorium affair, 219–21; and CCC, 126; and China, 179; and Citizenship Institute, 201–6; communism and, 88, 94–95, 100, 185, 215–16, 256n65; Creed of, 65–66, 184–85, 290n144, 296n54; and education, 216, 276n174; and elections, 218–19; end of, 192, 205–13, 226; establishment of, 57–58, 85–86, 88–97, 253n15; and funding issues, 148–49, 273n121; and HUAC, 295n53, 296nn56–57; Lash and, 213–17, 221–22, 302nn107,113; and leadership struggles, 213–17, 221–22; membership of, 96; Model Congress, 146–47, 150–51; and New

319

and, 89; and NYA, 130–32, 140; and
Scottsboro Boys, 79; and voting age,
52–53, 160; and war, 299n82; as youth
advocate, 7, 10–11, 124, 128, 150,
156, 235n58, 288nn112,126, 295n53,
297n57, 298n81, 301n93; and youth
unemployment, 26
Roosevelt, Franklin Delano: and ASU,
153; and compulsory service, 161;
on democracy, 248n76; and education, 147–48; Lash and, 137, 210, 215,
292n11, 304n148, 305n152; and NYA,
133–34; and racial issues, 75; and
youth, 10, 86, 96–97, 116, 130, 136,
150, 191–92, 292n7
Roosevelt, James, 150, 311n4
Roosevelt, Theodore, 89
Roosevelt administration: and youth,
125, 132–33, 209, 229; youth critiques
of, 11
Roosevelt Youth Club Movement, 145,
274n136
Ross, Carl, 216, 222–23
Ross, Irwin, 214

Samson, Leon, 310n207
Sarah Lawrence College, 152
Sarnoff, David, 130
Saxe, John G., 45
Scottsboro Boys, 61–83, 242n1, 245n18;
outcome of trials, 79–80, 250n101
Second Sino-Japanese War, 169–70
segregation. See racial issues
Selective Training and Service Act, 161,
278n228, 310n208
Sevareid, Eric, 103, 108–9, 113, 172,
182–83, 230
Shinn, Roger, 305n151
Simmons, Ozzie, 67
Simms, Winston, 70
Simon, Abbott, 142, 175, 183, 204
Smith, Michael B., 25
socialists/socialism: and American Youth
Act, 139; appeal of, 26–27; and AYC,
93, 224; Bell on, 121; and com-
munism, 97–101; divisions within,
258n87, 259n103; influence of, 34–
36; Lash and, 102, 197, 221, 259n91,
307n176; and leadership, 33; and peace,

104–5; and Popular Front, 101–2, 112,
117–19. See also Student League for
Industrial Democracy; Young People's
Socialist League
social organizations, 32
Southern Negro Youth Conference, 75
Soviet Union, 177, 258n81; AYC and,
211–12; influence of, 55–56; Lash
on, 197, 225, 279n5, 309n204; and
radicalism, 34; and Spanish Civil War,
163–64, 173, 283n64
Spanish Civil War, 163–87
The Spectator, 41, 126
Spivack, Robert, 52–54
Stalin, Josef, 36, 88, 97, 163, 173, 283n64
Stone, Irving, 54
Stone, Oliver, 181
Strack, Celeste, 6, 142, 265n221
Streator, George, 7, 72
strikes, 148–49; Lash on, 175; for peace,
105–7, 106f, 109–10, 112–15, 213,
264n199, 302n117; Reed Harris affair
and, 44–47; Spanish Civil War and,
166–67
Studebaker, John, 97, 129–30, 132–33,
159, 219, 276n193
The Student Advocate, 9, 167–70
Student Christian Movement, 119
Student Federalists, 161–62
Student League for Industrial Democ-
racy (SLID), 5, 32, 54, 236n88; and
ASU, 99–100, 115–16; and AYC, 93;
colleges and, 49; independence of, 99;
membership of, 54; and peace, 105,
107, 113, 115; and Popular Front,
113–14; and Scottsboro Boys, 65
students: and AYC, 88; rights of, Reed
Harris affair and, 40–60; and Scotts-
boro Boys, 62; and self-government,
153; and workers, 40–41
Students in Defense of Democracy
(SDD), 221, 223
Student Strike Against War, 15
Swarthmore, 152
Syracuse University, 69

Taber, John, 77
Taussig, Charles, 145; and American
Youth Act, 139; and HUAC, 198; Ilma

Taussig, Charles (*continued*)
and, 90; and labor, 140; and NYA,
130–32, 134, 136, 159, 277n206; and
racial issues, 76–77; on unemployment, 128; and youth, 270n61; on
youth vision, 32, 38, 125, 156–57
Thirties, youth concerns in, 2–3
Thomas, Hugh, 163, 279n4, 282n50,
286n94
Thomas, Norman, 54–55, 89, 92–93,
112, 145, 257n80, 302n117
transients, 63, 93–94
Trotskyites, 33, 98–100, 117, 119, 173
Tugwell, Rexford, 10, 233n9
Turner, John R., 70
Twenties, youth concerns in, 2–3, 232n6,
237n5, 263n190

umbrella groups, 4–5; establishment of, 87
unemployment, 25–27, 38, 124, 128,
234n39; and African Americans, 62–
63, 76; AYC and, 204; and radical-
ism, 34
Unitarian Youth, 212
United Mine Workers, 214
United Student Peace Committee
(USPC), 166, 174, 285n74
United Youth Committee to Aid Spanish
Democracy, 169
University of Kansas, 71
U.S. Office of Education (USOE), 129,
155, 219

Vandeman, A.W., 127
Vassar World Youth Congress, 154–55,
175–79, 186
Villard, Oswald Garrison, 90
vision of youth organizations, 6, 32, 230;
AYC Creed, 65–66, 184–85; Cadden
on, 301n92; Declaration of Rights
of American Youth, 143–44; World
Youth Congress and, 178
vocational training, 31–32, 125; AYA and,
137; CCC and, 127
volunteers, in Spanish Civil War, 170–73,
182–83
Voorhis, Jerry, 147, 296n57
voting age, 52–53, 160

Wagner, Robert F., 77, 112
Wagner Act, 153, 200
Wagner-Costigan Bill, 67
Wallace, Henry A., 90
Walsh, David, 129, 139
war: debates on, 173–87, 193–95, 201,
209–10, 214–17, 283n63, 284n68.
See also defense training; militarism;
pacifism
Warren, Frank, 258n89, 309n205
Watt, George, 282n41, 283n63
Watt, Ruth, 98, 292n11
Wechsler, James, 5; and American Youth
Act, 142–43; and ASU, 119–20; and
AYC, 92–93; on Butler, 44; on change
in beliefs, 240n97; on class, 40; on college conservatives, 56; and communism, 34–37, 92–93, 236n92, 279n5,
284n68, 287n101; and economic
issues, 27; on fascism, 165; and Harlan
County miners' strike, 21–23; and
HUAC, 59, 241n116; on leadership,
55; on Munich, 289n133; and peace,
104–5, 108–9, 115; and Popular Front,
102; and press, 9; and procedural issues,
286n88; and racial issues, 69; and religion, 8, 77–78; and Spanish Civil
War, 164, 167, 172; and student rights
issues, 45, 47–48, 50; and war debates,
174, 261n128, 263n181, 279n8; on
World Youth Congress, 178–79; and
WWII, 311n5; and YCL, 36–37
Weems, Frank, 246n36
Weiner, Mark, 242nn1–2, 245n18
Weiss, Max, 215
Wiggins, Lee, 305n151
Williams, Aubrey, 276n193; and AYC,
159; and defense training, 158–59,
277n206, 306n170; and NYA, 128,
131, 139, 141, 156–59, 162, 209,
219–20, 276n185, 310n3; and racial
issues, 76–77, 214–15, 249n84
Williams, Frances, 186, 205, 212, 219,
256n65, 291n150
Willkie, Wendell, 218
Wilson, Welford, 67–68
Winchell, Walter, 241n116
Wise, Raymond, 45
Witt, Herbert, 193, 195–96, 200, 215

women, and youth movement, 6–7
Woodring, Harry, 126
Works Progress Administration, 130
World War II, 191–226, 230, 291n156,
311n5; and funding, 156; McMichael
and, 204; Sevareid on, 183
World Youth Congress, Vassar, 154–55,
175–79, 186, 290n142
Wright, Wade, 78

Yard, Molly, 6, 8, 119, 181, 196; and lead-
ership struggles, 201, 211, 224; and
war debates, 194–95
Yergan, Max, 69
Young, Owen, 130
Young Communist League (YCL), 5, 32,
35, 97, 117–18, 193, 224; and AYC,
88; membership of, 34; Wechsler and,
36–37
Young Democrats, 32
Young Judea, 32, 212
Young Men's Christian Association
(YMCA), 4, 32, 54, 56; and AYC, 92;
and funding issues, 149; headquarters
of, 8; and NYA, 135; and racial issues,
66
Young Men's Vocational Foundation, 94
Young People's Peace Lobby, 287n107
Young People's Socialist League (YPSL),

5, 32, 97–99, 113–14, 117, 255n55,
258n87; and American Youth Act,
139; and AYC, 93, 308n194; guidelines
for, 265n215; and war debates, 218,
225–26
Young Republicans, 8, 32
Young Women's Christian Association
(YWCA), 4, 8, 32; and funding issues,
149; and NYA, 135; and racial issues,
66
youth: attitudes of, 21, 26; definition of, 2
youth activism, 1–18; nature of, 12–15;
scholarship on, 12–14
Youth Committee Against War, 213
youth organizations, 227–30; adult leaders
and, 213; categories of, 32–33; end
of, 192, 310n208; establishment of,
32; headquarters of, 8, 33; and New
Deal, 124–62; and Popular Front, 85–
123; resignations from, 212, 221–22,
289n134, 305n151; and Spanish Civil
War, 163–87; and World War II, 191–
226. See also vision of youth organizations
youth problem, adult views of, 38–39,
147–48

Zorbaugh, Harvey, 91, 95

ESE SELECT TITLES FROM EMPIRE STATE EDITIONS

Allen Jones with Mark Naison, *The Rat That Got Away: A Bronx Memoir*

Janet Grossbach Mayer, *As Bad as They Say? Three Decades of Teaching in the Bronx*

William Seraile, *Angels of Mercy: White Women and the History of New York's Colored Orphan Asylum*

Daniel Campo, *The Accidental Playground: Brooklyn Waterfront Narratives of the Undesigned and Unplanned*

Howard Eugene Johnson with Wendy Johnson, *A Dancer in the Revolution: Stretch Johnson, Harlem Communist at the Cotton Club*. Foreword by Mark D. Naison

Phillip Deery, *Red Apple: Communism and McCarthyism in Cold War New York*

Stephen Miller, *Walking New York: Reflections of American Writers from Walt Whitman to Teju Cole*

Tom Glynn, *Reading Publics: New York City's Public Libraries, 1754–1911*

Craig Saper, *The Amazing Adventures of Bob Brown: A Real-Life Zelig Who Wrote His Way Through the 20th Century*

R. Scott Hanson, *City of Gods: Religious Freedom, Immigration, and Pluralism in Flushing, Queens*. Foreword by Martin E. Marty

Dorothy Day and the Catholic Worker: The Miracle of Our Continuance. Edited, with an Introduction and Additional Text by Kate Hennessy, Photographs by Vivian Cherry, Text by Dorothy Day

Pamela Lewis, *Teaching While Black: A New Voice on Race and Education in New York City*

Mark Naison and Bob Gumbs, *Before the Fires: An Oral History of African American Life in the Bronx from the 1930s to the 1960s*

Robert Weldon Whalen, *Murder, Inc., and the Moral Life: Gangsters and Gangbusters in La Guardia's New York*

Joanne Witty and Henrik Krogius, *Brooklyn Bridge Park: A Dying Waterfront Transformed*

Sharon Egretta Sutton, *When Ivory Towers Were Black: A Story about Race in America's Cities and Universities*

David J. Goodwin, *Left Bank of the Hudson: Jersey City and the Artists of 111 1st Street*. Foreword by DW Gibson

Pamela Hanlon, *A Worldly Affair: New York, the United Nations, and the Story Behind Their Unlikely Bond*

For a complete list, visit www.empirestateeditions.com.